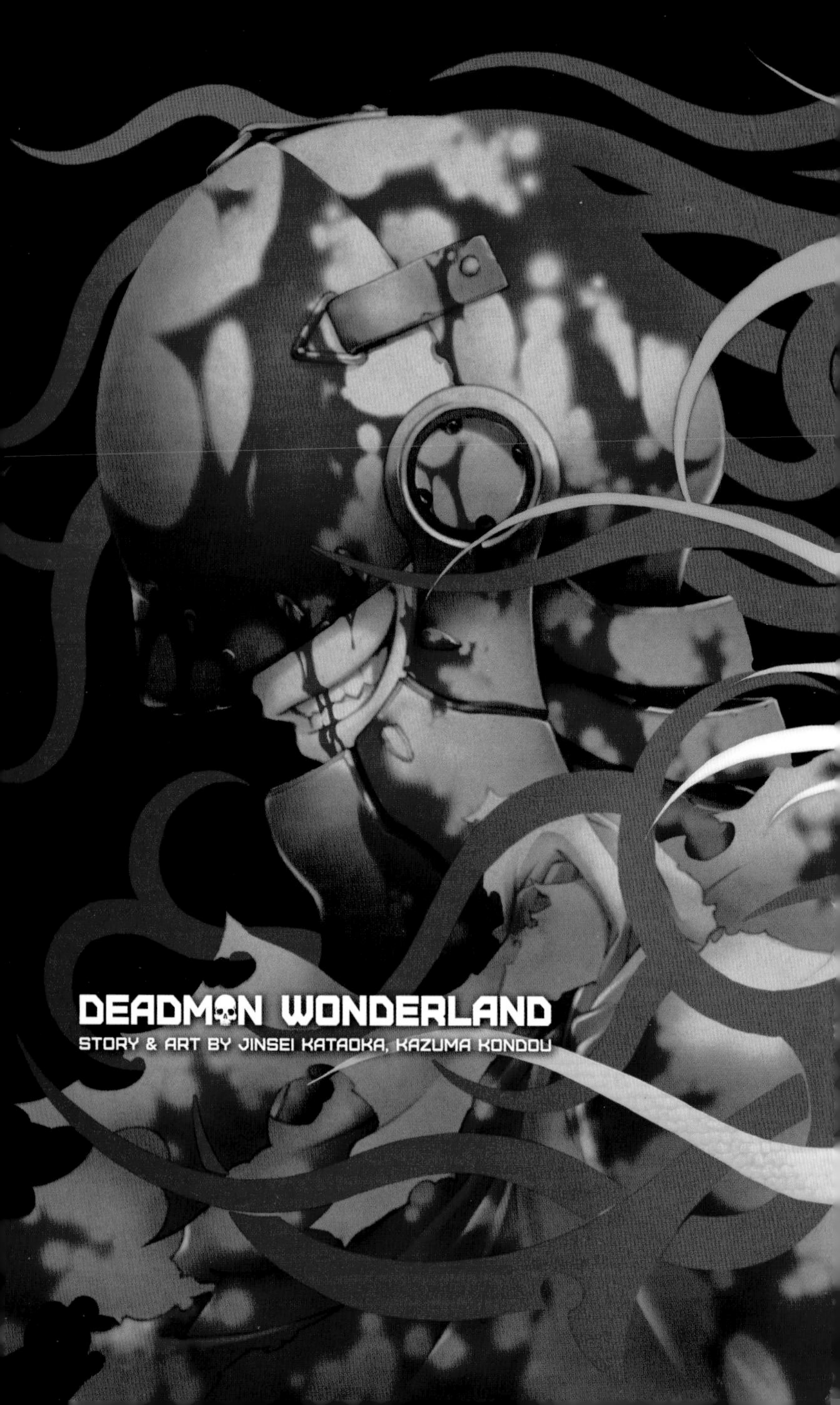
DEADMAN WONDERLAND
STORY & ART BY JINSEI KATAOKA, KAZUMA KONDOU

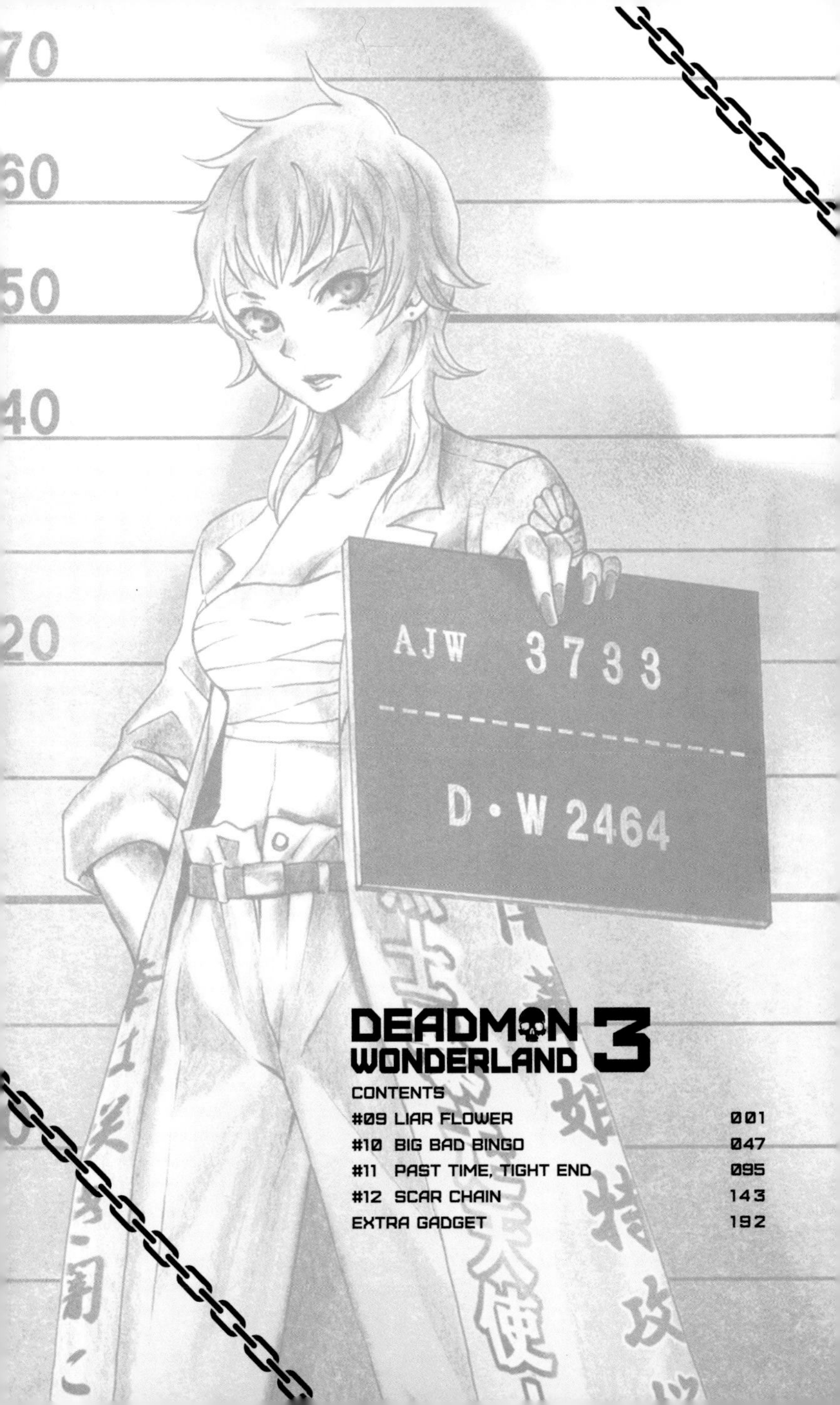
AJW 3733
D・W 2464

DEADMAN WONDERLAND 3

CONTENTS

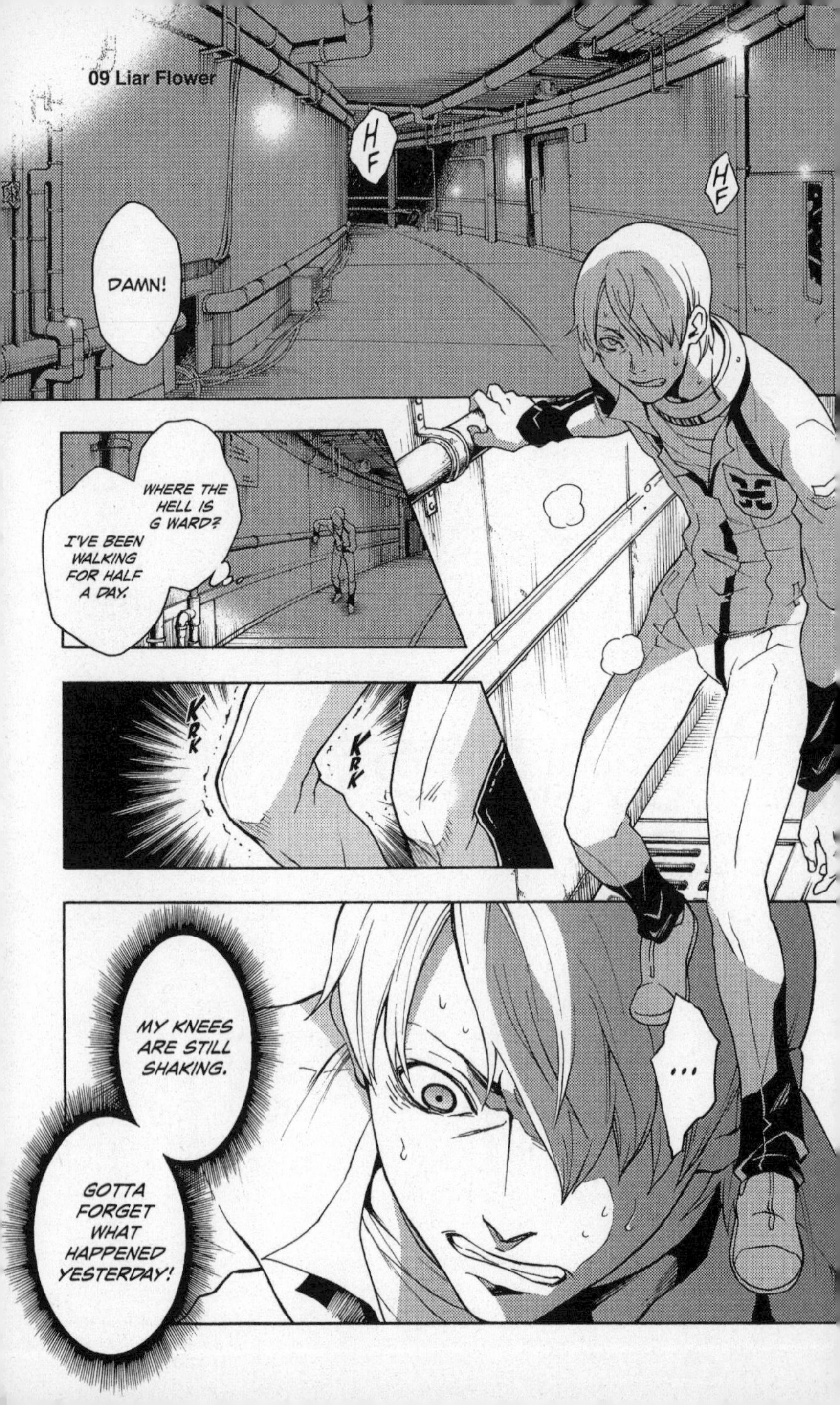
HF
HF
DAMN!
WHERE THE HELL IS G WARD? I'VE BEEN WALKING FOR HALF A DAY.
KRK
KRK
...
MY KNEES ARE STILL SHAKING.
GOTTA FORGET WHAT HAPPENED YESTERDAY!

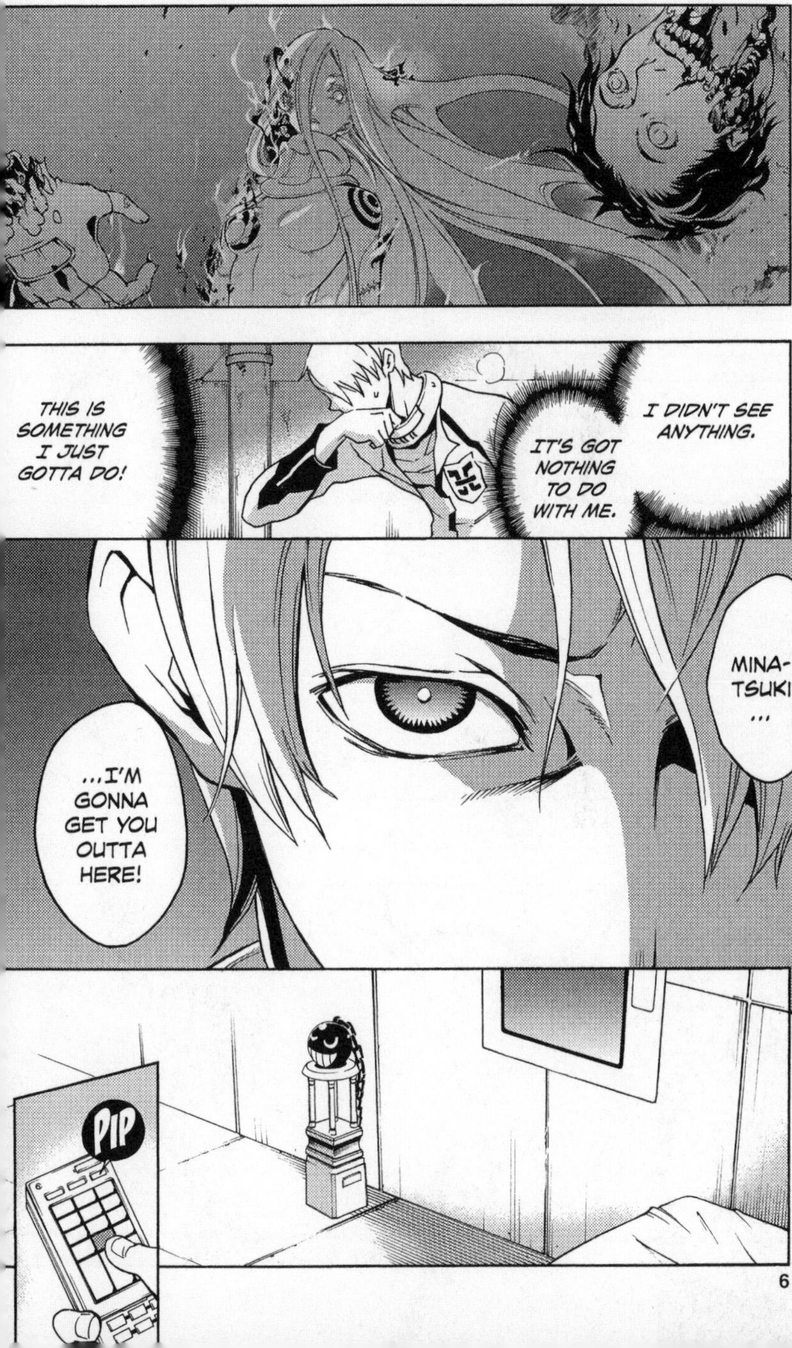
I DIDN'T SEE ANYTHING.
IT'S GOT NOTHING TO DO WITH ME.
THIS IS SOMETHING I JUST GOTTA DO!
MINA-TSUKI...
...I'M GONNA GET YOU OUTTA HERE!
PIP

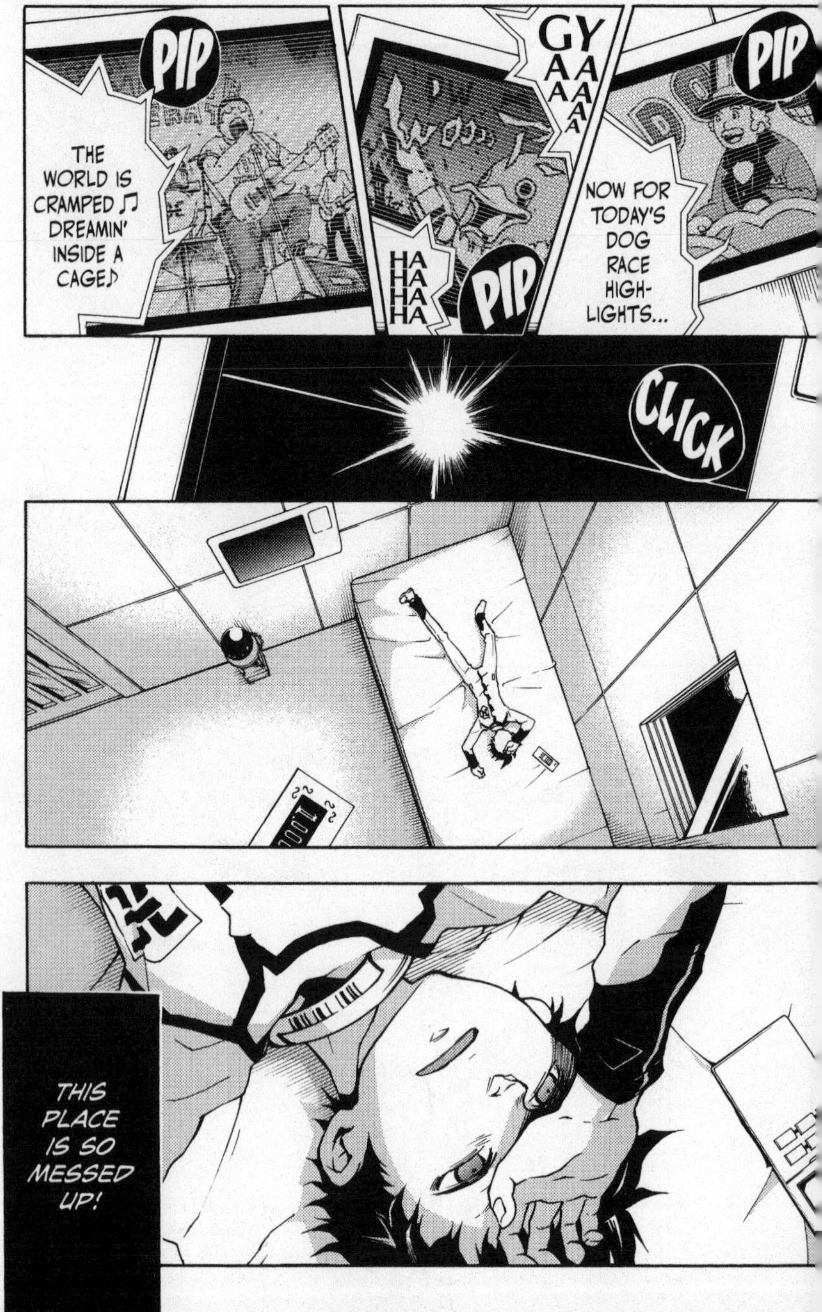
PIP
NOW FOR TODAY'S DOG RACE HIGH-LIGHTS...
GYAAAAAA
HAHAHAHA
PIP
PIP
THE WORLD IS CRAMPED ♫ DREAMIN' INSIDE A CAGE♪
CLICK
THIS PLACE IS SO MESSED UP!

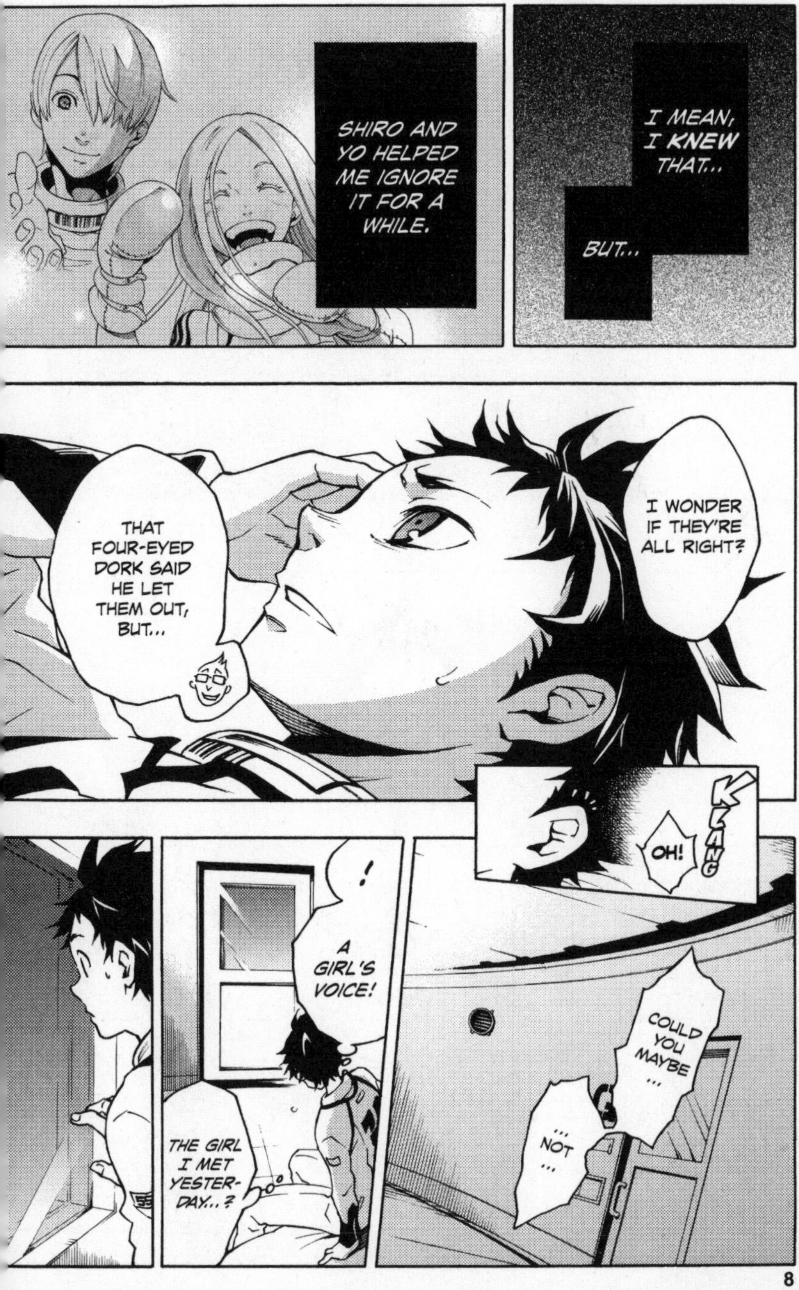
I MEAN, I KNEW THAT...
BUT...
SHIRO AND YO HELPED ME IGNORE IT FOR A WHILE.
I WONDER IF THEY'RE ALL RIGHT?
THAT FOUR-EYED DORK SAID HE LET THEM OUT, BUT...
KLANG
OH!
COULD YOU MAYBE ...
... NOT ...
!
A GIRL'S VOICE!
THE GIRL I MET YESTER-DAY...?

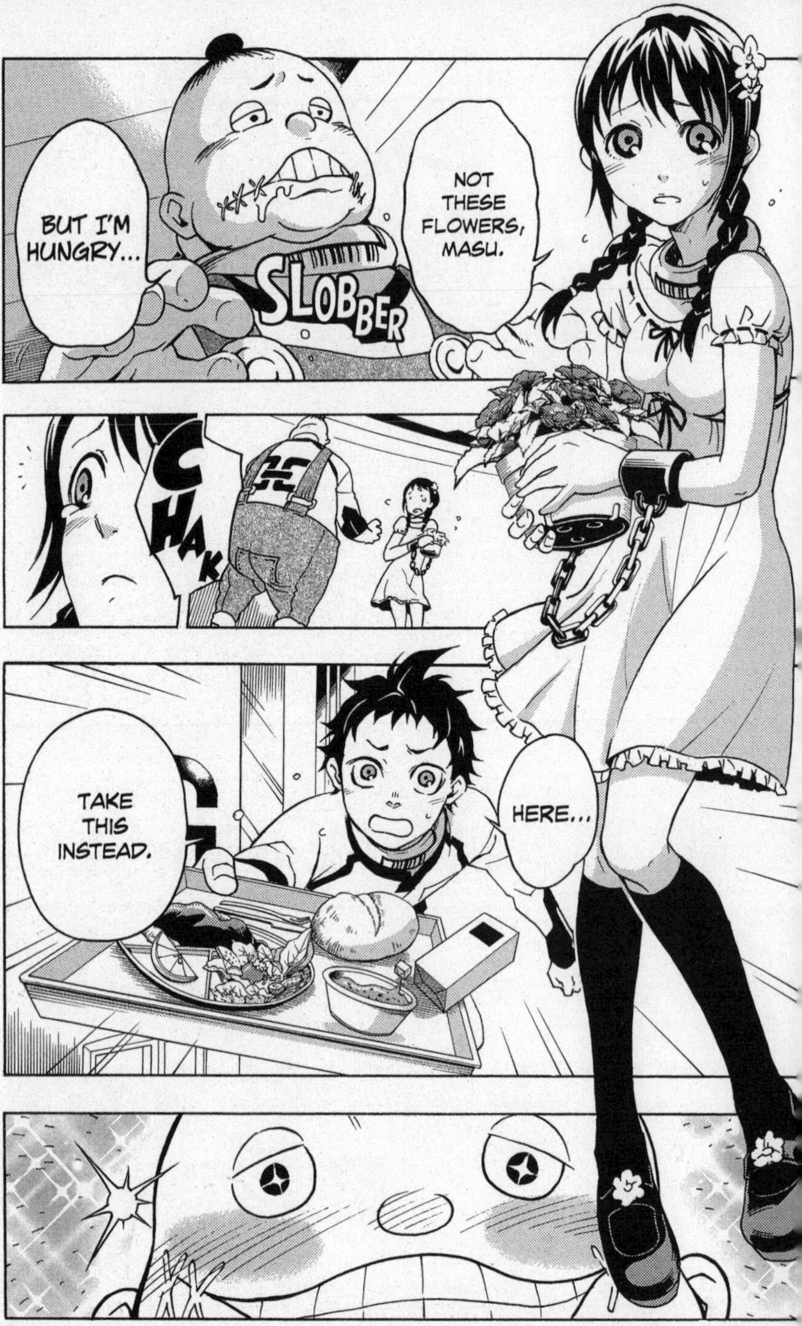
NOT THESE FLOWERS, MASU.
BUT I'M HUNGRY...
SLOBBER
CHAK
HERE...
TAKE THIS INSTEAD.

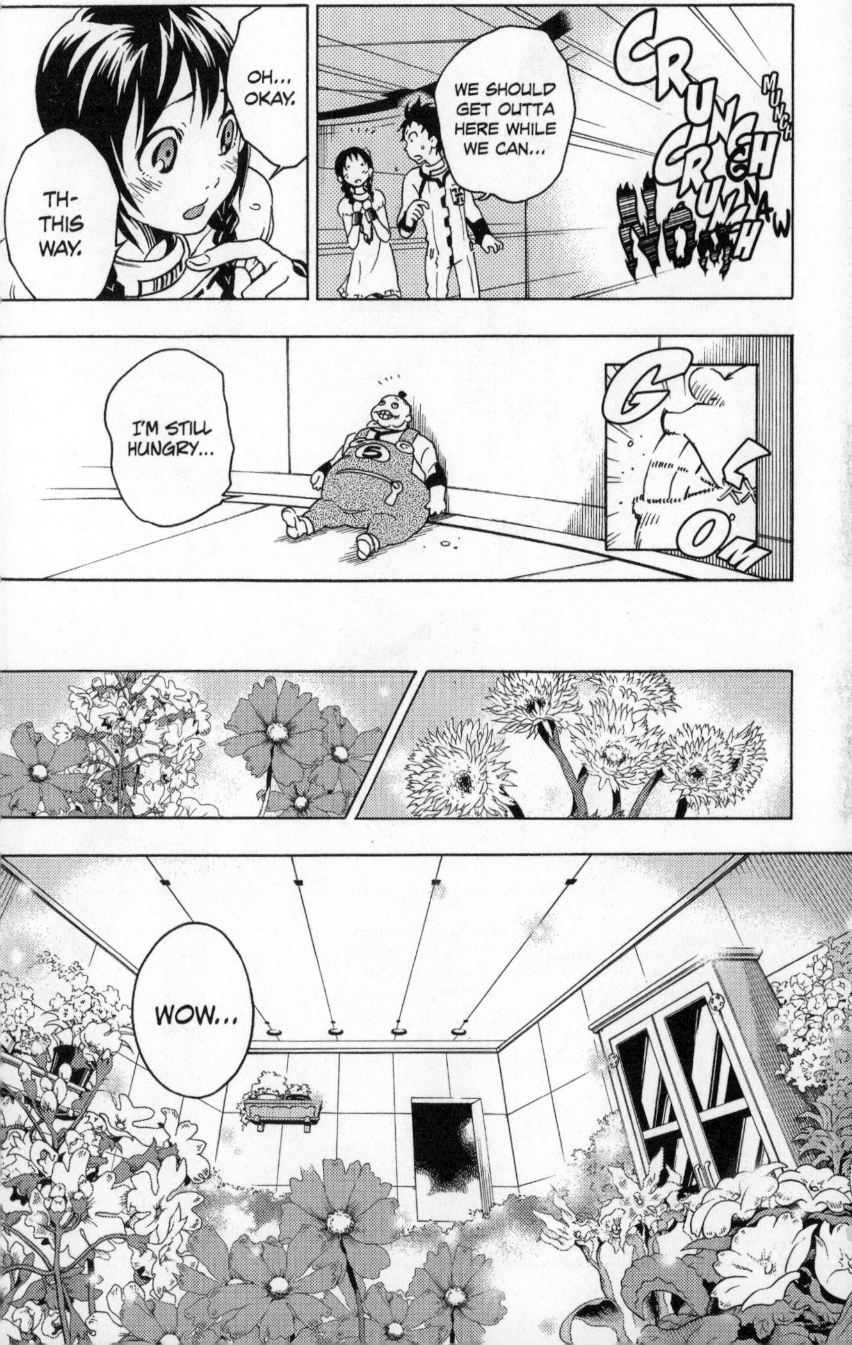
CRUNCH
MUNCH
CRUNCH
GNAW
WE SHOULD GET OUTTA HERE WHILE WE CAN...
OH... OKAY.
TH- THIS WAY.
I'M STILL HUNGRY...
WOW...

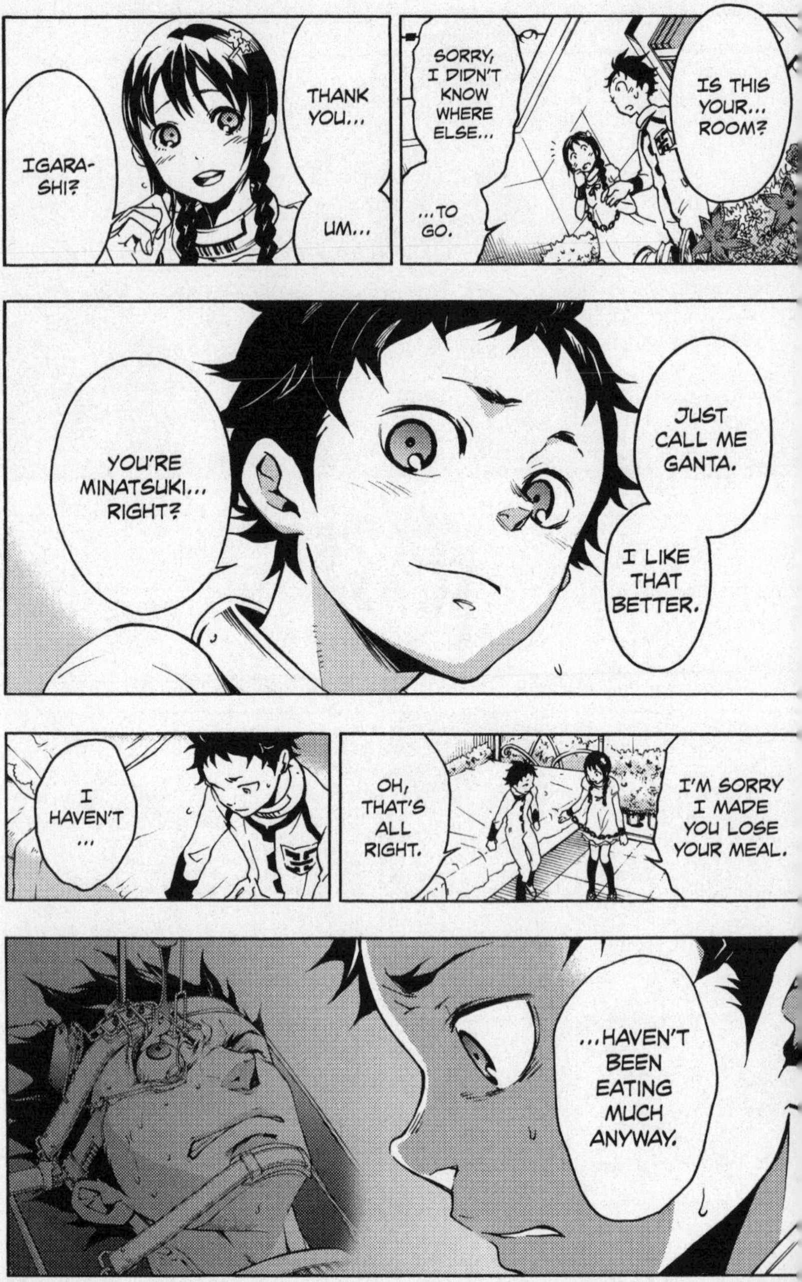
IS THIS YOUR... ROOM?
SORRY, I DIDN'T KNOW WHERE ELSE...
...TO GO.
THANK YOU...
UM...
IGARA-SHI?
JUST CALL ME GANTA.
I LIKE THAT BETTER.
YOU'RE MINATSUKI... RIGHT?
I'M SORRY I MADE YOU LOSE YOUR MEAL.
OH, THAT'S ALL RIGHT.
I HAVEN'T ...
...HAVEN'T BEEN EATING MUCH ANYWAY.

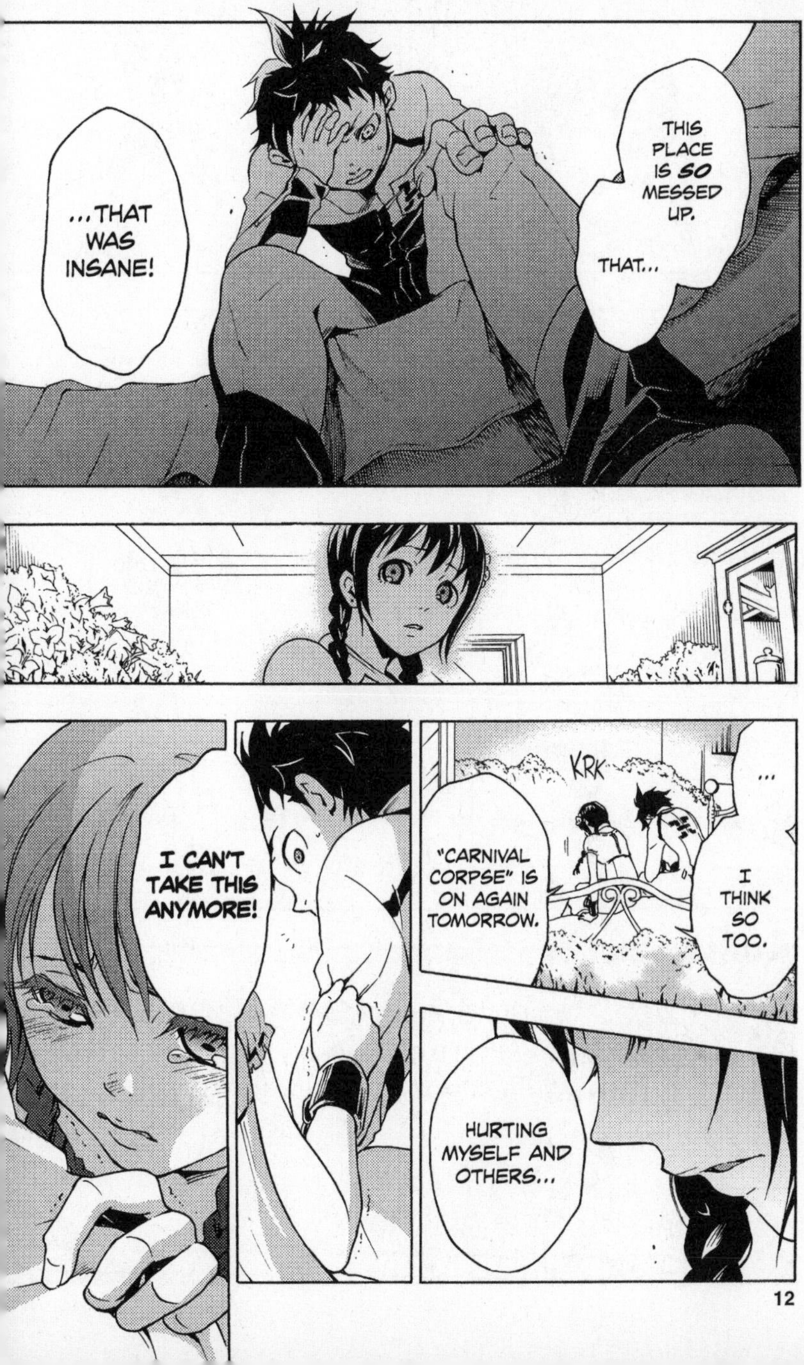
THIS PLACE IS *SO* MESSED UP.
THAT...
...THAT WAS INSANE!
...
I THINK SO TOO.
KRK
"CARNIVAL CORPSE" IS ON AGAIN TOMORROW.
HURTING MYSELF AND OTHERS...
I CAN'T TAKE THIS ANYMORE!

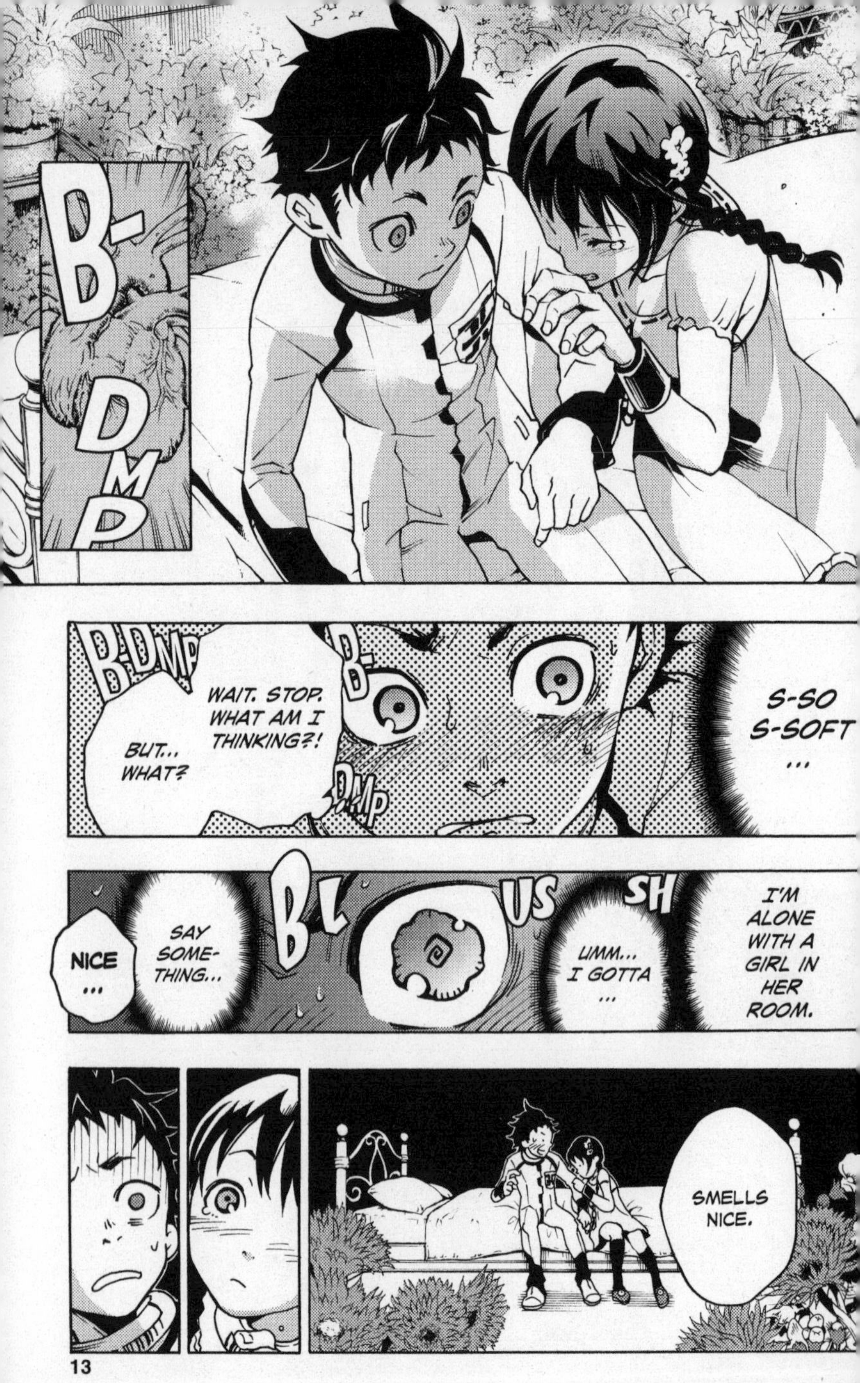
B-DMP
S-SO S-SOFT ...
B-DMP
WAIT. STOP. WHAT AM I THINKING?!
BUT... WHAT?
B-DMP
I'M ALONE WITH A GIRL IN HER ROOM.
UMM... I GOTTA ...
BLUSH
SAY SOME-THING...
NICE ...
SMELLS NICE.

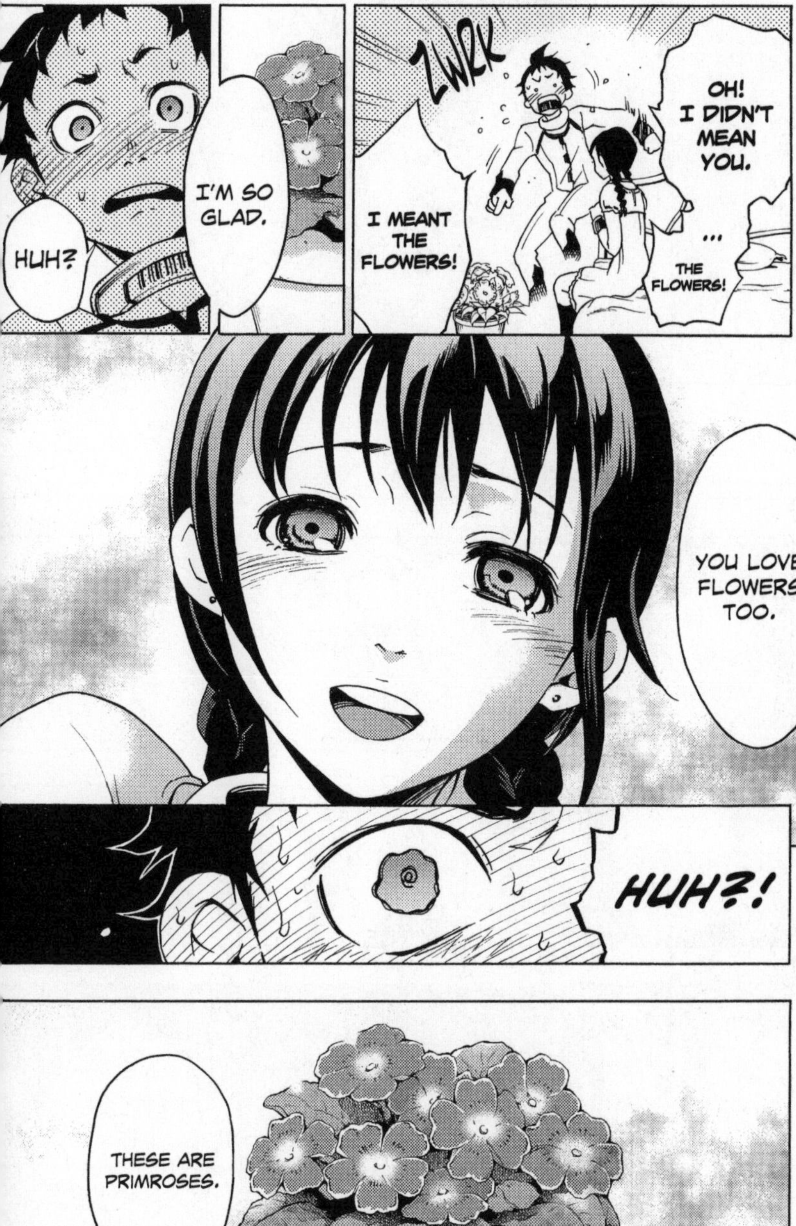
OH! I DIDN'T MEAN YOU.
ZWRK
... THE FLOWERS!
I MEANT THE FLOWERS!
I'M SO GLAD.
HUH?
YOU LOVE FLOWERS TOO.
HUH?!
THESE ARE PRIMROSES.

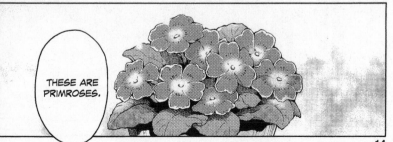

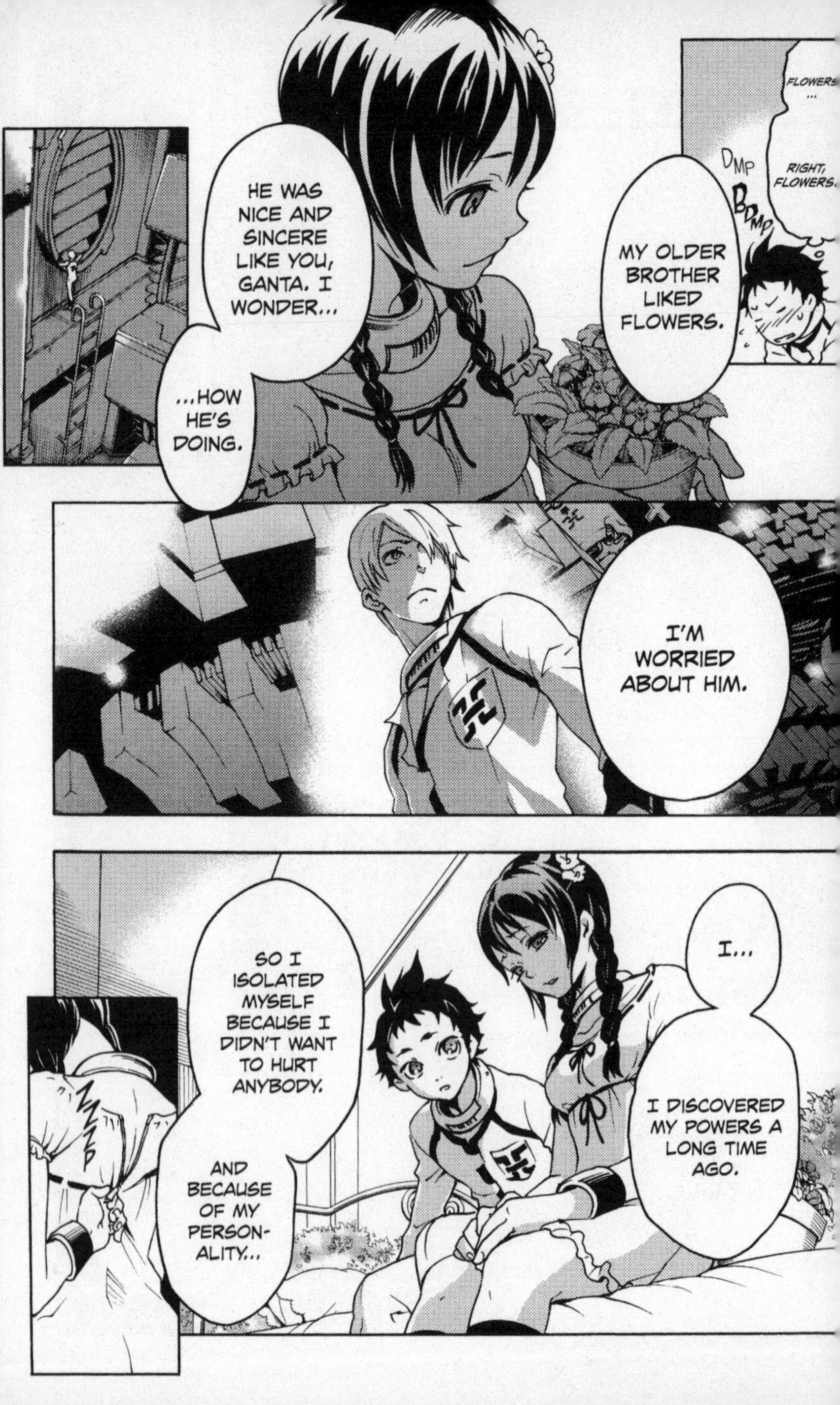
FLOWERS...
RIGHT, FLOWERS.
DMP
BDMP
MY OLDER BROTHER LIKED FLOWERS.
HE WAS NICE AND SINCERE LIKE YOU, GANTA. I WONDER...
...HOW HE'S DOING.
I'M WORRIED ABOUT HIM.
I...
I DISCOVERED MY POWERS A LONG TIME AGO.
SO I ISOLATED MYSELF BECAUSE I DIDN'T WANT TO HURT ANYBODY.
AND BECAUSE OF MY PERSON-ALITY...

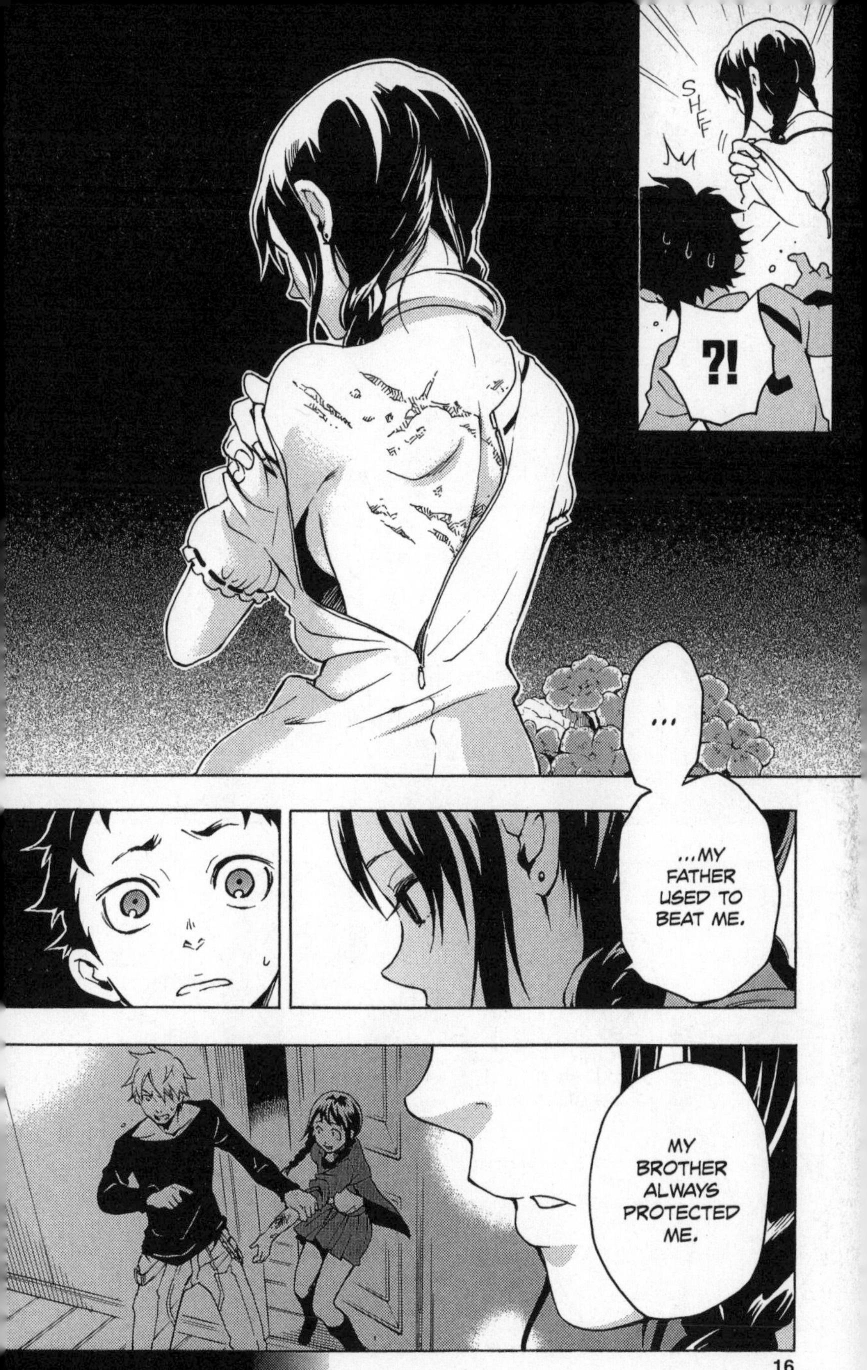
SHFF
?!
...
...MY FATHER USED TO BEAT ME.
MY BROTHER ALWAYS PROTECTED ME.

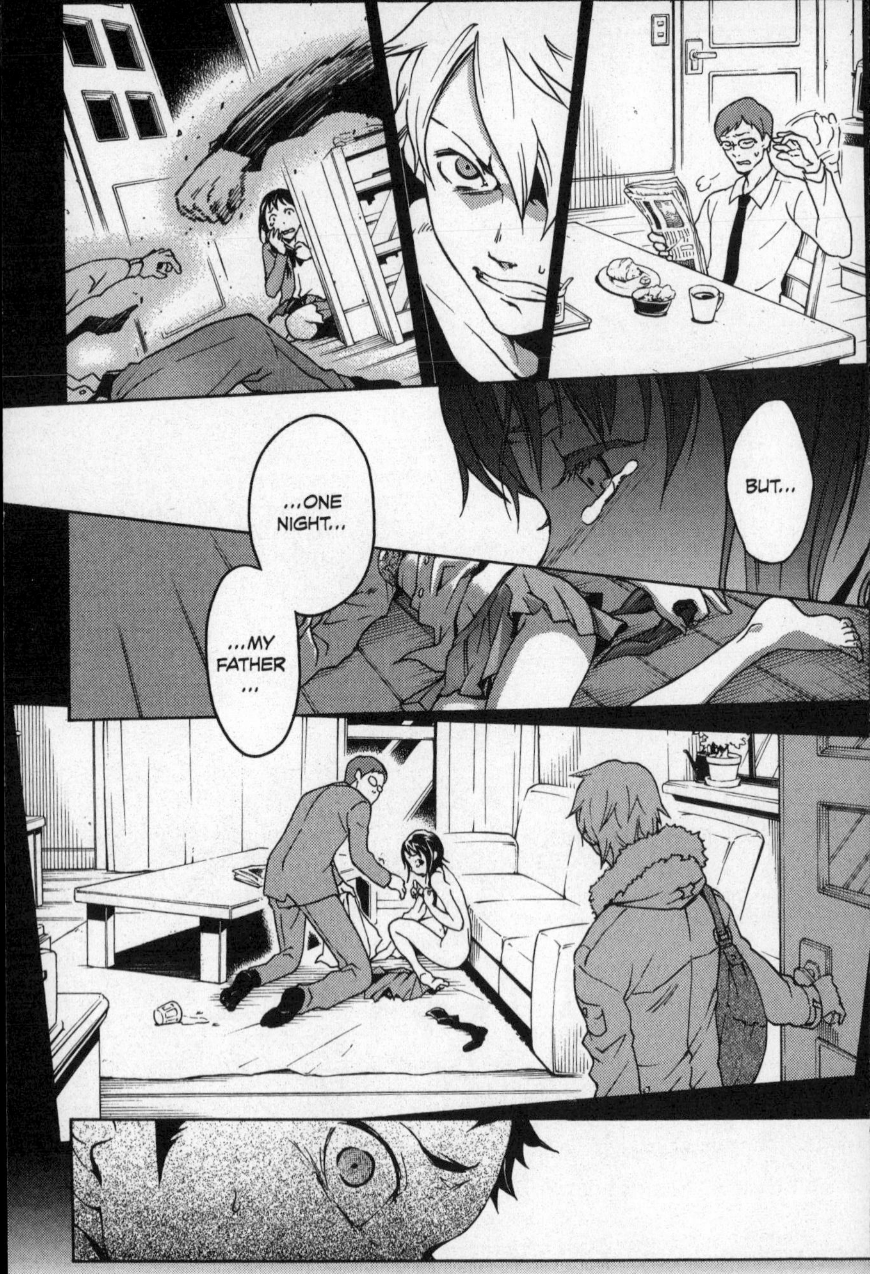
BUT...
...ONE NIGHT...
...MY FATHER ...

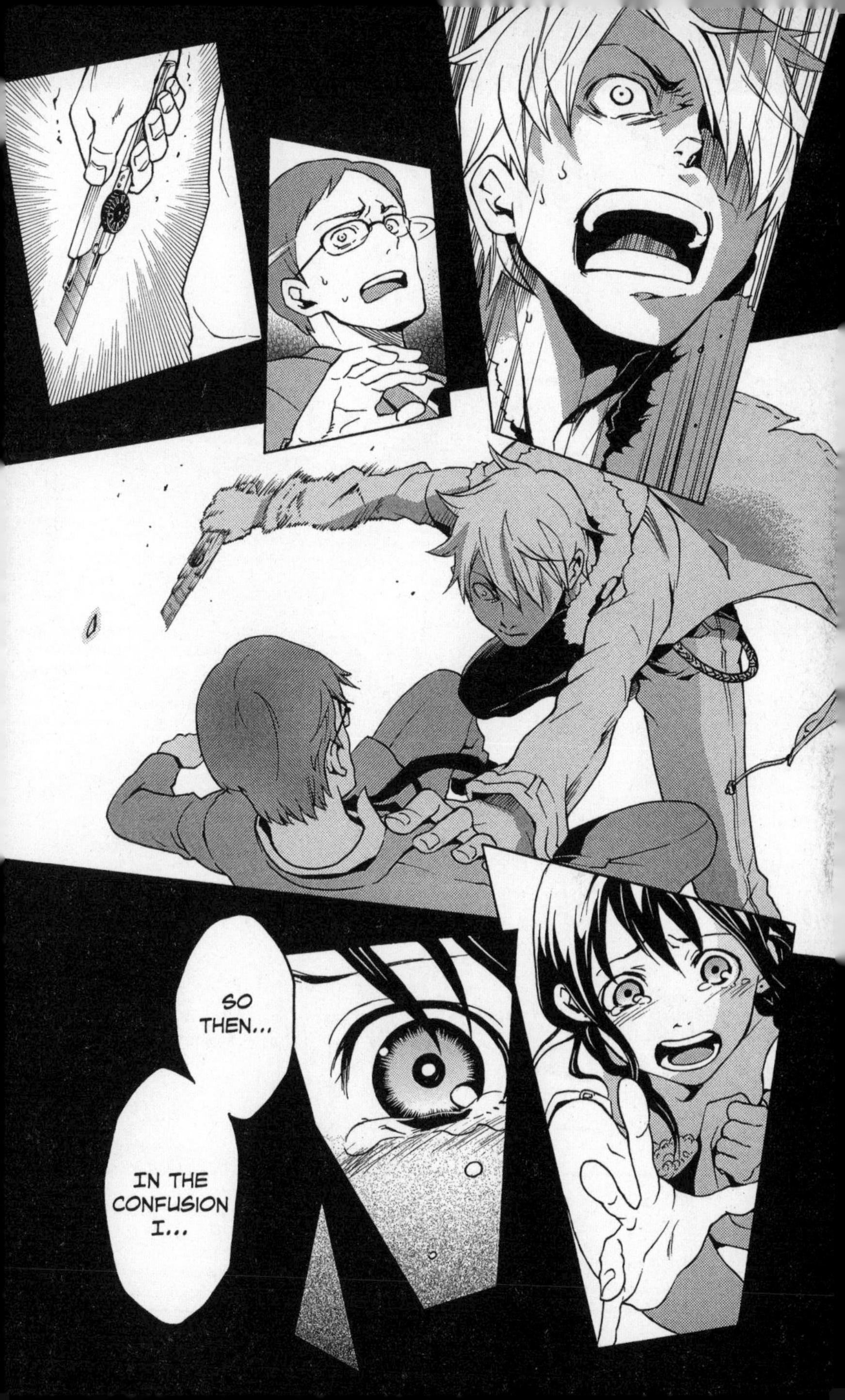
SO THEN...
IN THE CONFUSION I...

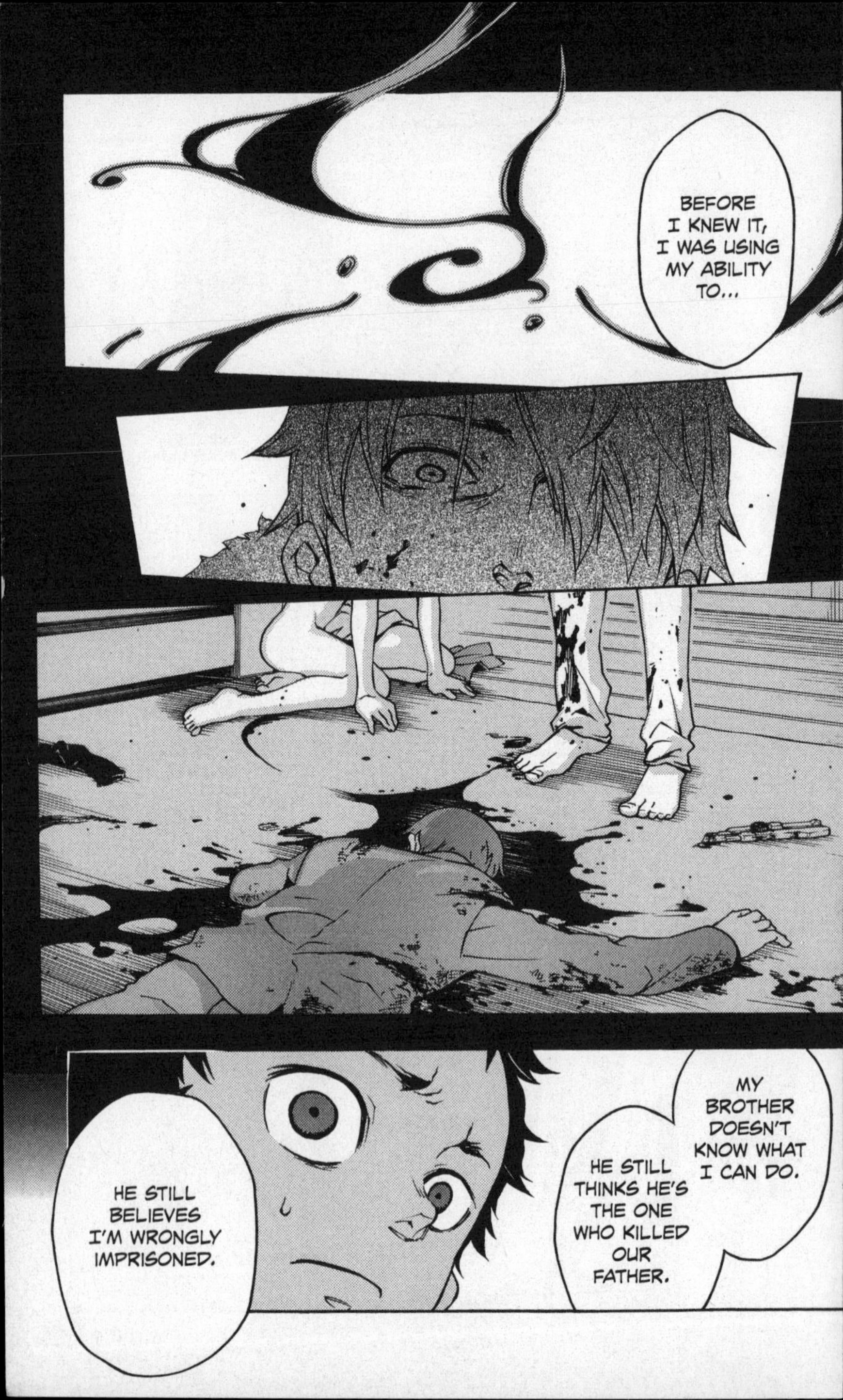
BEFORE I KNEW IT, I WAS USING MY ABILITY TO...
MY BROTHER DOESN'T KNOW WHAT I CAN DO.
HE STILL THINKS HE'S THE ONE WHO KILLED OUR FATHER.
HE STILL BELIEVES I'M WRONGLY IMPRISONED.

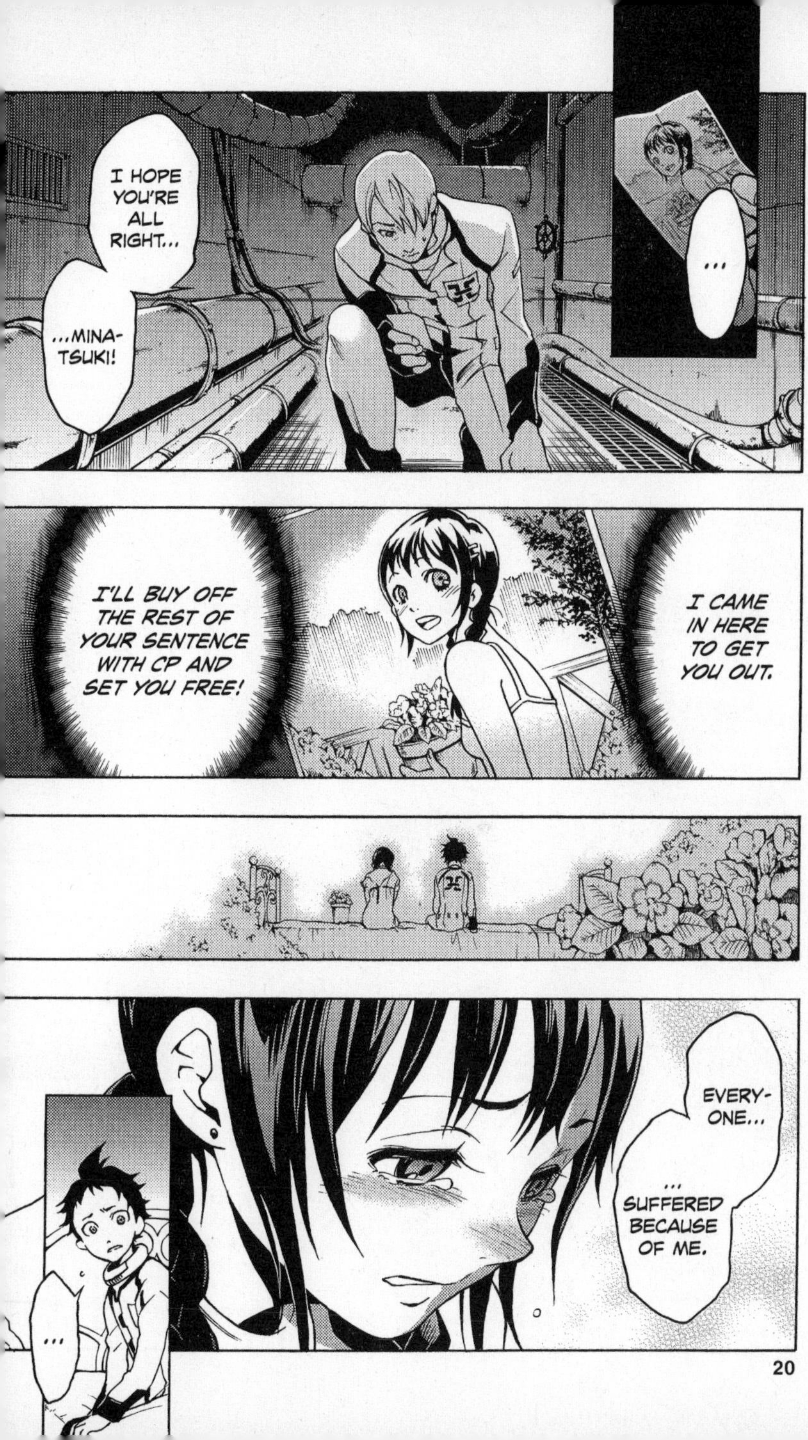
...
I HOPE YOU'RE ALL RIGHT...
...MINA-TSUKI!
I CAME IN HERE TO GET YOU OUT.
I'LL BUY OFF THE REST OF YOUR SENTENCE WITH CP AND SET YOU FREE!
EVERY-ONE...
... SUFFERED BECAUSE OF ME.
...

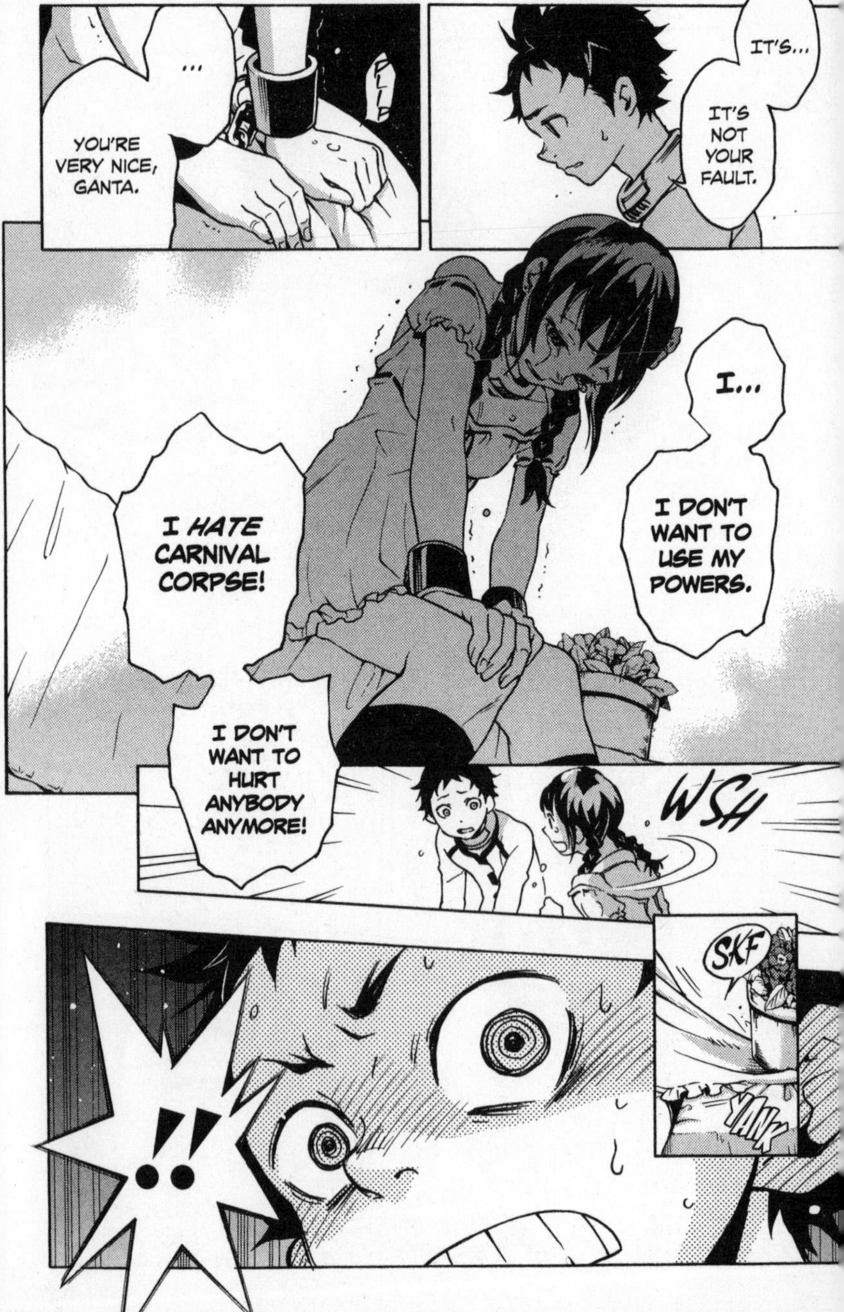
IT'S...
IT'S NOT YOUR FAULT.
...
YOU'RE VERY NICE, GANTA.
I...
I DON'T WANT TO USE MY POWERS.
I *HATE* CARNIVAL CORPSE!
I DON'T WANT TO HURT ANYBODY ANYMORE!
WSH
SKF
YANK
!!

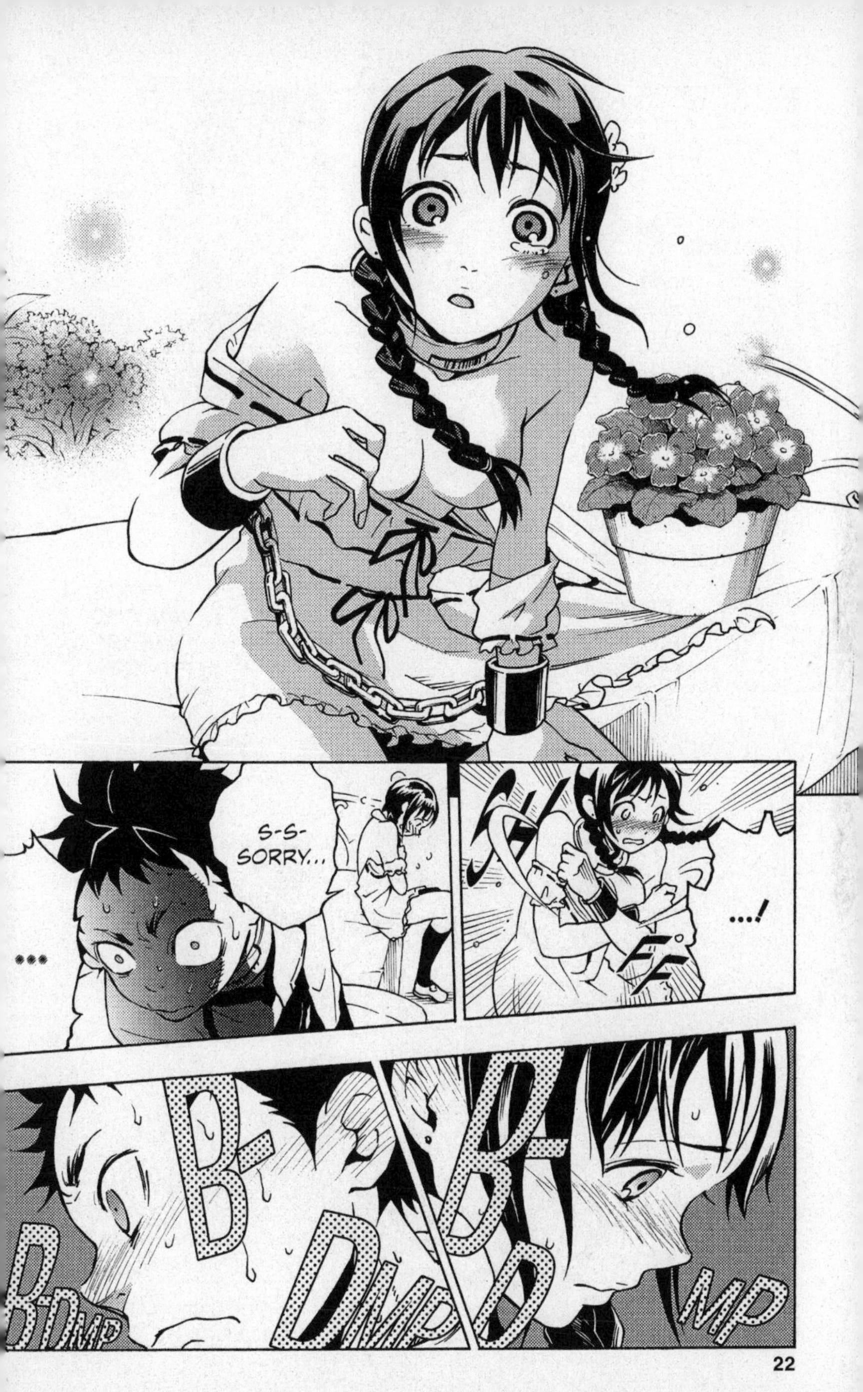
CH
FF
...!
S-S-SORRY...
...
B-
D-
MP
B-
DMP
B-DMP

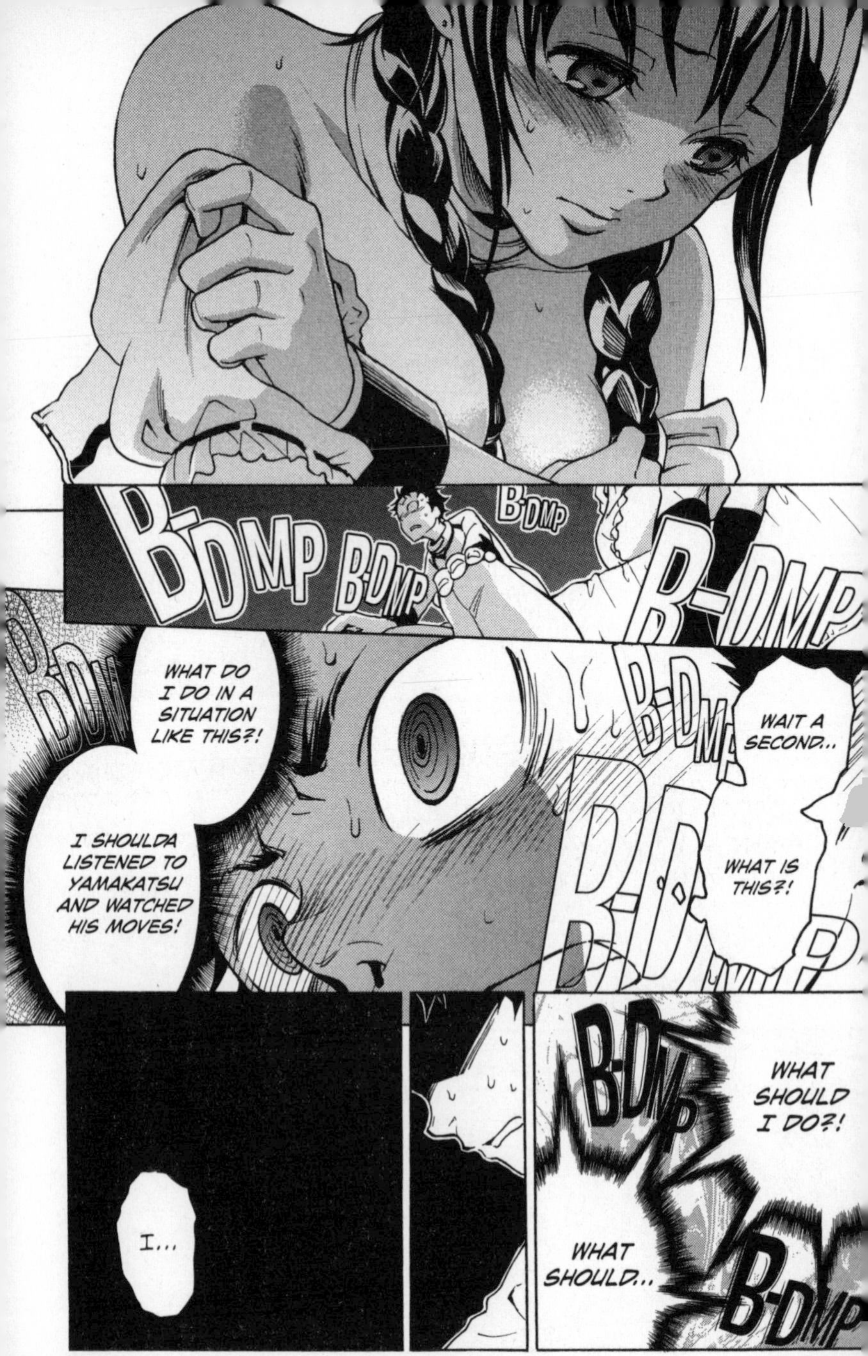
B-DMP
B-DMP
B-DMP
B-DMP
WAIT A SECOND...
WHAT IS THIS?!
WHAT DO I DO IN A SITUATION LIKE THIS?!
I SHOULDA LISTENED TO YAMAKATSU AND WATCHED HIS MOVES!
WHAT SHOULD I DO?!
B-DMP
WHAT SHOULD...
B-DMP
I...

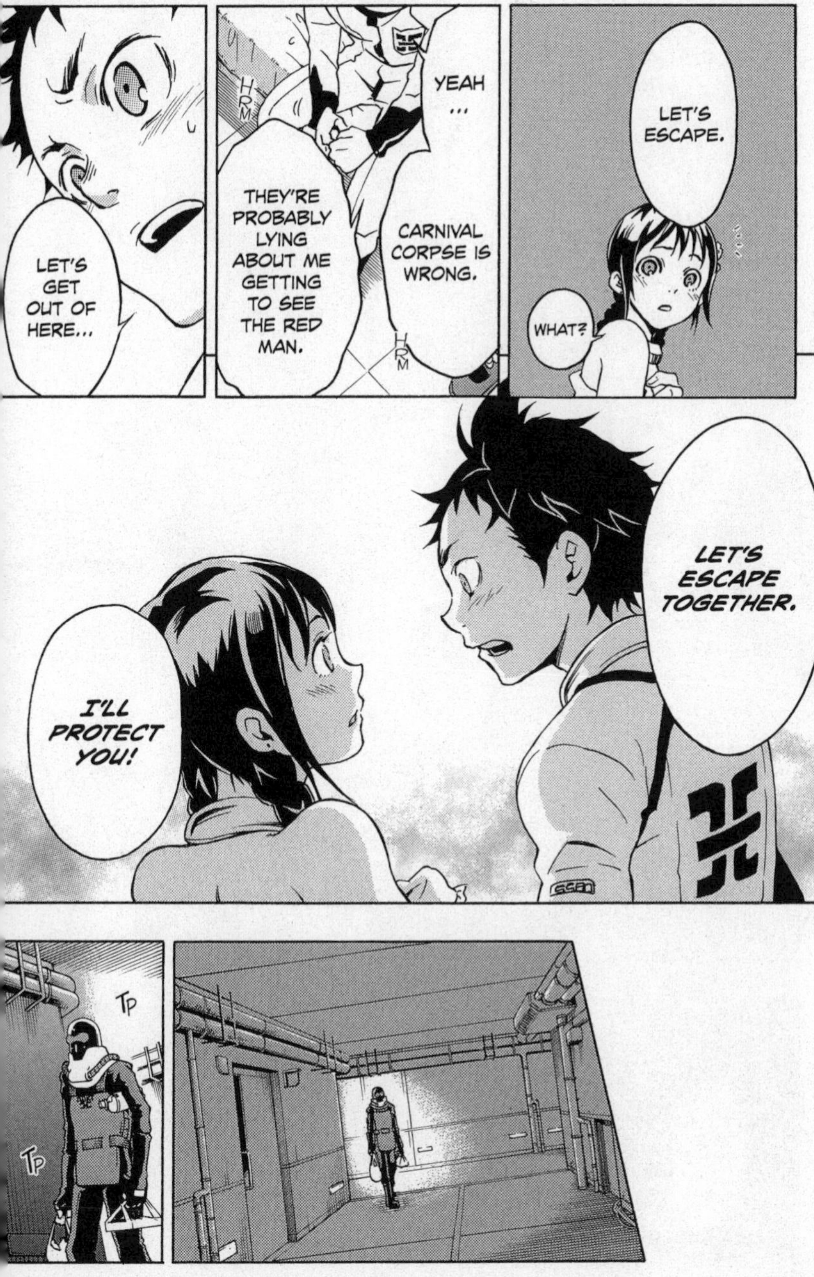
LET'S ESCAPE.
WHAT?
YEAH ...
CARNIVAL CORPSE IS WRONG.
HRM
THEY'RE PROBABLY LYING ABOUT ME GETTING TO SEE THE RED MAN.
HRM
LET'S GET OUT OF HERE...
LET'S ESCAPE TOGETHER.
I'LL PROTECT YOU!
TP
TP

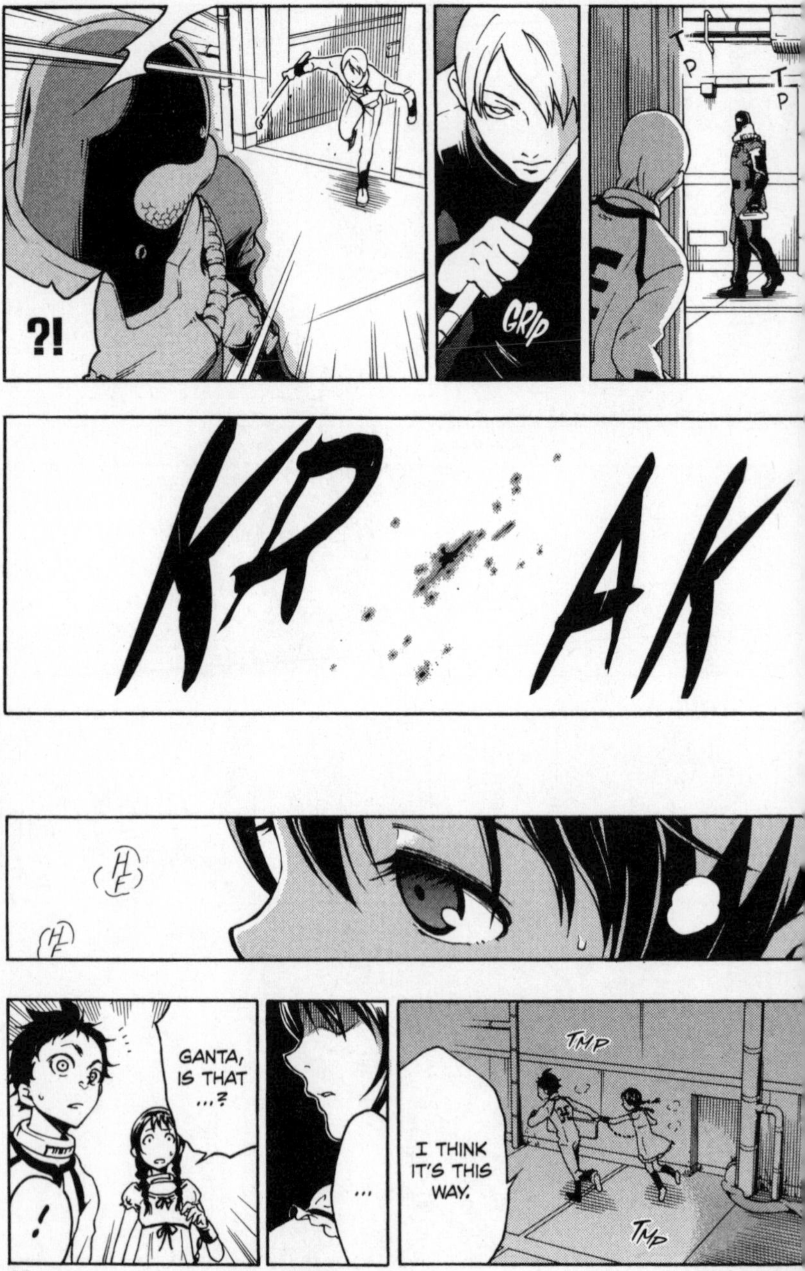
TP
TP
GRIP
?!
KRAK
HF
HF
TMP
I THINK IT'S THIS WAY.
TMP
...
GANTA, IS THAT ...?
!

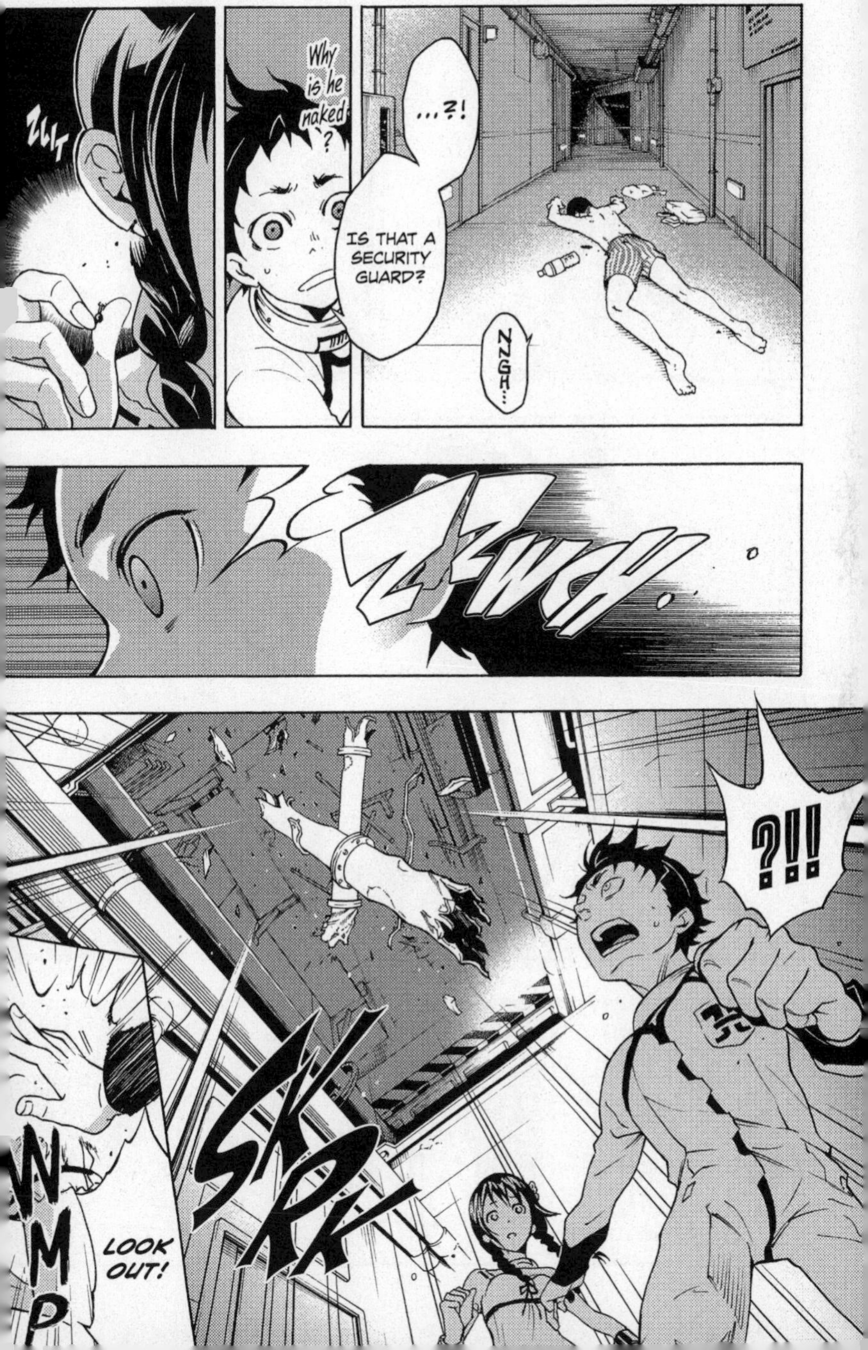
...?!
IS THAT A SECURITY GUARD?
NNGH...
Why is he naked?
ZLIT
ZWCH
?!!
SKRK
LOOK OUT!
NMP

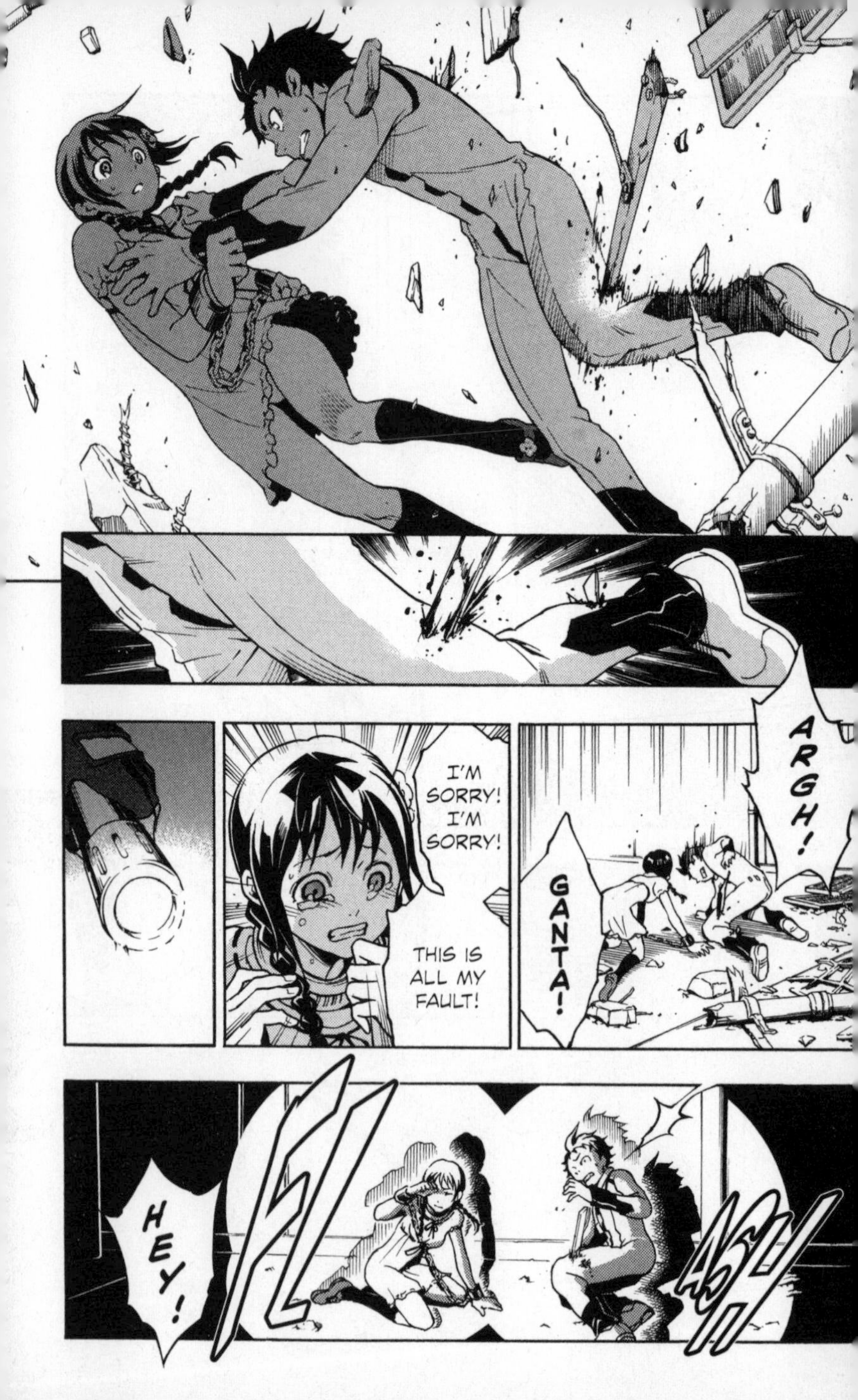
ARGH!
GANTA!
I'M SORRY! I'M SORRY!
THIS IS ALL MY FAULT!
FLASH
HEY!

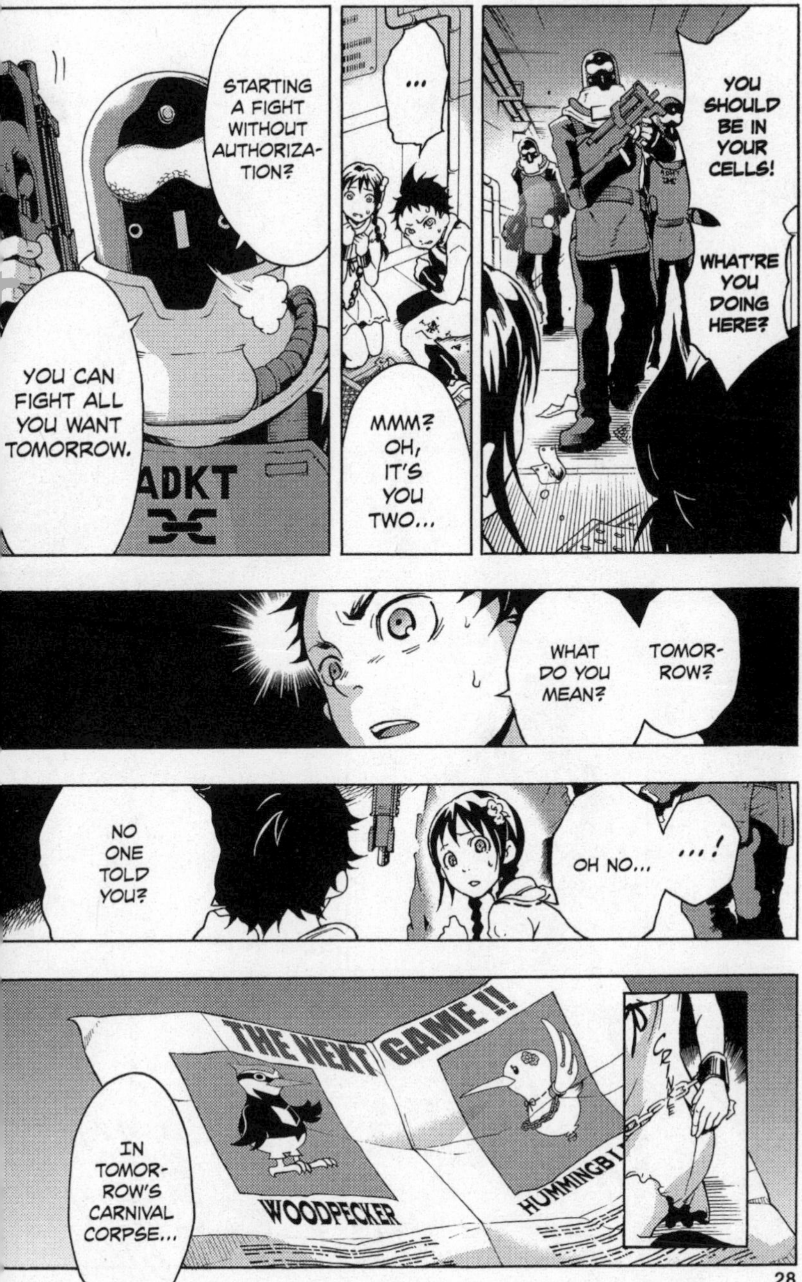
YOU SHOULD BE IN YOUR CELLS!
WHAT'RE YOU DOING HERE?
...
MMM? OH, IT'S YOU TWO...
STARTING A FIGHT WITHOUT AUTHORIZATION?
YOU CAN FIGHT ALL YOU WANT TOMORROW.
ADKT
TOMORROW?
WHAT DO YOU MEAN?
...!
OH NO...
NO ONE TOLD YOU?
CRINKLE
THE NEXT GAME!!
HUMMINGBI
WOODPECKER
IN TOMORROW'S CARNIVAL CORPSE...

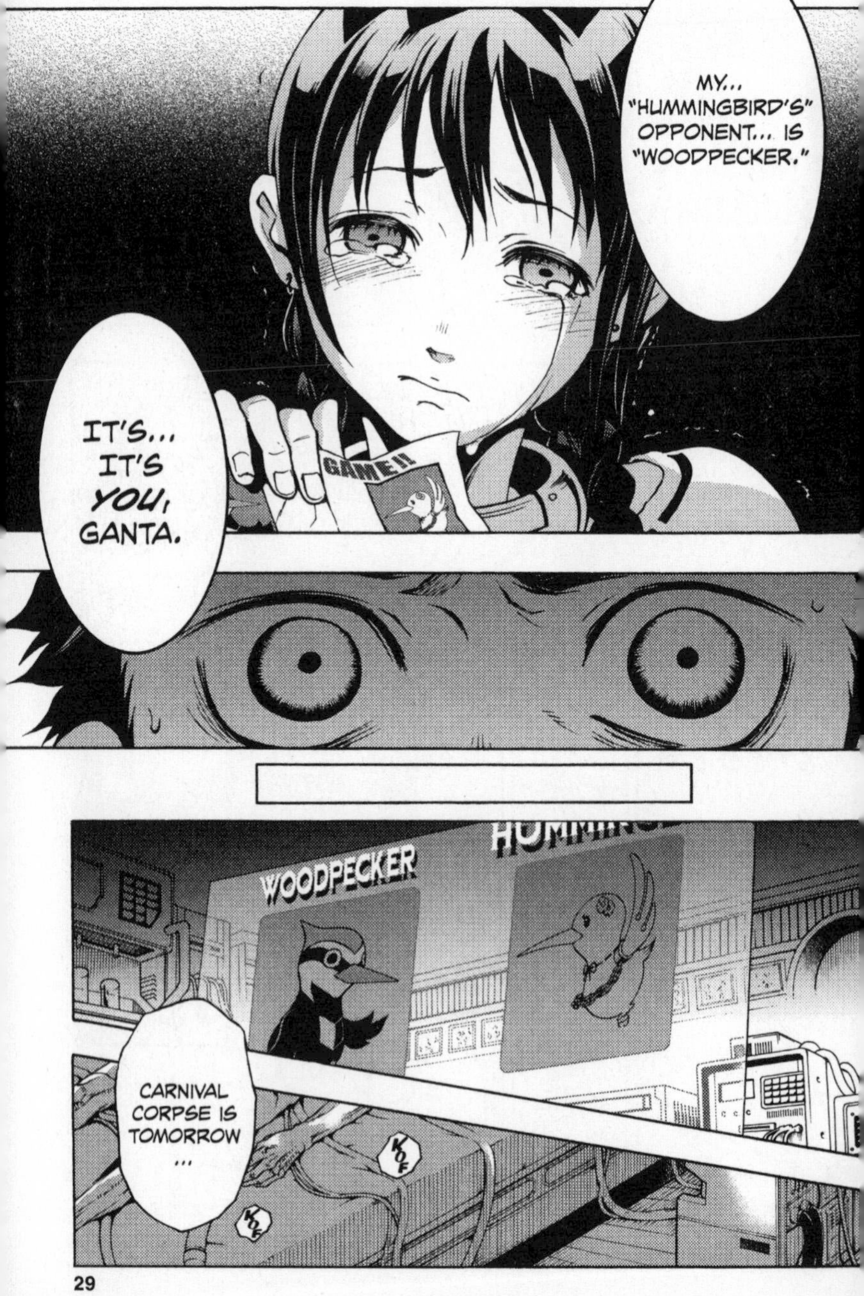
MY... "HUMMINGBIRD'S" OPPONENT... IS "WOODPECKER."
GAME!!
IT'S... IT'S *YOU*, GANTA.
WOODPECKER
CARNIVAL CORPSE IS TOMORROW ...
KOF
KOF

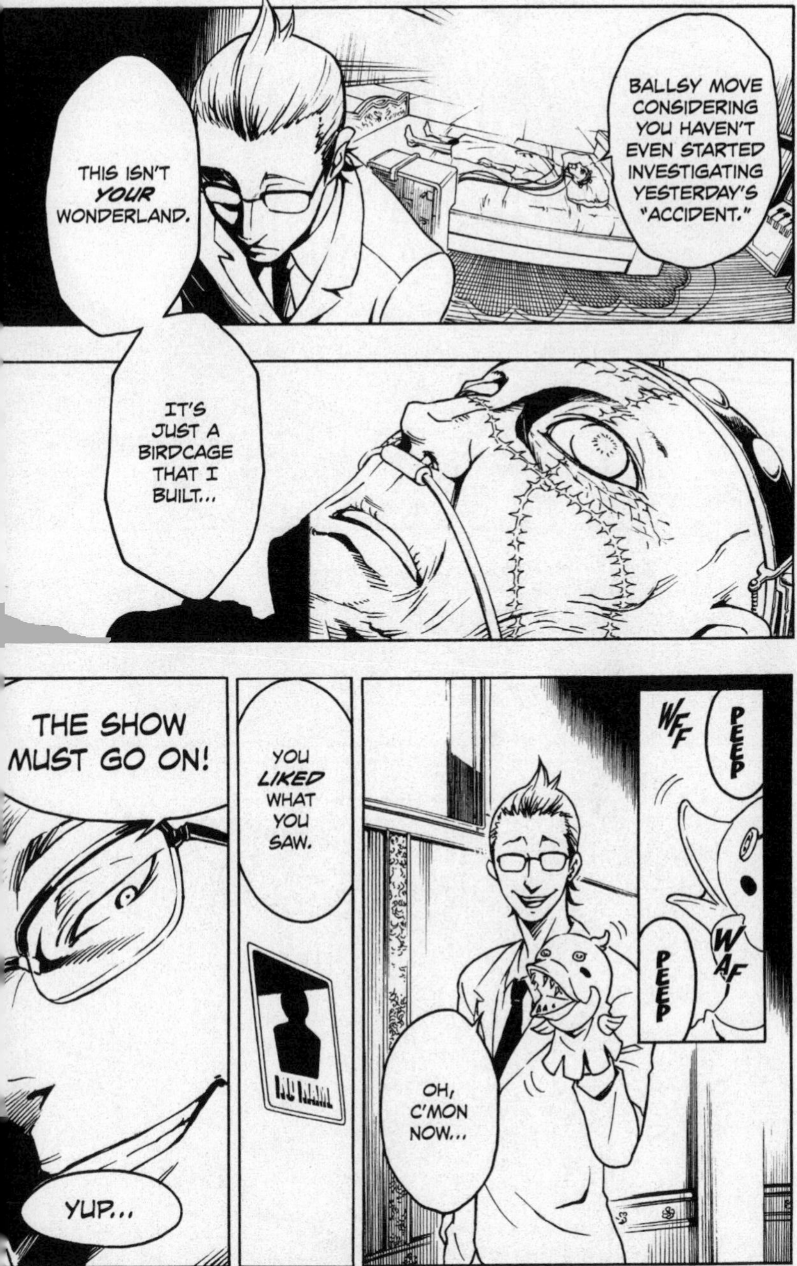
BALLSY MOVE CONSIDERING YOU HAVEN'T EVEN STARTED INVESTIGATING YESTERDAY'S "ACCIDENT."
THIS ISN'T *YOUR* WONDERLAND.
IT'S JUST A BIRDCAGE THAT I BUILT...
PEEP
WFF
WAF
PEEP
OH, C'MON NOW...
YOU *LIKED* WHAT YOU SAW.
THE SHOW MUST GO ON!
YUP...

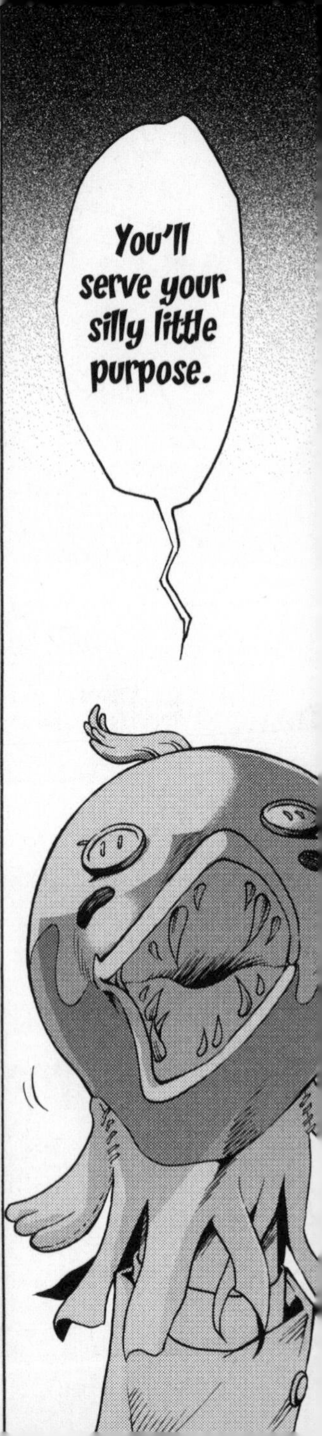
You'll serve your silly little purpose.

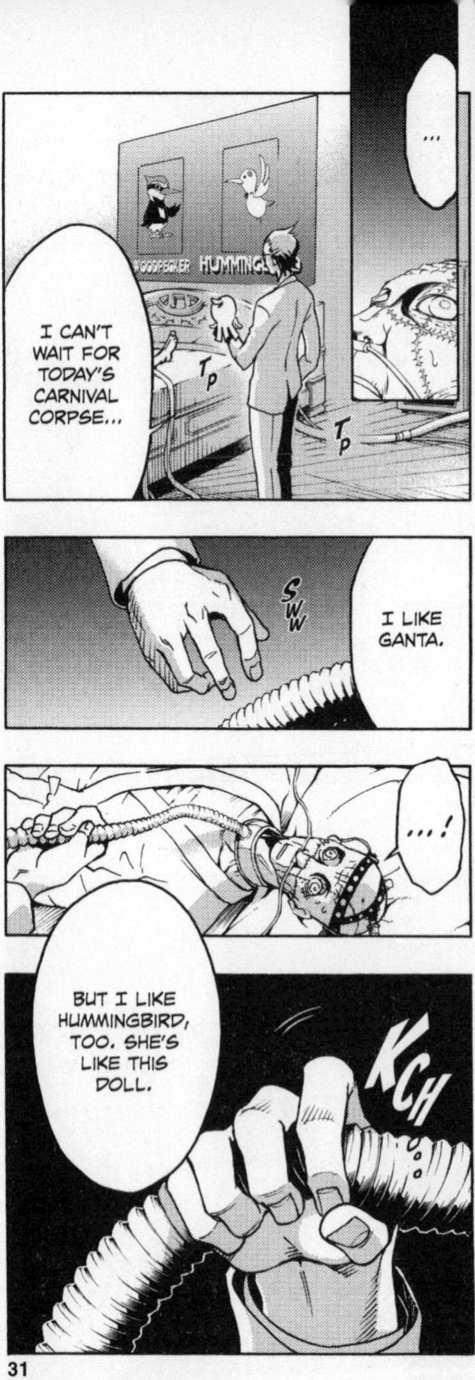
...
WOODPECKER
I CAN'T WAIT FOR TODAY'S CARNIVAL CORPSE...
TP
TP
I LIKE GANTA.
SWW
...!
BUT I LIKE HUMMINGBIRD, TOO. SHE'S LIKE THIS DOLL.
KCH

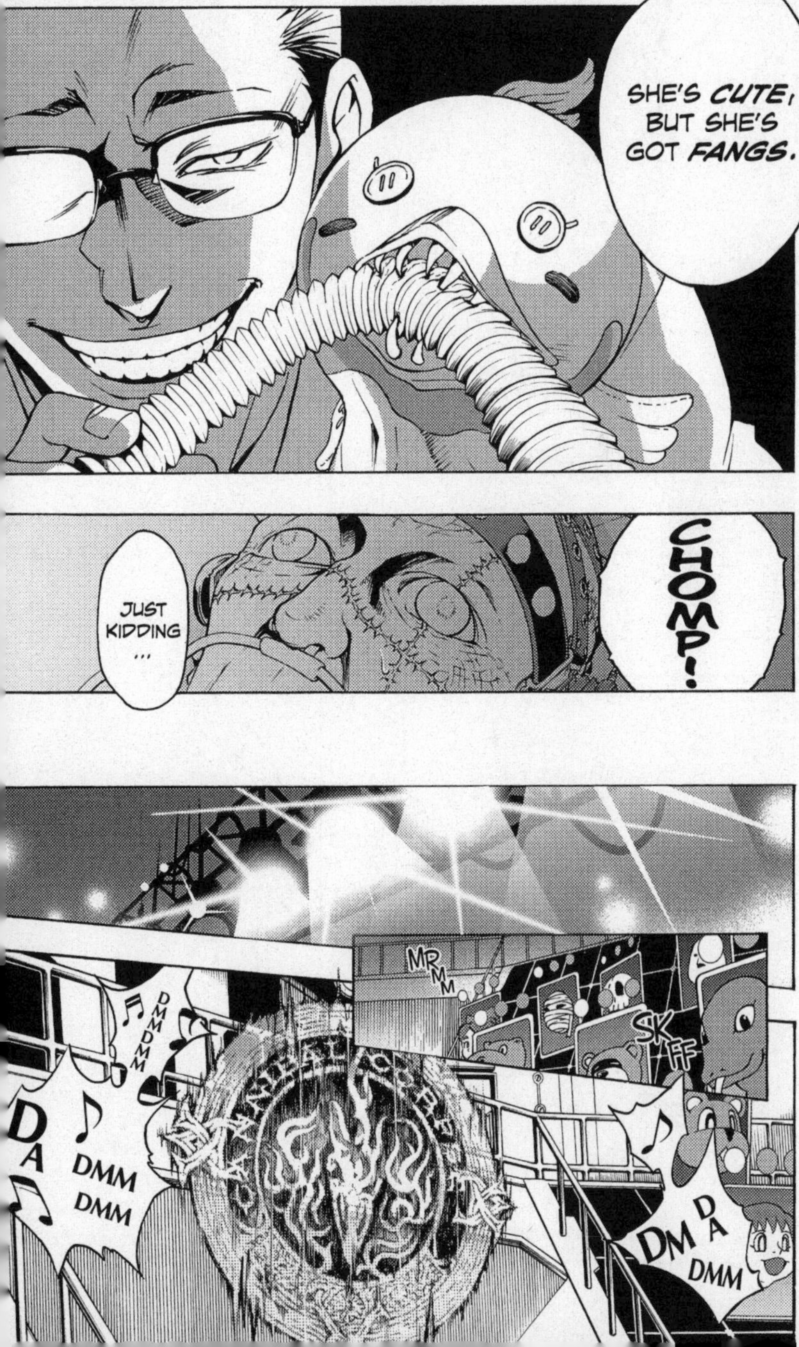
SHE'S CUTE, BUT SHE'S GOT FANGS.
CHOMP!
JUST KIDDING ...
SKFF
MRMM
DM DA DMM
DMMDMM
DA
DMM DMM

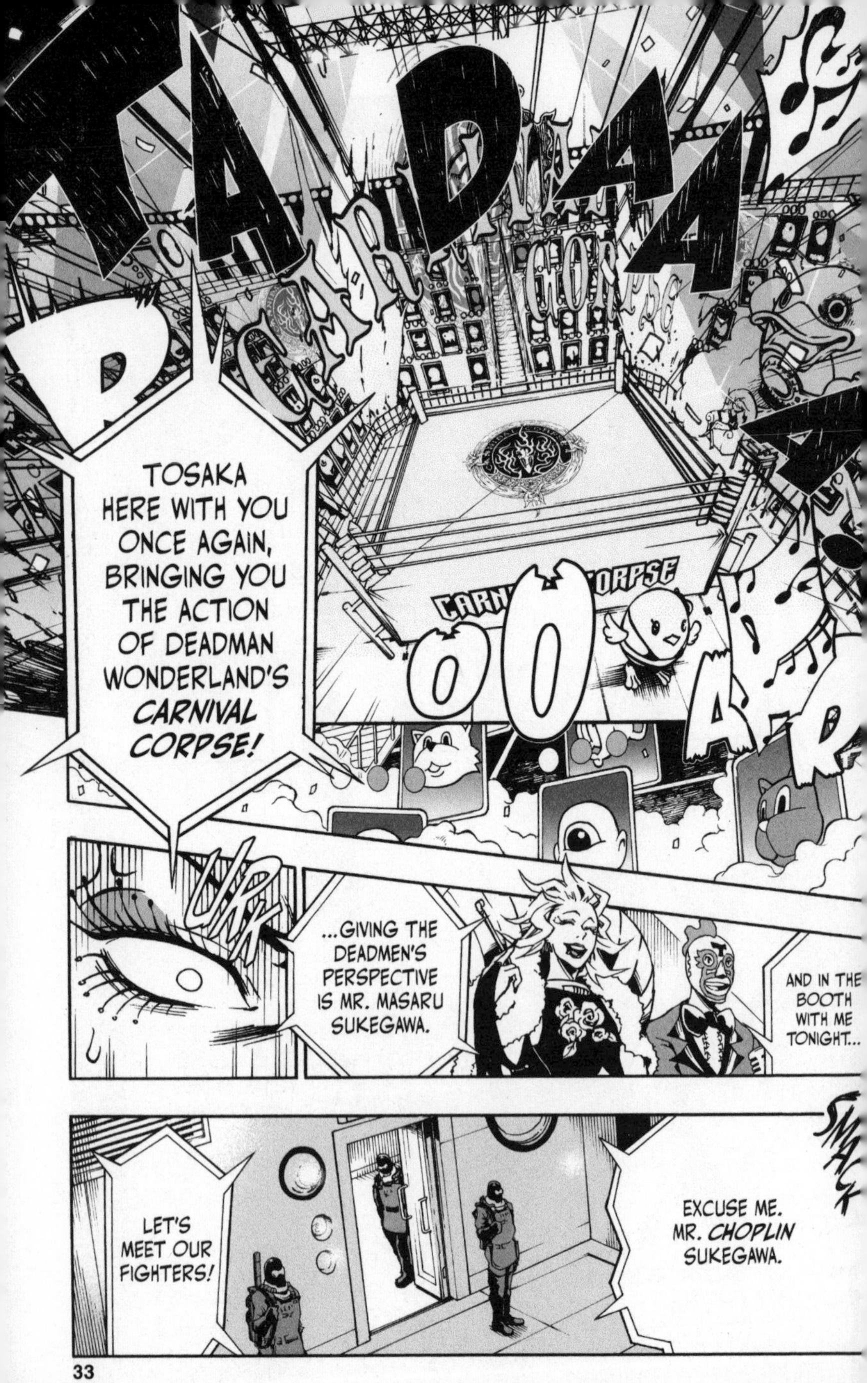

TOSAKA HERE WITH YOU ONCE AGAIN, BRINGING YOU THE ACTION OF DEADMAN WONDERLAND'S *CARNIVAL CORPSE!*
AND IN THE BOOTH WITH ME TONIGHT...
...GIVING THE DEADMEN'S PERSPECTIVE IS MR. MASARU SUKEGAWA.
URK
SMACK
EXCUSE ME. MR. *CHOPLIN* SUKEGAWA.
LET'S MEET OUR FIGHTERS!

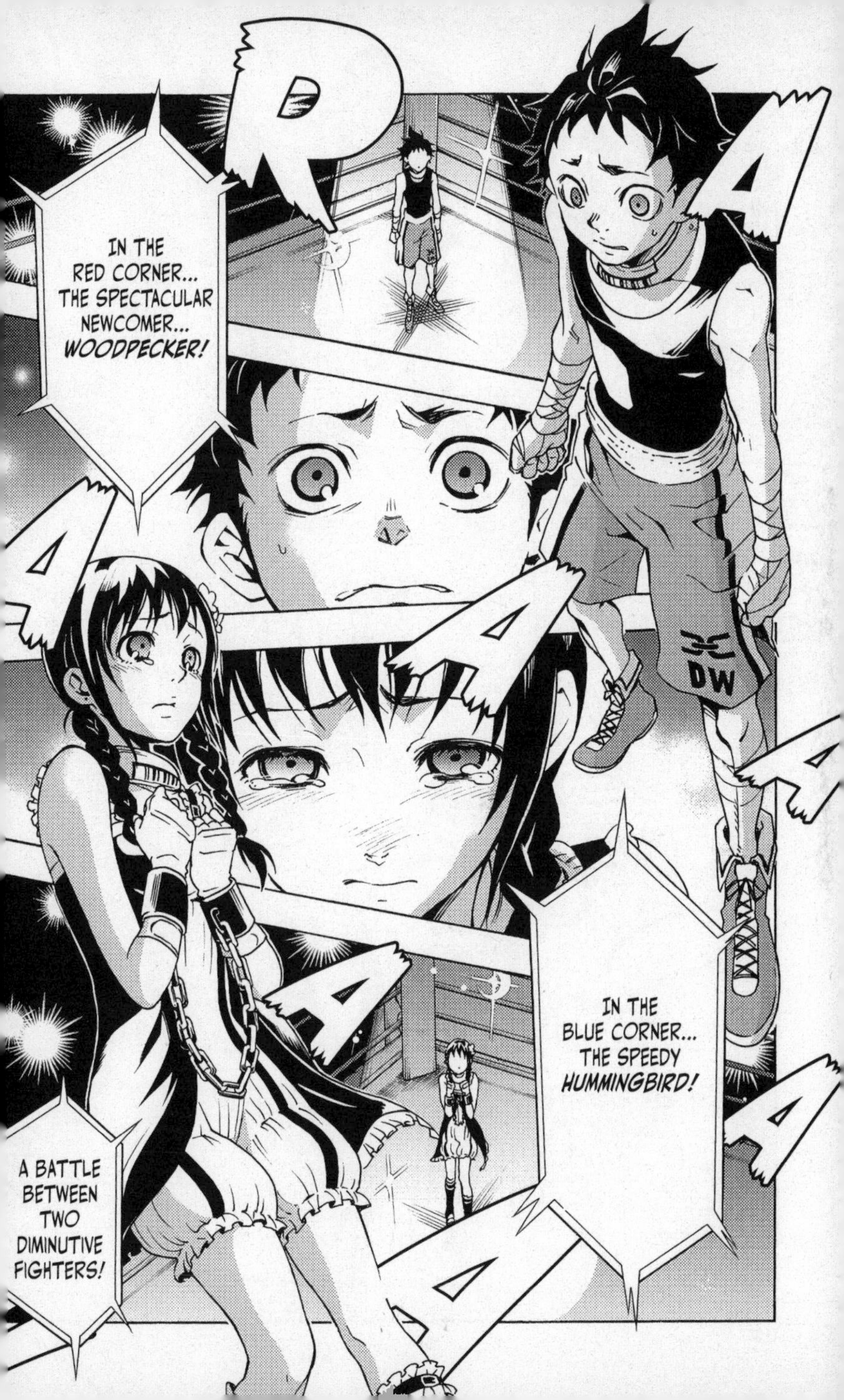
IN THE RED CORNER... THE SPECTACULAR NEWCOMER... *WOODPECKER!*
IN THE BLUE CORNER... THE SPEEDY *HUMMINGBIRD!*
A BATTLE BETWEEN TWO DIMINUTIVE FIGHTERS!

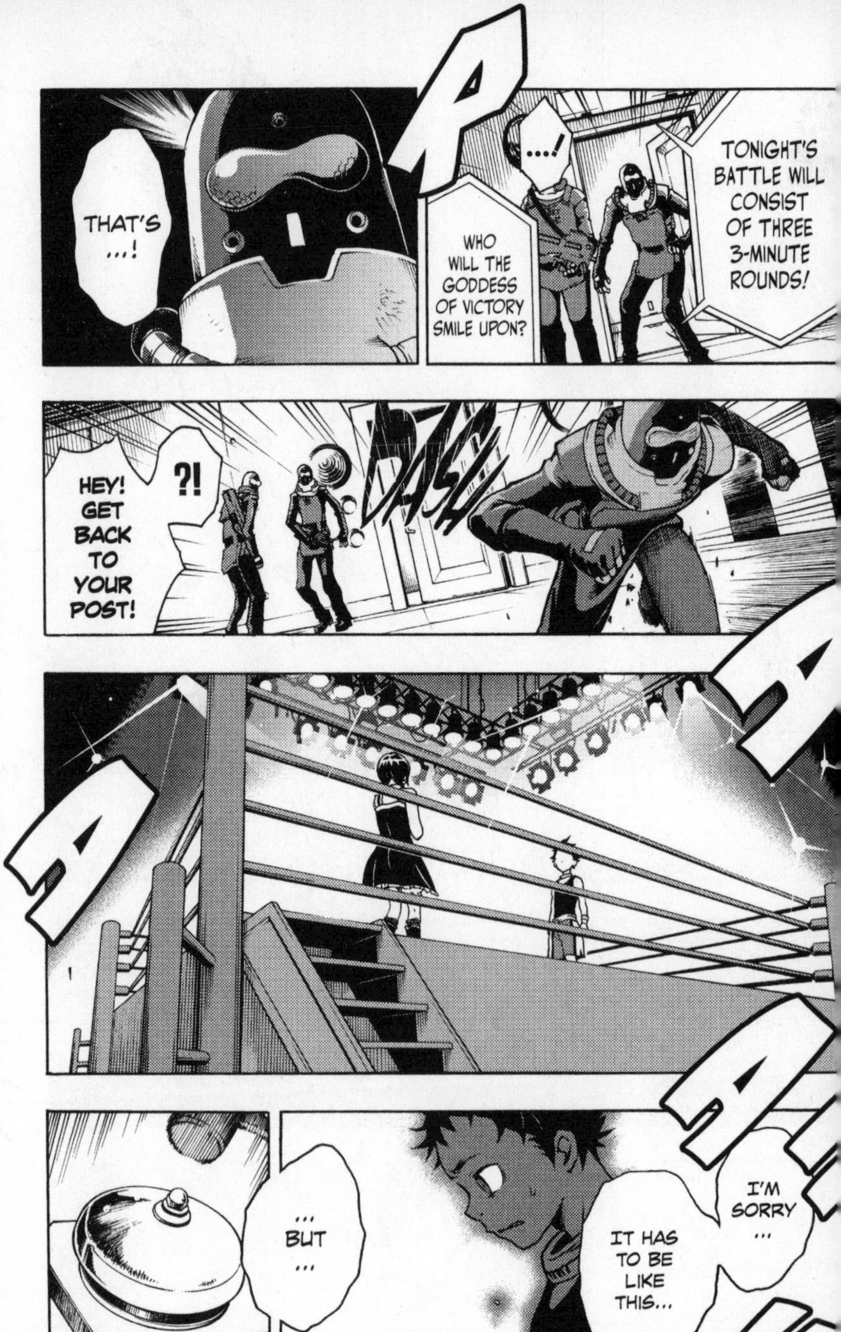
TONIGHT'S BATTLE WILL CONSIST OF THREE 3-MINUTE ROUNDS!
WHO WILL THE GODDESS OF VICTORY SMILE UPON?
....!
P
THAT'S ...!
DASH
?!
HEY! GET BACK TO YOUR POST!
I'M SORRY ...
IT HAS TO BE LIKE THIS...
... BUT ...

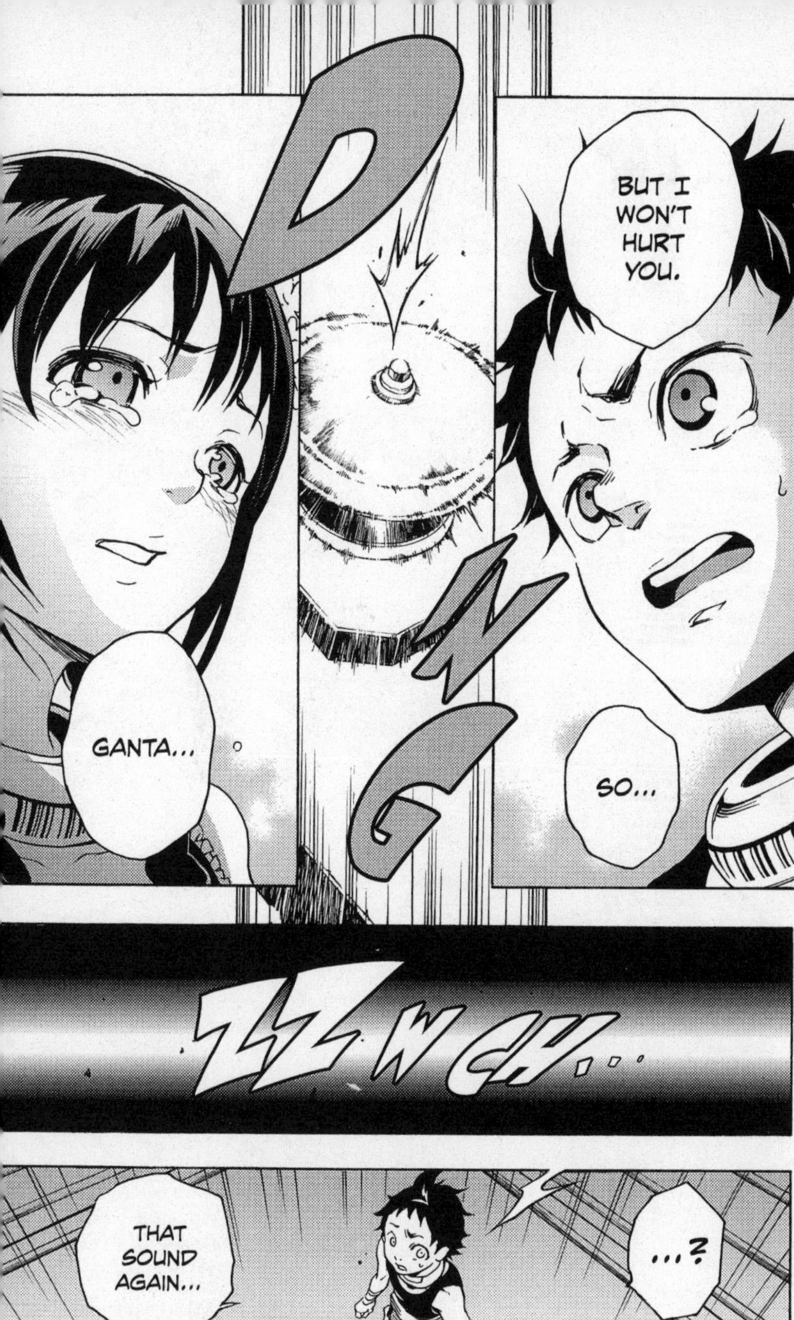
BUT I WON'T HURT YOU.
SO...
DNG
GANTA...
ZZWCH...
...?
THAT SOUND AGAIN...

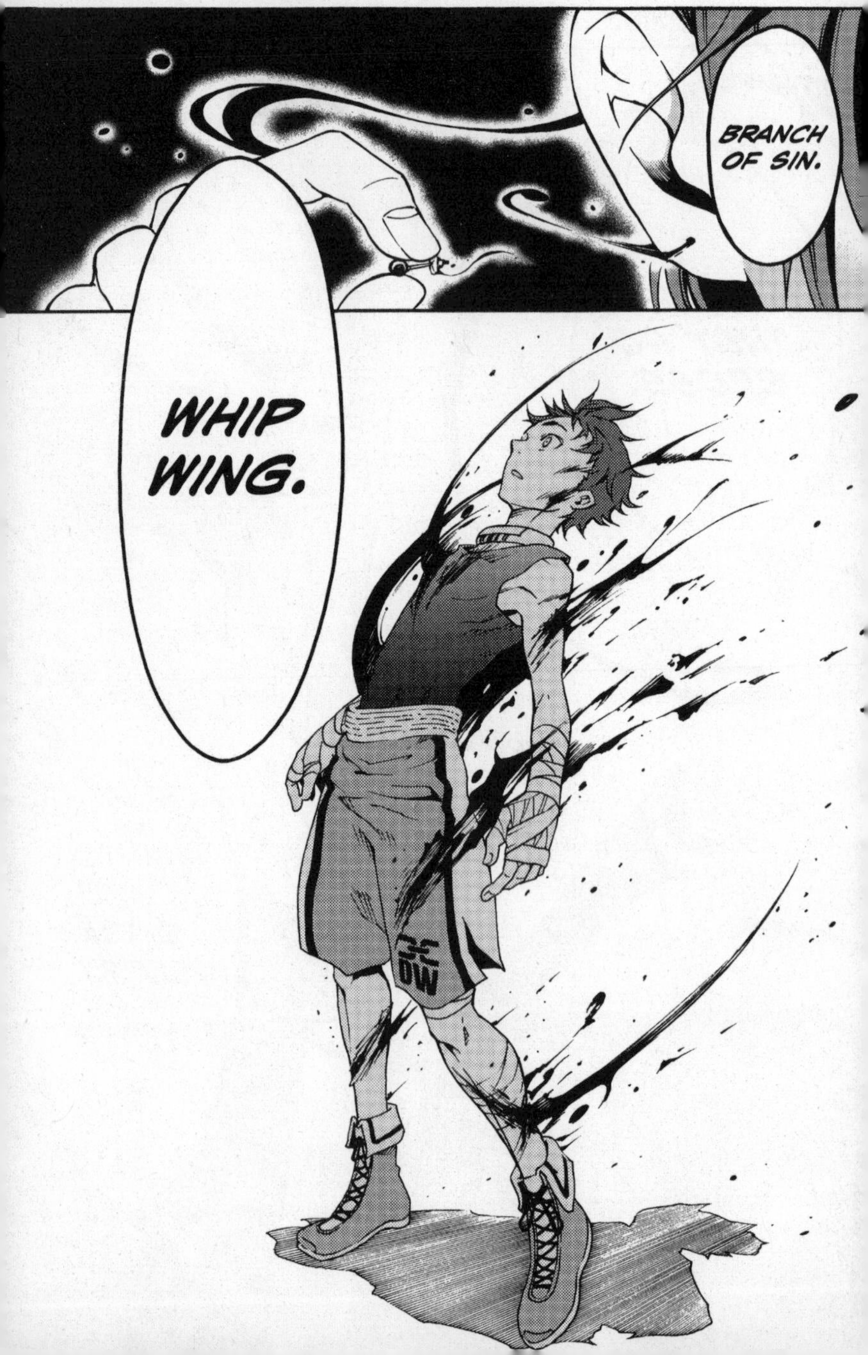
BRANCH OF SIN.
WHIP WING.

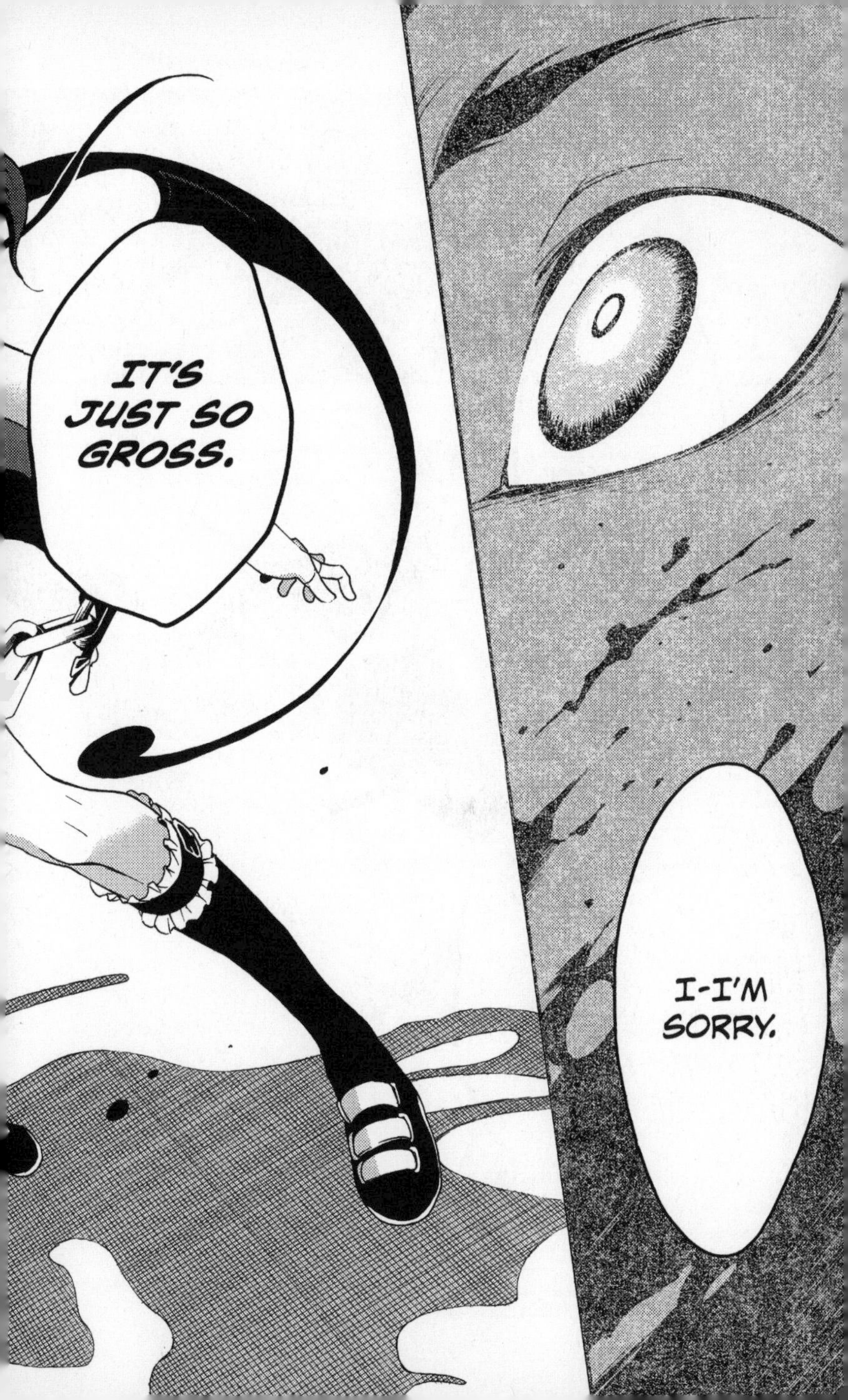
I-I'M SORRY.
IT'S JUST SO GROSS.

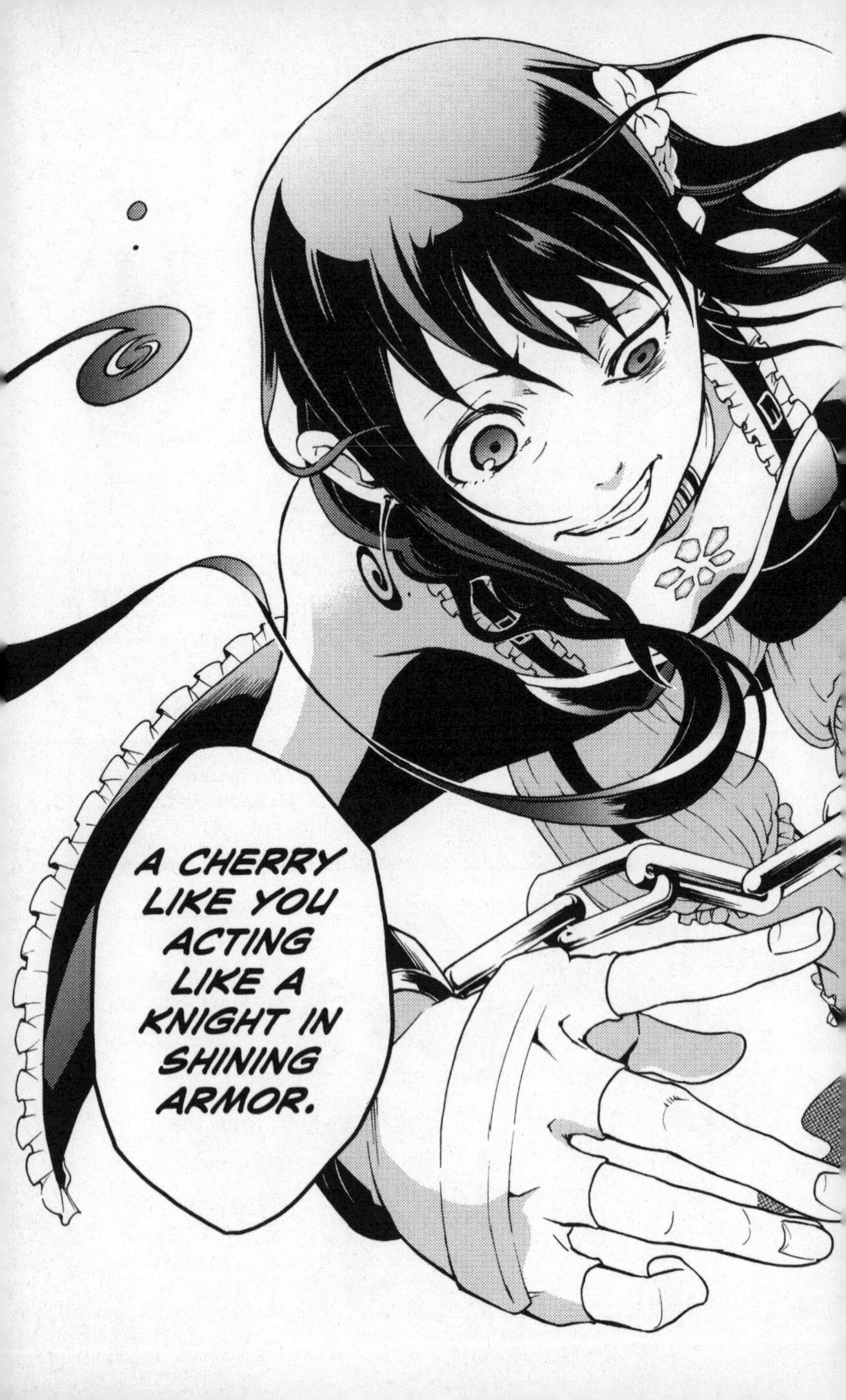
A CHERRY LIKE YOU ACTING LIKE A KNIGHT IN SHINING ARMOR.

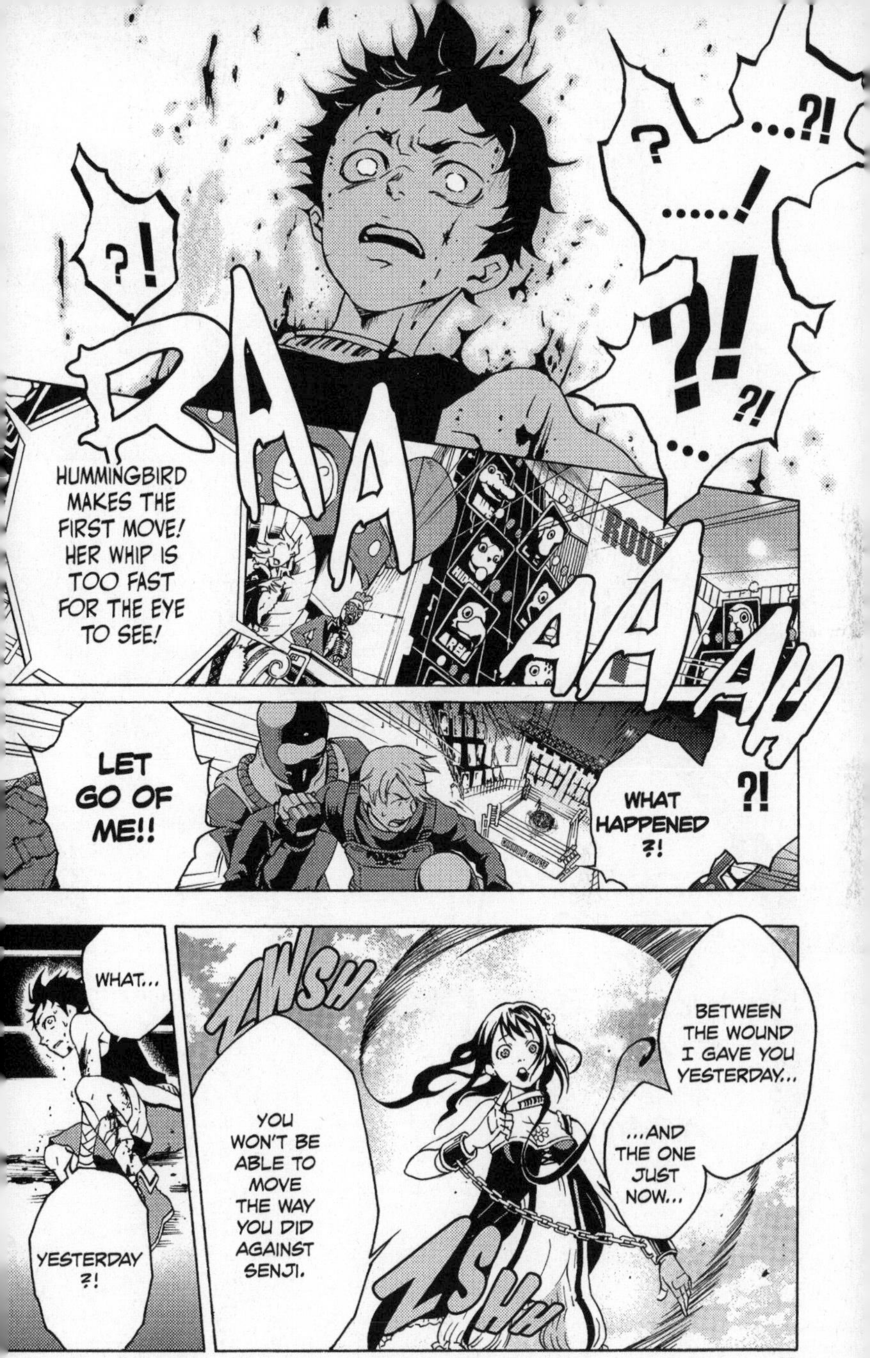
...?!
?
.....!
?!
?!
...
?!
HUMMINGBIRD MAKES THE FIRST MOVE! HER WHIP IS TOO FAST FOR THE EYE TO SEE!
RAAAAAAH
?!
WHAT HAPPENED ?!
LET GO OF ME!!
BETWEEN THE WOUND I GAVE YOU YESTERDAY...
...AND THE ONE JUST NOW...
YOU WON'T BE ABLE TO MOVE THE WAY YOU DID AGAINST SENJI.
ZWSH
ZSHH
WHAT...
YESTERDAY ?!

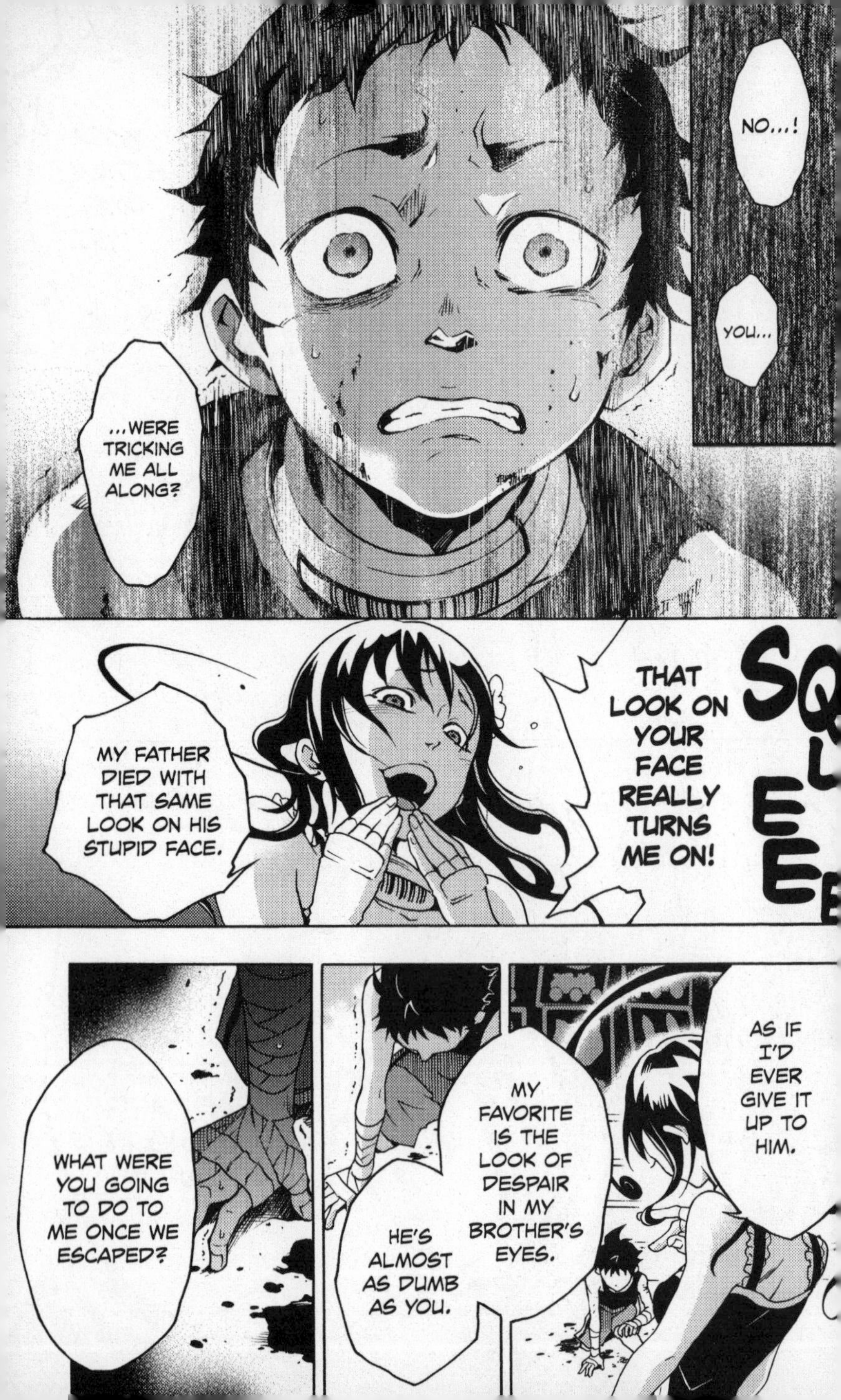
NO...!
YOU...
...WERE TRICKING ME ALL ALONG?
THAT LOOK ON YOUR FACE REALLY TURNS ME ON!
MY FATHER DIED WITH THAT SAME LOOK ON HIS STUPID FACE.
AS IF I'D EVER GIVE IT UP TO HIM.
MY FAVORITE IS THE LOOK OF DESPAIR IN MY BROTHER'S EYES.
HE'S ALMOST AS DUMB AS YOU.
WHAT WERE YOU GOING TO DO TO ME ONCE WE ESCAPED?

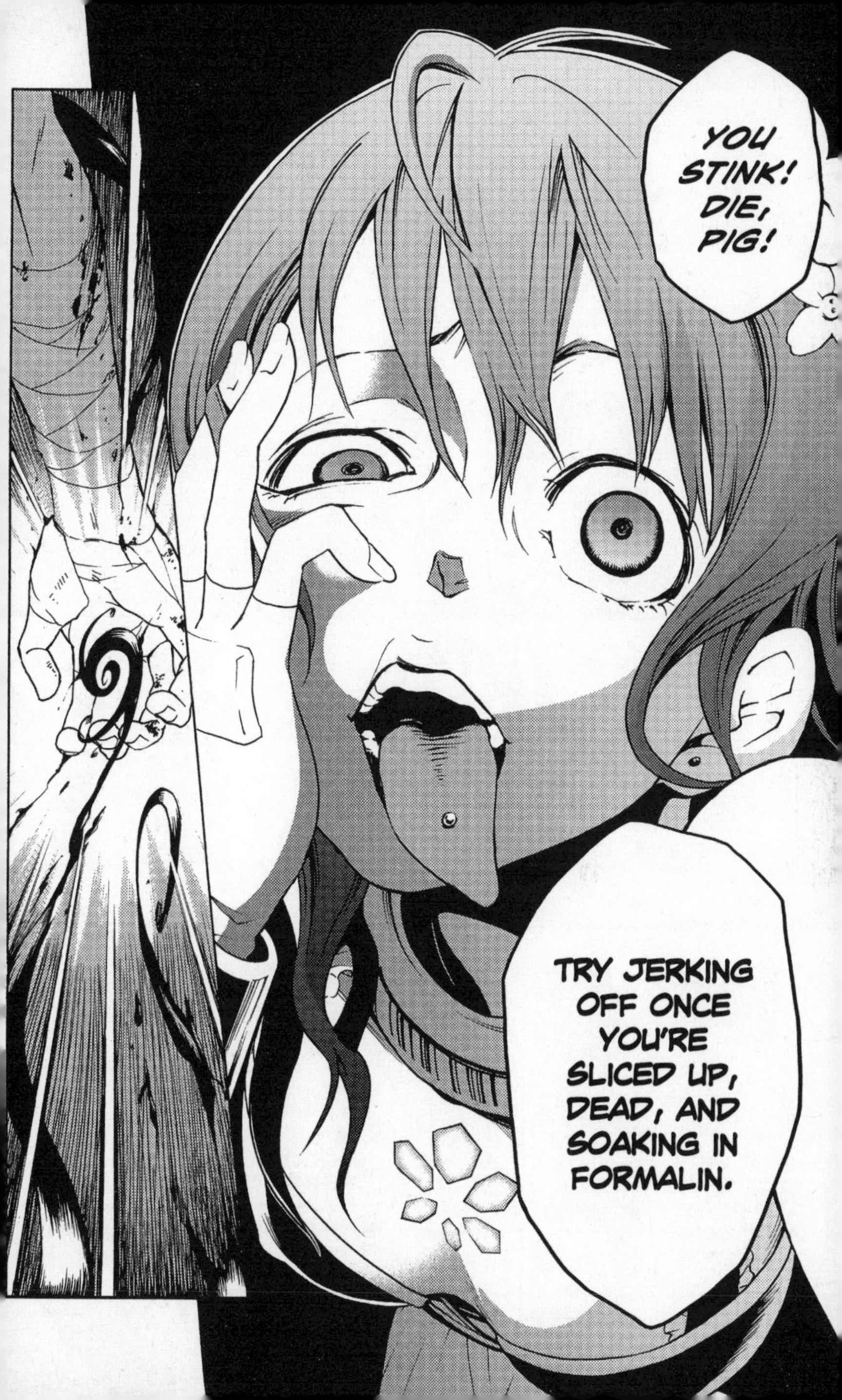
YOU STINK! DIE, PIG!
TRY JERKING OFF ONCE YOU'RE SLICED UP, DEAD, AND SOAKING IN FORMALIN.

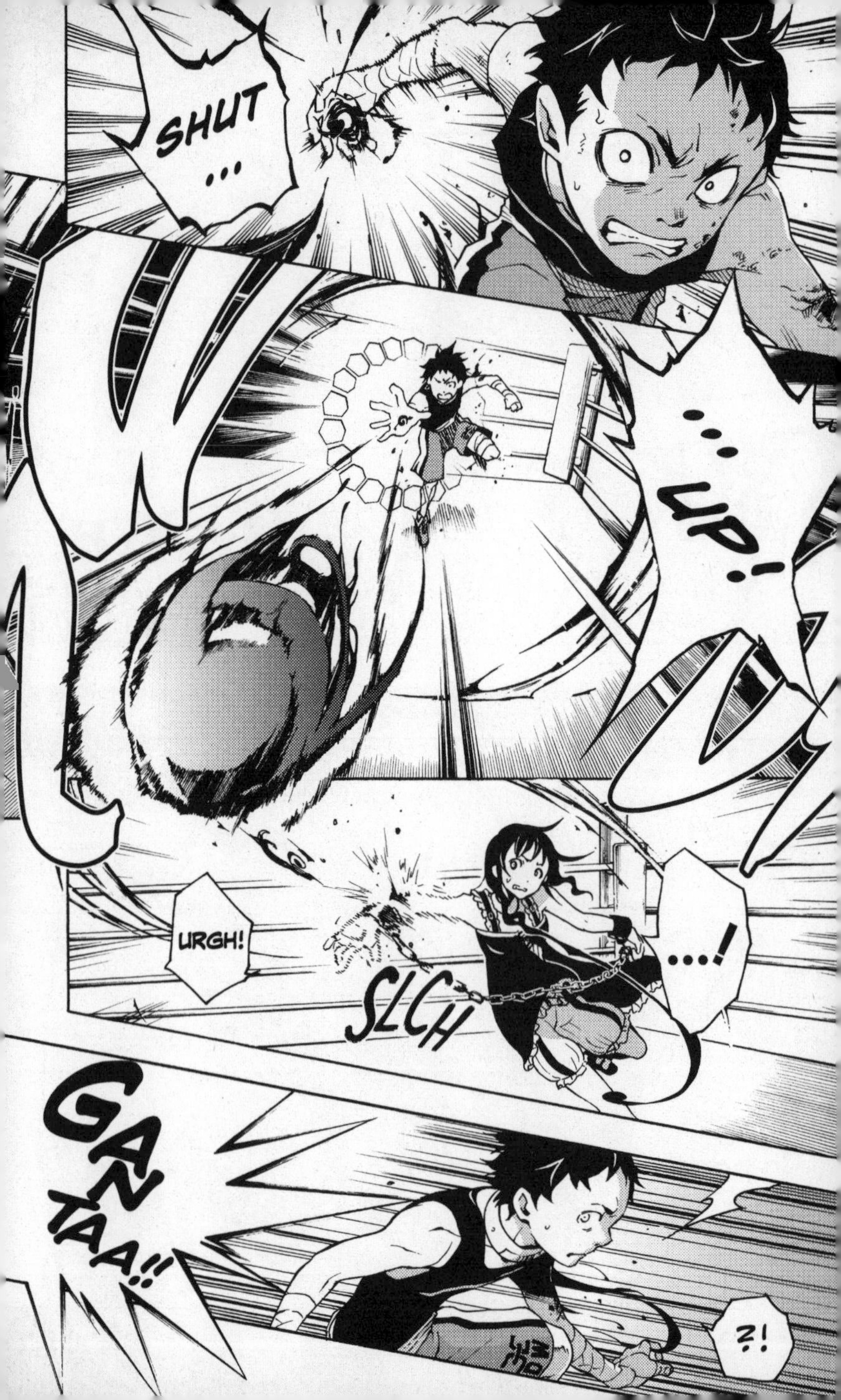
SHUT ...
... UP!!
....!
SLCH
URGH!
GANTAA!!
?!

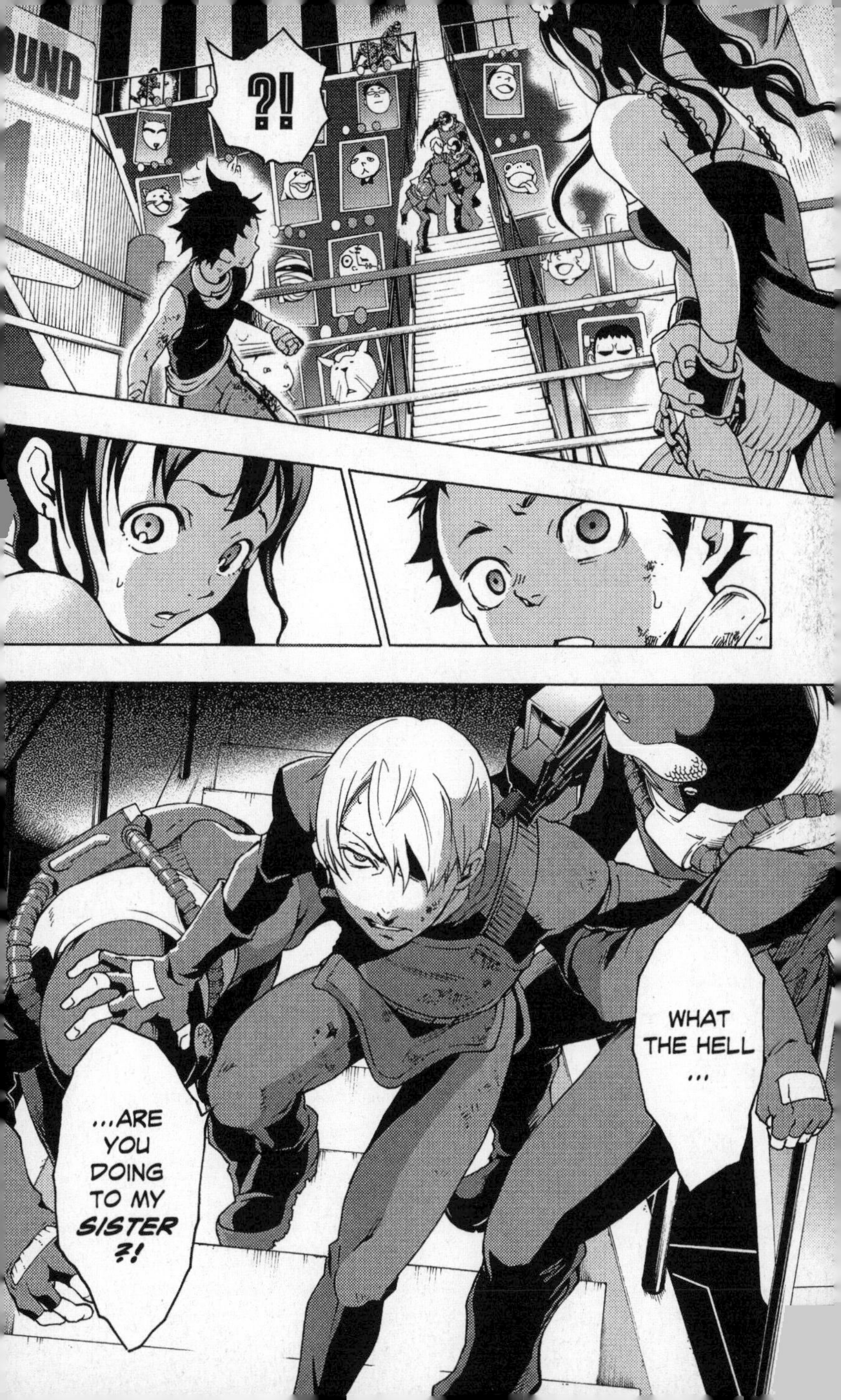
?!
WHAT THE HELL ...
...ARE YOU DOING TO MY SISTER ?!

DEAD
MAN WONDER LAND

DEAD
MAN WONDER LAND

DEAD
MAN WONDER LAND

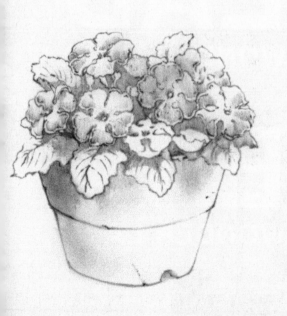

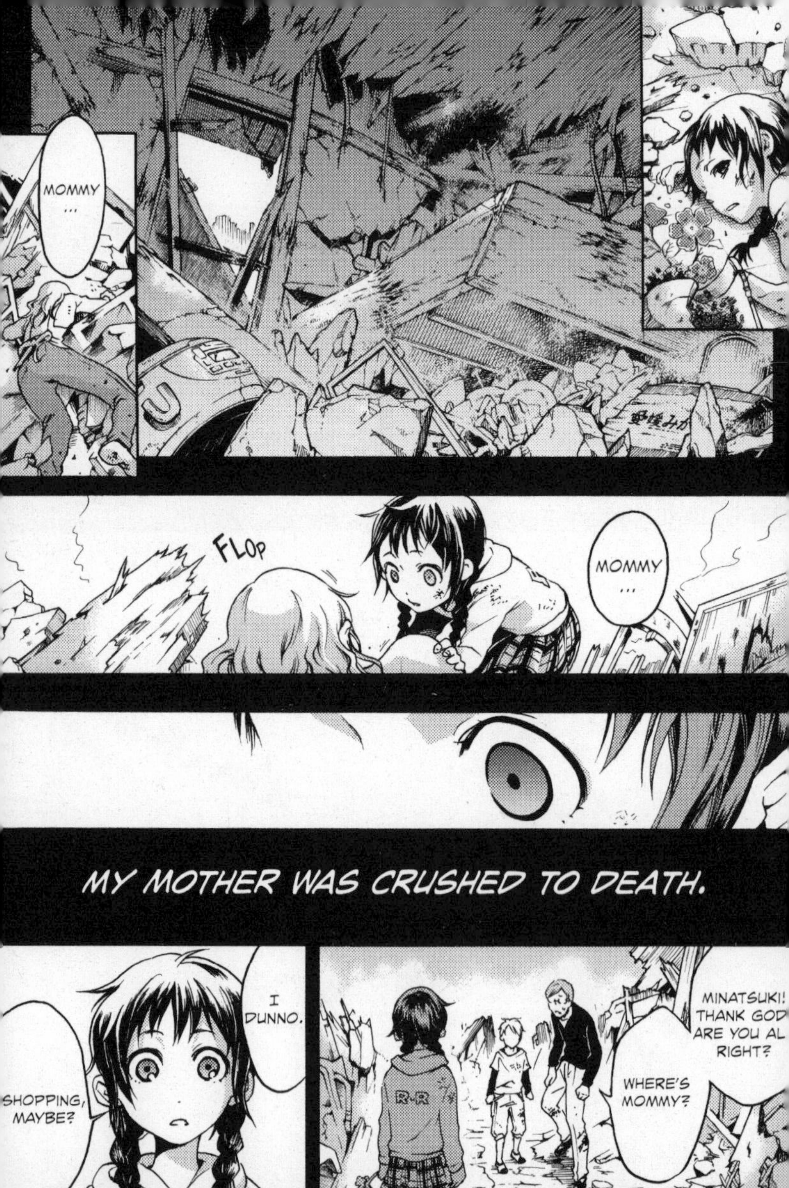
MOMMY ...
MOMMY ...
FLOP
MY MOTHER WAS CRUSHED TO DEATH.
MINATSUKI! THANK GOD ARE YOU AL RIGHT?
WHERE'S MOMMY?
I DUNNO.
SHOPPING, MAYBE?

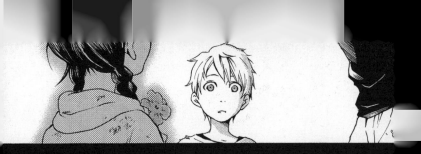

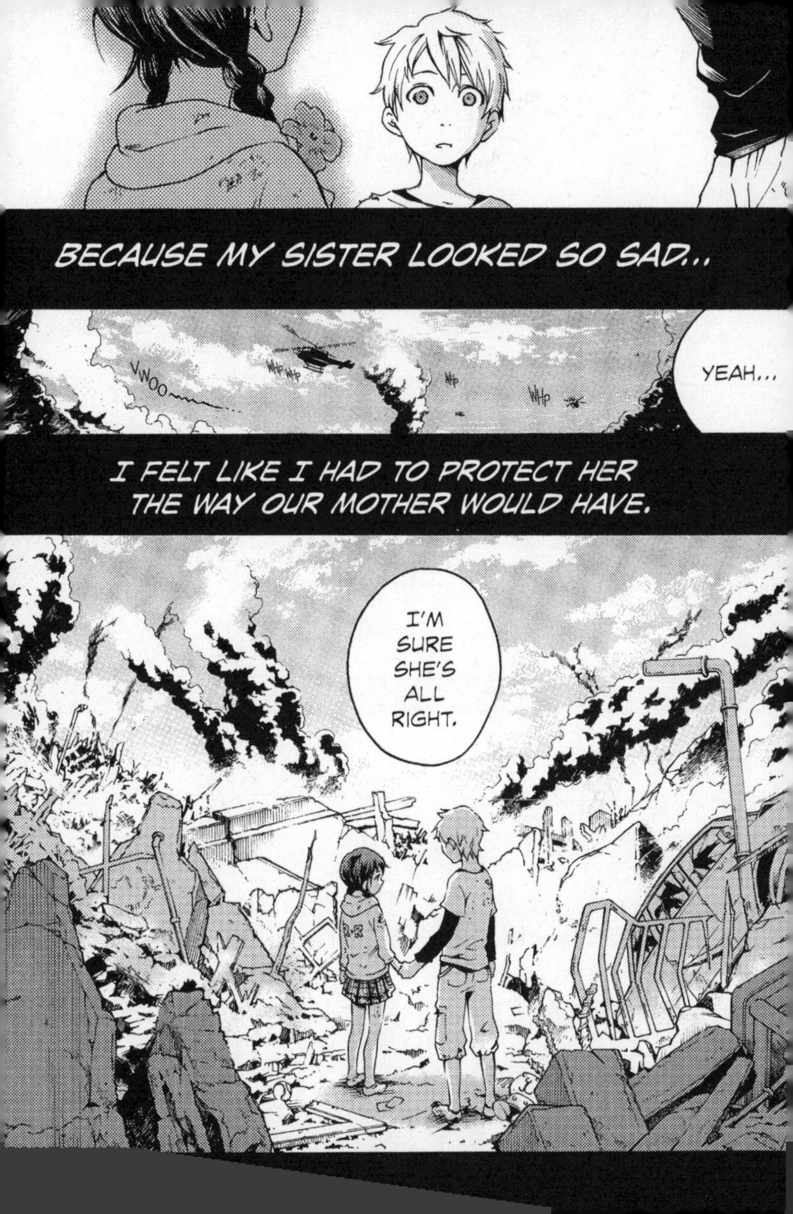
BECAUSE MY SISTER LOOKED SO SAD...
YEAH...
WHP
WHP
WHP WHP
VWOO...
I FELT LIKE I HAD TO PROTECT HER THE WAY OUR MOTHER WOULD HAVE.
I'M SURE SHE'S ALL RIGHT.

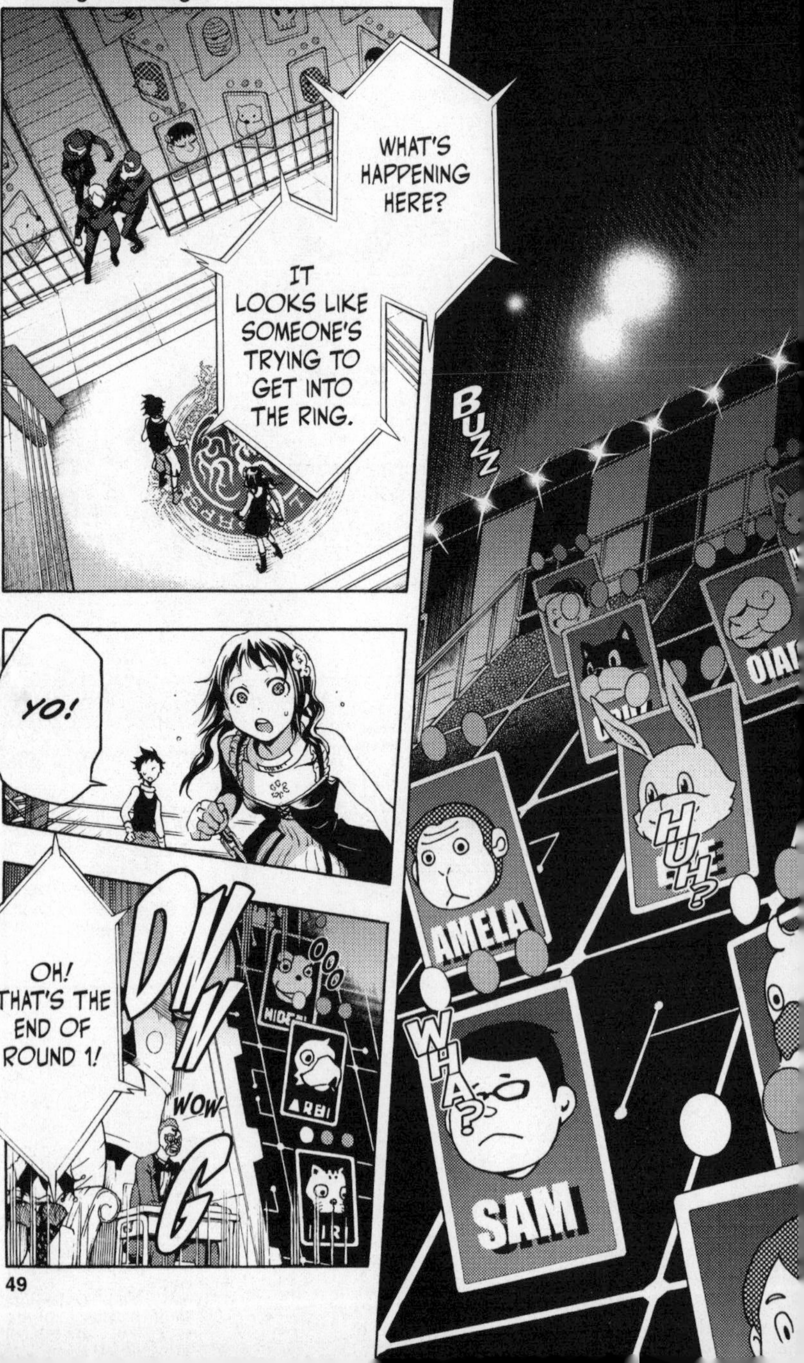
BUZZ
AMELA
HUH?
WHA?
SAM
WHAT'S HAPPENING HERE?
IT LOOKS LIKE SOMEONE'S TRYING TO GET INTO THE RING.
YO!
OH! THAT'S THE END OF ROUND 1!
DING
WOW

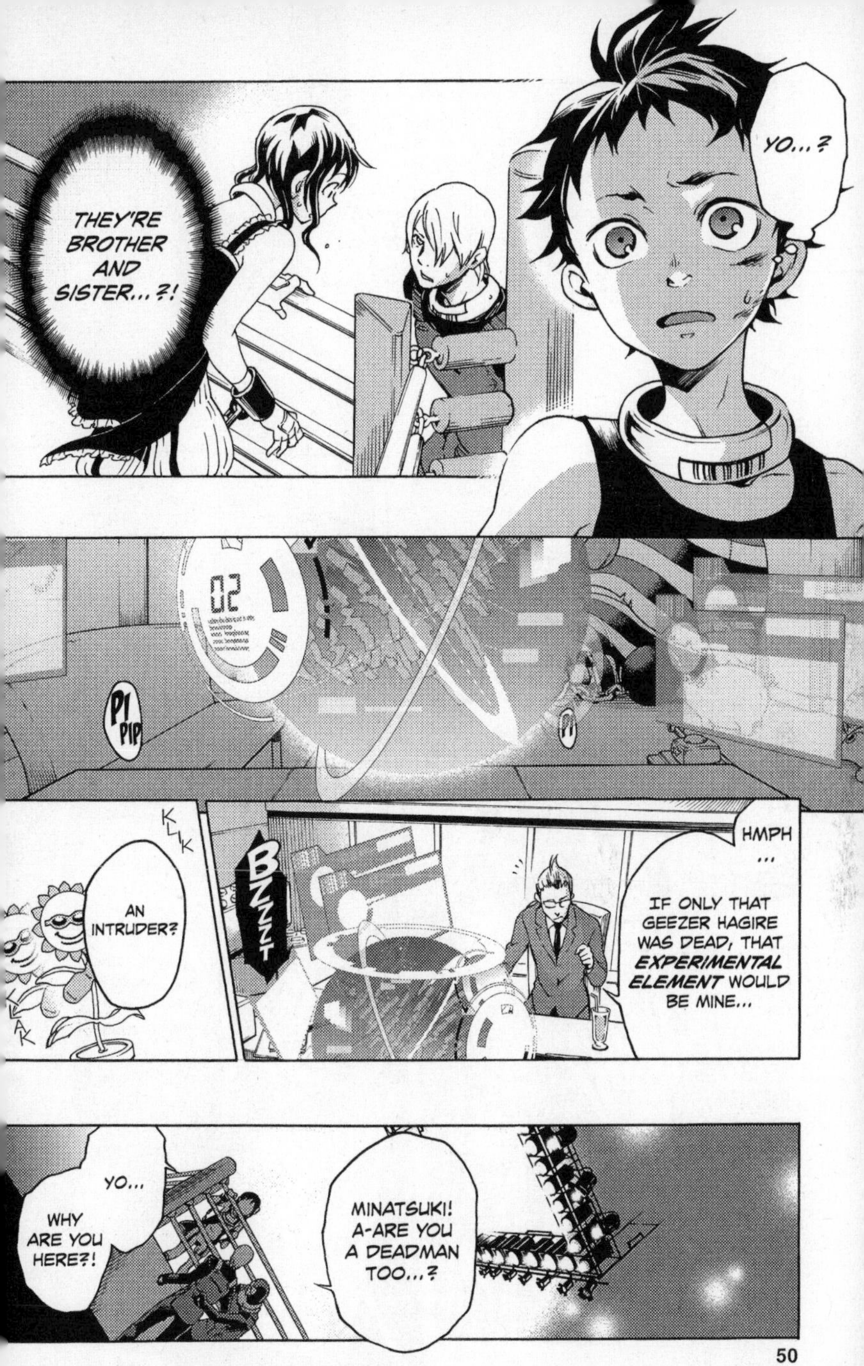
YO...?
THEY'RE BROTHER AND SISTER...?!
PI
PI PIP
HMPH...
IF ONLY THAT GEEZER HAGIRE WAS DEAD, THAT EXPERIMENTAL ELEMENT WOULD BE MINE...
BZZZT
KLIK
AN INTRUDER?
KLAK
MINATSUKI! A-ARE YOU A DEADMAN TOO...?
YO... WHY ARE YOU HERE?!

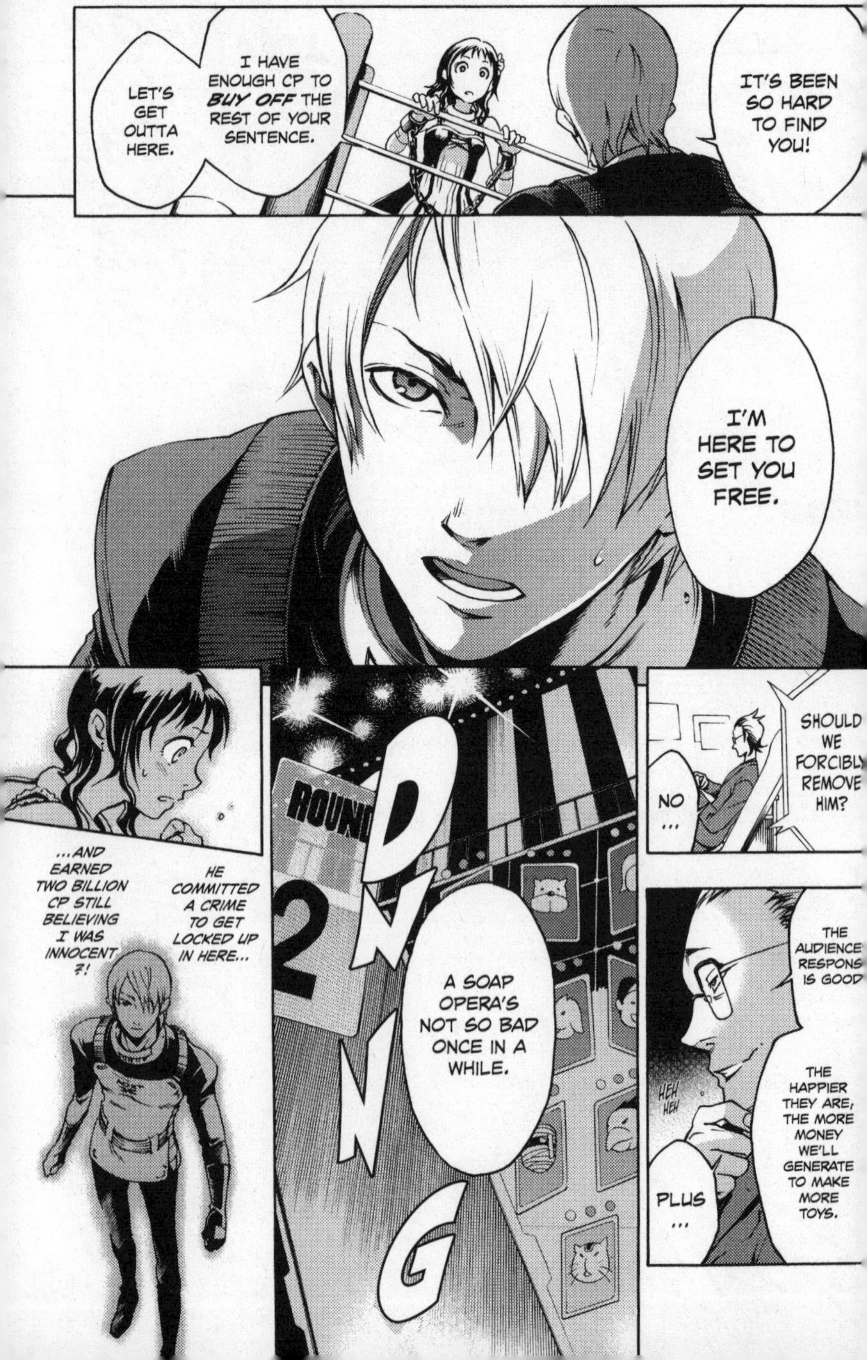
IT'S BEEN SO HARD TO FIND YOU!
I HAVE ENOUGH CP TO BUY OFF THE REST OF YOUR SENTENCE.
LET'S GET OUTTA HERE.
I'M HERE TO SET YOU FREE.
SHOULD WE FORCIBL REMOVE HIM?
NO ...
THE AUDIENCE RESPONS IS GOOD
HEH HEH
THE HAPPIER THEY ARE, THE MORE MONEY WE'LL GENERATE TO MAKE MORE TOYS.
PLUS ...
A SOAP OPERA'S NOT SO BAD ONCE IN A WHILE.
ROUN
2
DNNG
HE COMMITTED A CRIME TO GET LOCKED UP IN HERE...
...AND EARNED TWO BILLION CP STILL BELIEVING I WAS INNOCENT?!

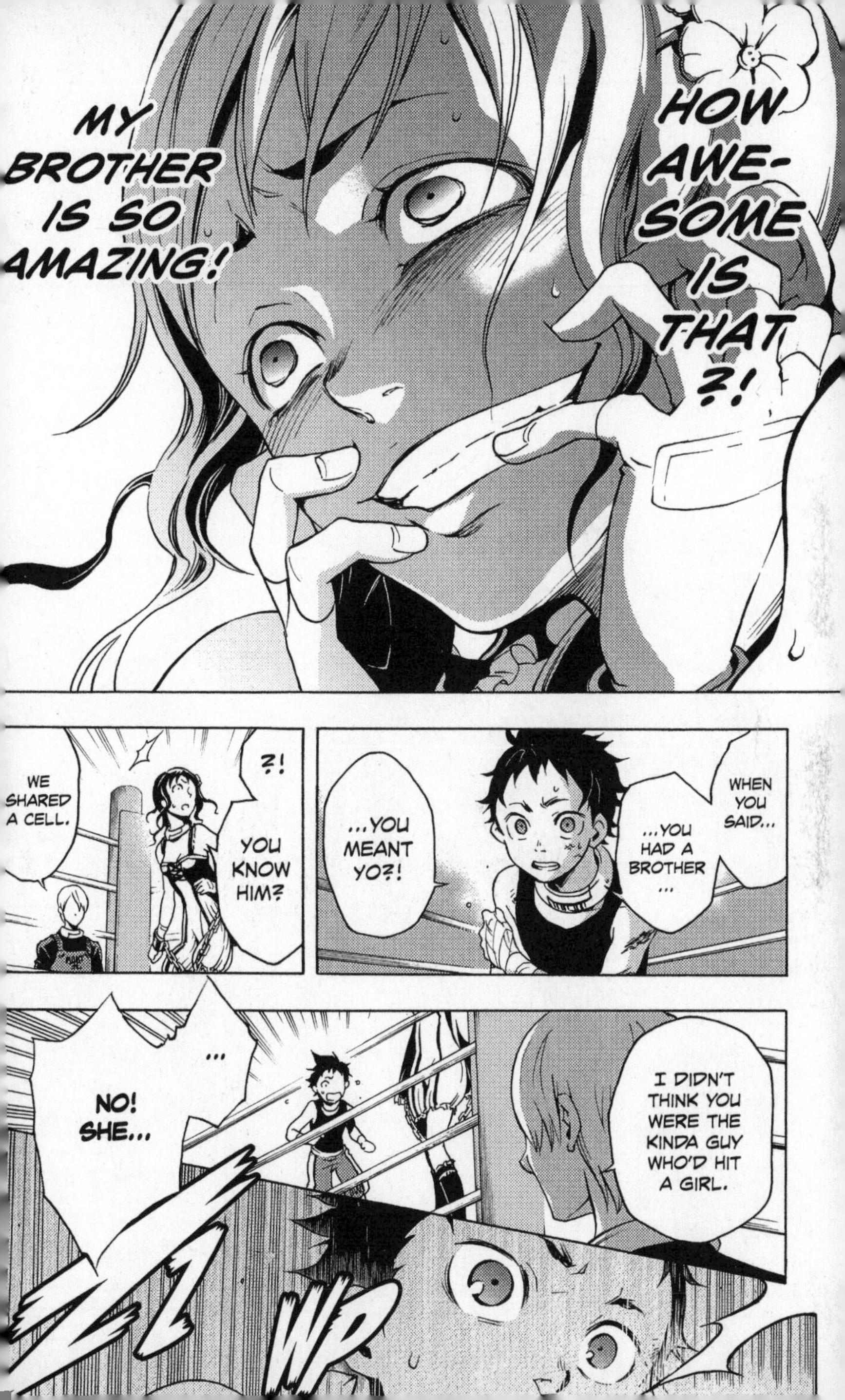
HOW AWE-SOME IS THAT?!
MY BROTHER IS SO AMAZING!
WHEN YOU SAID...
...YOU HAD A BROTHER ...
...YOU MEANT YO?!
?!
YOU KNOW HIM?
WE SHARED A CELL.
I DIDN'T THINK YOU WERE THE KINDA GUY WHO'D HIT A GIRL.
...
NO! SHE...

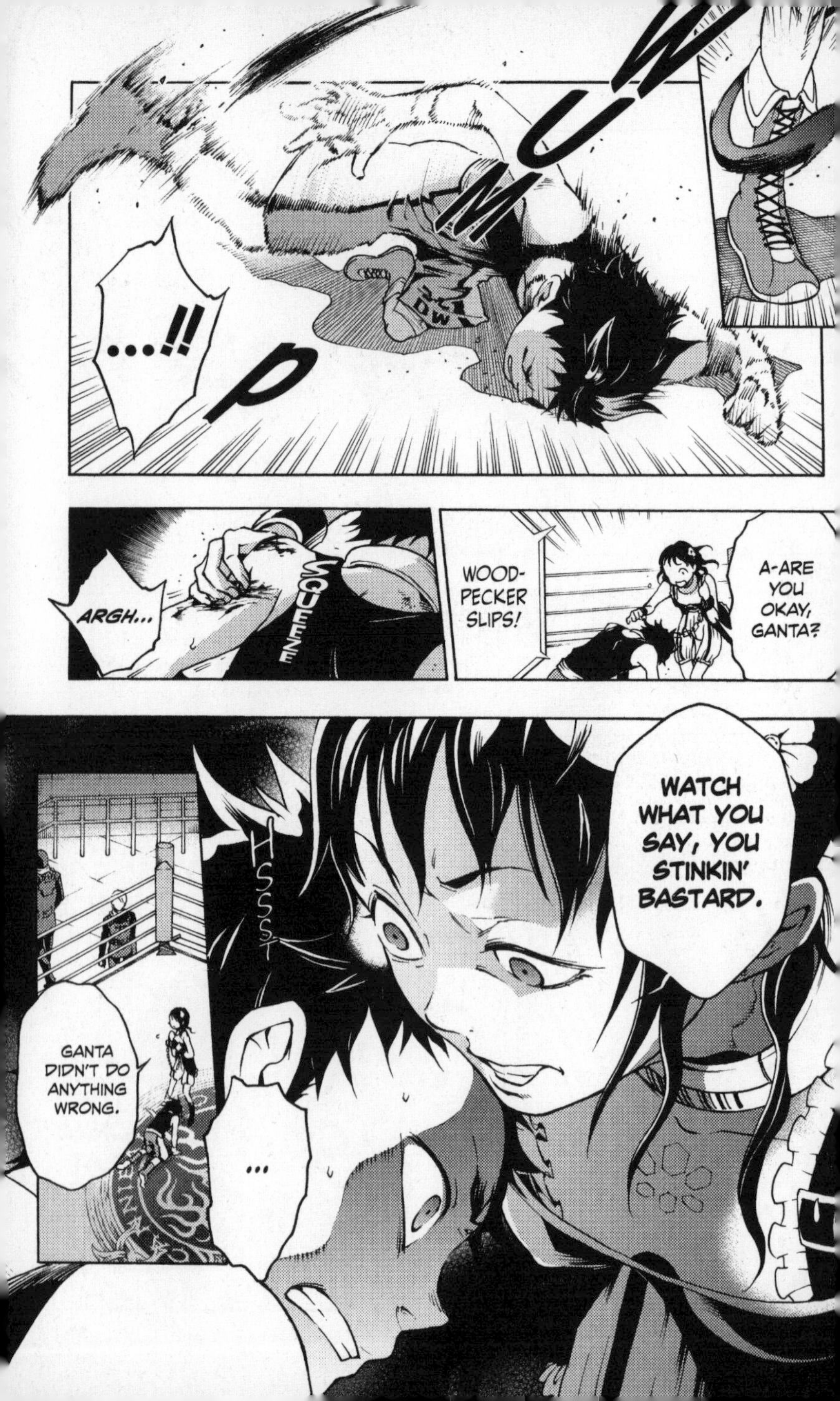

WUMP
...!!
A-ARE YOU OKAY, GANTA?
WOOD-PECKER SLIPS!
SQUEEENE
ARGH...
WATCH WHAT YOU SAY, YOU STINKIN' BASTARD.
HSSSST
...
GANTA DIDN'T DO ANYTHING WRONG.

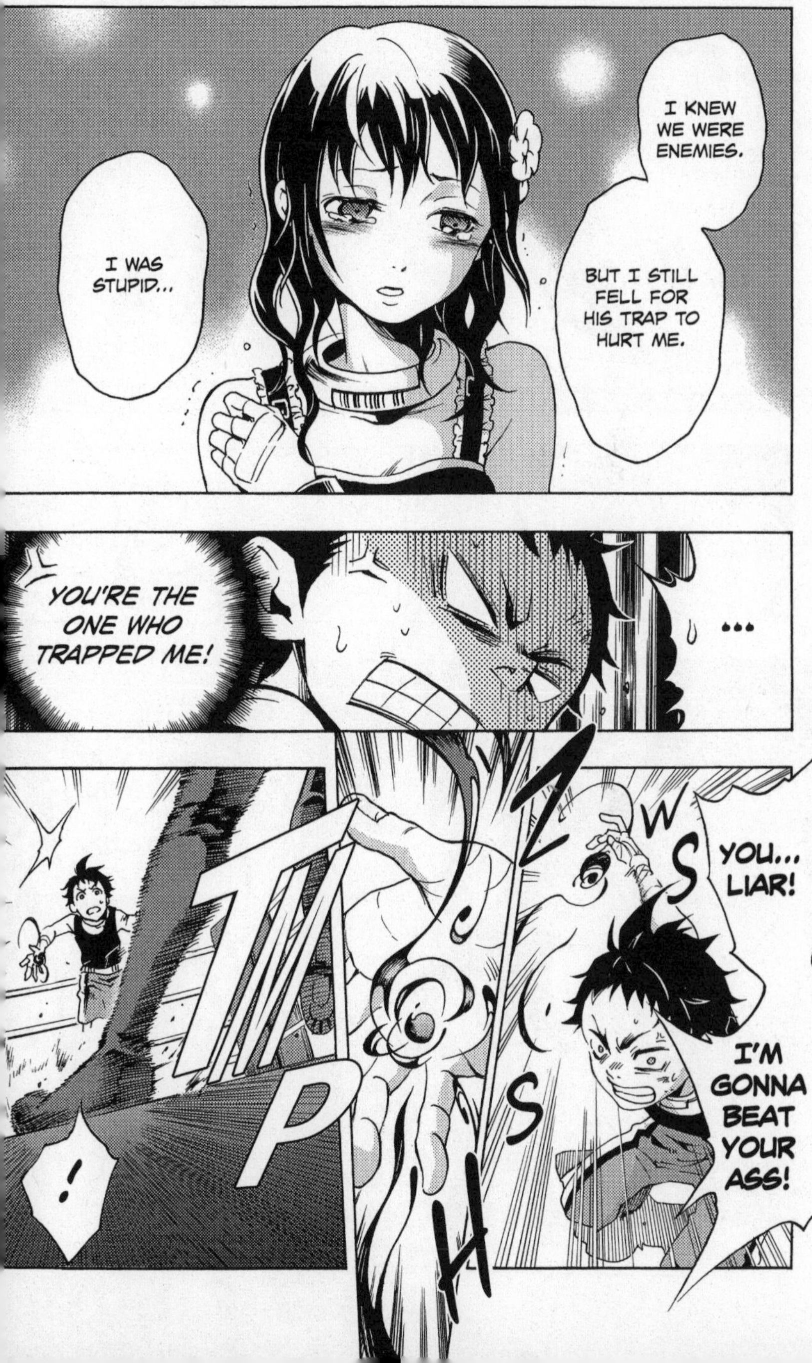
I KNEW WE WERE ENEMIES.
BUT I STILL FELL FOR HIS TRAP TO HURT ME.
I WAS STUPID...
...
YOU'RE THE ONE WHO TRAPPED ME!
YOU... LIAR!
I'M GONNA BEAT YOUR ASS!
!

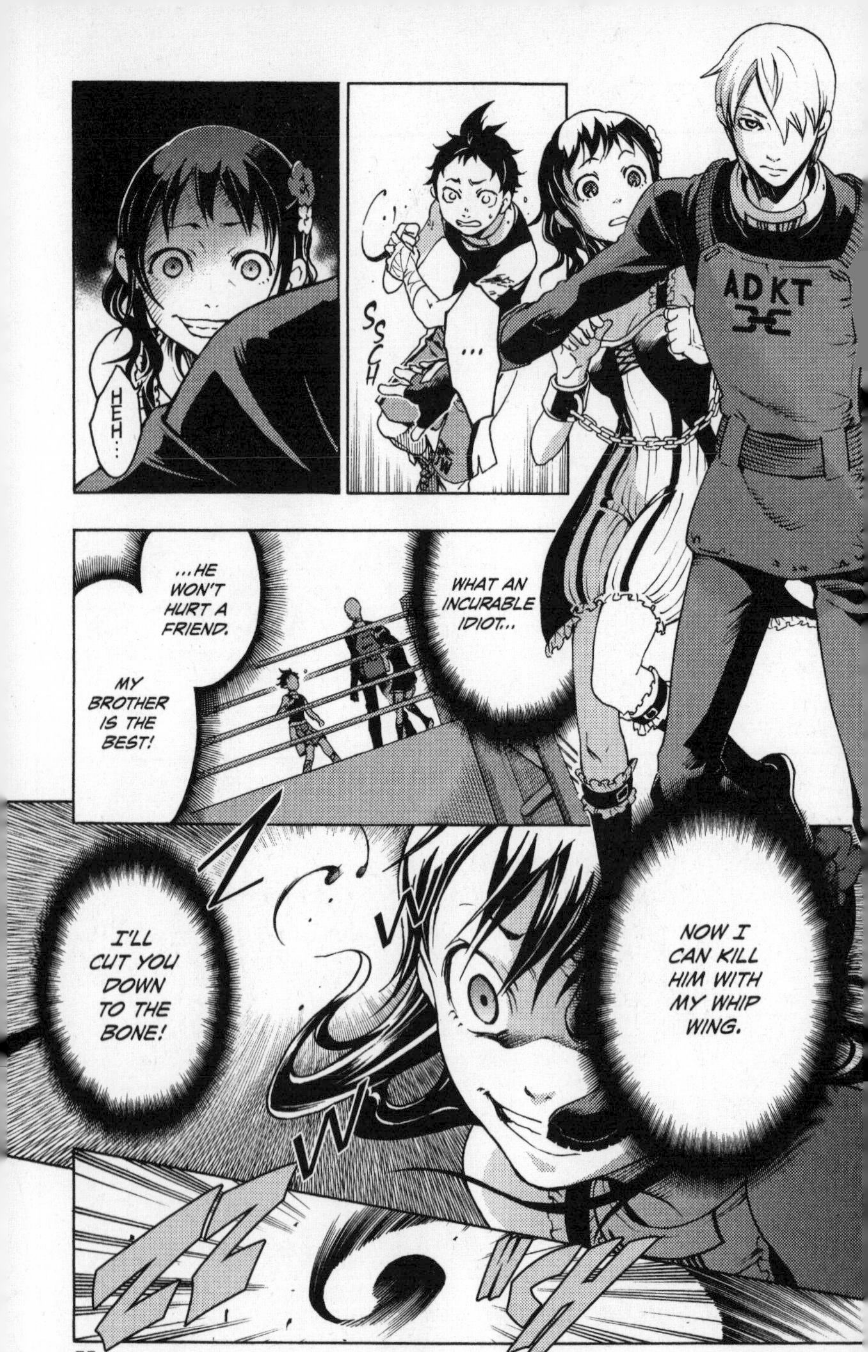
SSCH
...
HEH...
WHAT AN INCURABLE IDIOT...
...HE WON'T HURT A FRIEND.
MY BROTHER IS THE BEST!
NOW I CAN KILL HIM WITH MY WHIP WING.
I'LL CUT YOU DOWN TO THE BONE!

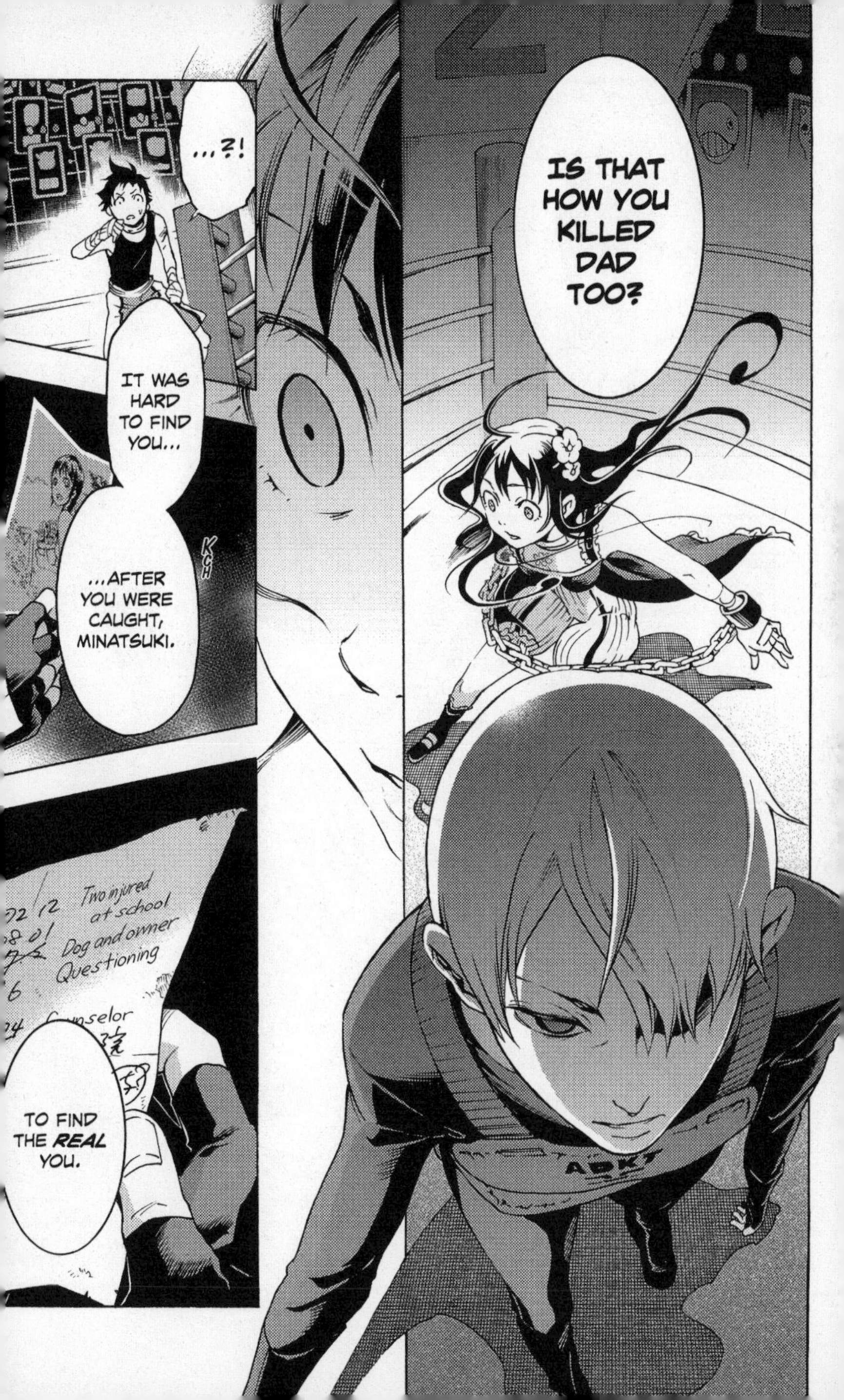
IS THAT HOW YOU KILLED DAD TOO?
...?!
IT WAS HARD TO FIND YOU...
...AFTER YOU WERE CAUGHT, MINATSUKI.
KCH
Two injured at school
Dog and owner
Questioning
TO FIND THE *REAL* YOU.

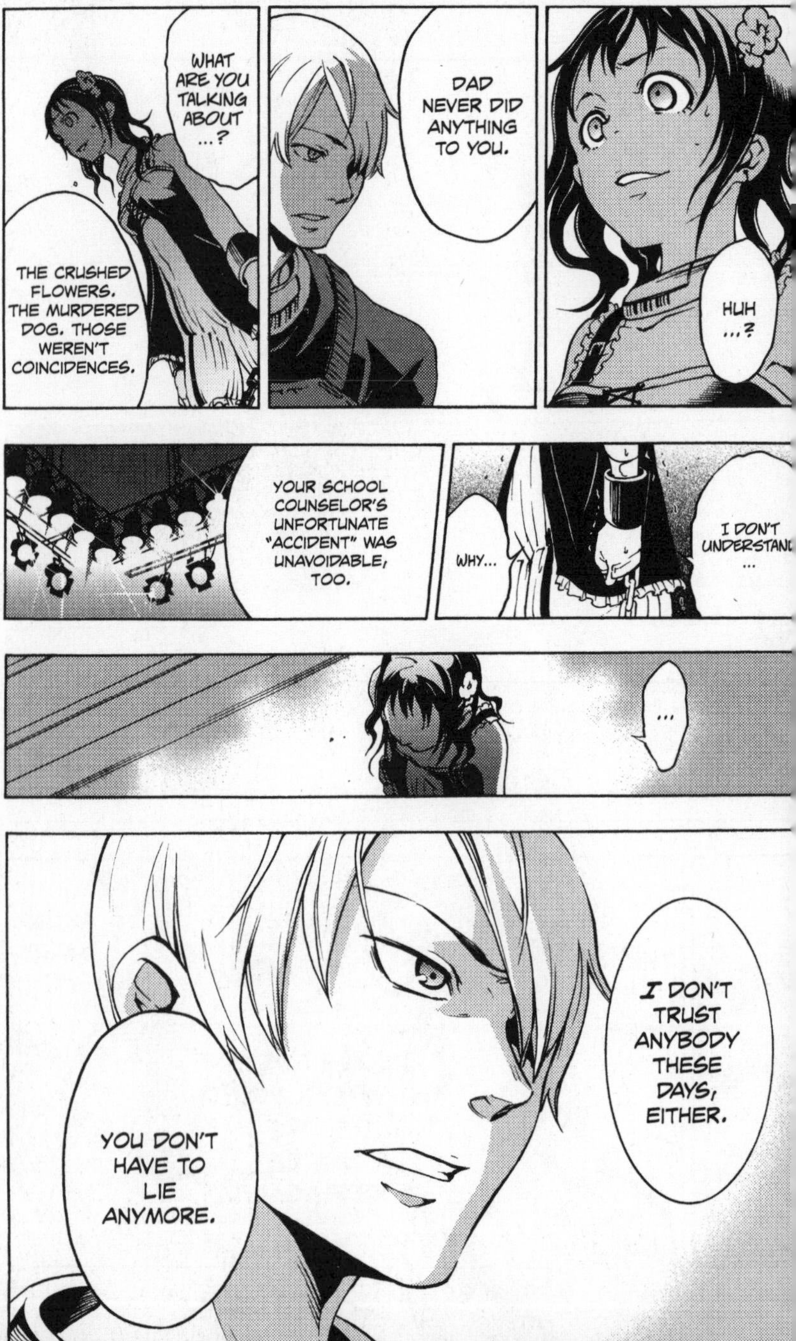
HUH ...?
DAD NEVER DID ANYTHING TO YOU.
WHAT ARE YOU TALKING ABOUT ...?
THE CRUSHED FLOWERS. THE MURDERED DOG. THOSE WEREN'T COINCIDENCES.
I DON'T UNDERSTAND ...
WHY...
YOUR SCHOOL COUNSELOR'S UNFORTUNATE "ACCIDENT" WAS UNAVOIDABLE, TOO.
...
I DON'T TRUST ANYBODY THESE DAYS, EITHER.
YOU DON'T HAVE TO LIE ANYMORE.

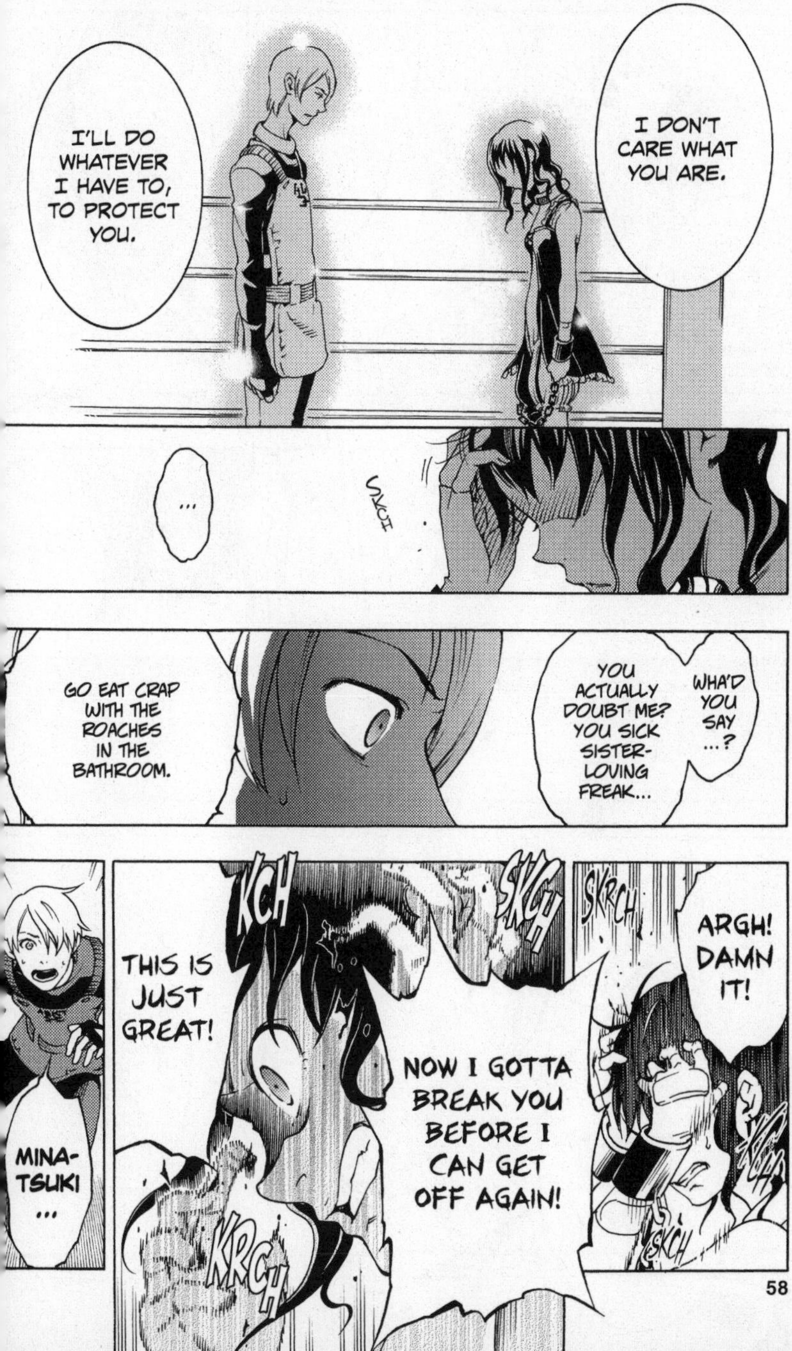
I DON'T CARE WHAT YOU ARE.
I'LL DO WHATEVER I HAVE TO, TO PROTECT YOU.
SKCH
...
WHA'D YOU SAY ...?
YOU ACTUALLY DOUBT ME? YOU SICK SISTER-LOVING FREAK...
GO EAT CRAP WITH THE ROACHES IN THE BATHROOM.
ARGH! DAMN IT!
SKRCH
SKCH
SKCH
KCH
THIS IS JUST GREAT!
NOW I GOTTA BREAK YOU BEFORE I CAN GET OFF AGAIN!
KRCH
MINA-TSUKI ...

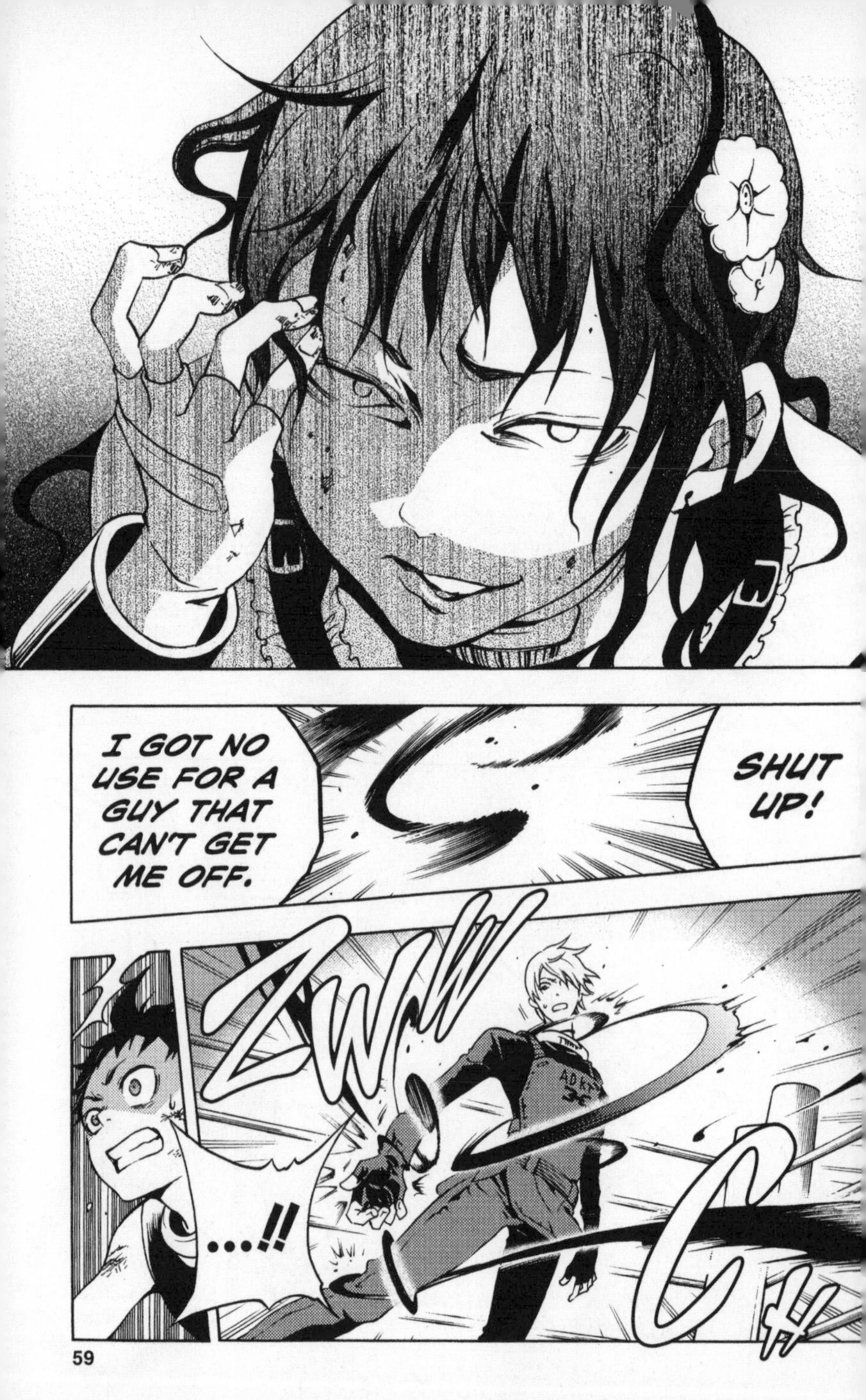
SHUT UP!
I GOT NO USE FOR A GUY THAT CAN'T GET ME OFF.
...!!

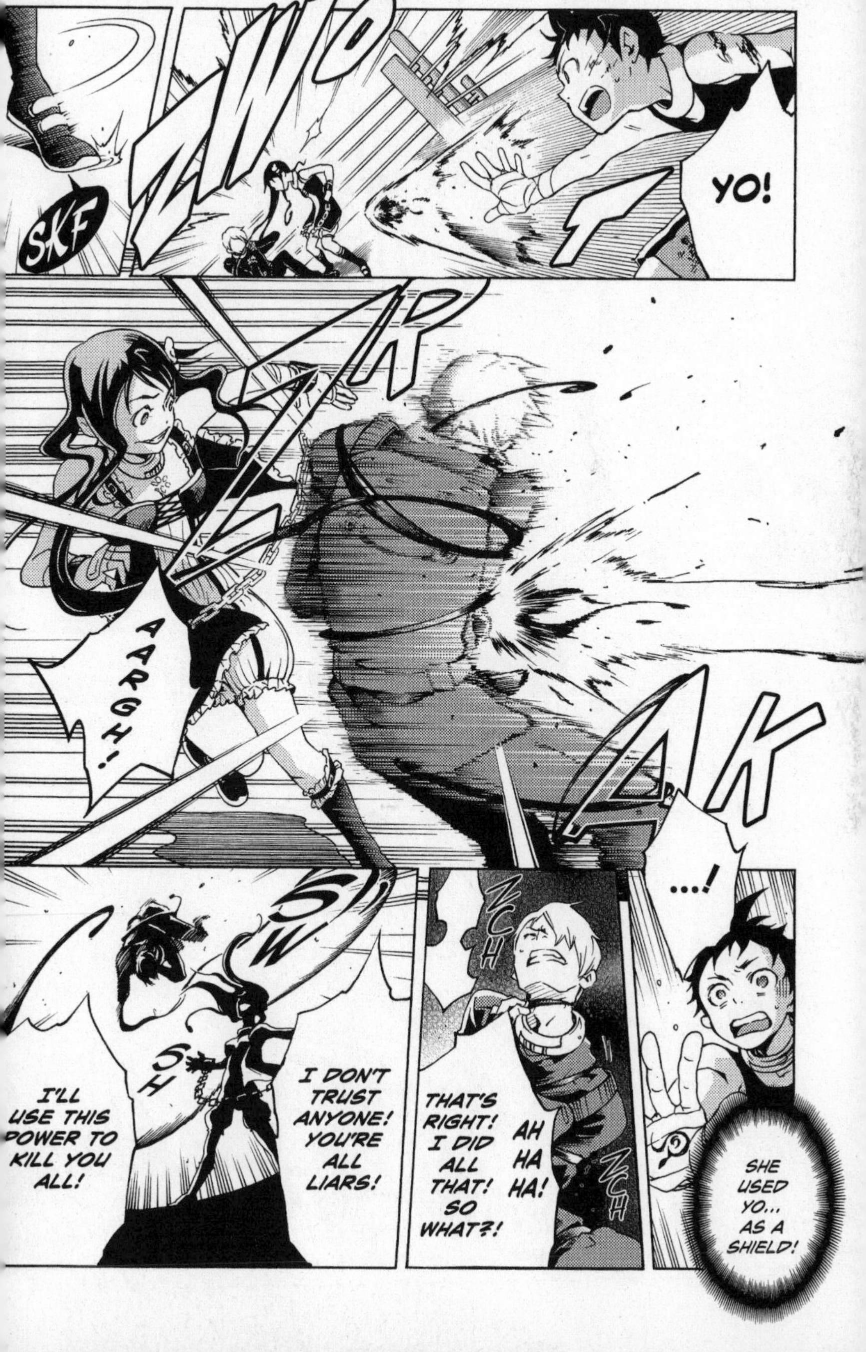
YO!
SKF
AARGH!
...!
SHE USED YO... AS A SHIELD!
NCH
THAT'S RIGHT! I DID ALL THAT! SO WHAT?!
AH HA HA!
NCH
I DON'T TRUST ANYONE! YOU'RE ALL LIARS!
SH
I'LL USE THIS POWER TO KILL YOU ALL!

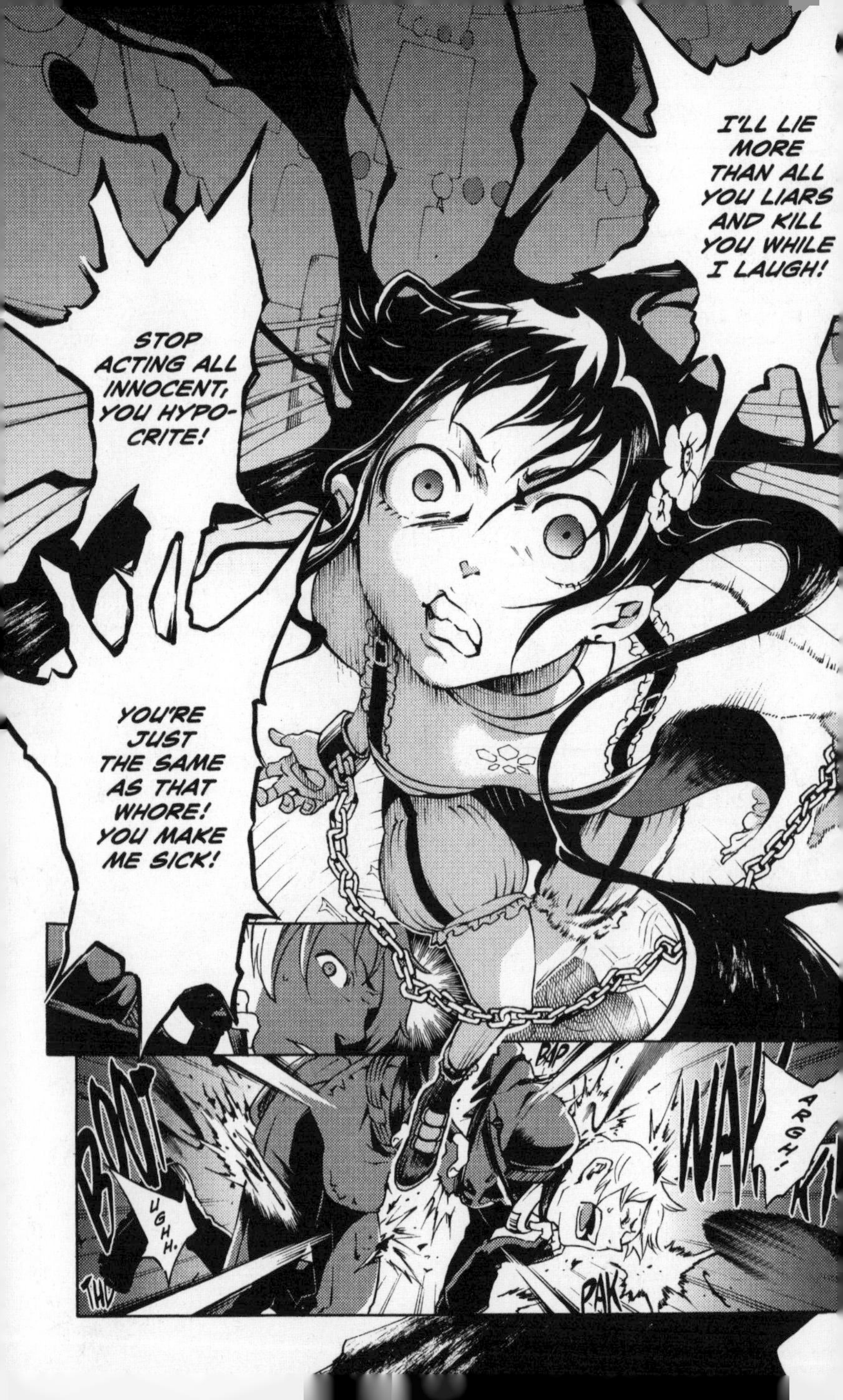
I'LL LIE MORE THAN ALL YOU LIARS AND KILL YOU WHILE I LAUGH!
STOP ACTING ALL INNOCENT, YOU HYPOCRITE!
YOU'RE JUST THE SAME AS THAT WHORE! YOU MAKE ME SICK!
BAP
ARGH!
WAK
PAK
BOO
UGHH.
THU

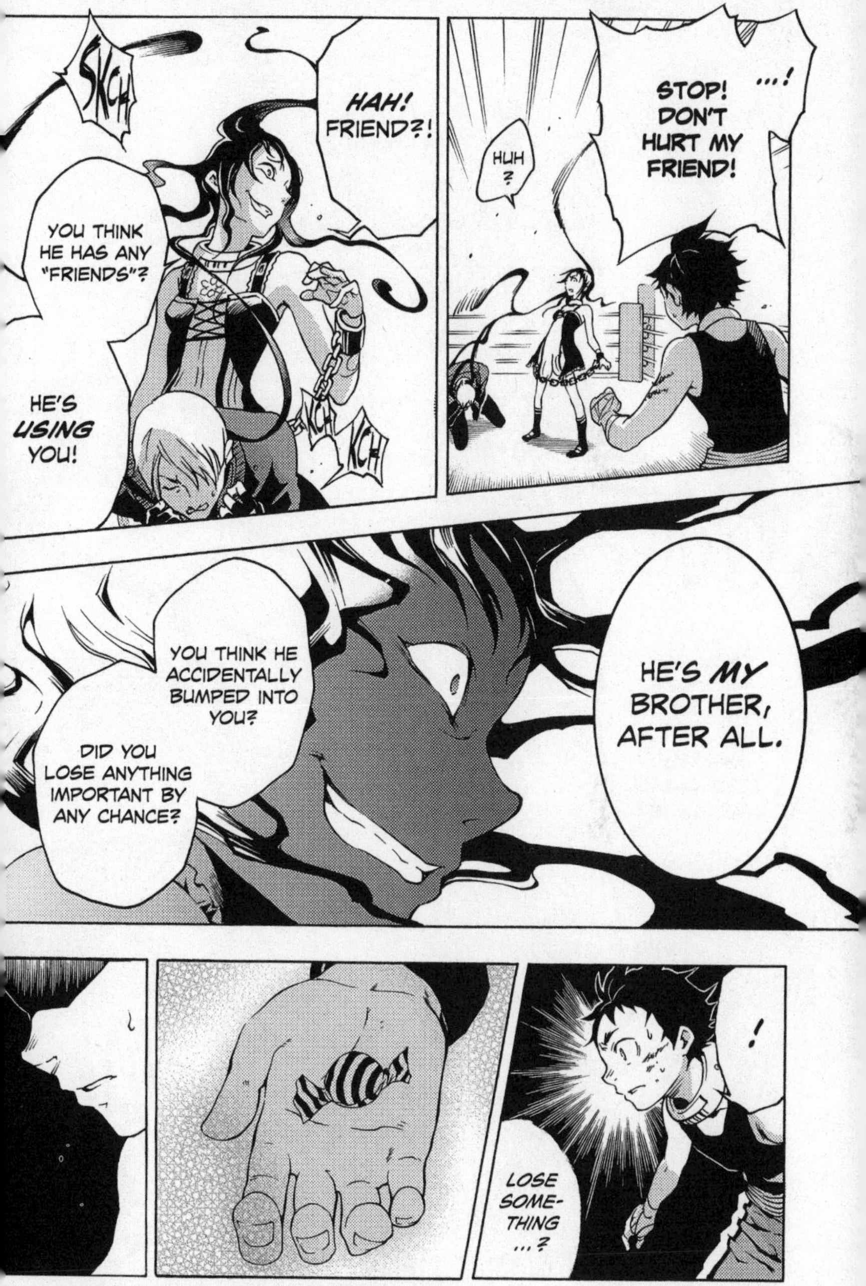
...!
STOP! DON'T HURT MY FRIEND!
HUH?
HAH! FRIEND?!
SKCH
YOU THINK HE HAS ANY "FRIENDS"?
KCH
KCH
HE'S *USING* YOU!
HE'S *MY* BROTHER, AFTER ALL.
YOU THINK HE ACCIDENTALLY BUMPED INTO YOU?
DID YOU LOSE ANYTHING IMPORTANT BY ANY CHANCE?
!
LOSE SOME-THING ...?

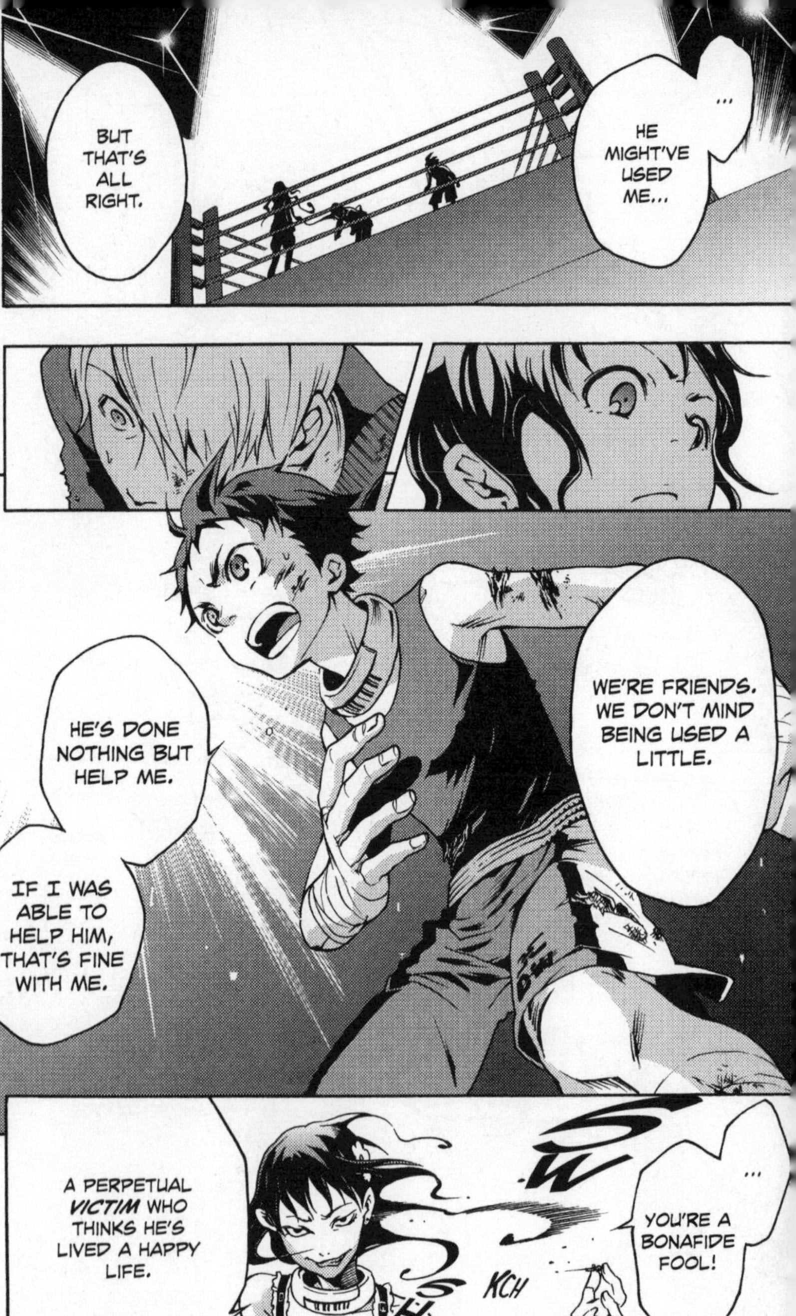
...
HE MIGHT'VE USED ME...
BUT THAT'S ALL RIGHT.
WE'RE FRIENDS. WE DON'T MIND BEING USED A LITTLE.
HE'S DONE NOTHING BUT HELP ME.
IF I WAS ABLE TO HELP HIM, THAT'S FINE WITH ME.
...
YOU'RE A BONAFIDE FOOL!
SW
SH
KCH
A PERPETUAL *VICTIM* WHO THINKS HE'S LIVED A HAPPY LIFE.

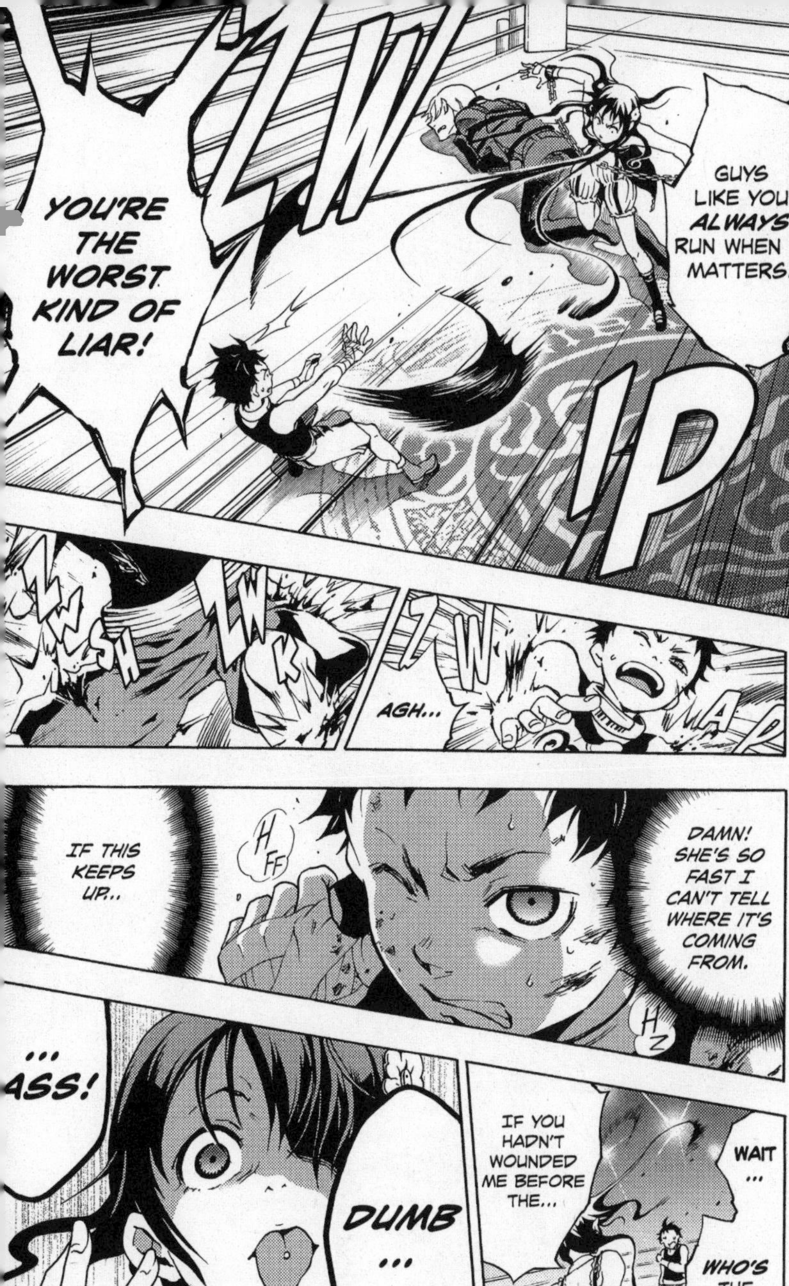
GUYS LIKE YOU ALWAYS RUN WHEN IT MATTERS.
YOU'RE THE WORST KIND OF LIAR!
AGH...
DAMN! SHE'S SO FAST I CAN'T TELL WHERE IT'S COMING FROM.
IF THIS KEEPS UP...
WAIT... WHO'S THE LIAR?!
IF YOU HADN'T WOUNDED ME BEFORE THE...
DUMB...
...ASS!

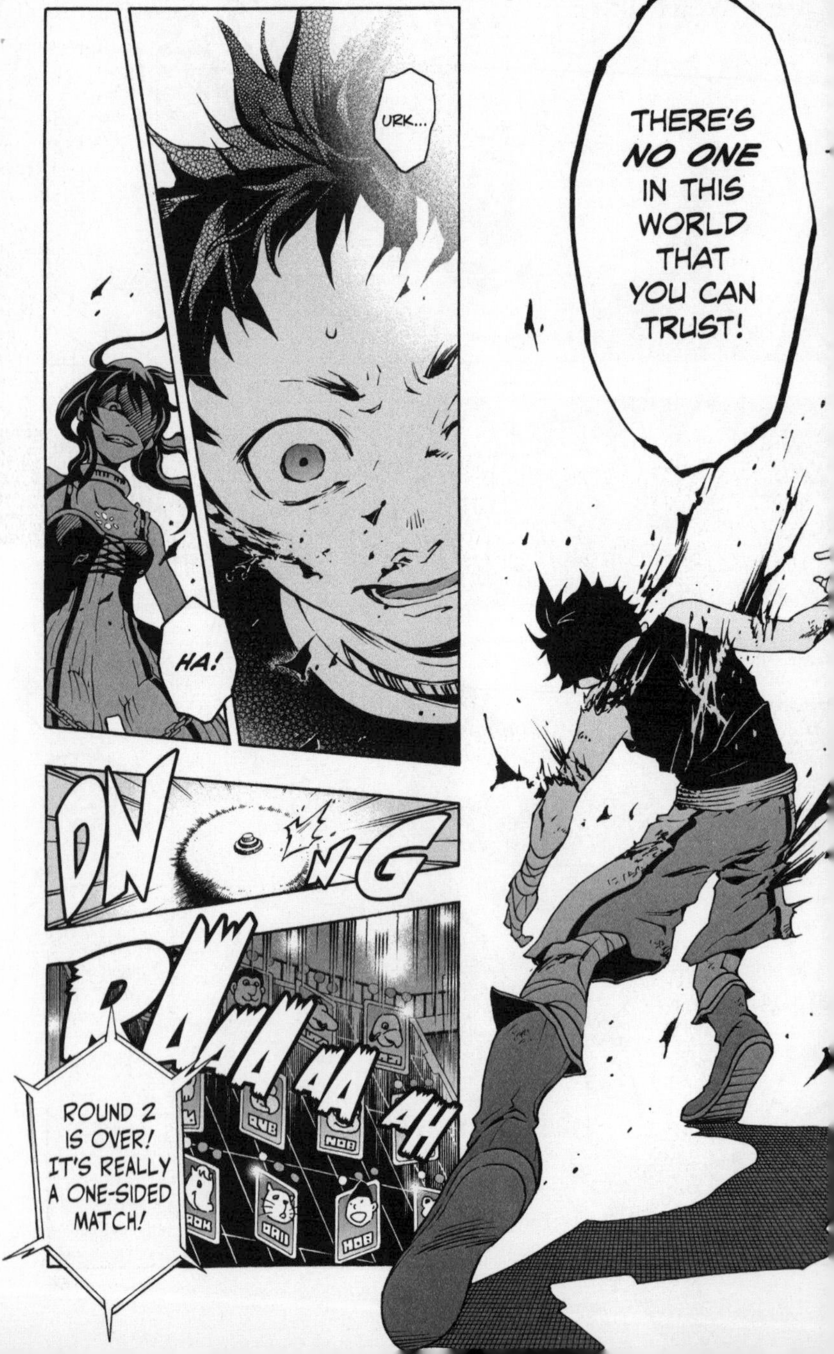
THERE'S *NO ONE* IN THIS WORLD THAT YOU CAN TRUST!
URK...
HA!
DN NG
RAAAA AA AH
ROUND 2 IS OVER! IT'S REALLY A ONE-SIDED MATCH!

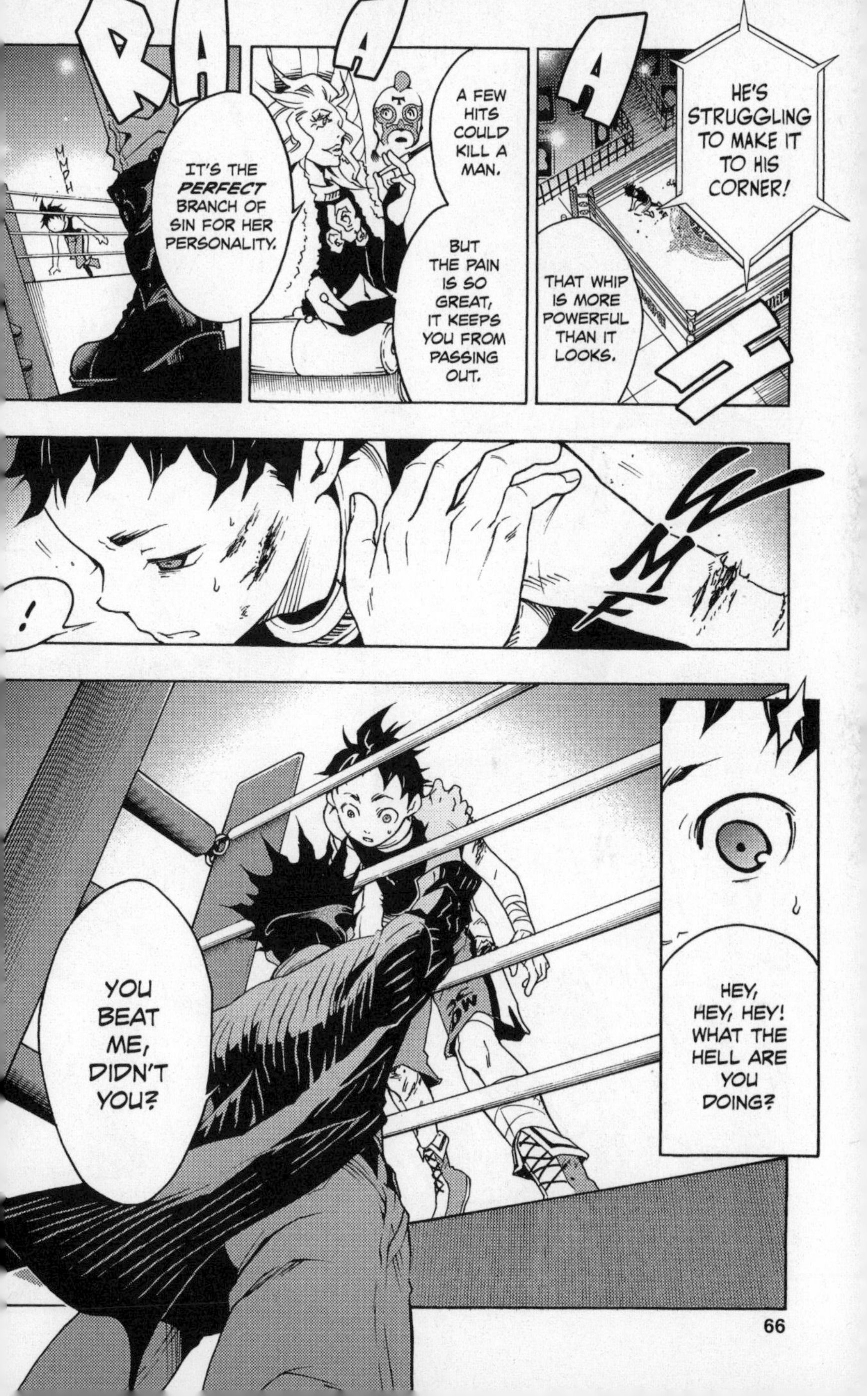

RAAAH
HE'S STRUGGLING TO MAKE IT TO HIS CORNER!
THAT WHIP IS MORE POWERFUL THAN IT LOOKS.
A FEW HITS COULD KILL A MAN.
BUT THE PAIN IS SO GREAT, IT KEEPS YOU FROM PASSING OUT.
IT'S THE *PERFECT* BRANCH OF SIN FOR HER PERSONALITY.
MMPH
WMF
!
HEY, HEY, HEY! WHAT THE HELL ARE YOU DOING?
YOU BEAT ME, DIDN'T YOU?

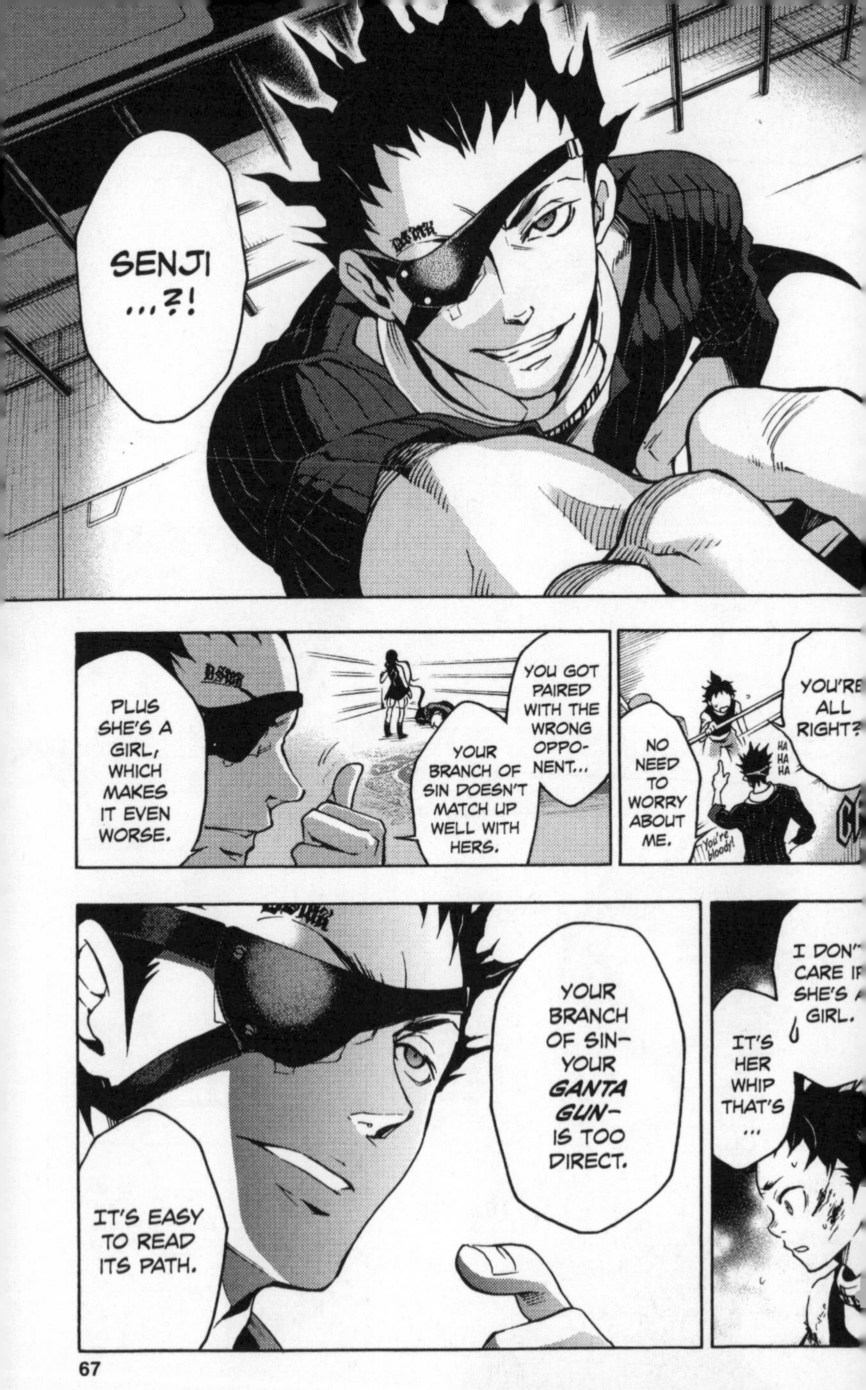
SENJI ...?!
YOU'RE ALL RIGHT?!
HA HA HA
NO NEED TO WORRY ABOUT ME.
You're bloody!
YOU GOT PAIRED WITH THE WRONG OPPONENT...
YOUR BRANCH OF SIN DOESN'T MATCH UP WELL WITH HERS.
PLUS SHE'S A GIRL, WHICH MAKES IT EVEN WORSE.
I DON'T CARE IF SHE'S A GIRL.
IT'S HER WHIP THAT'S ...
YOUR BRANCH OF SIN- YOUR *GANTA GUN*- IS TOO DIRECT.
IT'S EASY TO READ ITS PATH.

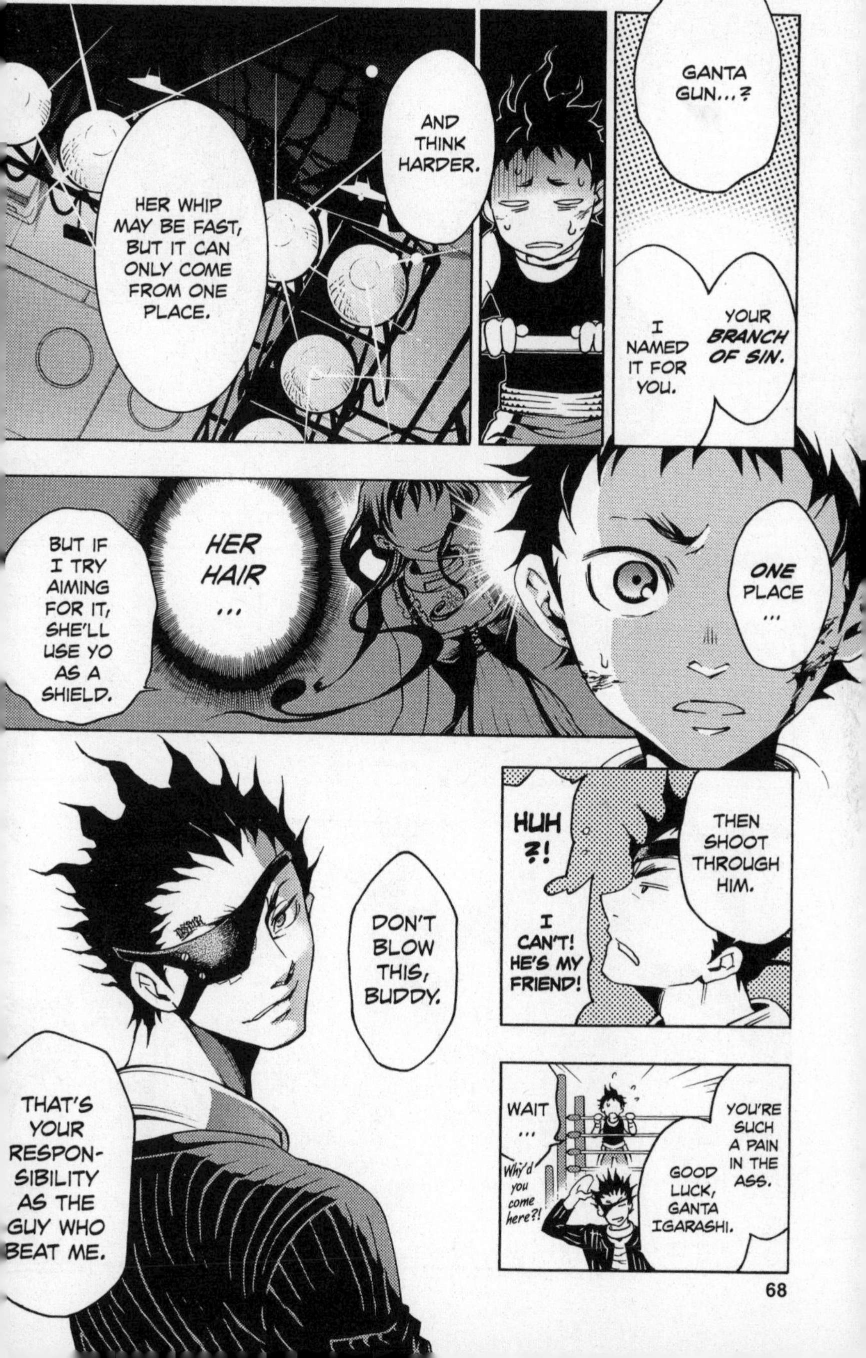
GANTA GUN...?
YOUR BRANCH OF SIN.
I NAMED IT FOR YOU.
AND THINK HARDER.
HER WHIP MAY BE FAST, BUT IT CAN ONLY COME FROM ONE PLACE.
ONE PLACE...
HER HAIR...
BUT IF I TRY AIMING FOR IT, SHE'LL USE YO AS A SHIELD.
THEN SHOOT THROUGH HIM.
HUH?!
I CAN'T! HE'S MY FRIEND!
YOU'RE SUCH A PAIN IN THE ASS.
GOOD LUCK, GANTA IGARASHI.
WAIT...
Why'd you come here?!
DON'T BLOW THIS, BUDDY.
THAT'S YOUR RESPON-SIBILITY AS THE GUY WHO BEAT ME.

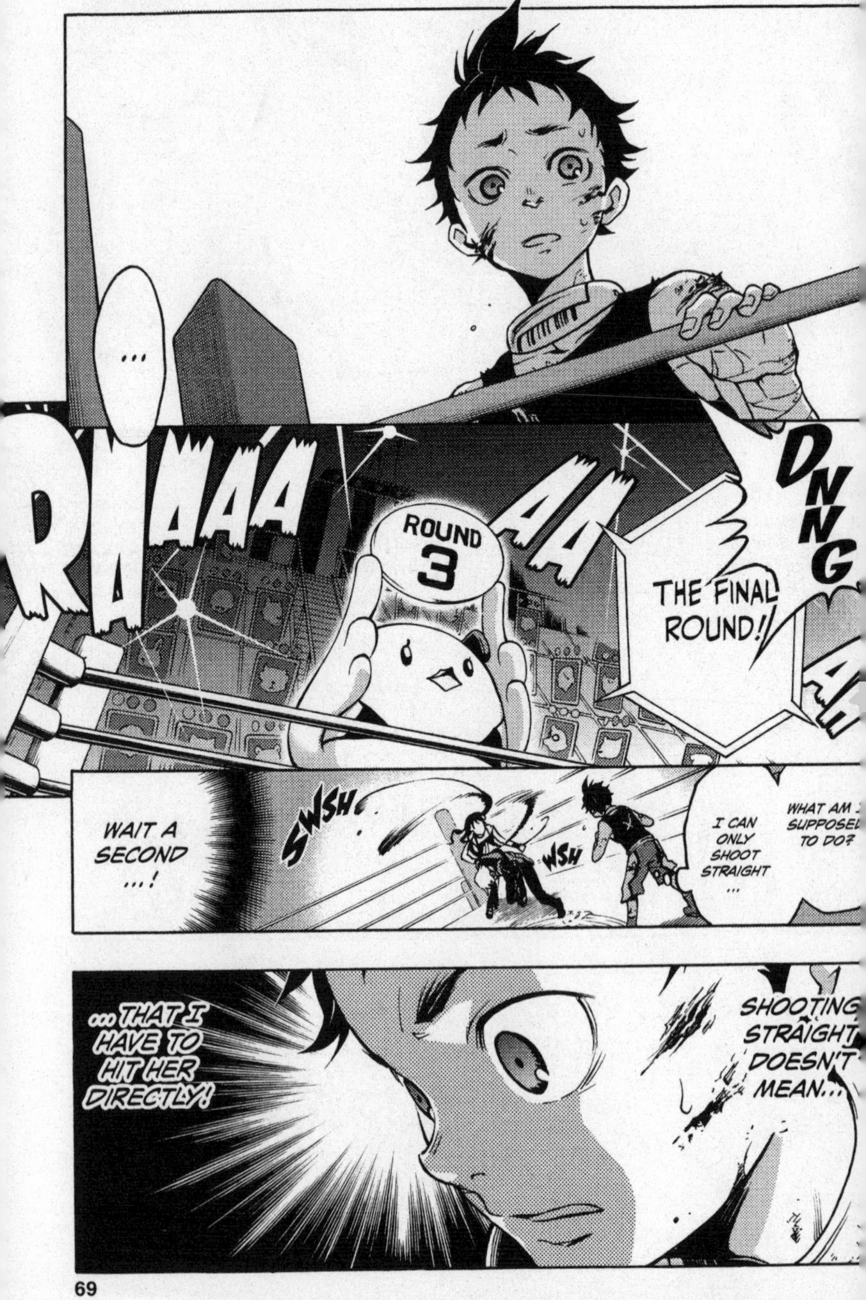
...
DNNG
THE FINAL ROUND!
ROUND 3
RAAAAAAA
WHAT AM I SUPPOSED TO DO?
I CAN ONLY SHOOT STRAIGHT ...
WSH
SWSH
WAIT A SECOND ...!
SHOOTING STRAIGHT DOESN'T MEAN...
...THAT I HAVE TO HIT HER DIRECTLY!

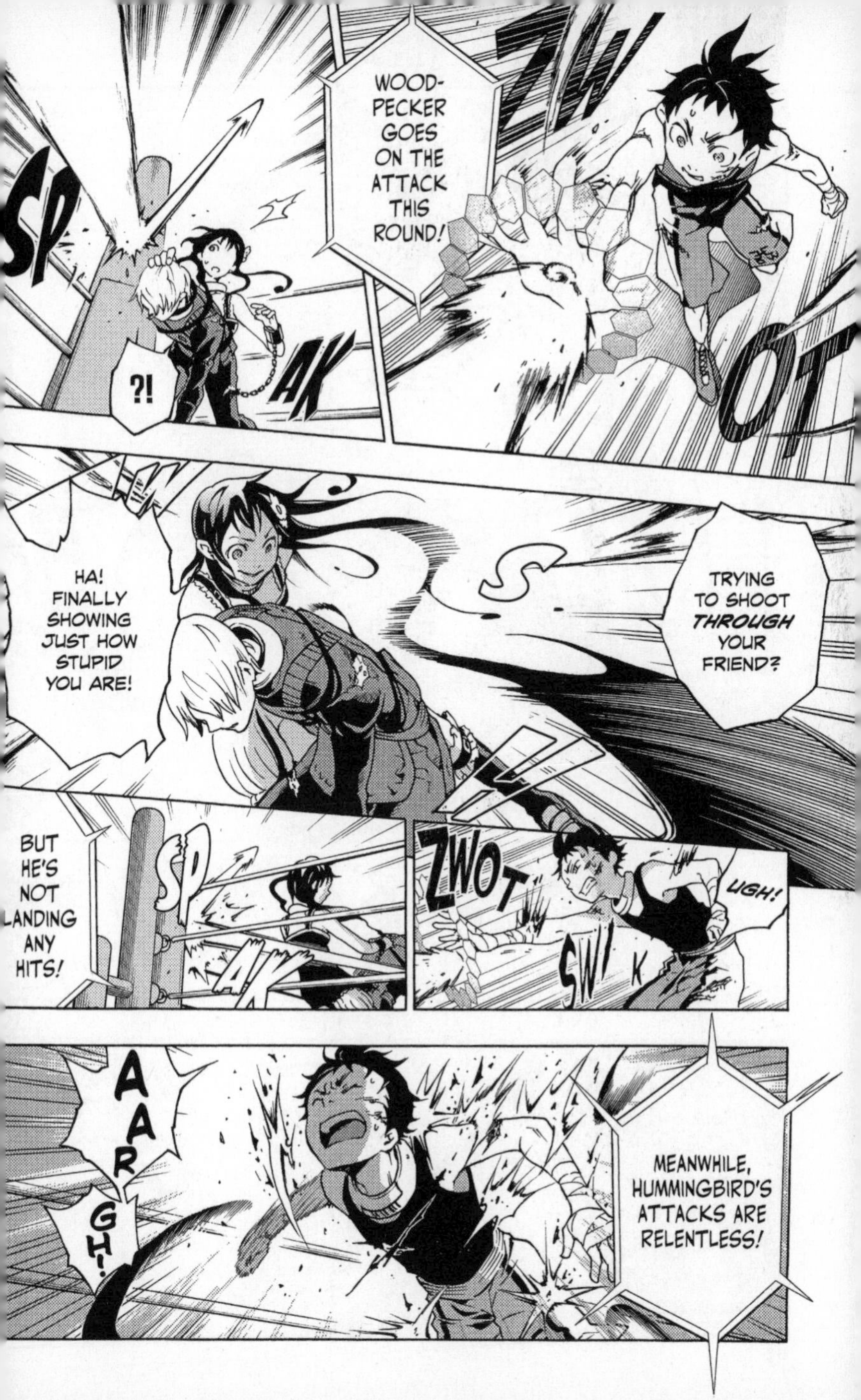
ZW
WOOD-PECKER GOES ON THE ATTACK THIS ROUND!
SP
?!
AK
OT
TRYING TO SHOOT *THROUGH* YOUR FRIEND?
S
HA! FINALLY SHOWING JUST HOW STUPID YOU ARE!
ZWOT
UGH!
SWI K
SP
AK
BUT HE'S NOT LANDING ANY HITS!
MEANWHILE, HUMMINGBIRD'S ATTACKS ARE RELENTLESS!
AARGH!

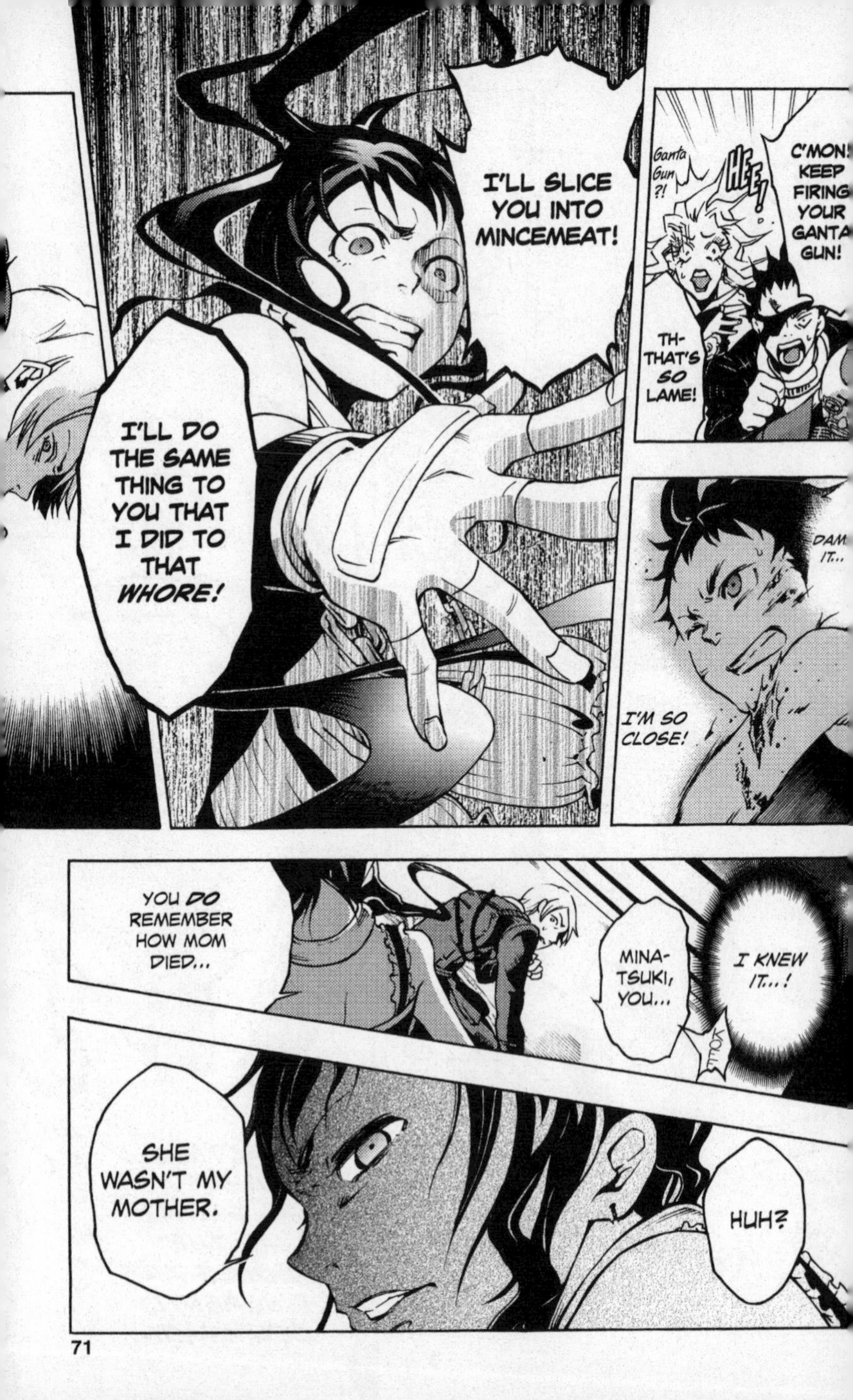
C'MON! KEEP FIRING YOUR GANTA GUN!
HEE!
Ganta Gun?!
TH-THAT'S SO LAME!
DAM IT...
I'M SO CLOSE!
I'LL SLICE YOU INTO MINCEMEAT!
I'LL DO THE SAME THING TO YOU THAT I DID TO THAT WHORE!
I KNEW IT...!
MINA-TSUKI, YOU...
YOU DO REMEMBER HOW MOM DIED...
HUH?
SHE WASN'T MY MOTHER.

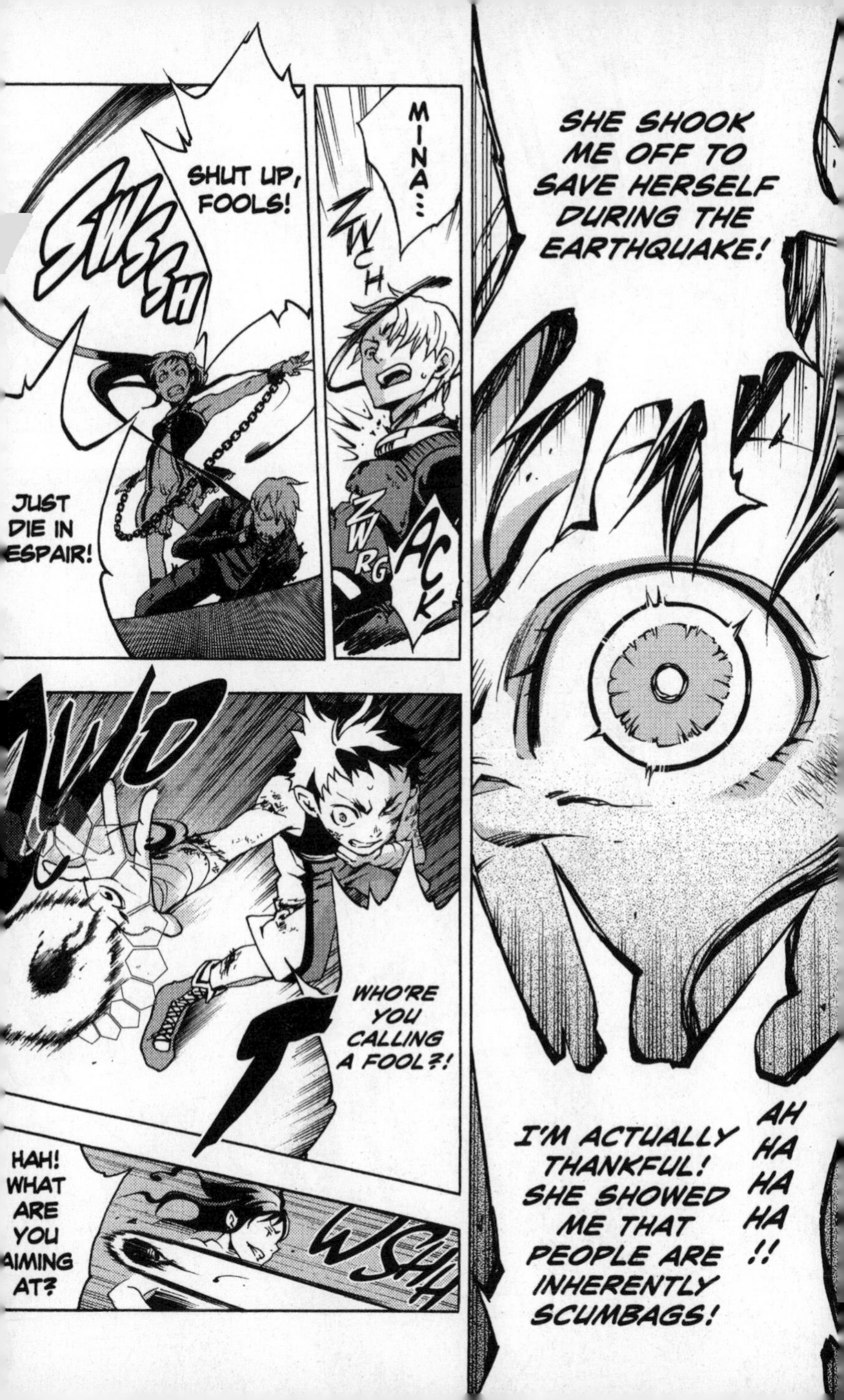
SHE SHOOK ME OFF TO SAVE HERSELF DURING THE EARTHQUAKE!
AH HA HA HA!!
I'M ACTUALLY THANKFUL! SHE SHOWED ME THAT PEOPLE ARE INHERENTLY SCUMBAGS!
MINA...
ZWRG
WACK
SHUT UP, FOOLS!
JUST DIE IN ESPAIR!
WHO'RE YOU CALLING A FOOL?!
WSH
HAH! WHAT ARE YOU AIMING AT?

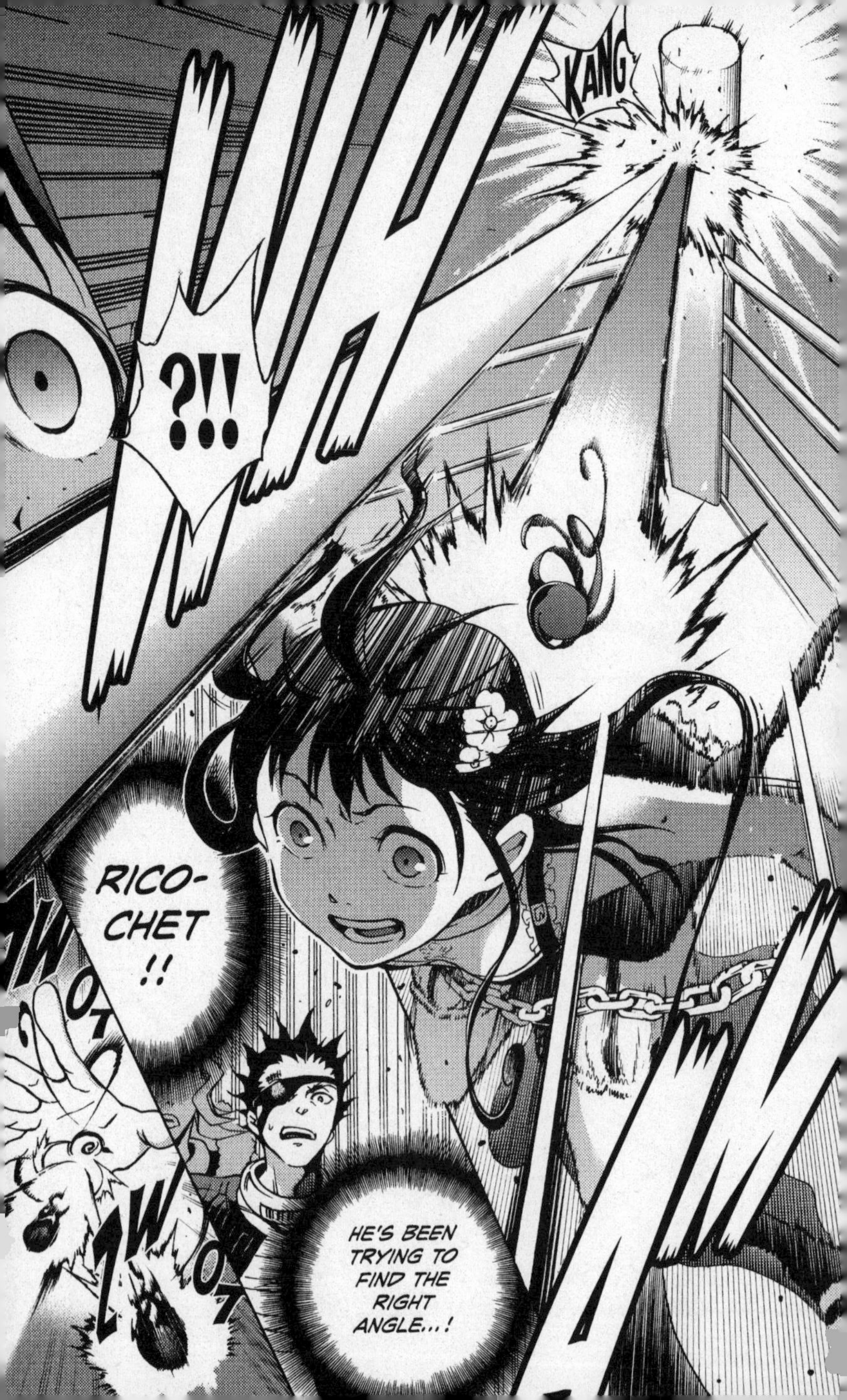
KANG
?!!
RICO-
CHET
!!
ZWOT
ZWOT
HE'S BEEN TRYING TO FIND THE RIGHT ANGLE...!

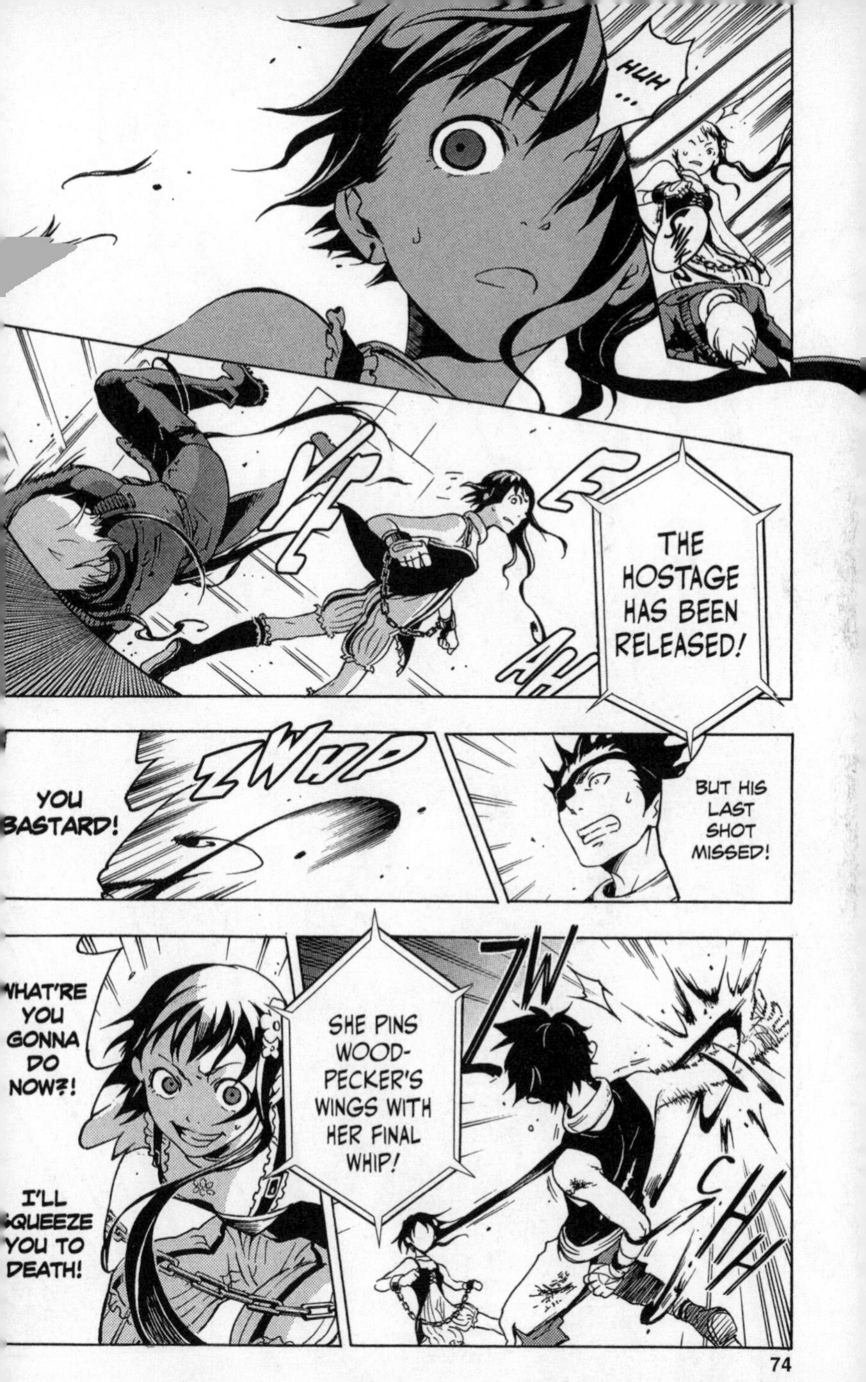

HUH ...
THE HOSTAGE HAS BEEN RELEASED!
BUT HIS LAST SHOT MISSED!
ZWHIP
YOU BASTARD!
SHE PINS WOOD-PECKER'S WINGS WITH HER FINAL WHIP!
WHAT'RE YOU GONNA DO NOW?!
I'LL SQUEEZE YOU TO DEATH!

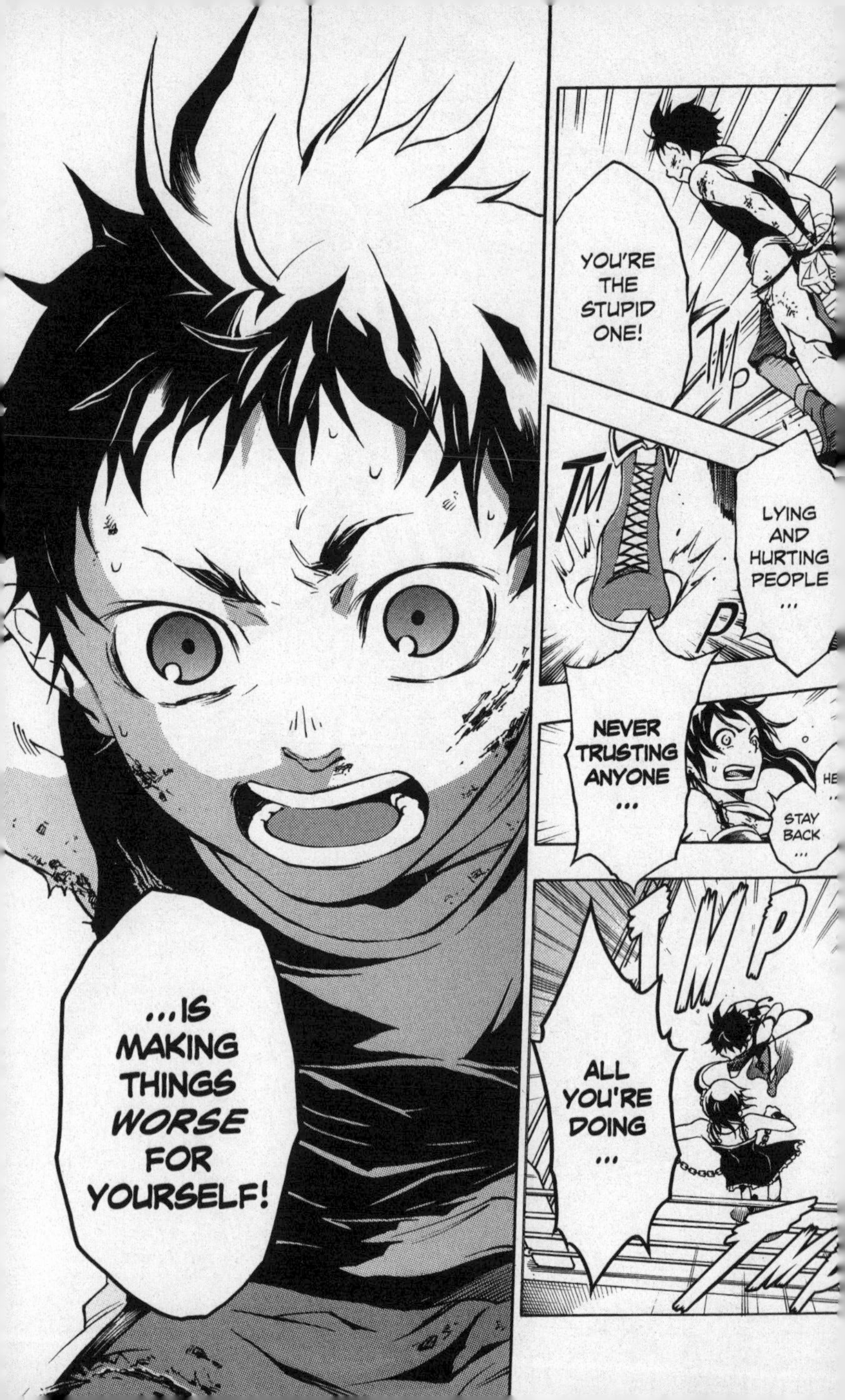
YOU'RE THE STUPID ONE!
TMP
TM
P
LYING AND HURTING PEOPLE ...
STAY BACK ...
NEVER TRUSTING ANYONE ...
TMP
ALL YOU'RE DOING ...
...IS MAKING THINGS *WORSE* FOR YOURSELF!

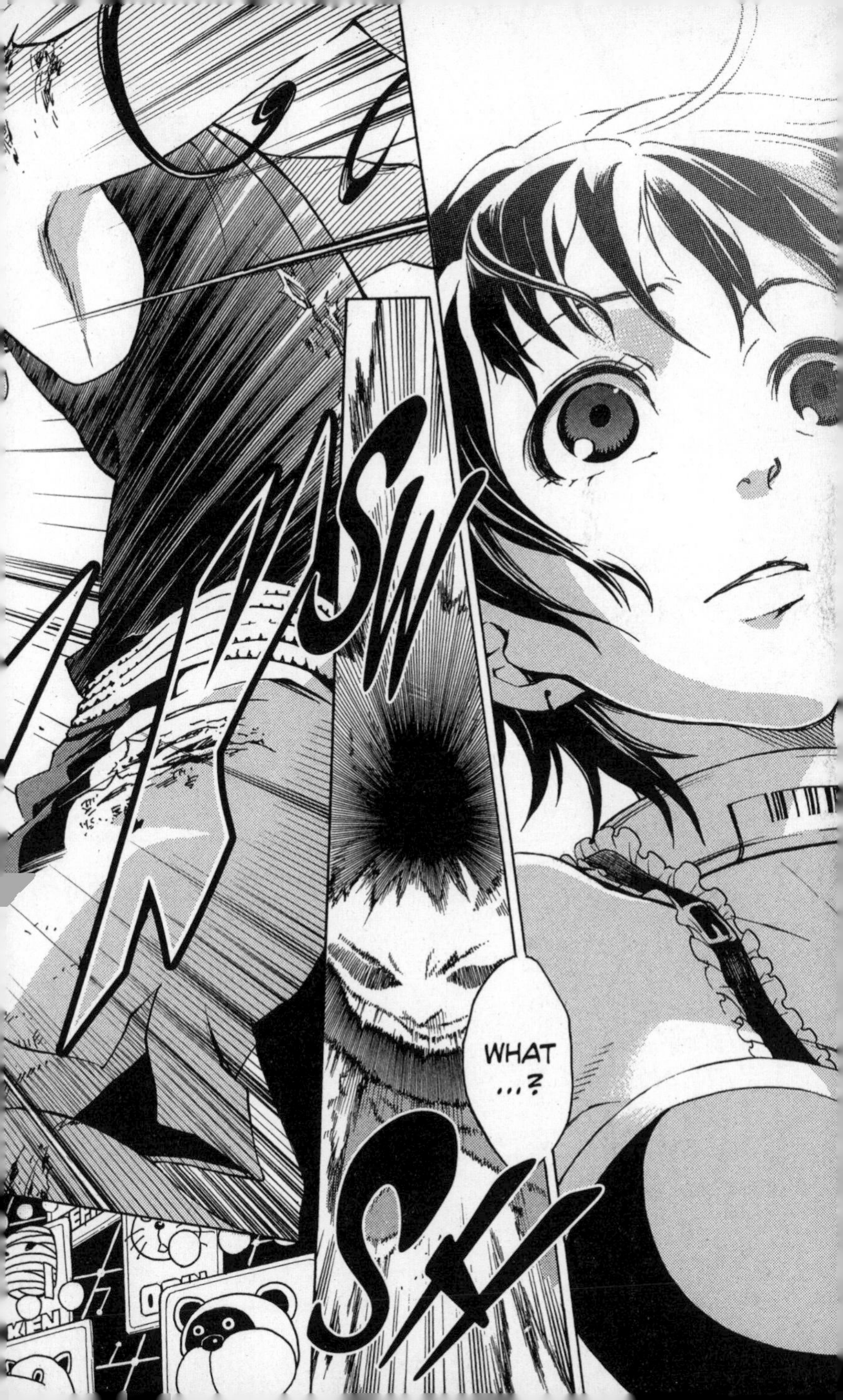
WHAT ...?
SWSH

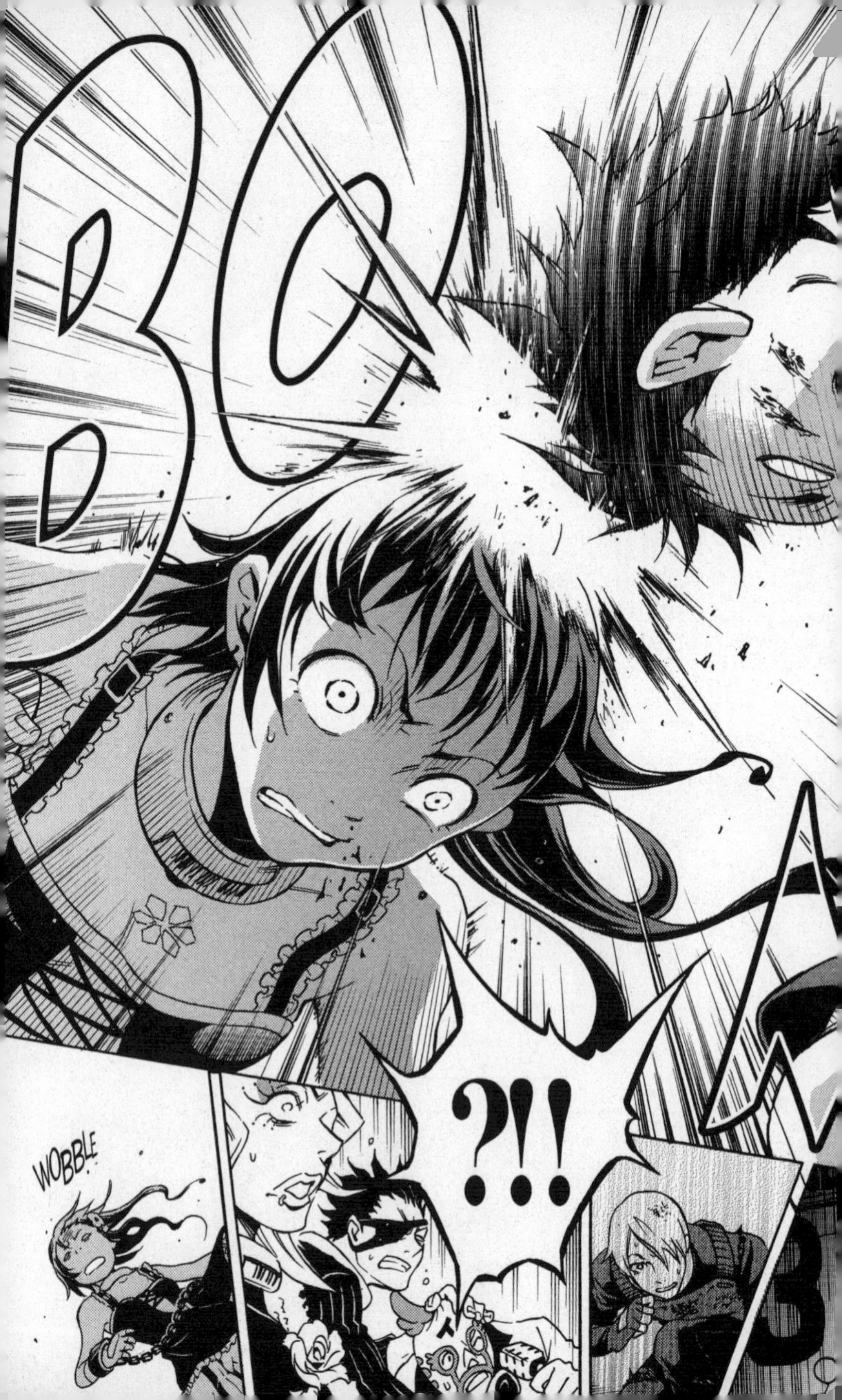
?!!
WOBBLE

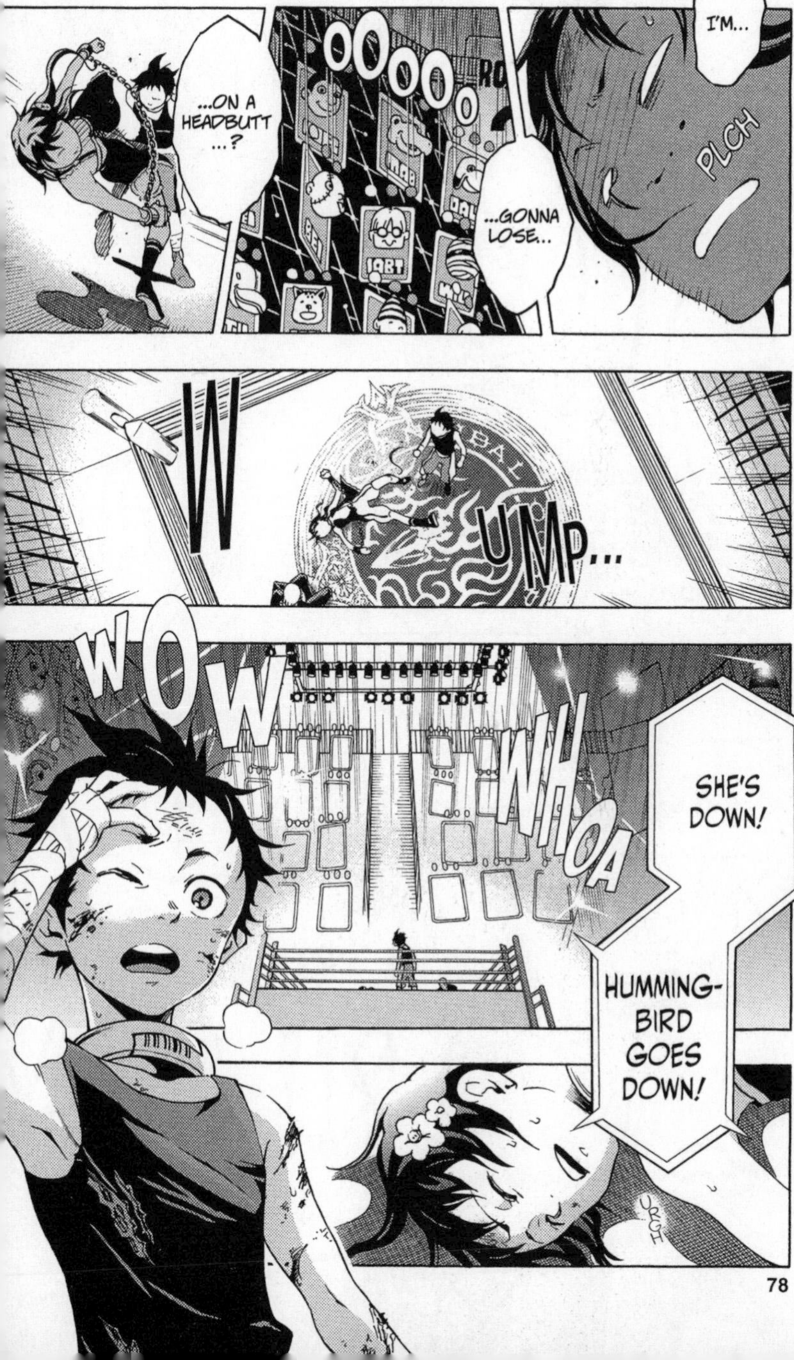

I'M...
PLCH
...GONNA LOSE...
OOOOO
...ON A HEADBUTT ...?
WUMP...
SHE'S DOWN!
HUMMING-BIRD GOES DOWN!
WHOA
WOW
URGH

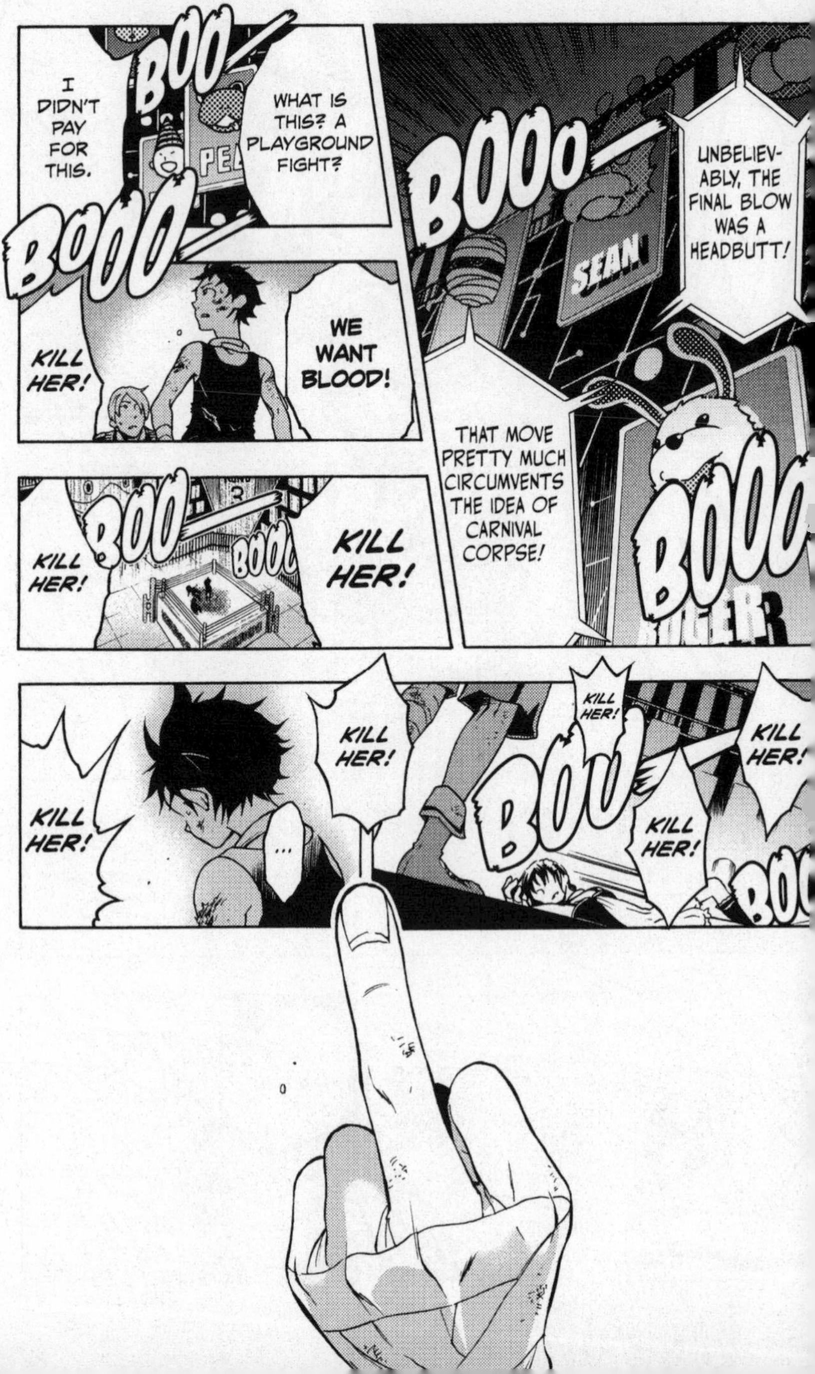

BOOO—
UNBELIEV-ABLY, THE FINAL BLOW WAS A HEADBUTT!
SEAN
THAT MOVE PRETTY MUCH CIRCUMVENTS THE IDEA OF CARNIVAL CORPSE!
BOOO
BOO—
WHAT IS THIS? A PLAYGROUND FIGHT?
I DIDN'T PAY FOR THIS.
BOOO
WE WANT BLOOD!
KILL HER!
KILL HER!
BOOO
BOO
KILL HER!
KILL HER!
BOO
KILL HER!
KILL HER!
BOO
KILL HER!
...
KILL HER!

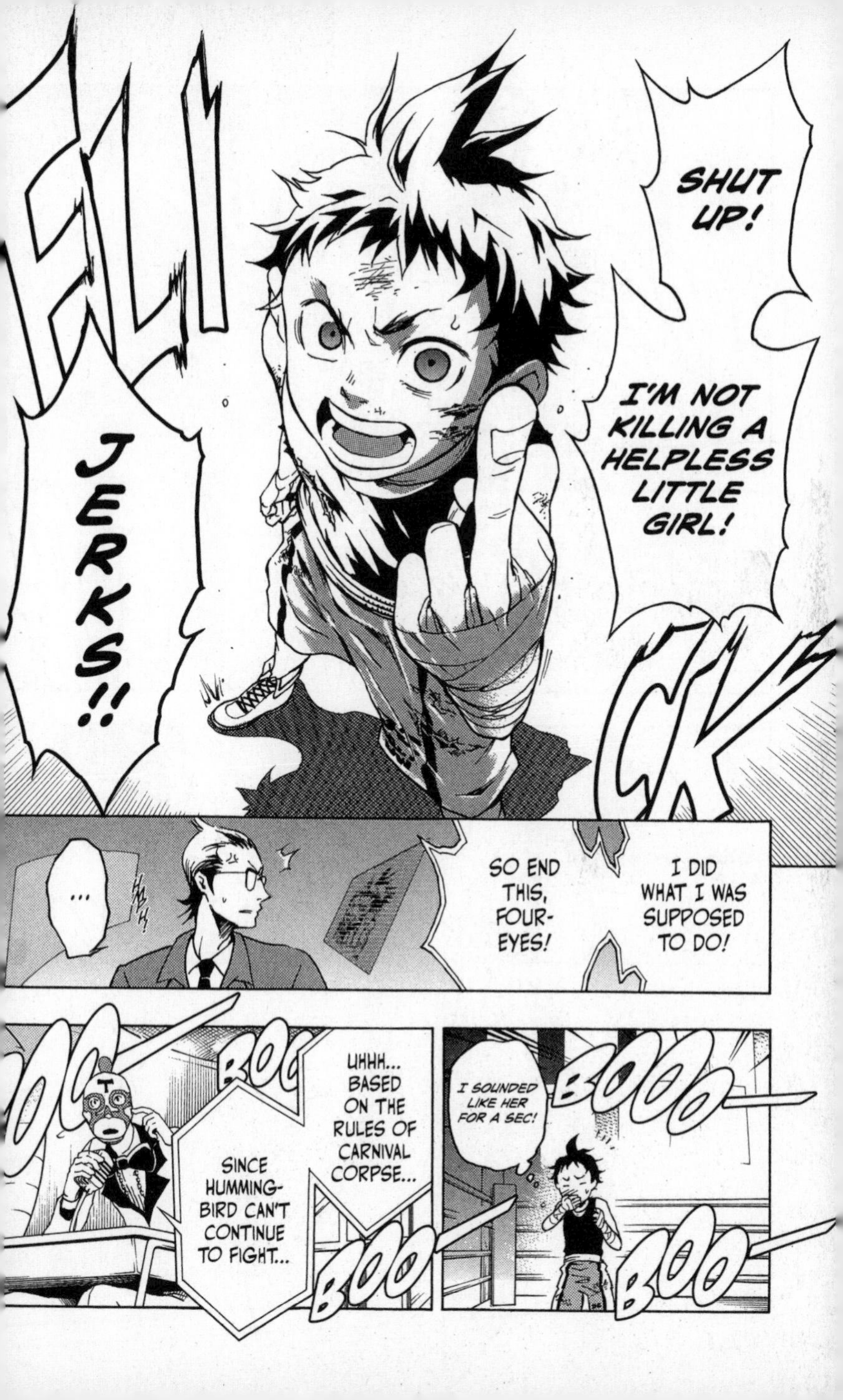
SHUT UP!
I'M NOT KILLING A HELPLESS LITTLE GIRL!
JERKS!!
I DID WHAT I WAS SUPPOSED TO DO!
SO END THIS, FOUR-EYES!
...
BOOO
I SOUNDED LIKE HER FOR A SEC!
BOO
UHHH... BASED ON THE RULES OF CARNIVAL CORPSE...
SINCE HUMMING-BIRD CAN'T CONTINUE TO FIGHT...
BOO

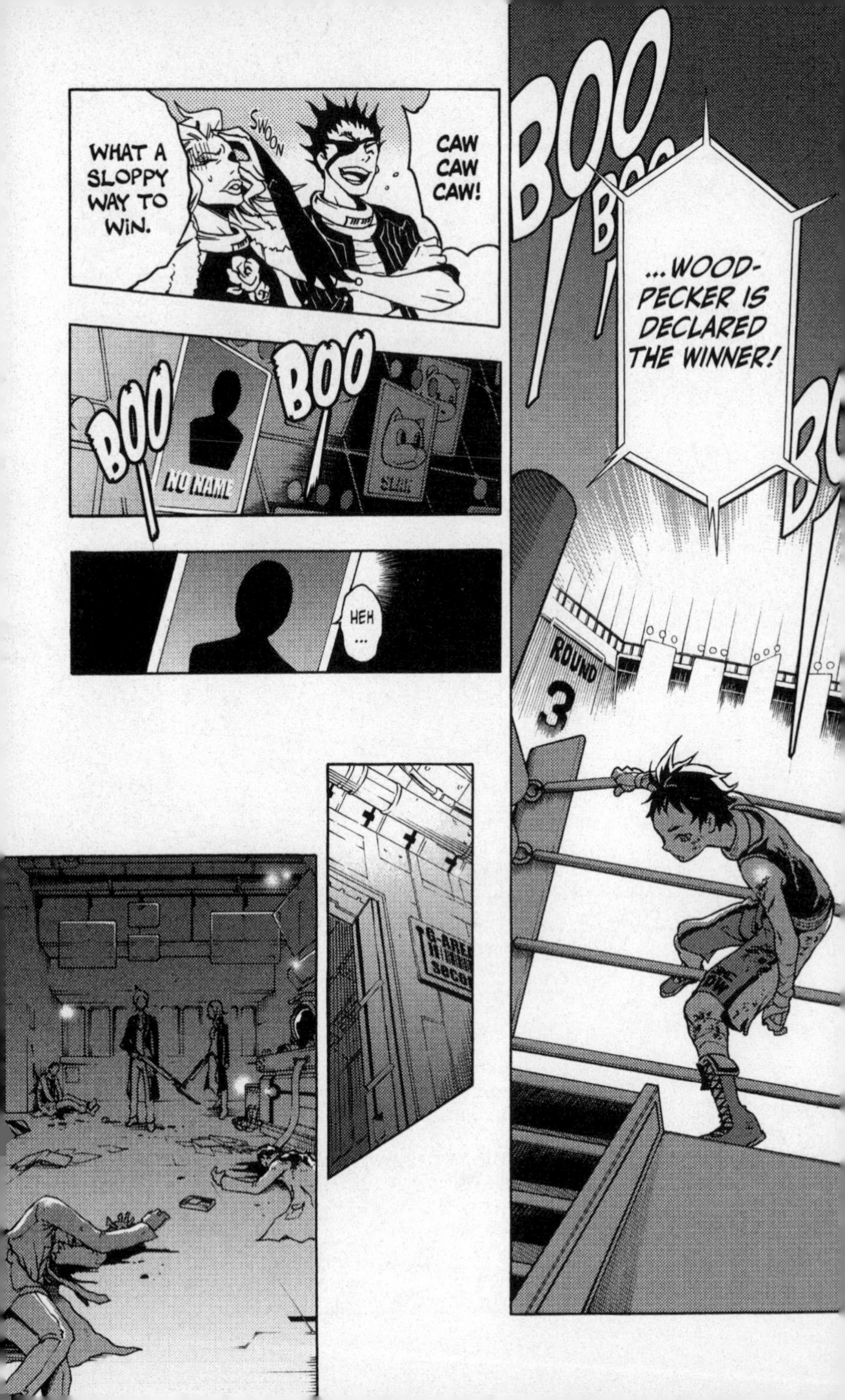
BOO
BOO
...WOOD-PECKER IS DECLARED THE WINNER!
ROUND 3
CAW CAW CAW!
SWOON
WHAT A SLOPPY WAY TO WIN.
BOO
NO NAME
BOO
HEH ...

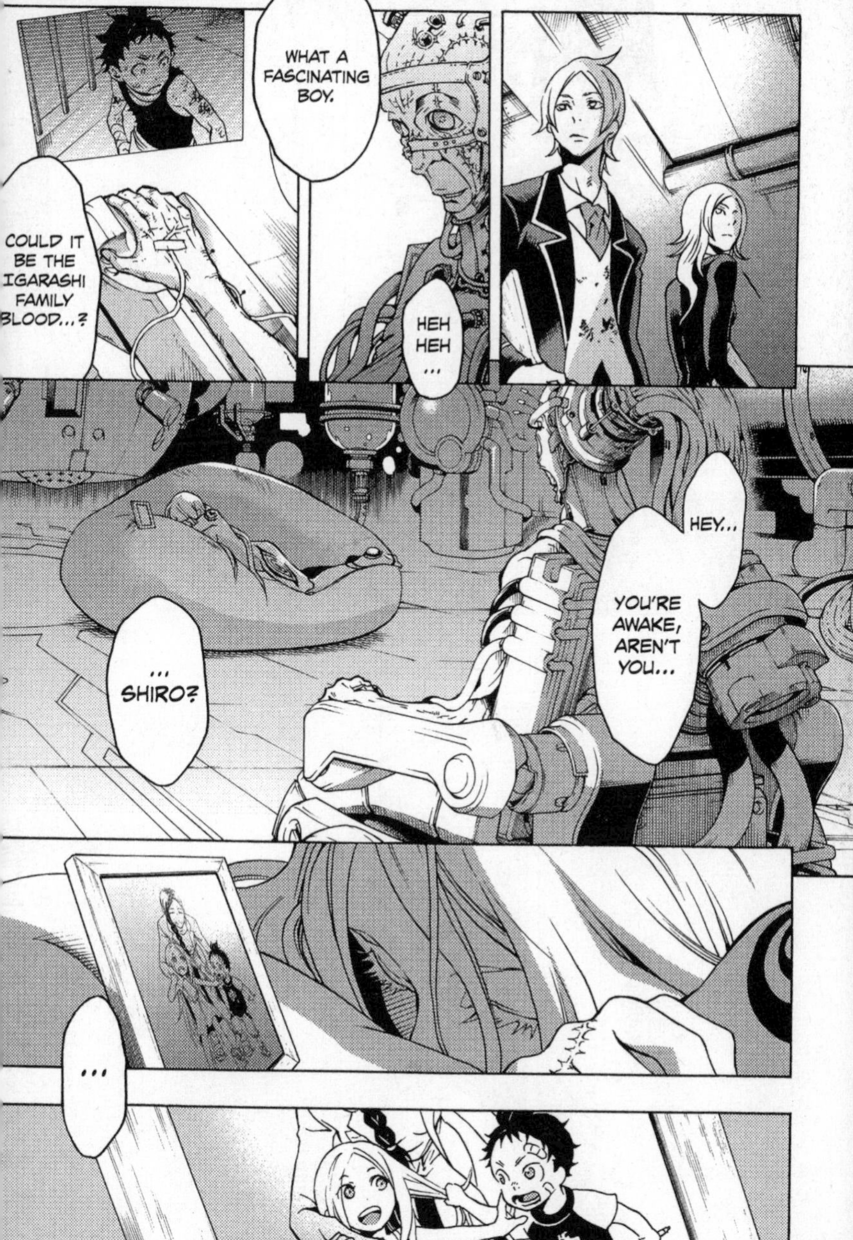

WHAT A FASCINATING BOY.
HEH HEH ...
COULD IT BE THE IGARASHI FAMILY BLOOD...?
HEY...
YOU'RE AWAKE, AREN'T YOU...
... SHIRO?
...

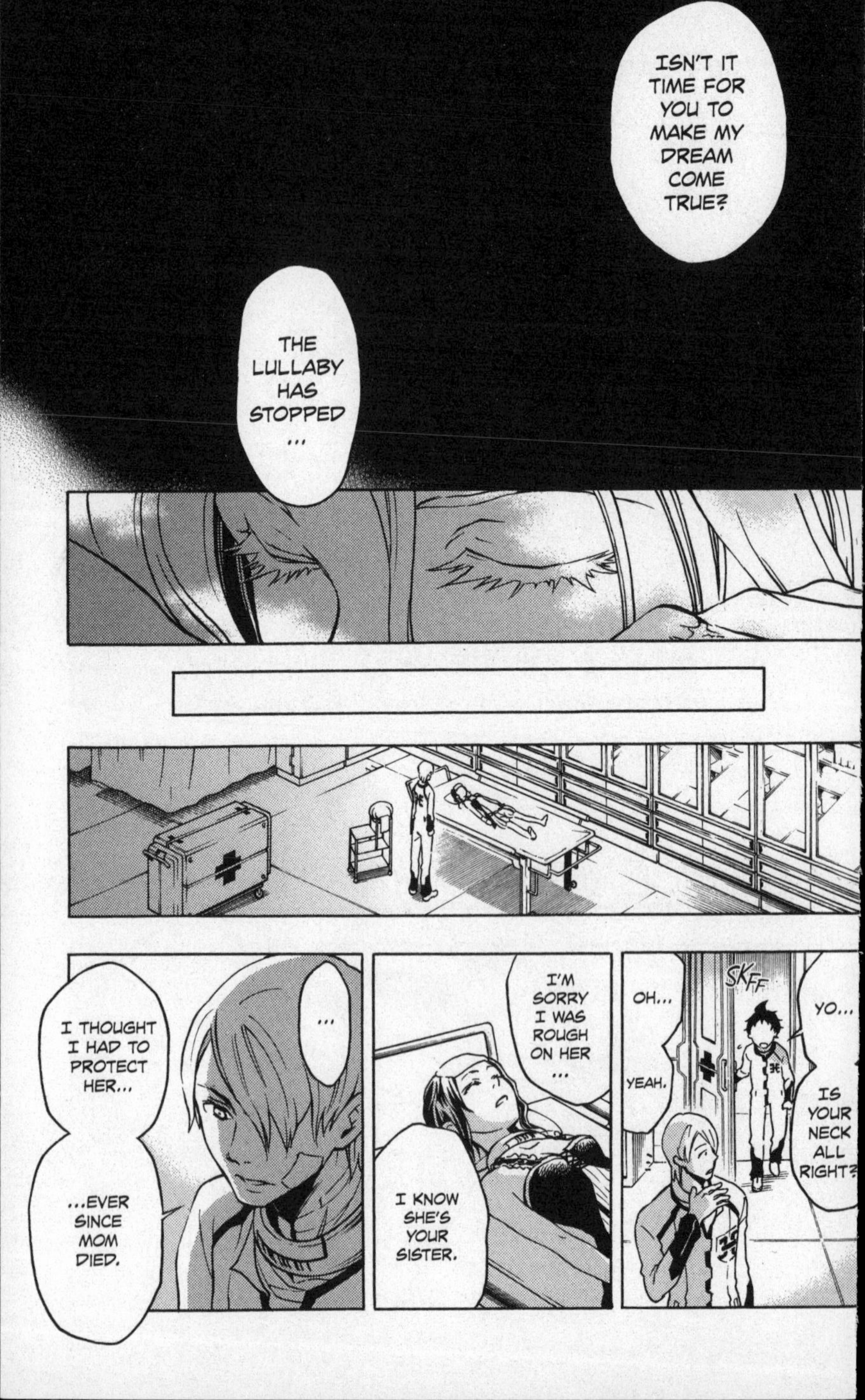
ISN'T IT TIME FOR YOU TO MAKE MY DREAM COME TRUE?
THE LULLABY HAS STOPPED ...
SKFF
YO...
OH...
IS YOUR NECK ALL RIGHT?
YEAH.
I'M SORRY I WAS ROUGH ON HER ...
I KNOW SHE'S YOUR SISTER.
...
I THOUGHT I HAD TO PROTECT HER...
...EVER SINCE MOM DIED.

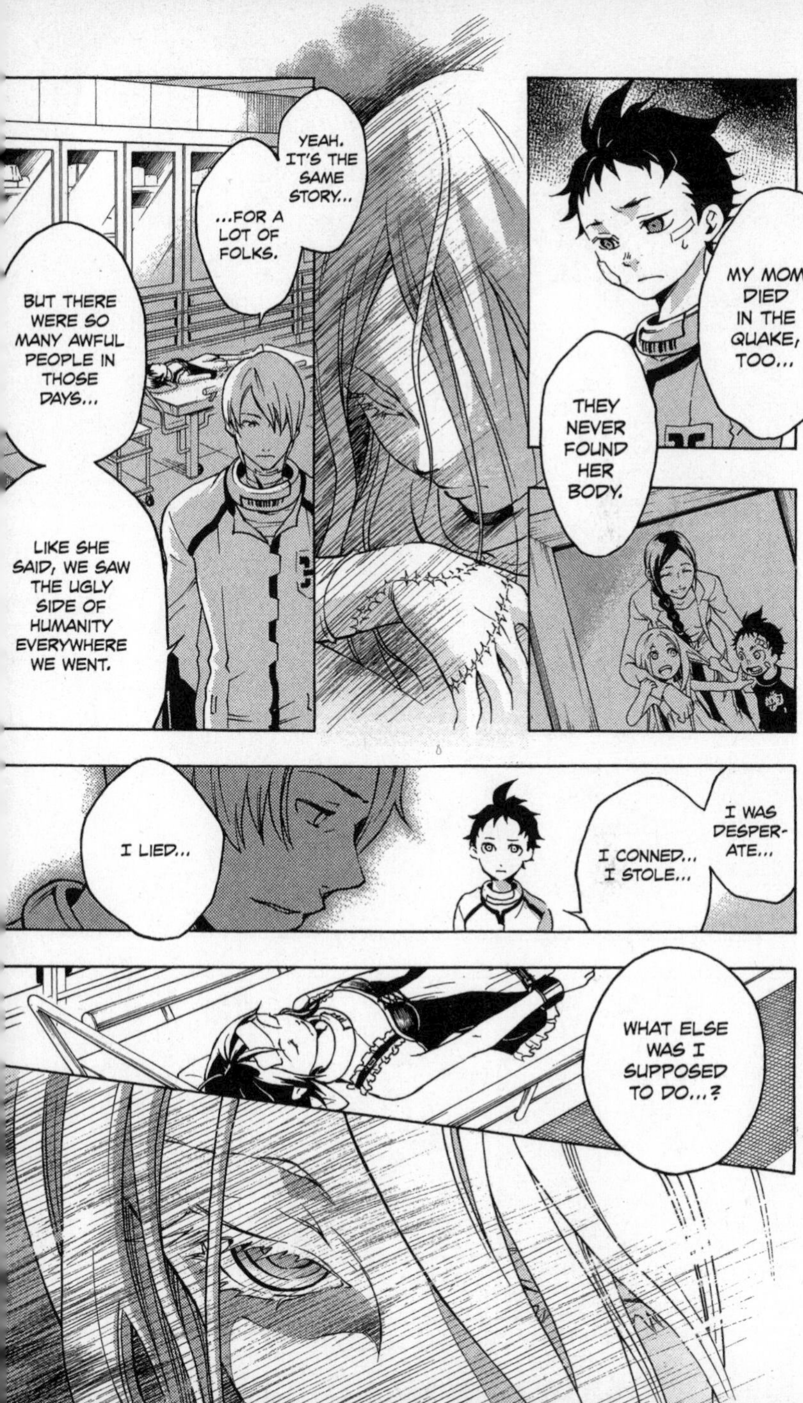
MY MOM DIED IN THE QUAKE, TOO...
THEY NEVER FOUND HER BODY.
YEAH. IT'S THE SAME STORY...
...FOR A LOT OF FOLKS.
BUT THERE WERE SO MANY AWFUL PEOPLE IN THOSE DAYS...
LIKE SHE SAID, WE SAW THE UGLY SIDE OF HUMANITY EVERYWHERE WE WENT.
I WAS DESPER-ATE...
I CONNED... I STOLE...
I LIED...
WHAT ELSE WAS I SUPPOSED TO DO...?

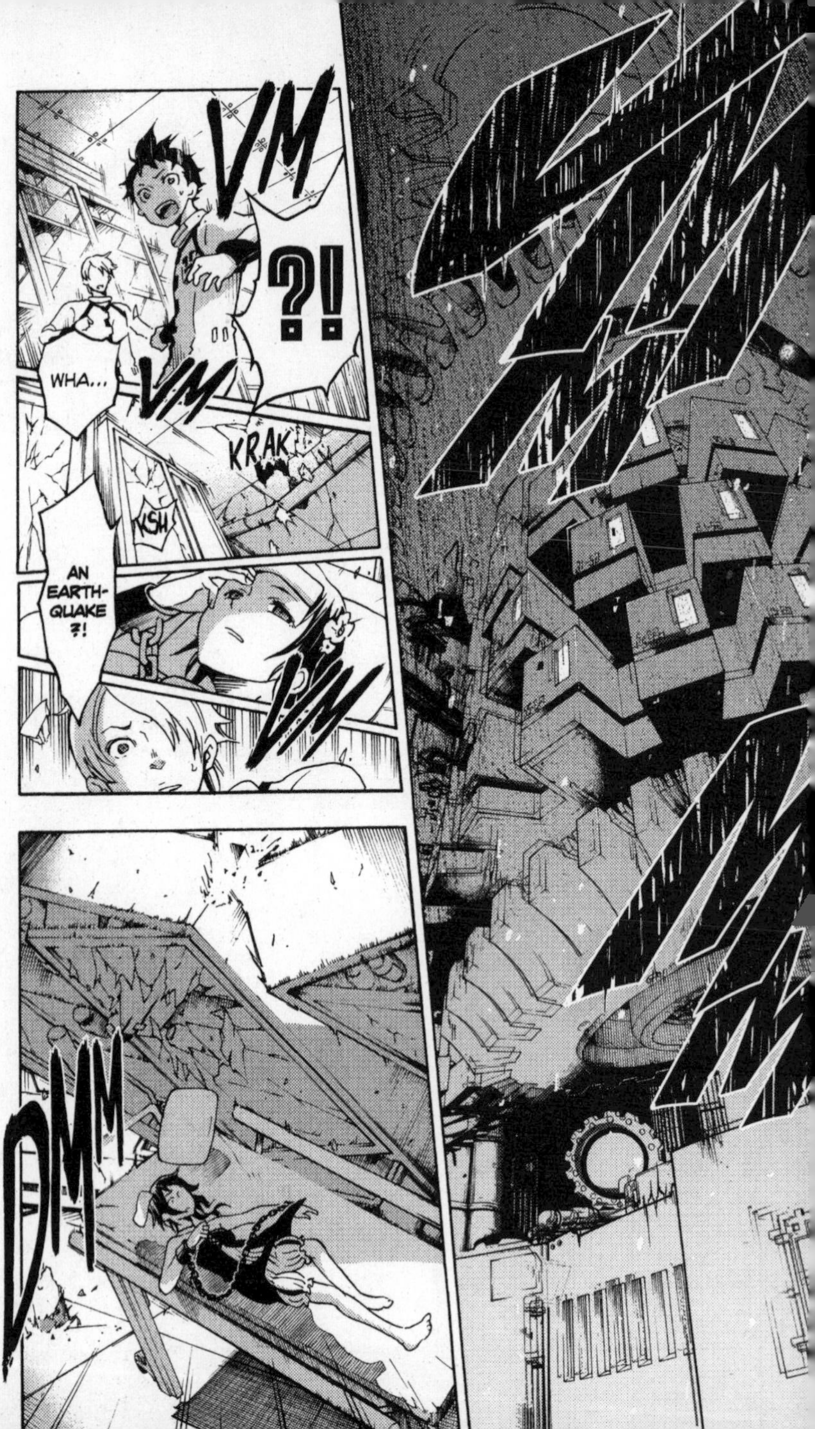
VM
?!
WHA...
VM
KRAK
KSH
AN EARTH-QUAKE?!
VM
DMM

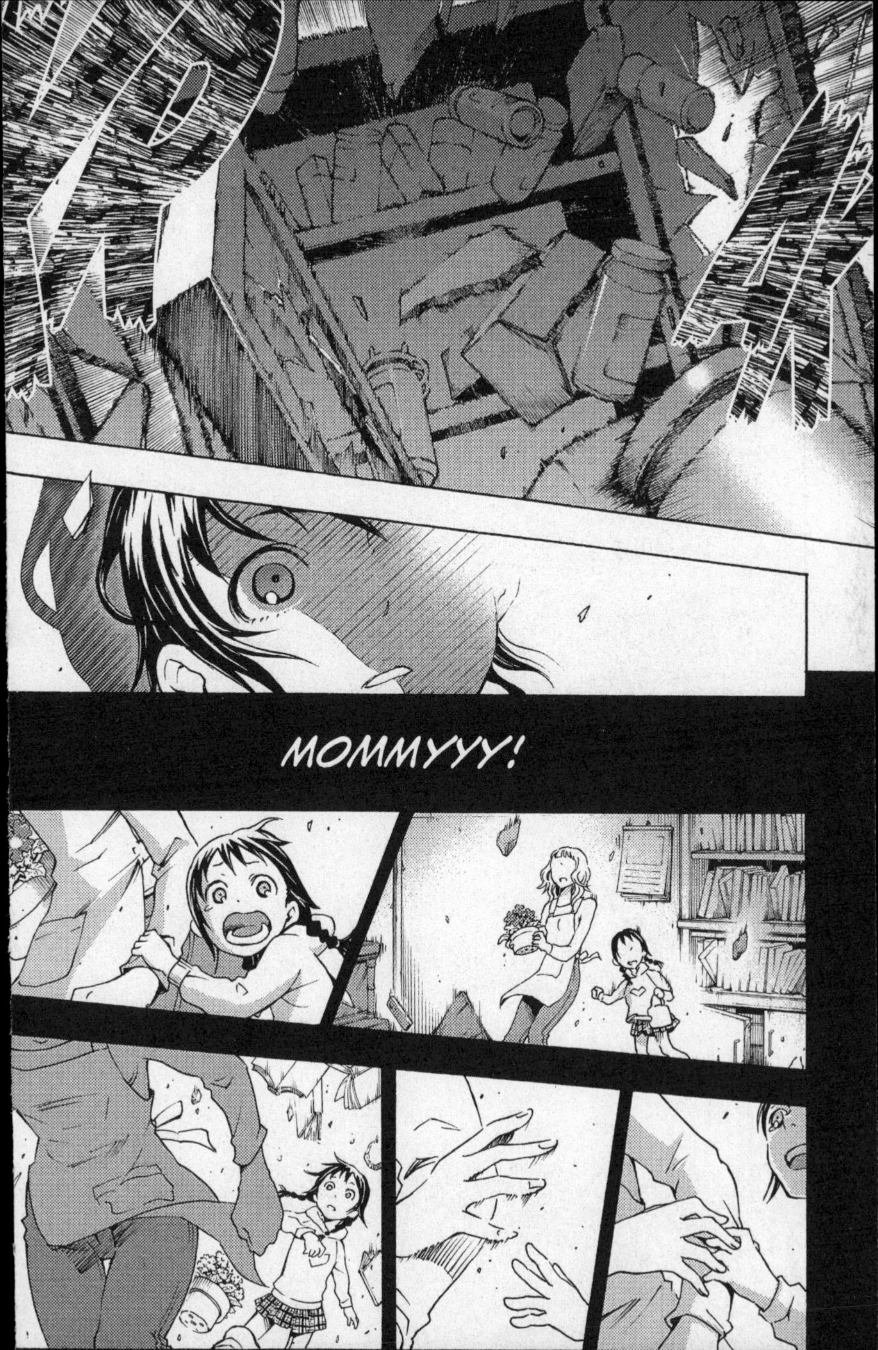
MOMMYYY!

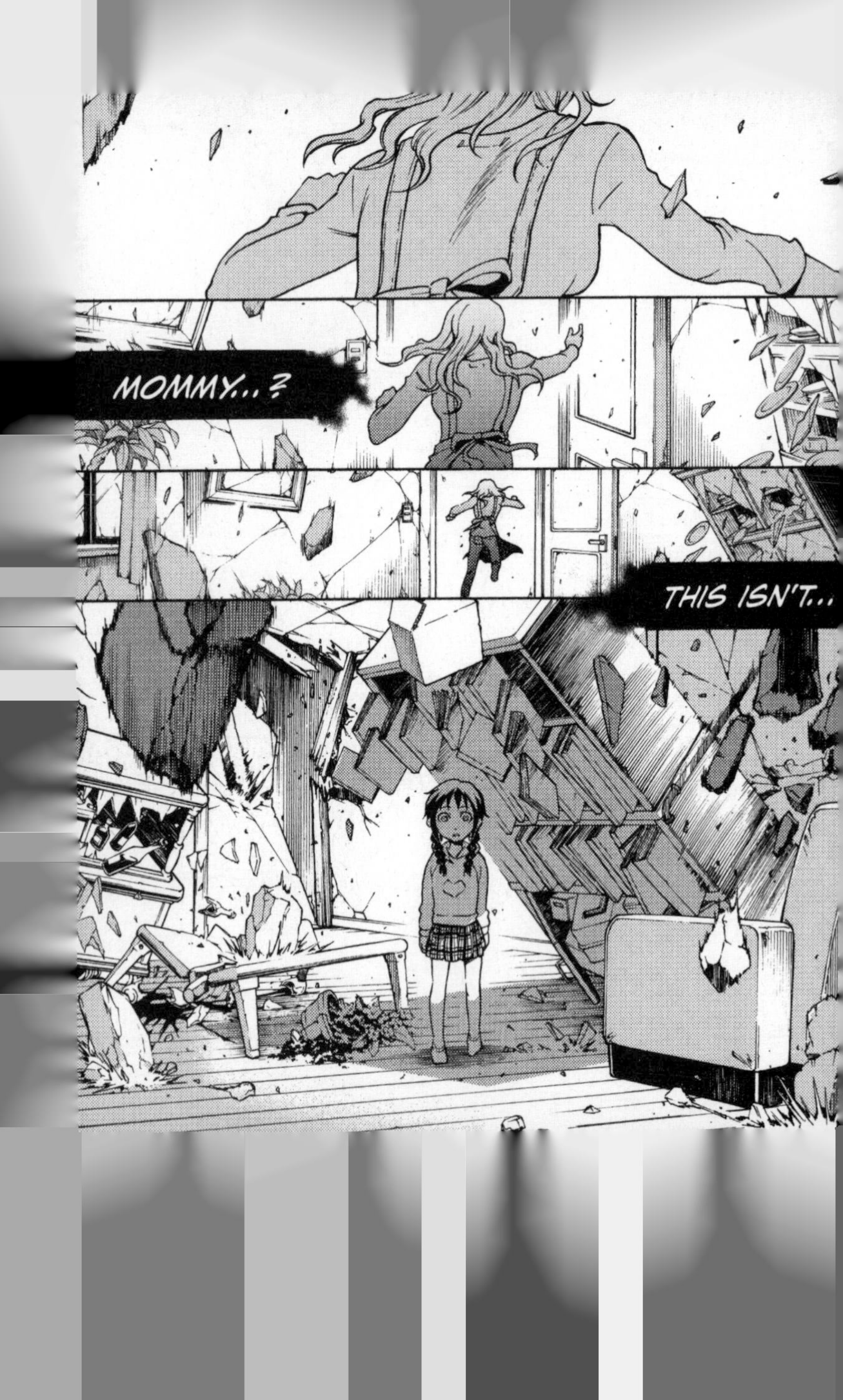
MOMMY...?
THIS ISN'T...

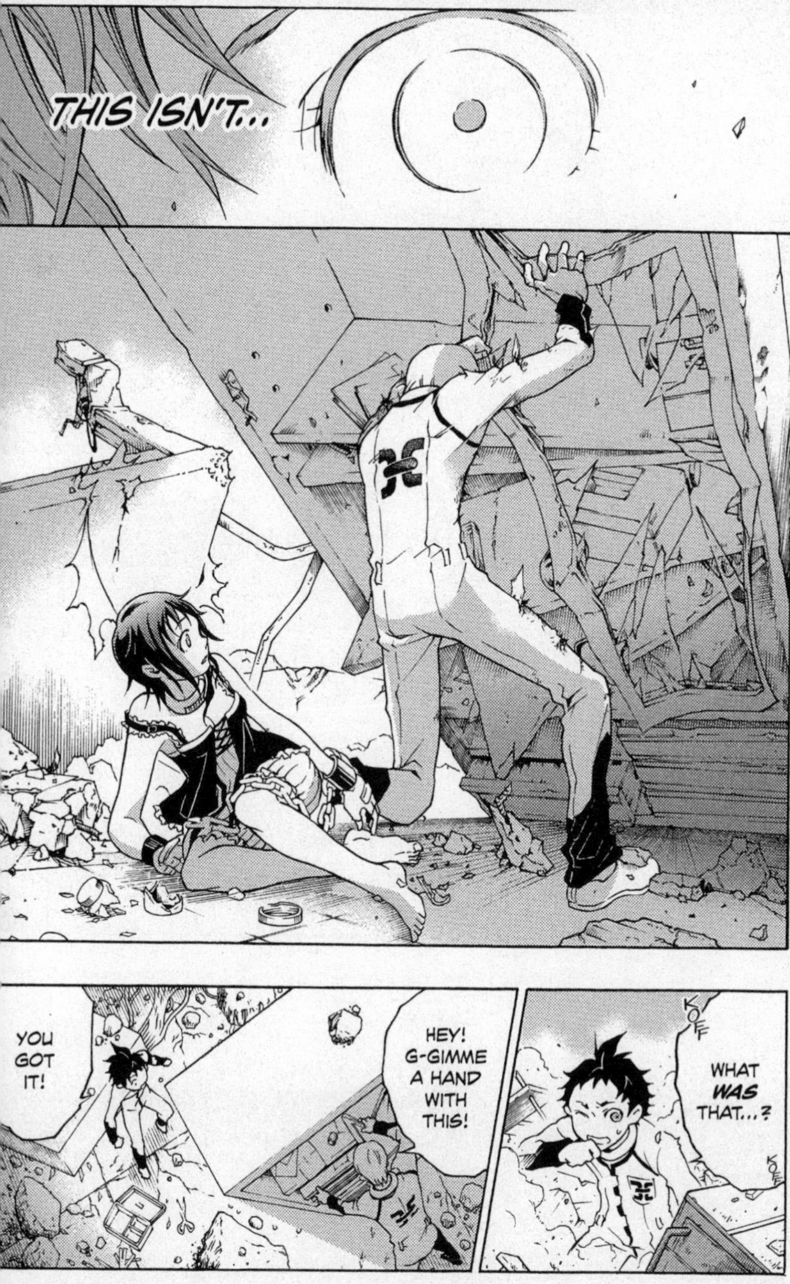
THIS ISN'T...
KOFF
WHAT *WAS* THAT...?
KOFF
HEY! G-GIMME A HAND WITH THIS!
YOU GOT IT!

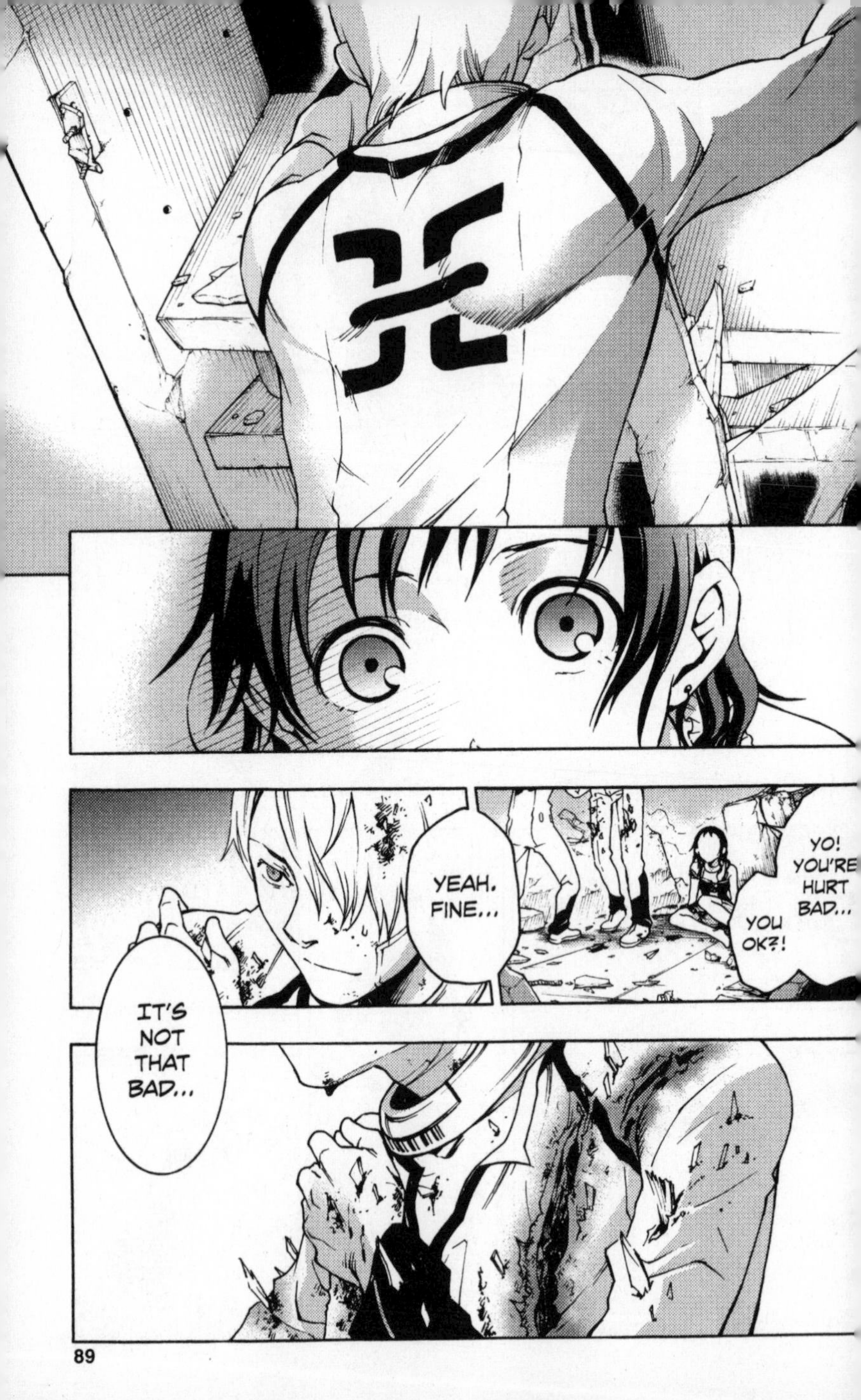
YO! YOU'RE HURT BAD...
YOU OK?!
YEAH. FINE...
IT'S NOT THAT BAD...

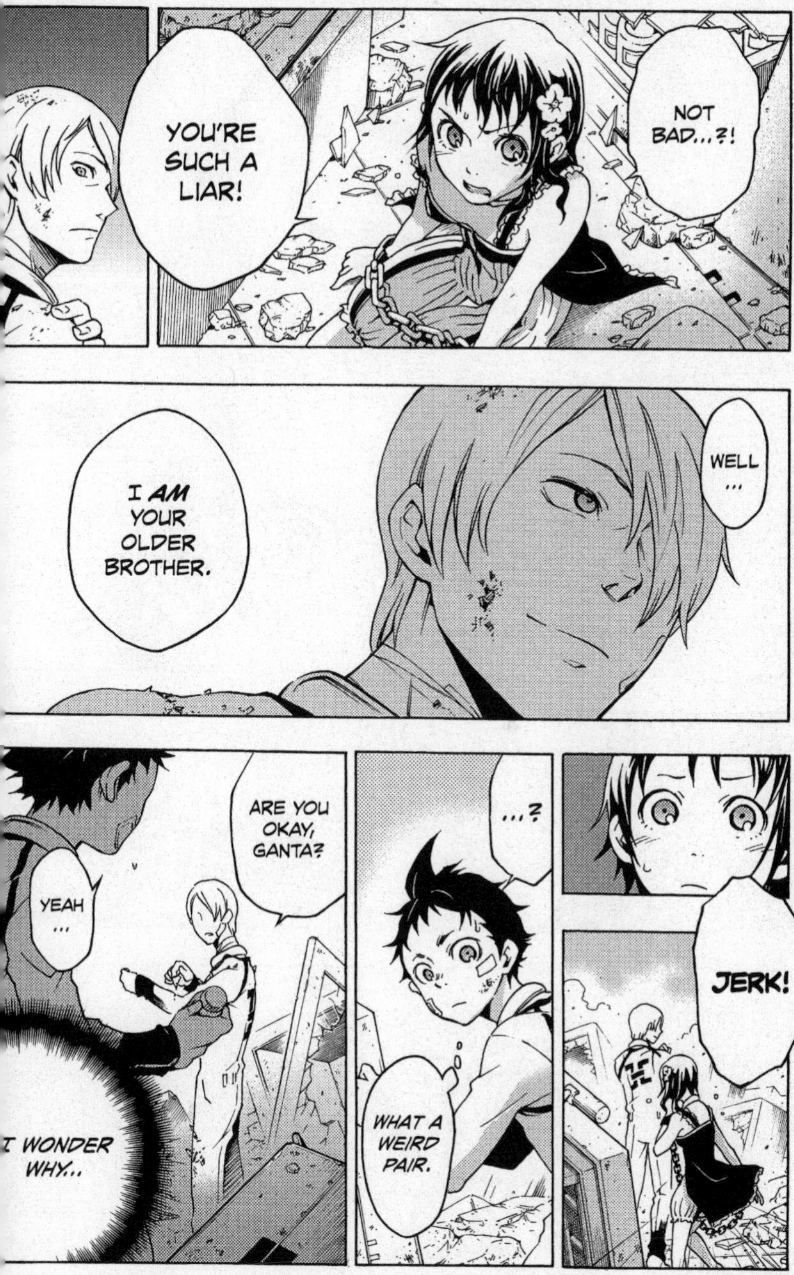
NOT BAD...?!
YOU'RE SUCH A LIAR!
WELL...
I *AM* YOUR OLDER BROTHER.
JERK!
...?
WHAT A WEIRD PAIR.
ARE YOU OKAY, GANTA?
YEAH...
I WONDER WHY...

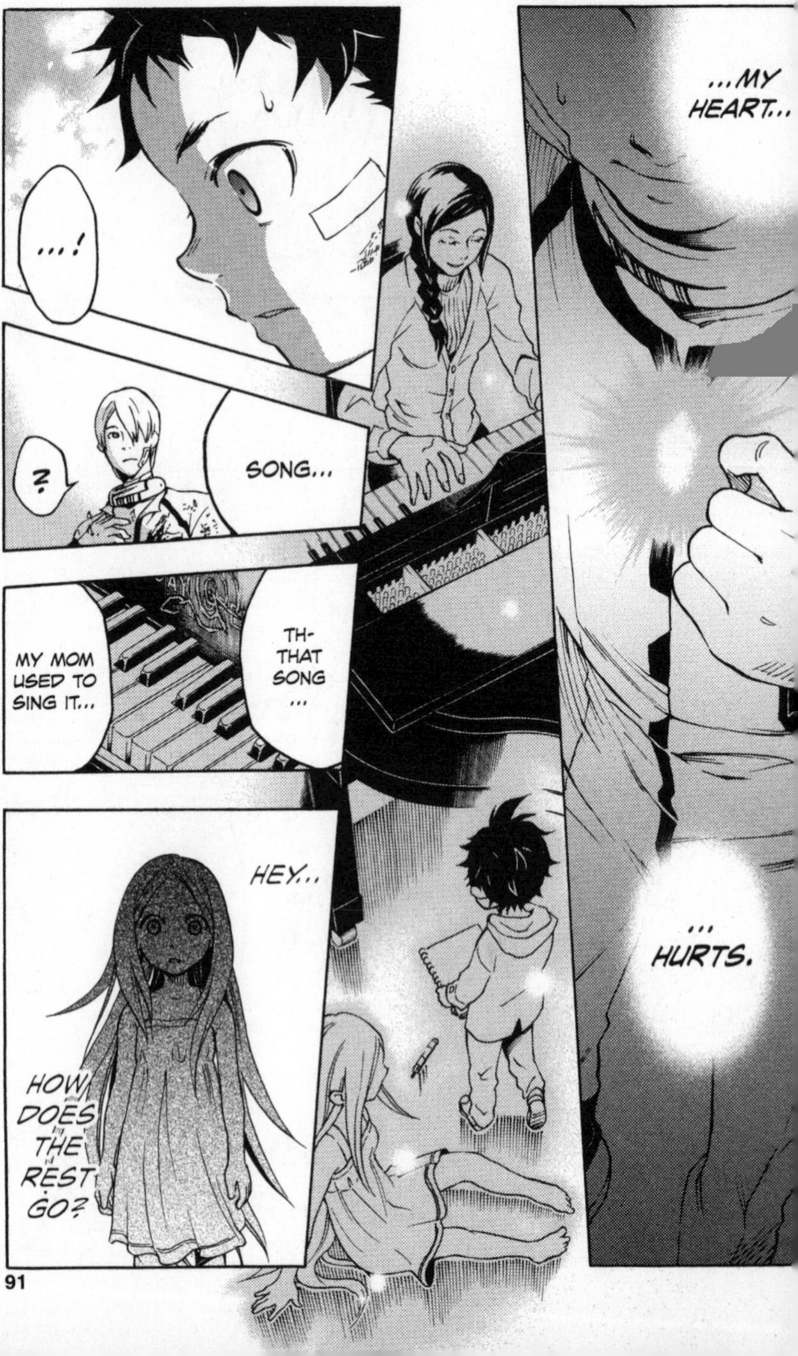

...MY HEART...
...HURTS.
...!
SONG...
?
TH-THAT SONG...
MY MOM USED TO SING IT...
HEY...
HOW DOES THE REST GO?

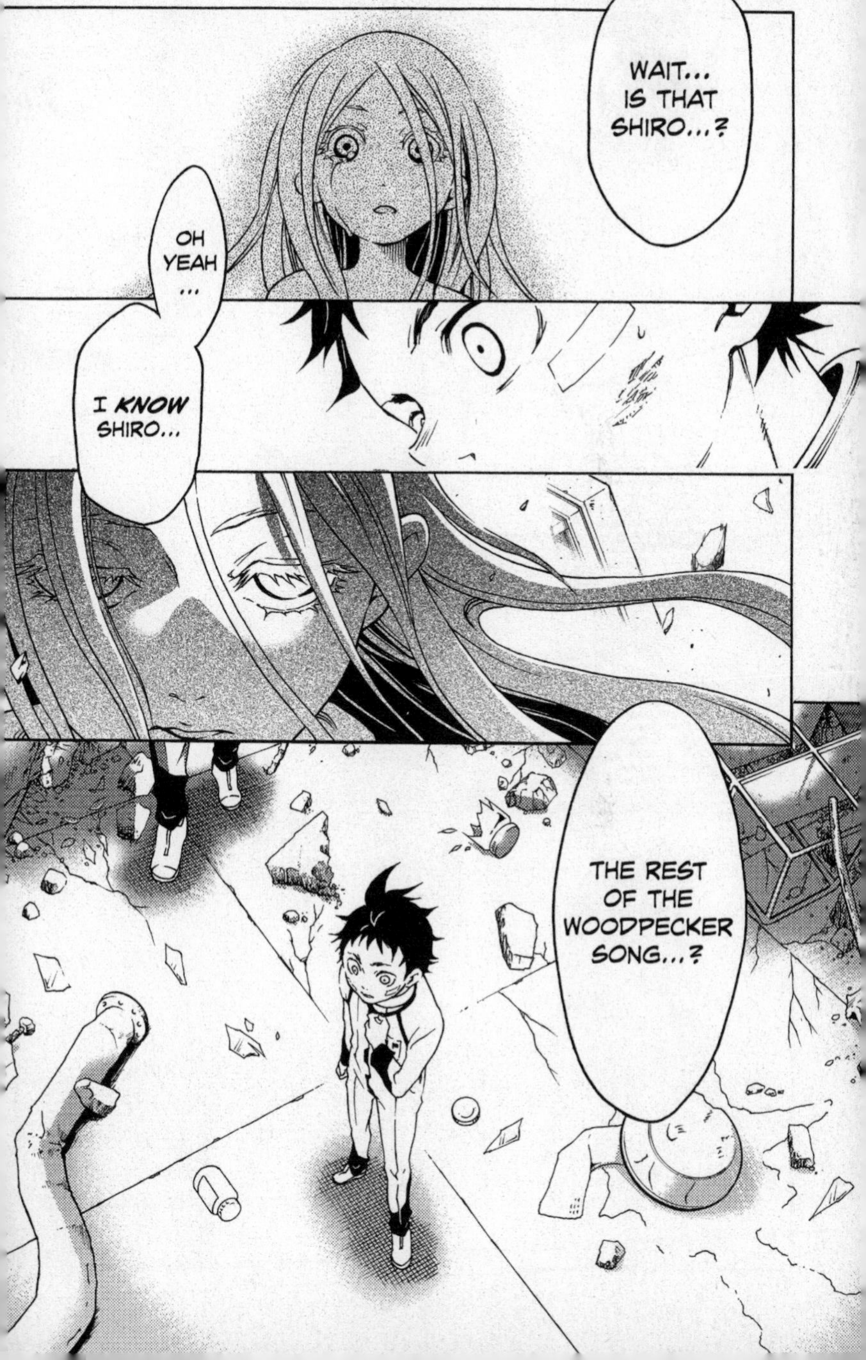
WAIT... IS THAT SHIRO...?
OH YEAH ...
I KNOW SHIRO...
THE REST OF THE WOODPECKER SONG...?

ONDER WO
LAND

DEAD
MAN
ONDER WO
LAND

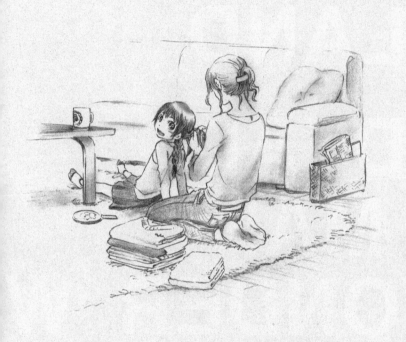

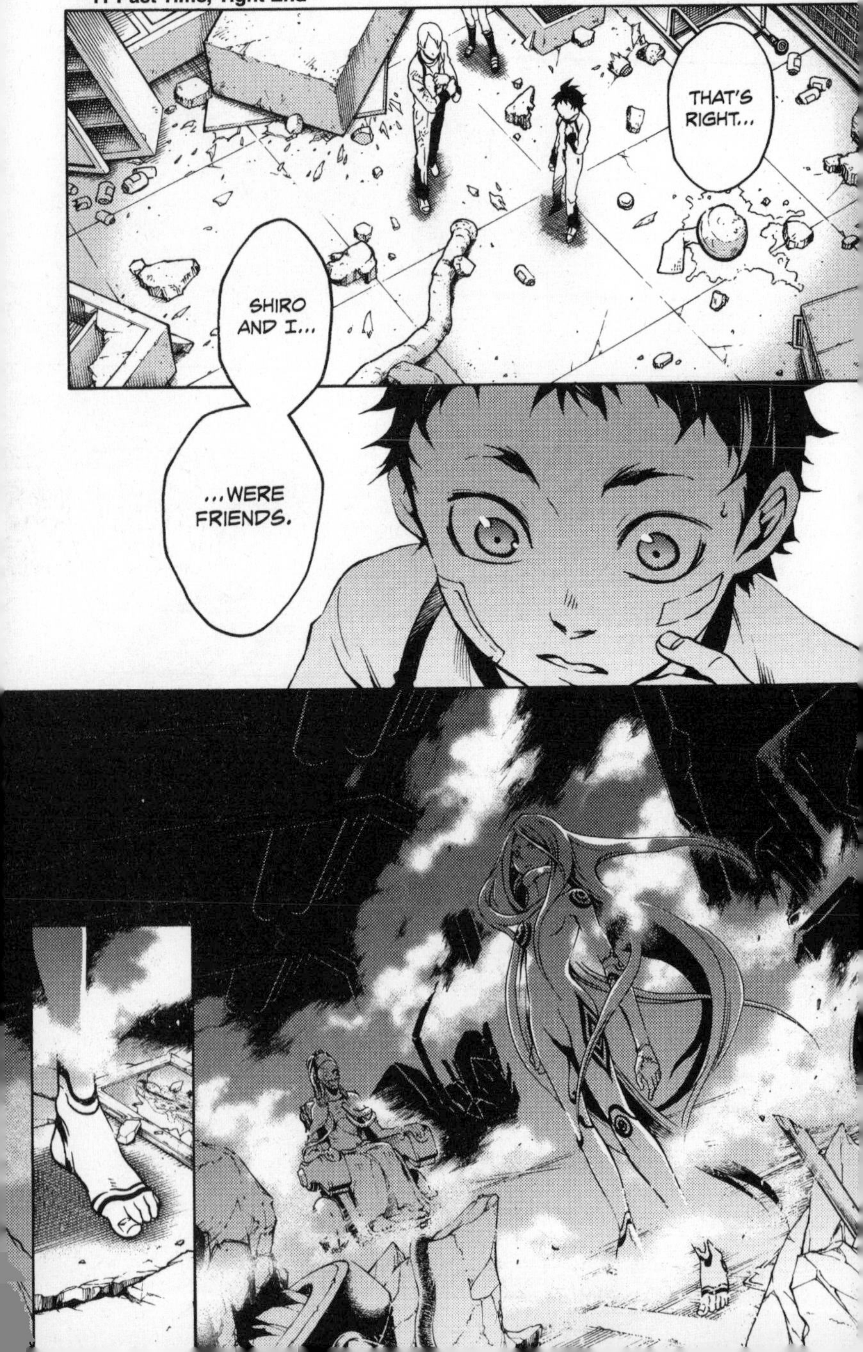
THAT'S RIGHT...
SHIRO AND I...
...WERE FRIENDS.

11 Past Time, Tight End

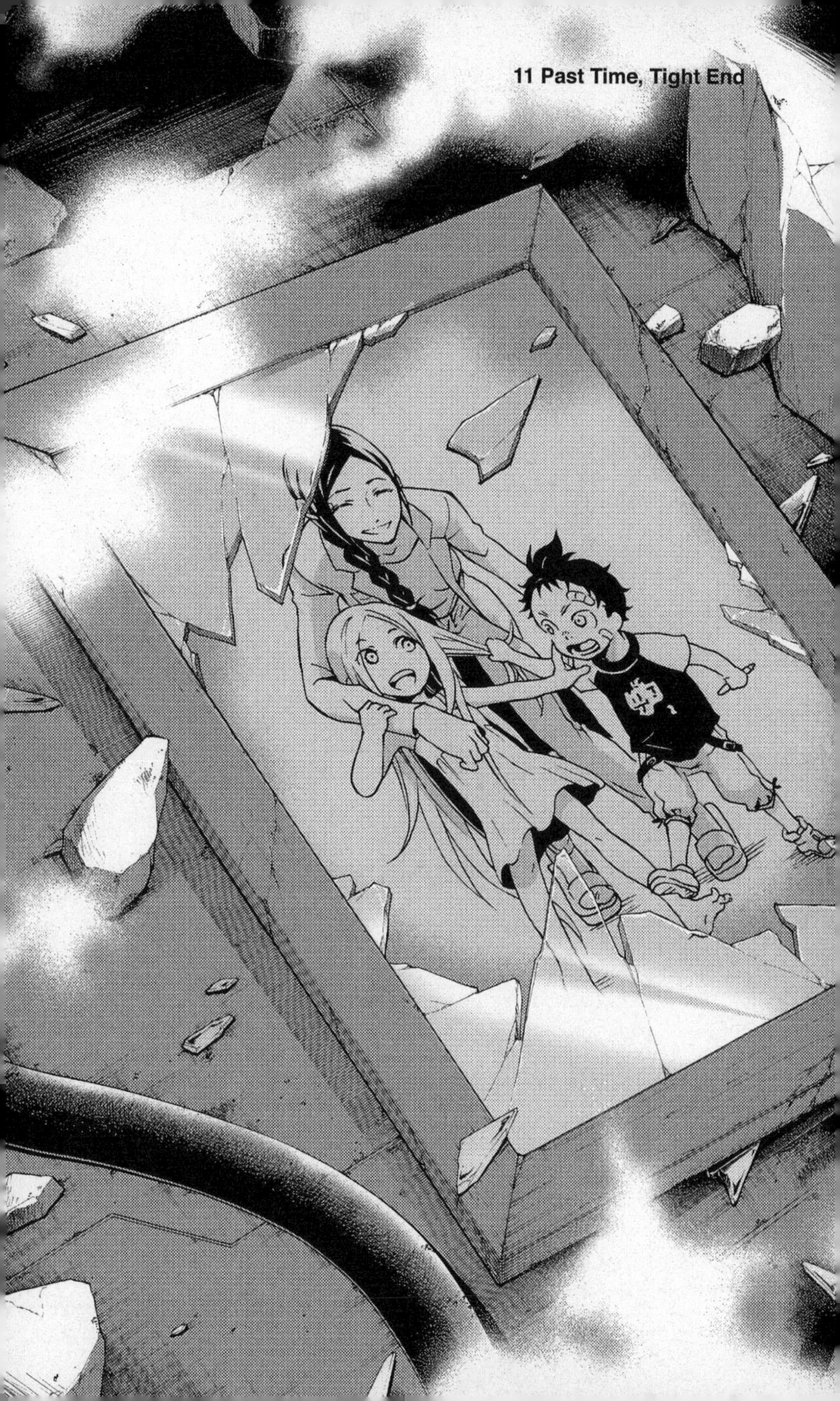

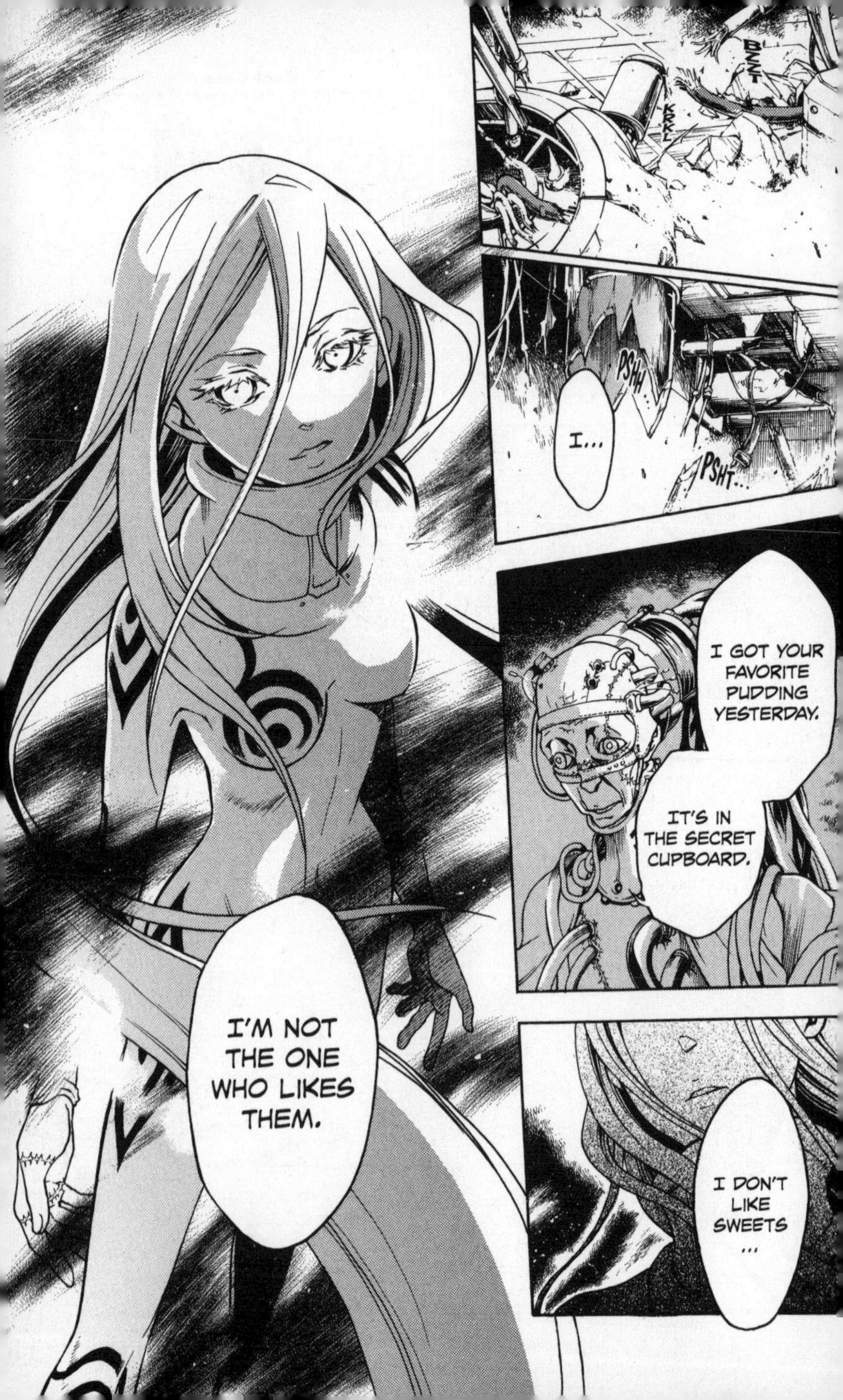
BZZT
KRKL
PSHH
I...
PSHT...
I GOT YOUR FAVORITE PUDDING YESTERDAY.
IT'S IN THE SECRET CUPBOARD.
I DON'T LIKE SWEETS ...
I'M NOT THE ONE WHO LIKES THEM.

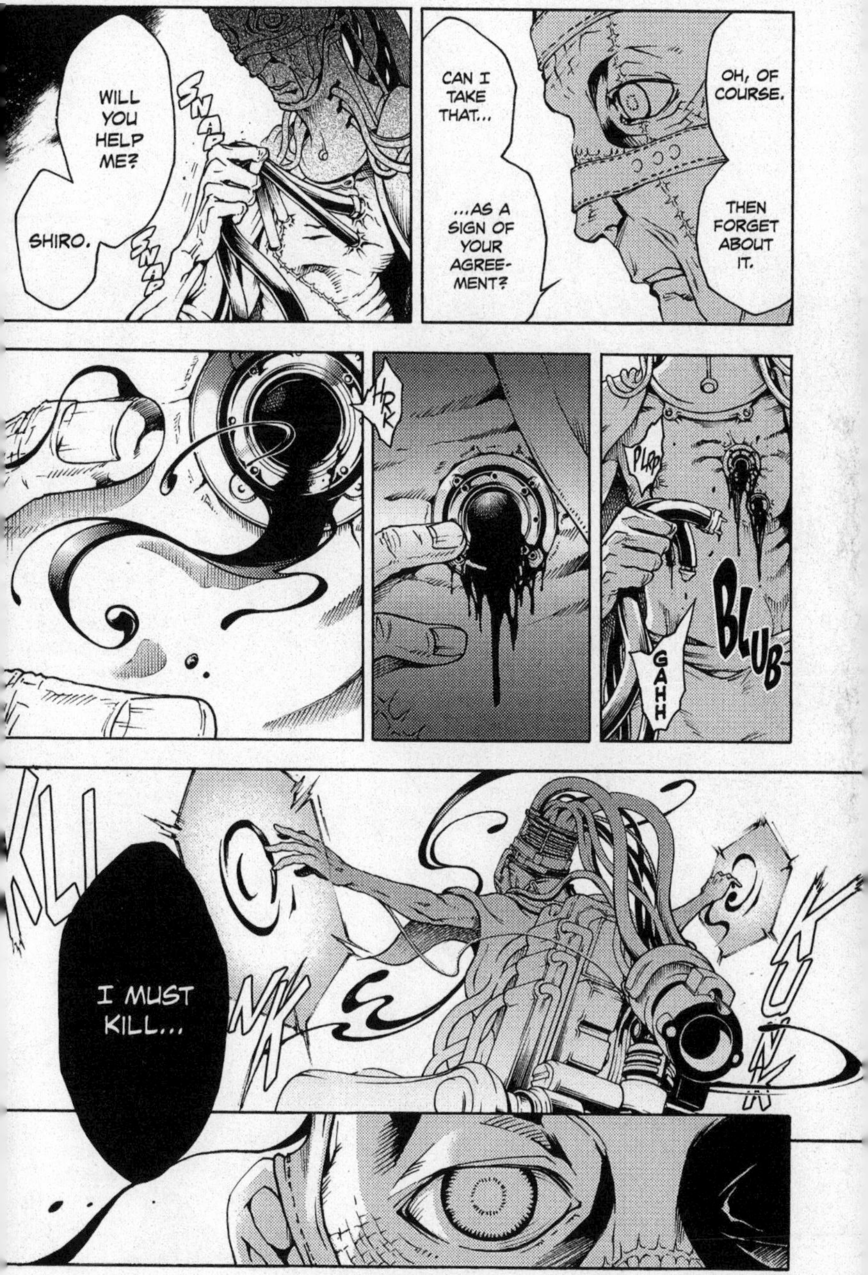
OH, OF COURSE.
THEN FORGET ABOUT IT.
CAN I TAKE THAT...
...AS A SIGN OF YOUR AGREEMENT?
WILL YOU HELP ME?
SNAP
SHIRO.
SNAP
PLRP
BLUB
GAHH
HRK
I MUST KILL...

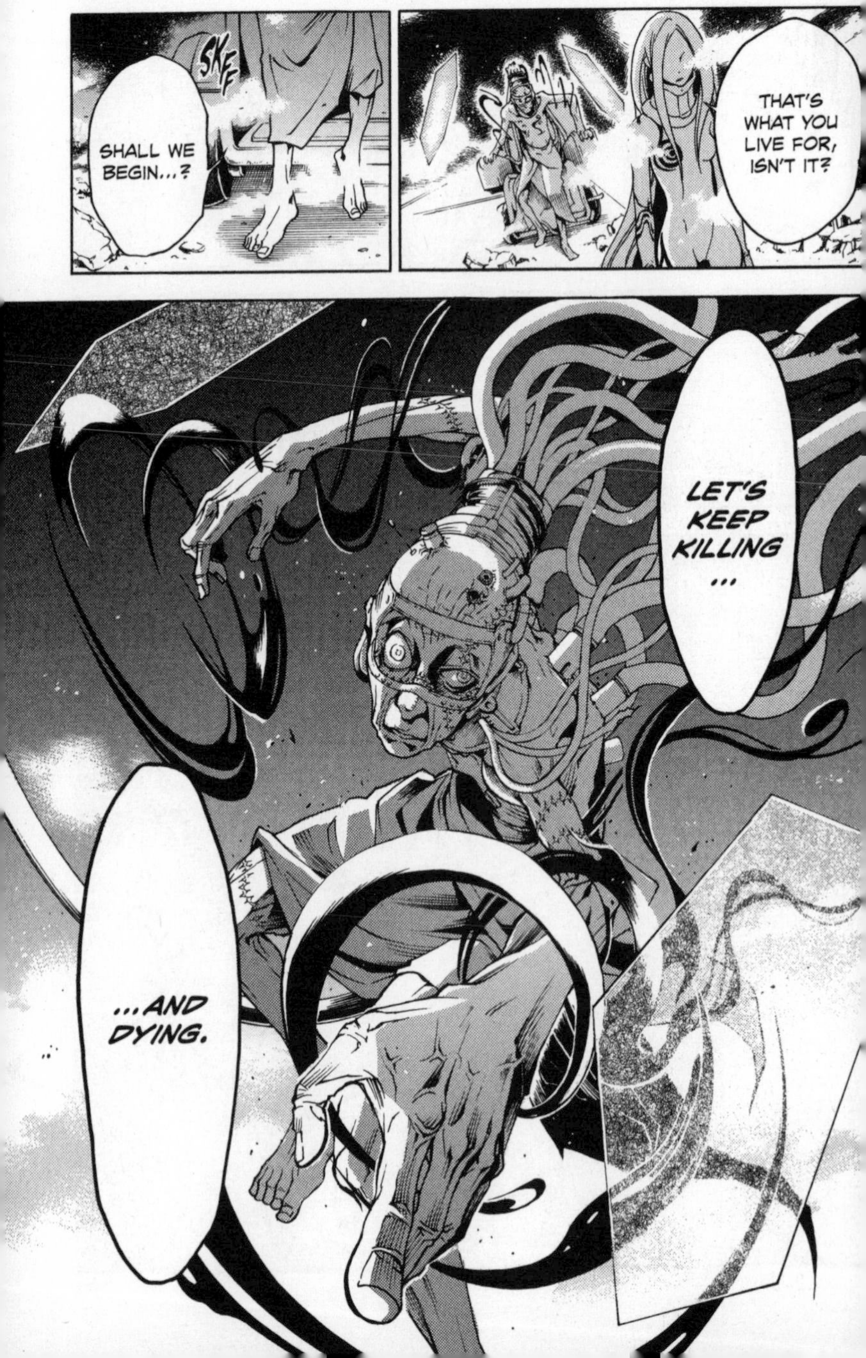
THAT'S WHAT YOU LIVE FOR, ISN'T IT?
SKFF
SHALL WE BEGIN...?
LET'S KEEP KILLING ...
...AND DYING.

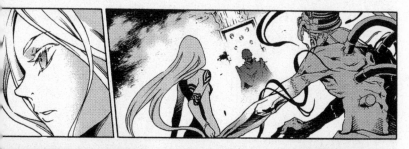

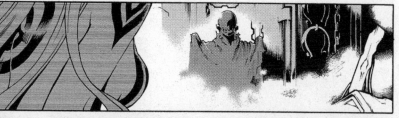

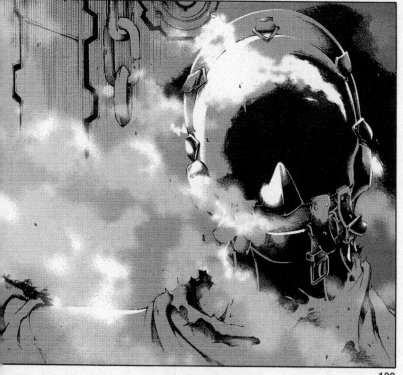

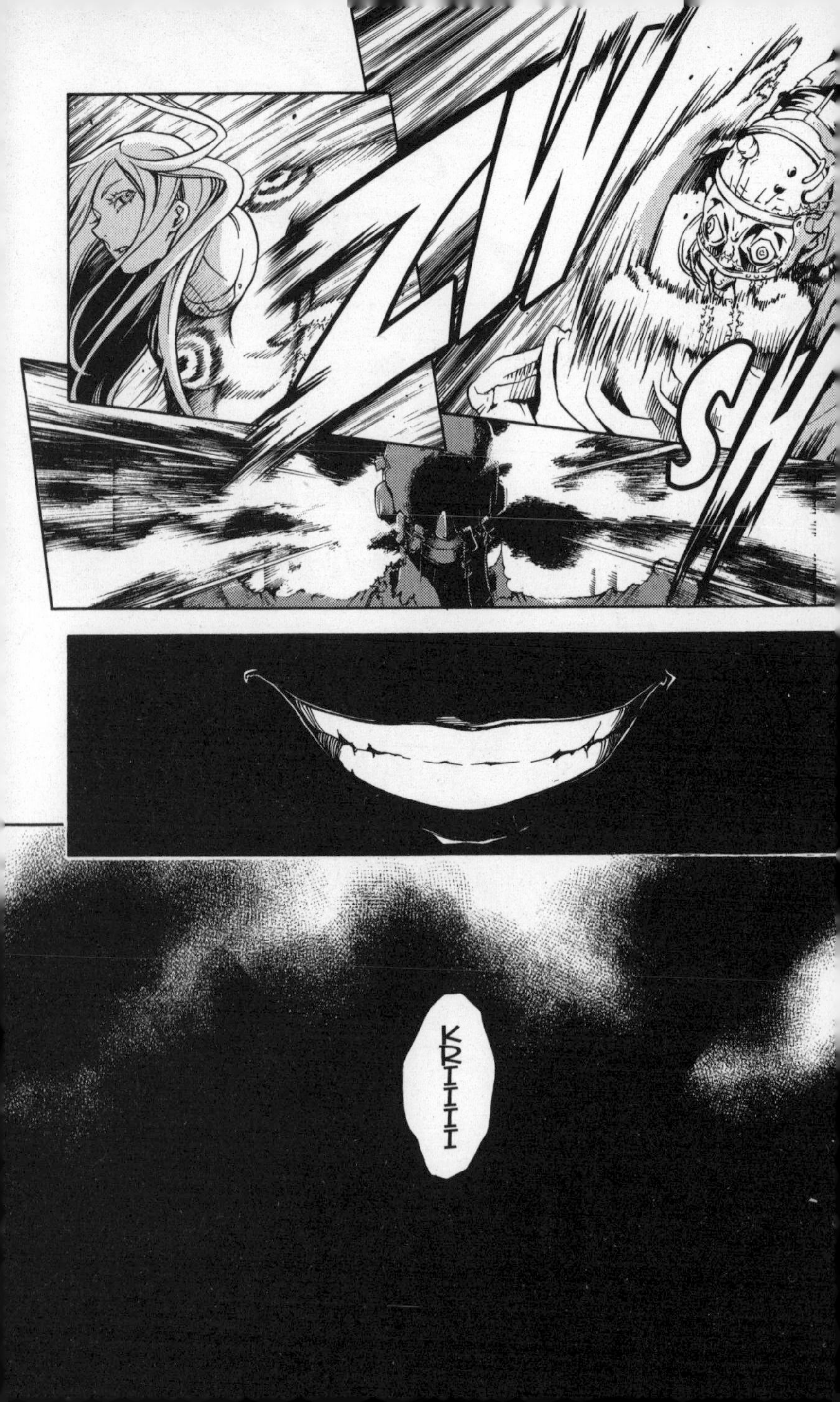
ZAN
SH
KRIIII

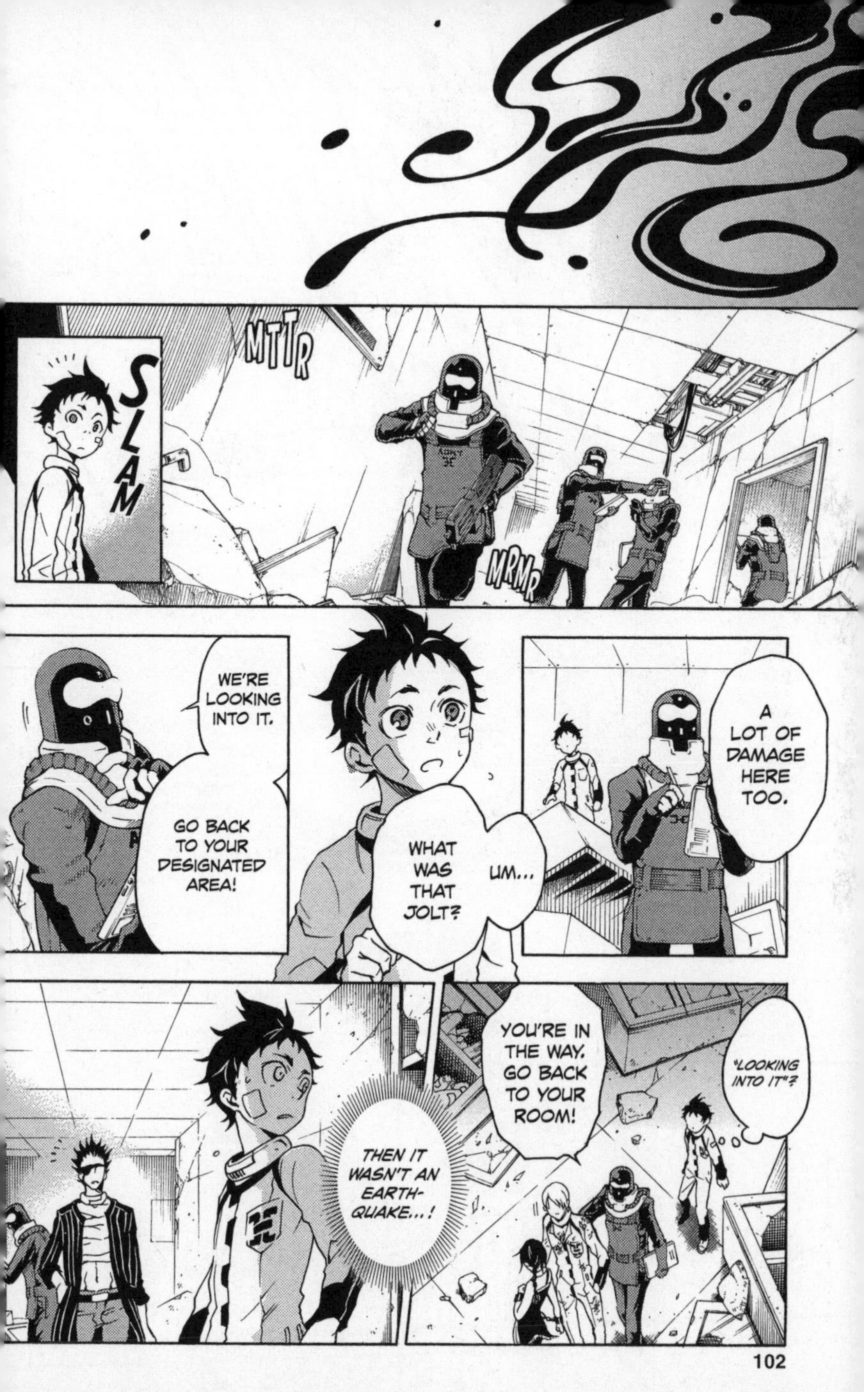
MTTR
MRMR
SLAM
A LOT OF DAMAGE HERE TOO.
UM...
WHAT WAS THAT JOLT?
WE'RE LOOKING INTO IT.
GO BACK TO YOUR DESIGNATED AREA!
"LOOKING INTO IT"?
YOU'RE IN THE WAY. GO BACK TO YOUR ROOM!
THEN IT WASN'T AN EARTH-QUAKE...!

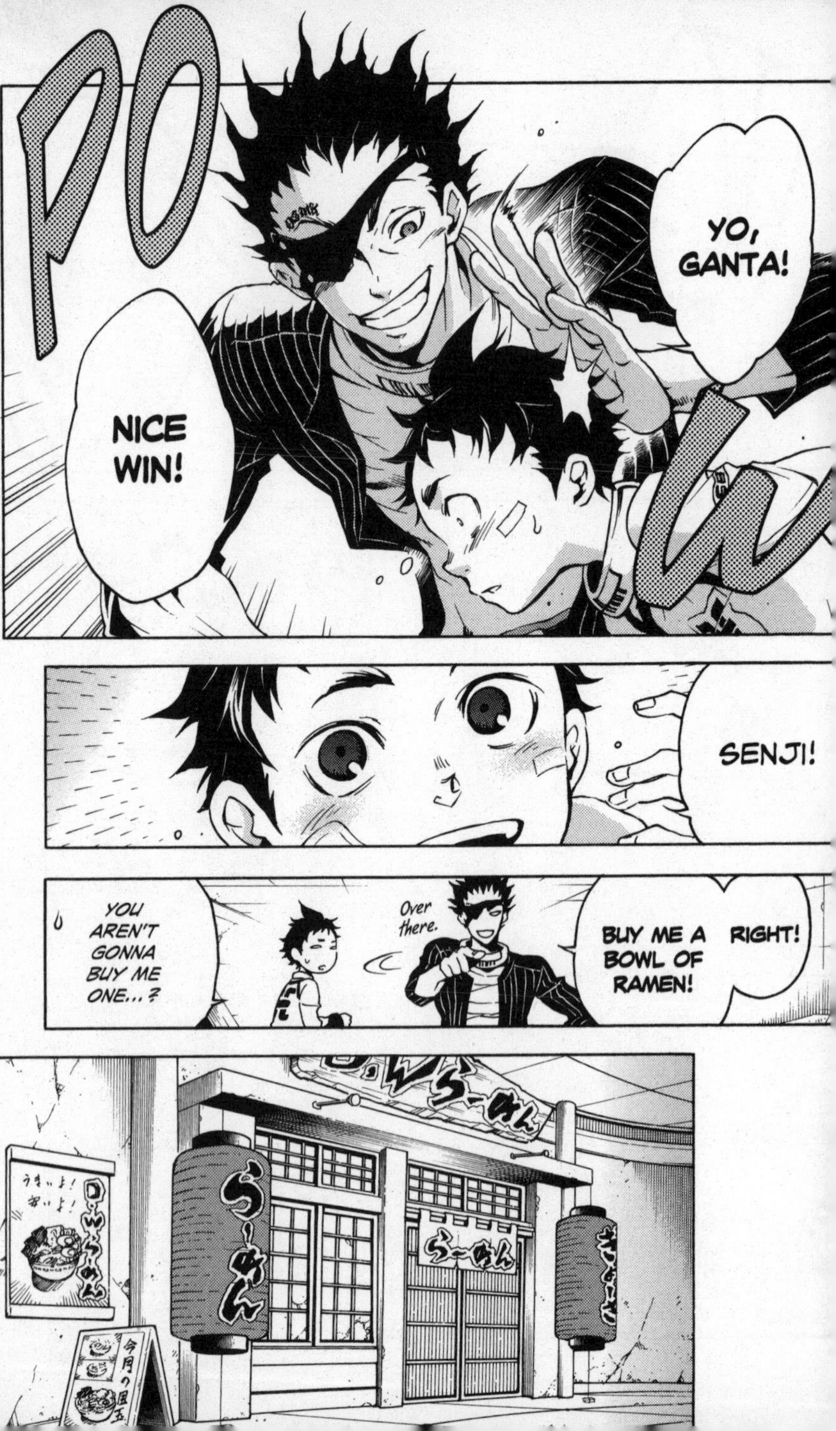
YO, GANTA!
NICE WIN!
POW
SENJI!
RIGHT!
BUY ME A BOWL OF RAMEN!
Over there.
YOU AREN'T GONNA BUY ME ONE...?
らーめん
らーめん

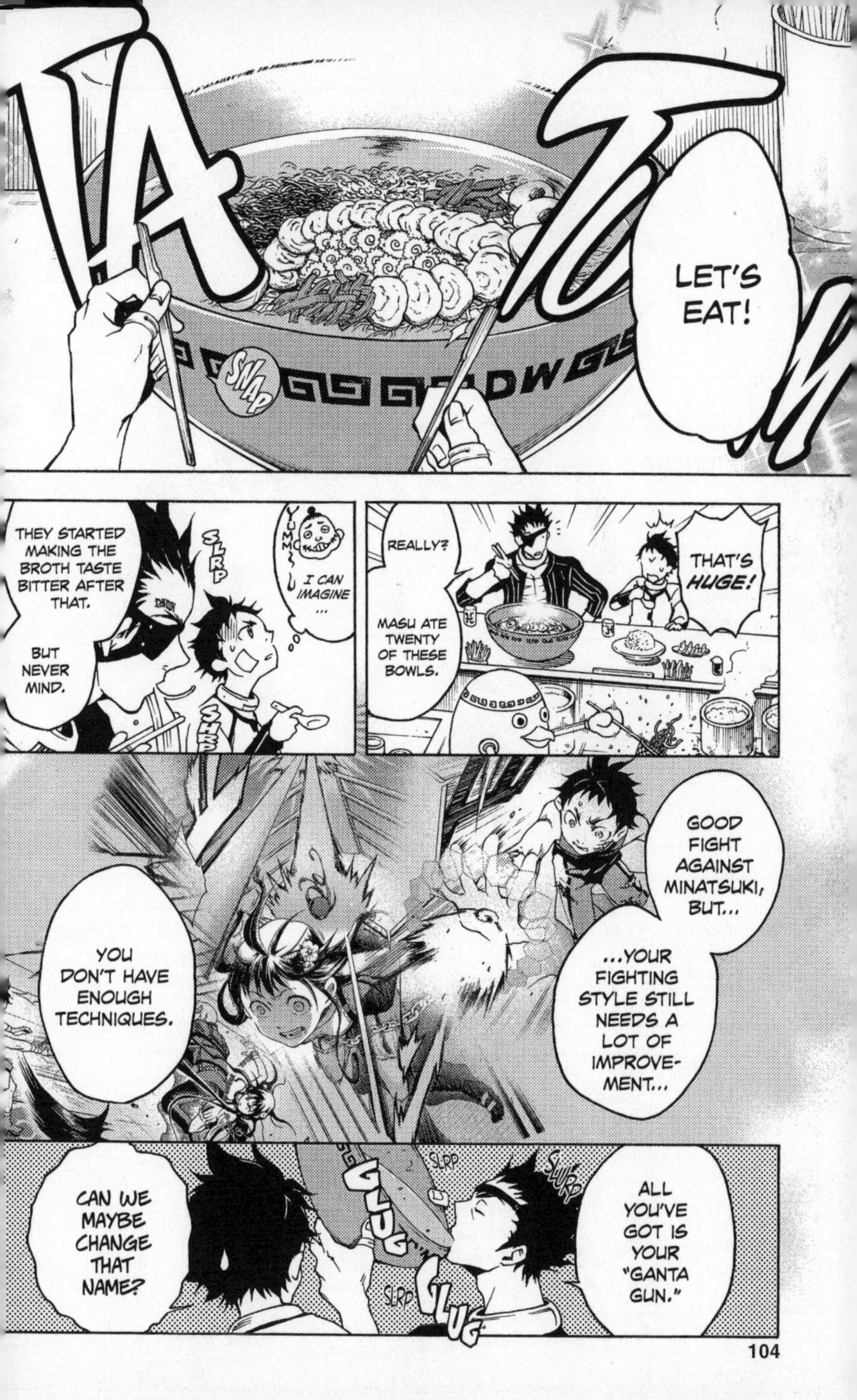

LET'S EAT!
SNAP
THAT'S HUGE!
REALLY?
MASU ATE TWENTY OF THESE BOWLS.
YUMM...
I CAN IMAGINE ...
SLRP
THEY STARTED MAKING THE BROTH TASTE BITTER AFTER THAT.
BUT NEVER MIND.
SHRP
GOOD FIGHT AGAINST MINATSUKI, BUT...
...YOUR FIGHTING STYLE STILL NEEDS A LOT OF IMPROVEMENT...
YOU DON'T HAVE ENOUGH TECHNIQUES.
SLURP
ALL YOU'VE GOT IS YOUR "GANTA GUN."
SLRP
GLUG
SLRP
GLUG
CAN WE MAYBE CHANGE THAT NAME?

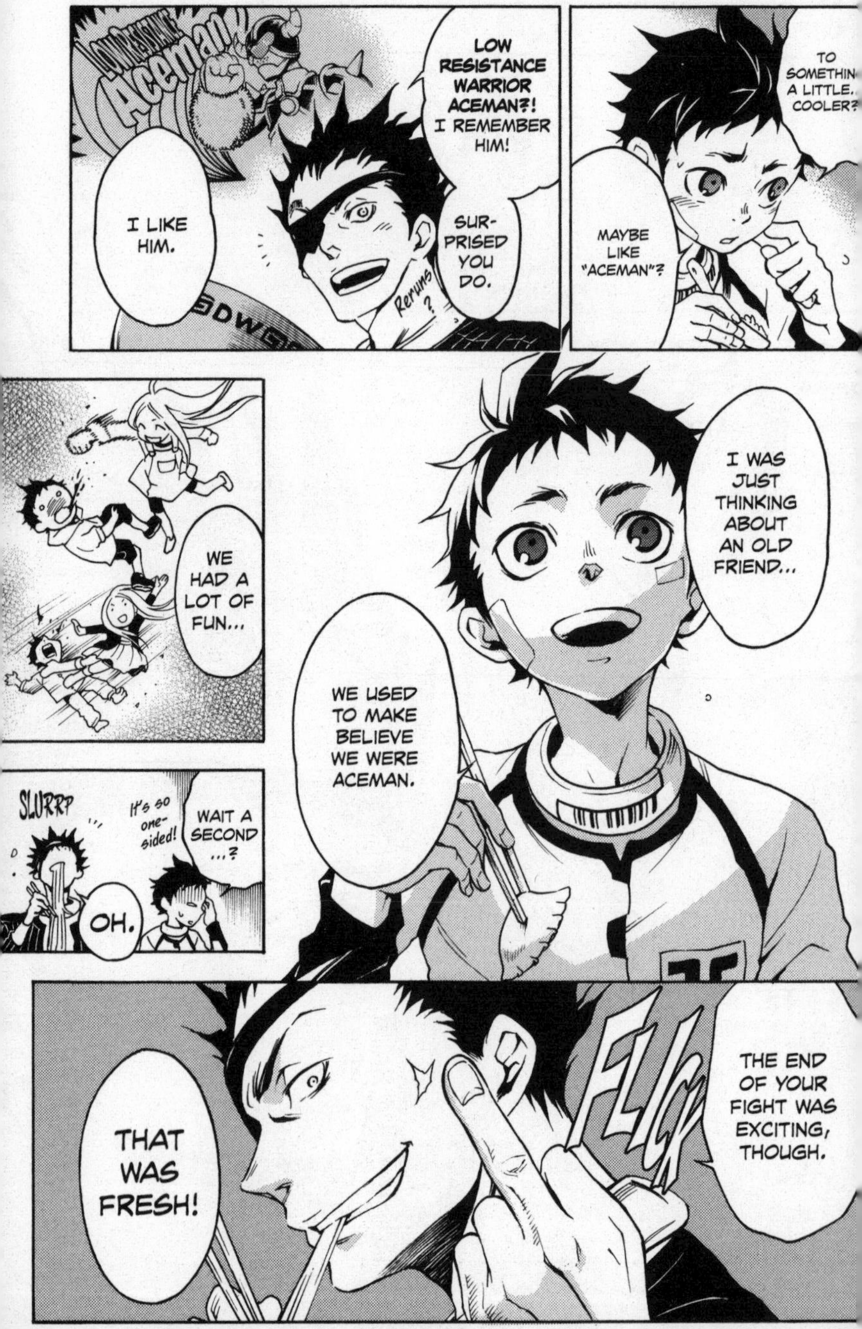
TO SOMETHIN A LITTLE... COOLER?
MAYBE LIKE "ACEMAN"?
LOW RESISTANCE WARRIOR ACEMAN?! I REMEMBER HIM!
SUR-PRISED YOU DO.
Reruns?
I LIKE HIM.
LOW RESISTANCE Aceman!!
I WAS JUST THINKING ABOUT AN OLD FRIEND...
WE USED TO MAKE BELIEVE WE WERE ACEMAN.
WE HAD A LOT OF FUN...
WAIT A SECOND ...?
It's so one-sided!
SLURRP
OH.
THE END OF YOUR FIGHT WAS EXCITING, THOUGH.
FLICK
THAT WAS FRESH!

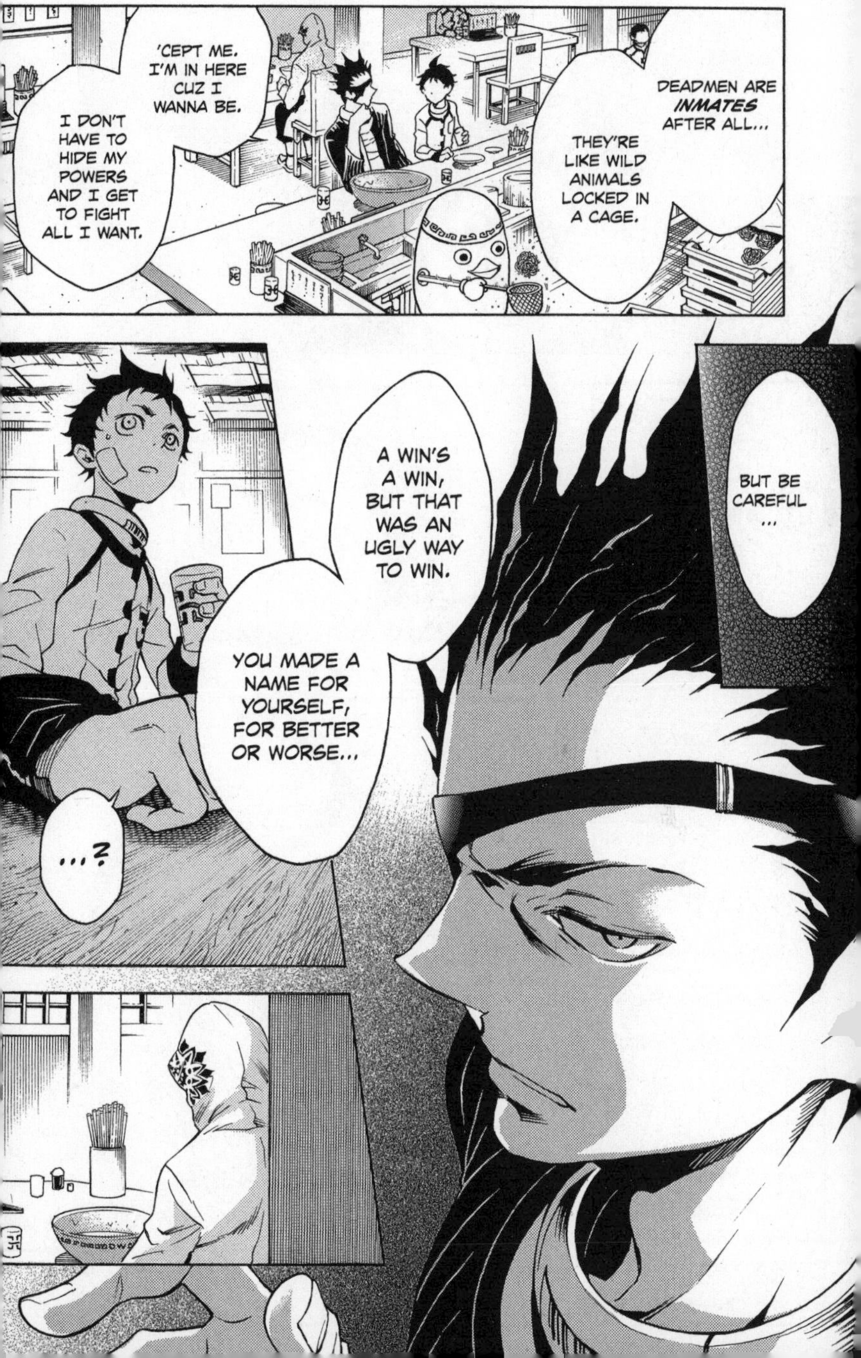
DEADMEN ARE *INMATES* AFTER ALL...
THEY'RE LIKE WILD ANIMALS LOCKED IN A CAGE.
'CEPT ME. I'M IN HERE CUZ I WANNA BE.
I DON'T HAVE TO HIDE MY POWERS AND I GET TO FIGHT ALL I WANT.
BUT BE CAREFUL...
A WIN'S A WIN, BUT THAT WAS AN UGLY WAY TO WIN.
YOU MADE A NAME FOR YOURSELF, FOR BETTER OR WORSE...
...?

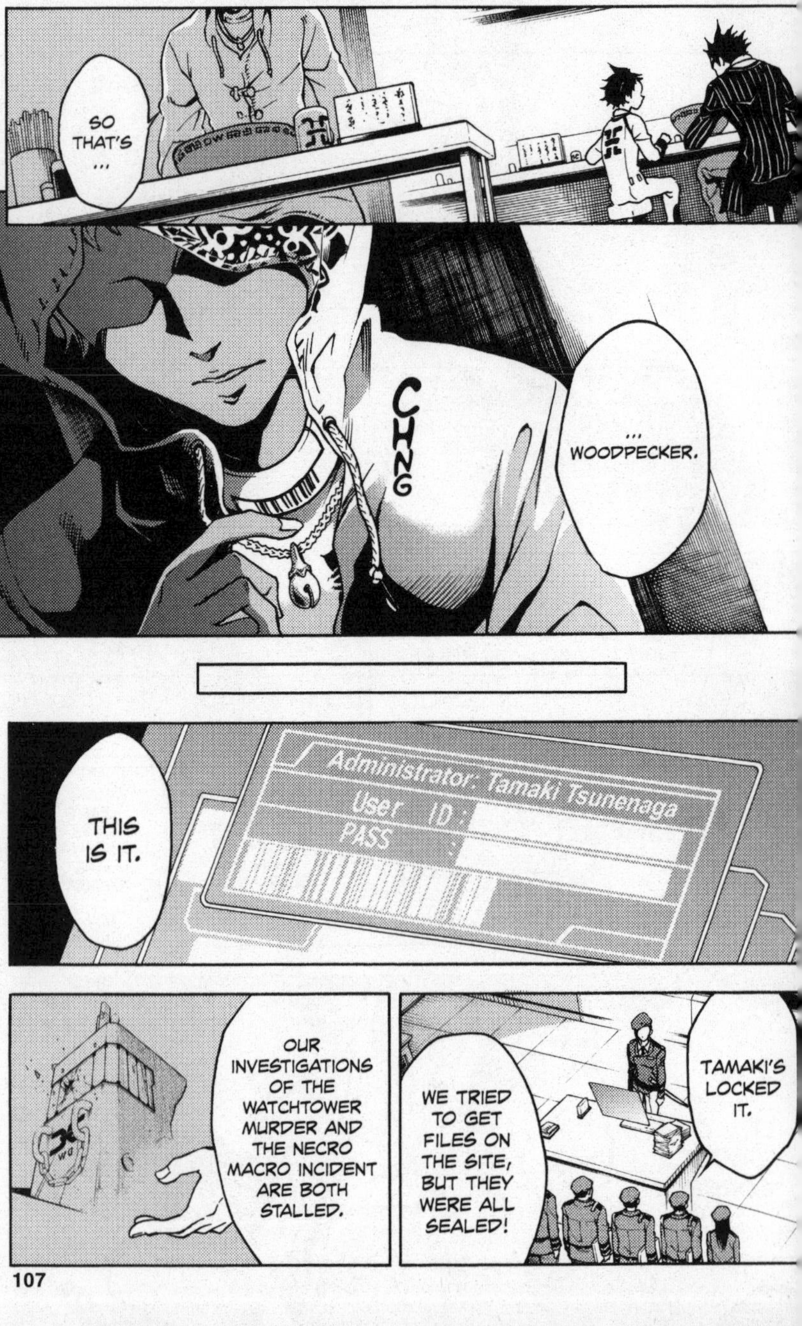
SO THAT'S ...
CHNG
... WOODPECKER.
THIS IS IT.
Administrator: Tamaki Tsunenaga
User ID:
PASS :
TAMAKI'S LOCKED IT.
WE TRIED TO GET FILES ON THE SITE, BUT THEY WERE ALL SEALED!
OUR INVESTIGATIONS OF THE WATCHTOWER MURDER AND THE NECRO MACRO INCIDENT ARE BOTH STALLED.

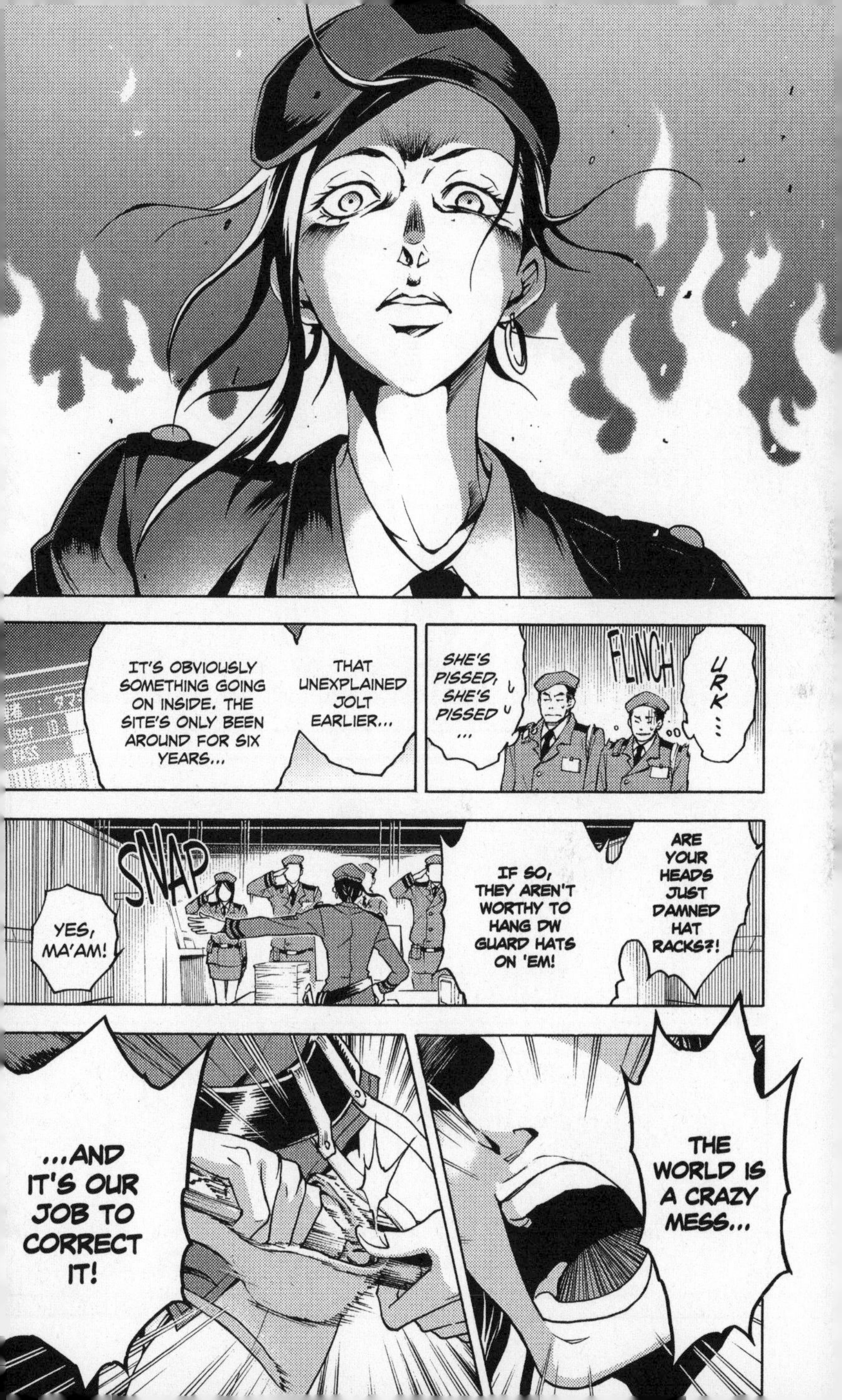
URK...
FLINCH
SHE'S PISSED, SHE'S PISSED...
THAT UNEXPLAINED JOLT EARLIER...
IT'S OBVIOUSLY SOMETHING GOING ON INSIDE. THE SITE'S ONLY BEEN AROUND FOR SIX YEARS...
ARE YOUR HEADS JUST DAMNED HAT RACKS?!
IF SO, THEY AREN'T WORTHY TO HANG DW GUARD HATS ON 'EM!
SNAP
YES, MA'AM!
THE WORLD IS A CRAZY MESS...
...AND IT'S OUR JOB TO CORRECT IT!

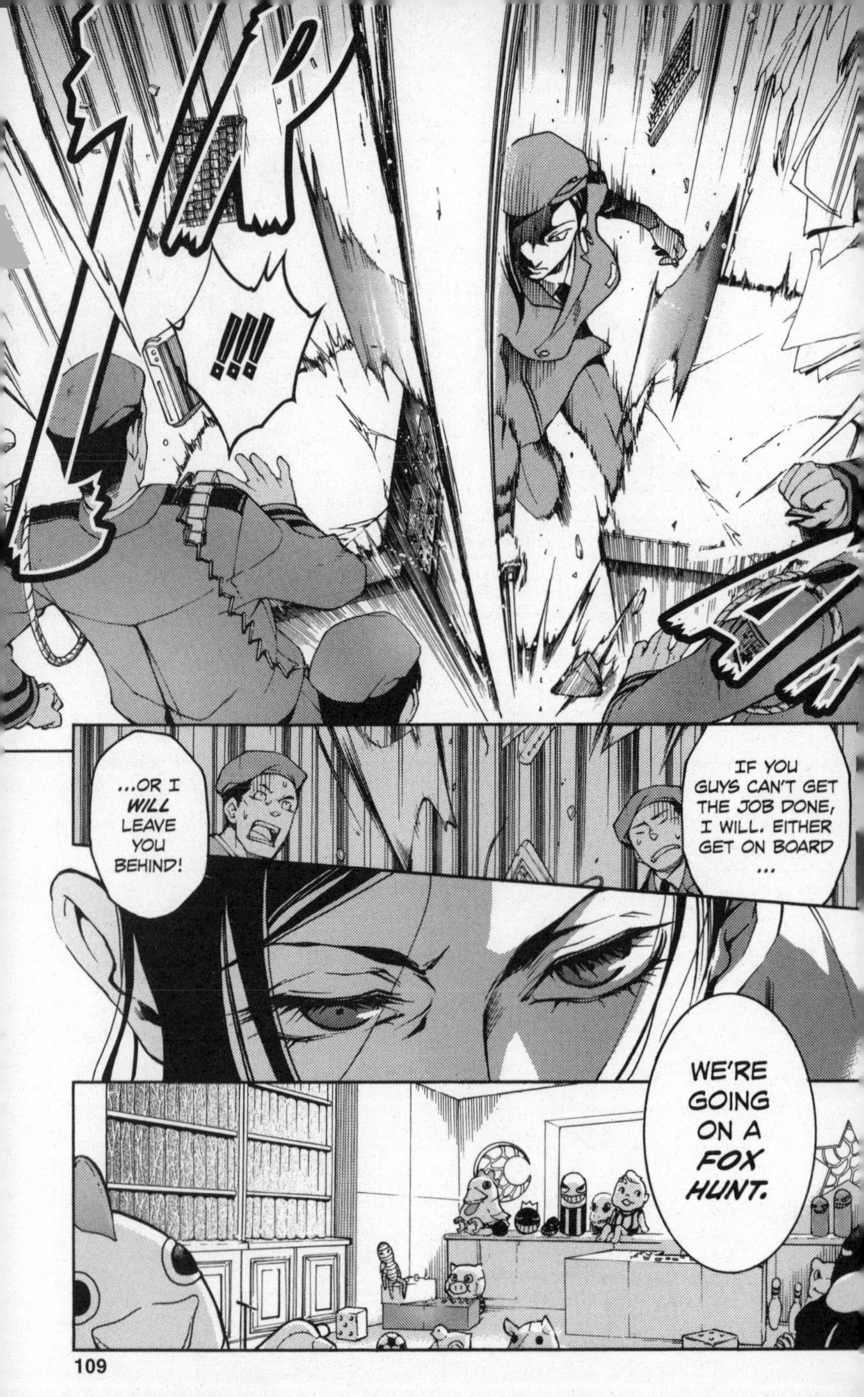
!!!!
IF YOU GUYS CAN'T GET THE JOB DONE, I WILL. EITHER GET ON BOARD ...
...OR I *WILL* LEAVE YOU BEHIND!
WE'RE GOING ON A *FOX HUNT.*

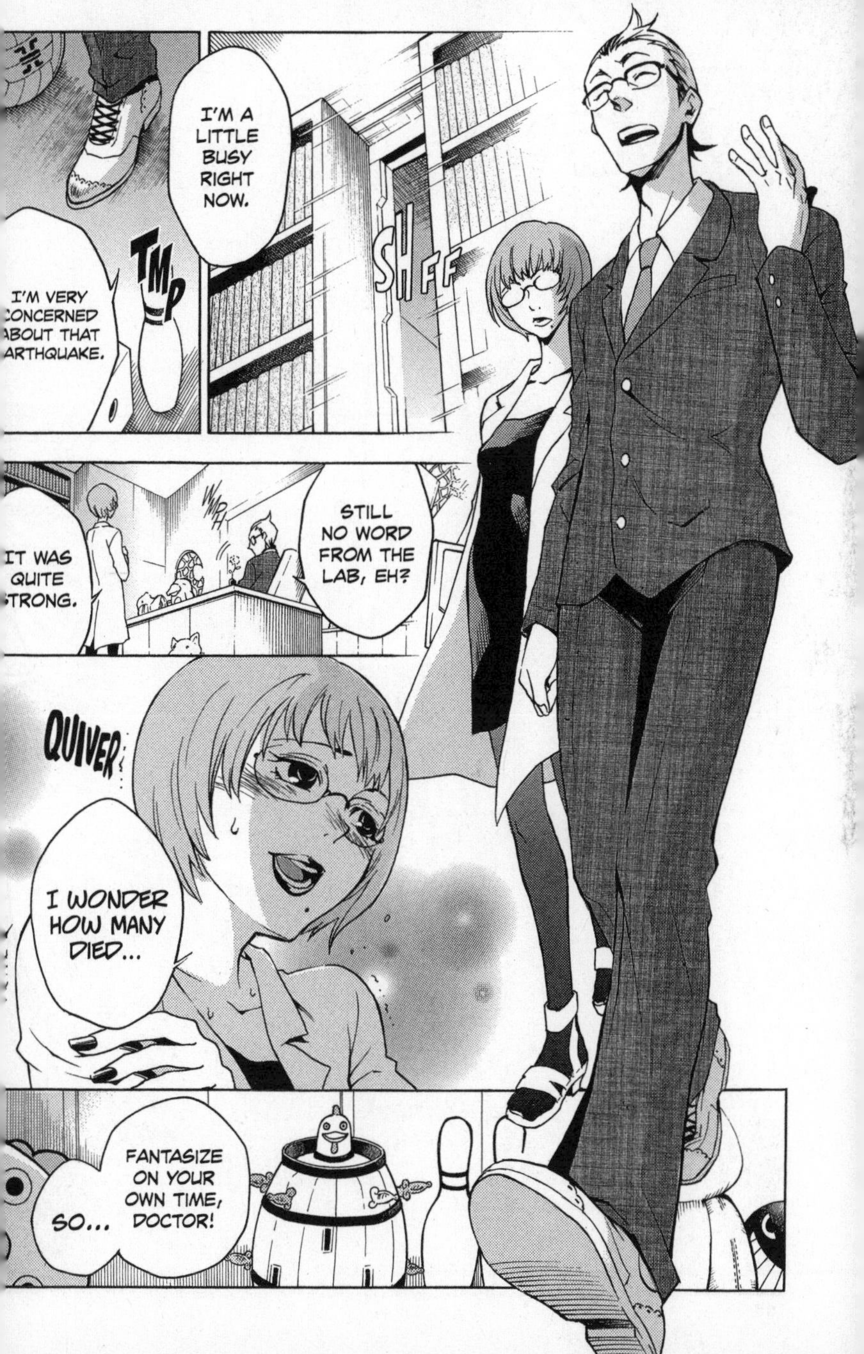
I'M A LITTLE BUSY RIGHT NOW.
SHFF
TMP
I'M VERY CONCERNED ABOUT THAT ARTHQUAKE.
STILL NO WORD FROM THE LAB, EH?
WHPH
IT WAS QUITE STRONG.
QUIVER
I WONDER HOW MANY DIED...
FANTASIZE ON YOUR OWN TIME, DOCTOR!
SO...

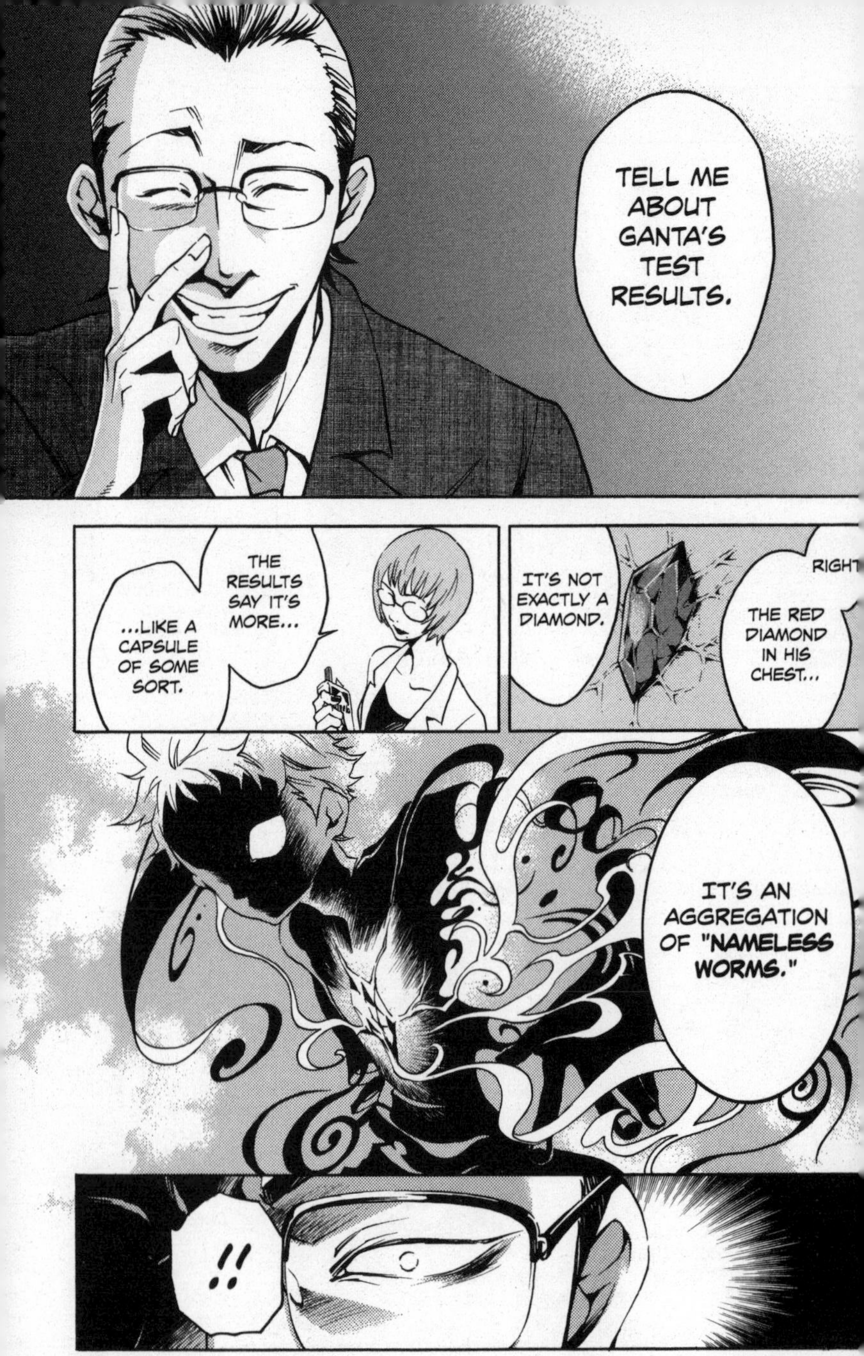
TELL ME ABOUT GANTA'S TEST RESULTS.
RIGHT
THE RED DIAMOND IN HIS CHEST...
IT'S NOT EXACTLY A DIAMOND.
THE RESULTS SAY IT'S MORE...
...LIKE A CAPSULE OF SOME SORT.
IT'S AN AGGREGATION OF "**NAMELESS WORMS.**"
!!

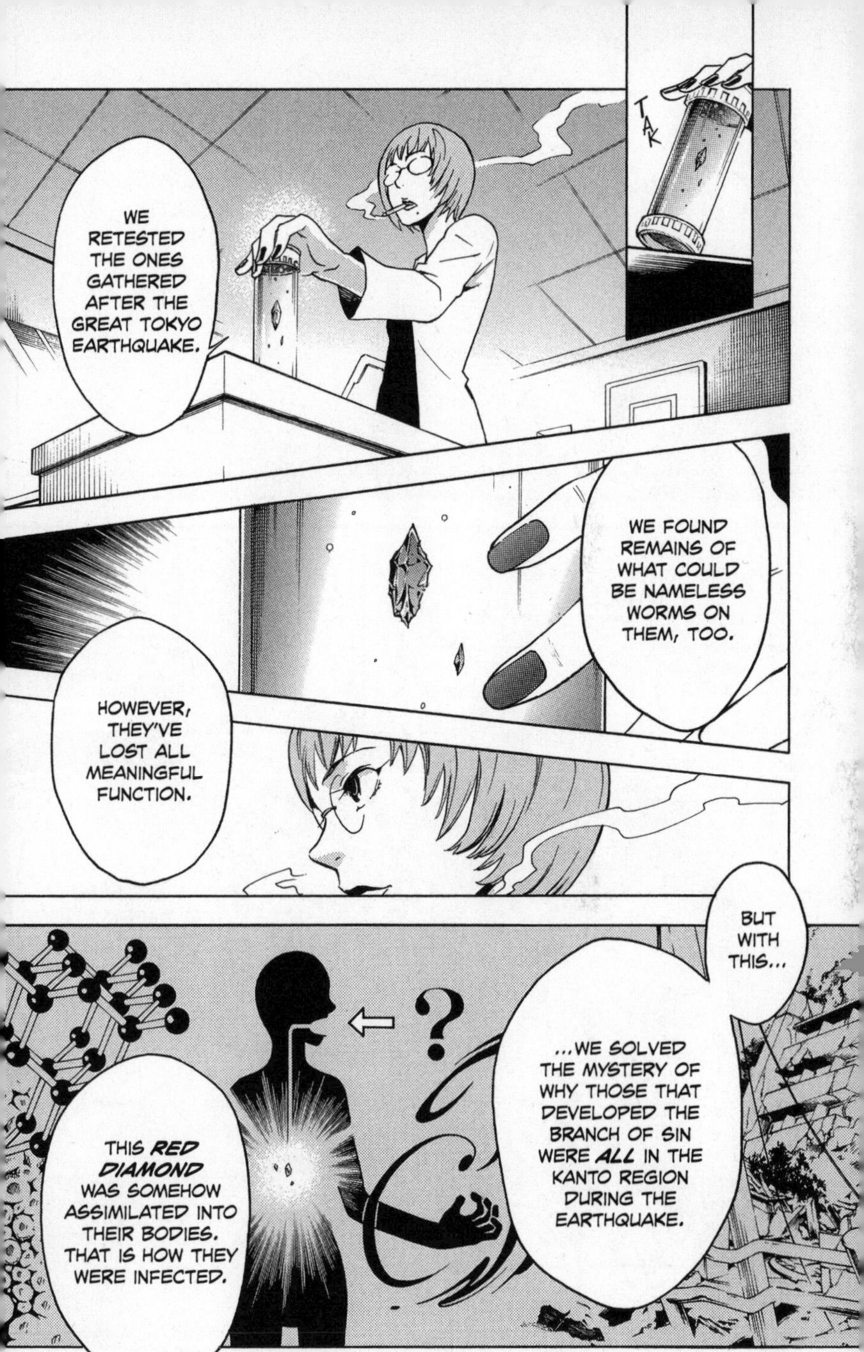
TAK
WE RETESTED THE ONES GATHERED AFTER THE GREAT TOKYO EARTHQUAKE.
WE FOUND REMAINS OF WHAT COULD BE NAMELESS WORMS ON THEM, TOO.
HOWEVER, THEY'VE LOST ALL MEANINGFUL FUNCTION.
BUT WITH THIS...
...WE SOLVED THE MYSTERY OF WHY THOSE THAT DEVELOPED THE BRANCH OF SIN WERE *ALL* IN THE KANTO REGION DURING THE EARTHQUAKE.
?
THIS *RED DIAMOND* WAS SOMEHOW ASSIMILATED INTO THEIR BODIES. THAT IS HOW THEY WERE INFECTED.

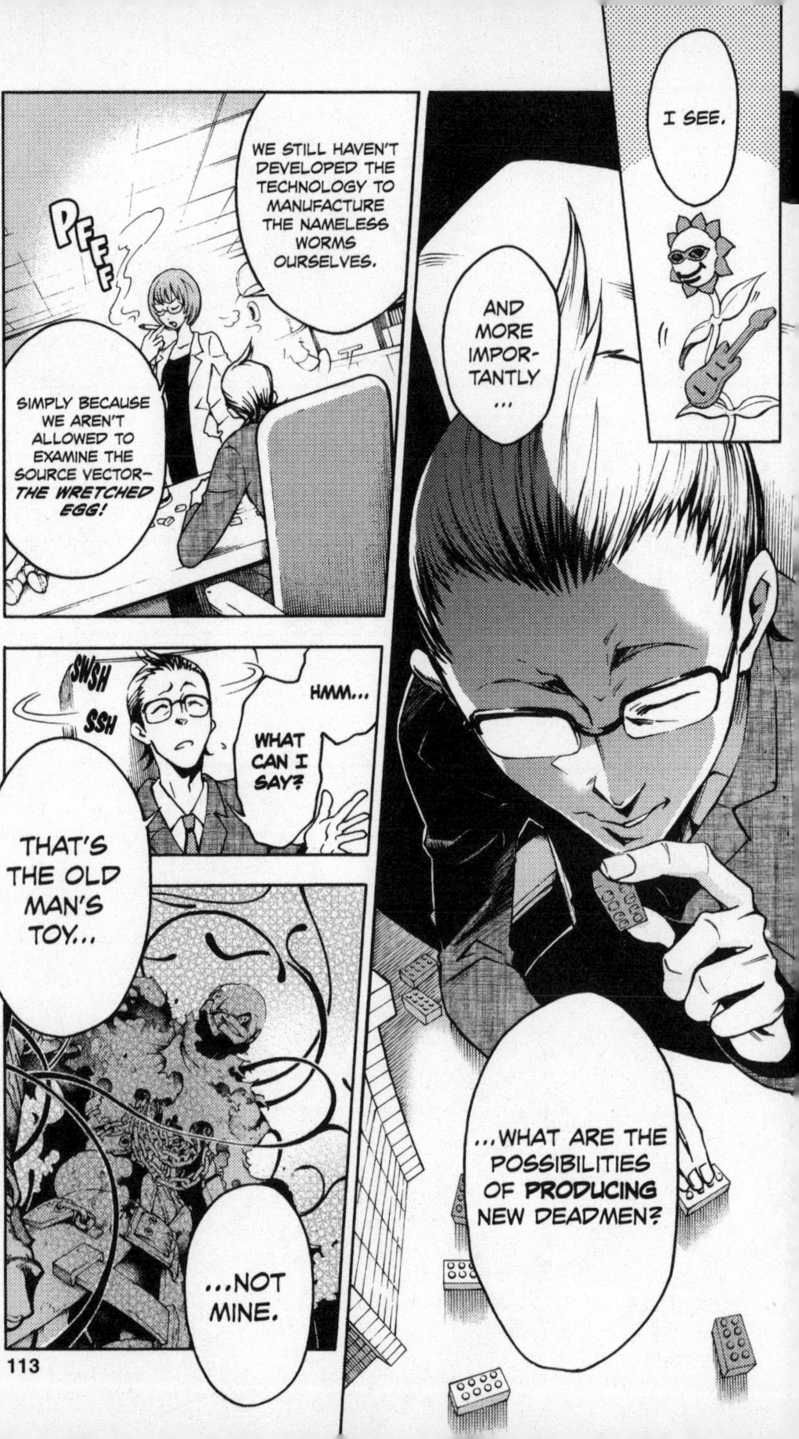
I SEE.
AND MORE IMPORTANTLY...
...WHAT ARE THE POSSIBILITIES OF PRODUCING NEW DEADMEN?
WE STILL HAVEN'T DEVELOPED THE TECHNOLOGY TO MANUFACTURE THE NAMELESS WORMS OURSELVES.
PFFF
SIMPLY BECAUSE WE AREN'T ALLOWED TO EXAMINE THE SOURCE VECTOR—*THE WRETCHED EGG!*
HMM...
WHAT CAN I SAY?
SWSH
SSH
THAT'S THE OLD MAN'S TOY...
...NOT MINE.

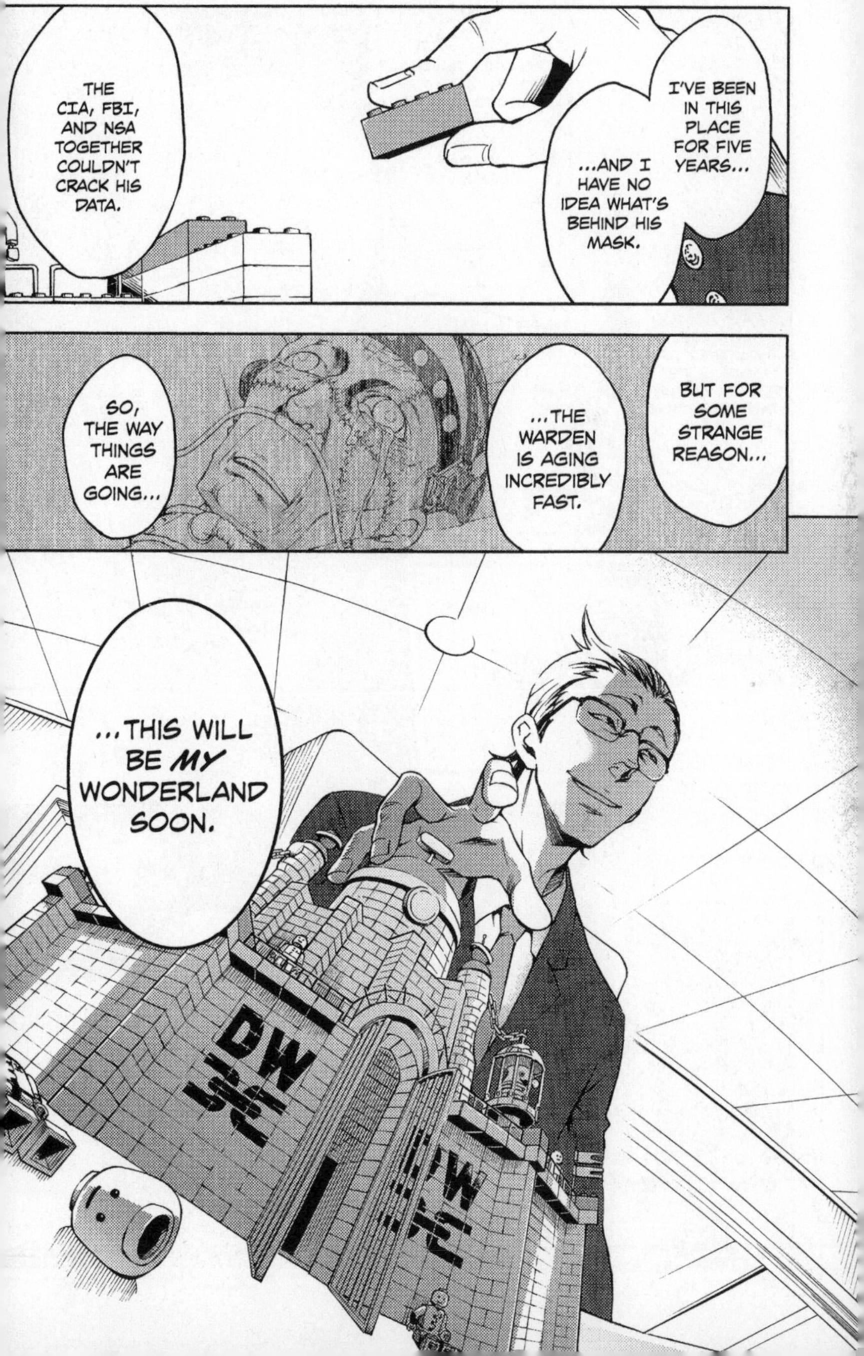
I'VE BEEN IN THIS PLACE FOR FIVE YEARS...
...AND I HAVE NO IDEA WHAT'S BEHIND HIS MASK.
THE CIA, FBI, AND NSA TOGETHER COULDN'T CRACK HIS DATA.
BUT FOR SOME STRANGE REASON...
...THE WARDEN IS AGING INCREDIBLY FAST.
SO, THE WAY THINGS ARE GOING...
...THIS WILL BE *MY* WONDERLAND SOON.
DW

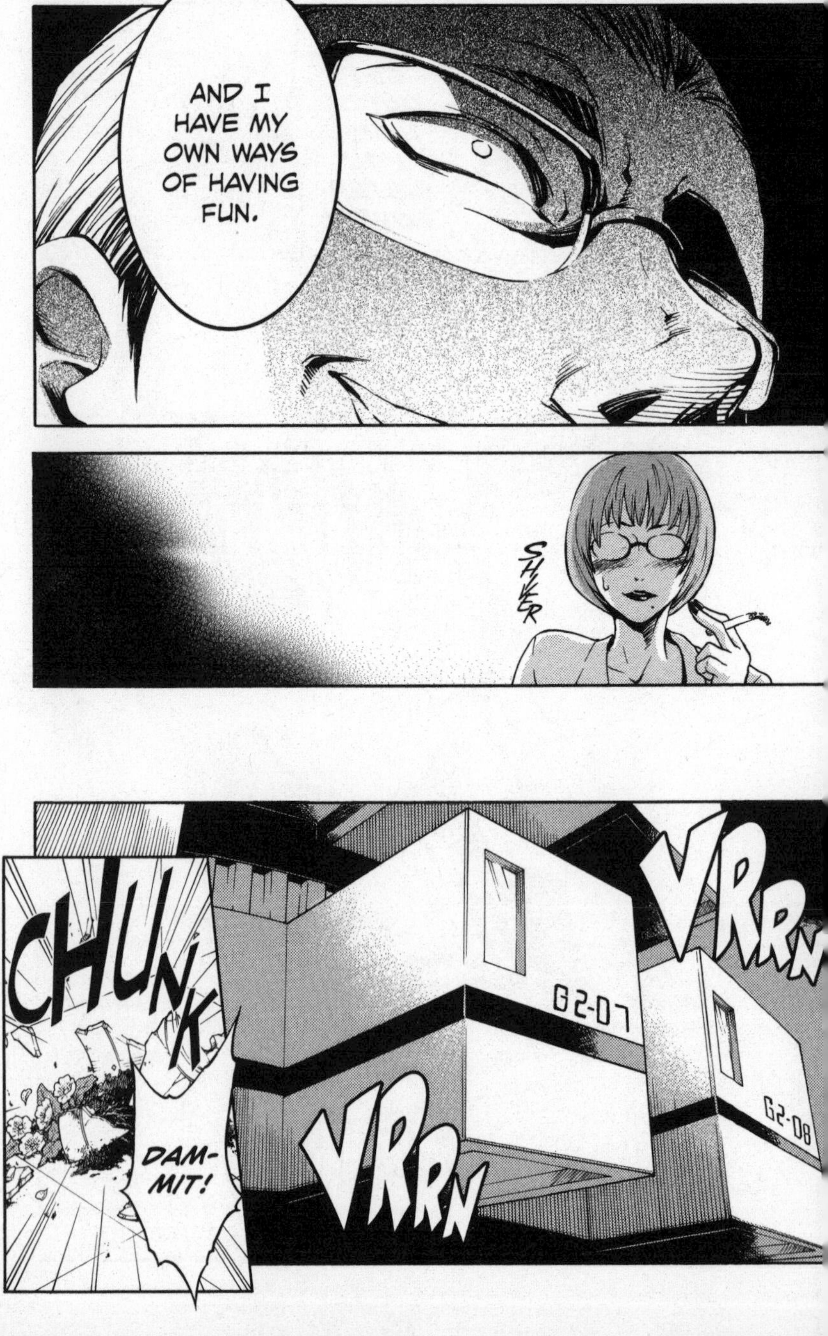
AND I HAVE MY OWN WAYS OF HAVING FUN.
SHIVER
VRRN
CHUNK
VRRN
DAM-MIT!

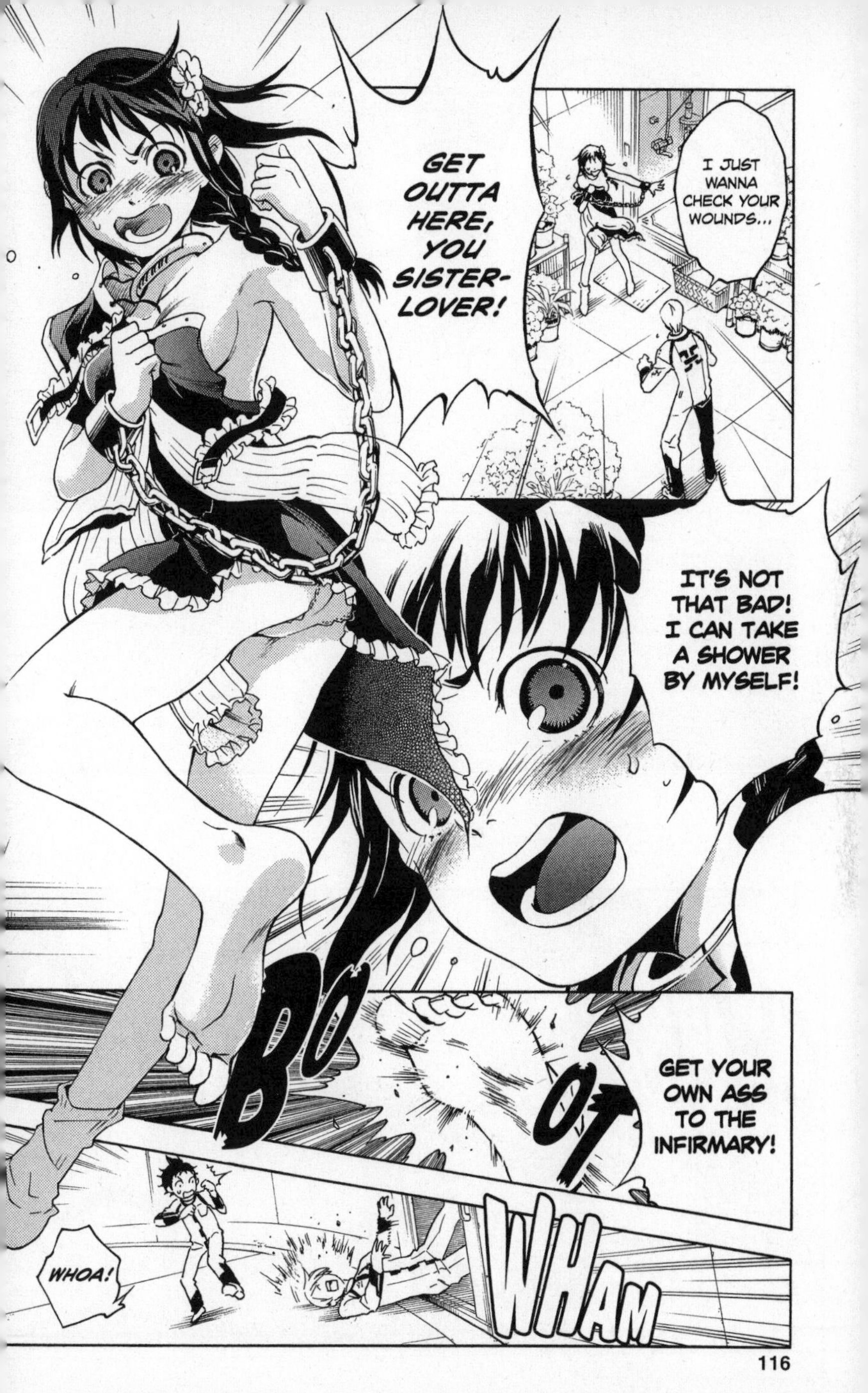
I JUST WANNA CHECK YOUR WOUNDS...
GET OUTTA HERE, YOU SISTER-LOVER!
IT'S NOT THAT BAD! I CAN TAKE A SHOWER BY MYSELF!
BOOT
GET YOUR OWN ASS TO THE INFIRMARY!
WHAM
WHOA!

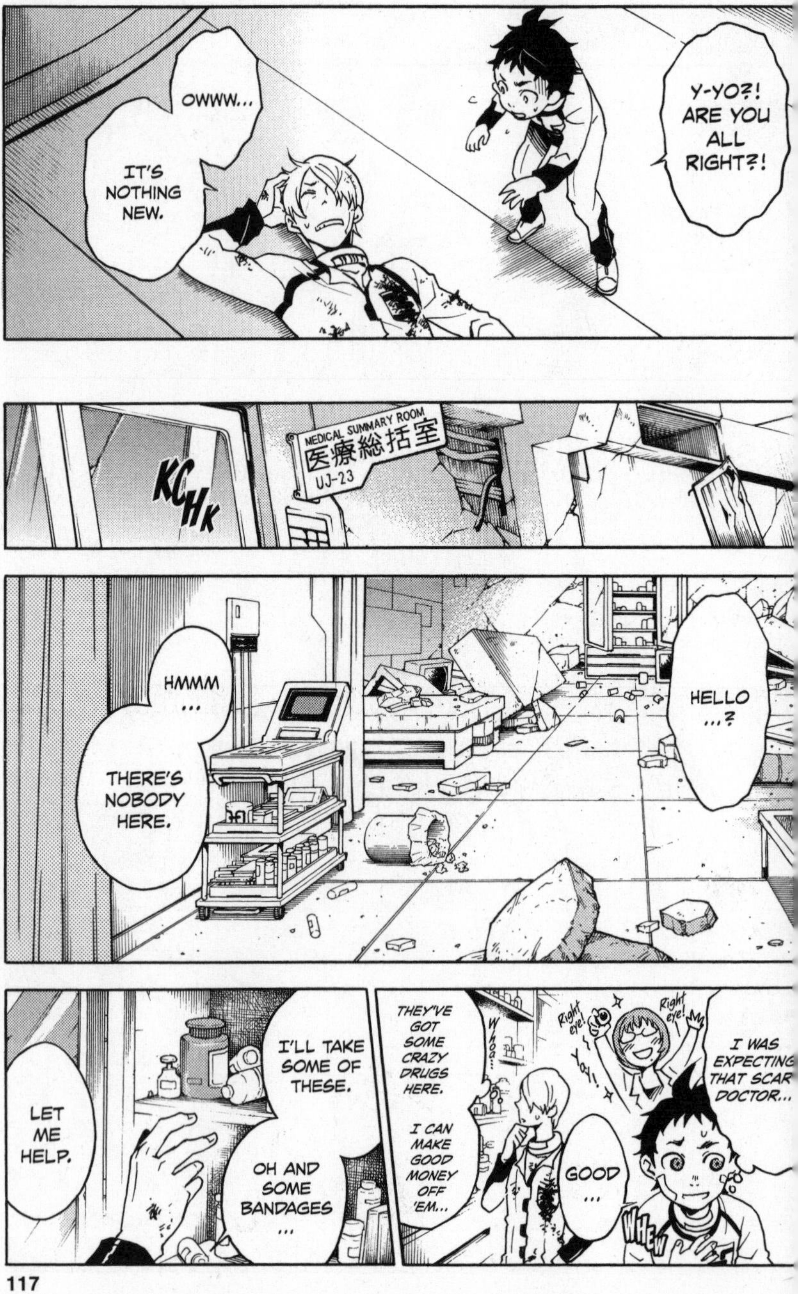
Y-YO?! ARE YOU ALL RIGHT?!
OWWW...
IT'S NOTHING NEW.
MEDICAL SUMMARY ROOM
医療総括室
UJ-23
KCHK
HELLO ...?
HMMM ...
THERE'S NOBODY HERE.
I WAS EXPECTING THAT SCAR DOCTOR...
Right eye!
Right eye!
Yay!!
Whoa...
GOOD ...
WHEW
THEY'VE GOT SOME CRAZY DRUGS HERE.
I CAN MAKE GOOD MONEY OFF 'EM...
I'LL TAKE SOME OF THESE.
OH AND SOME BANDAGES ...
LET ME HELP.

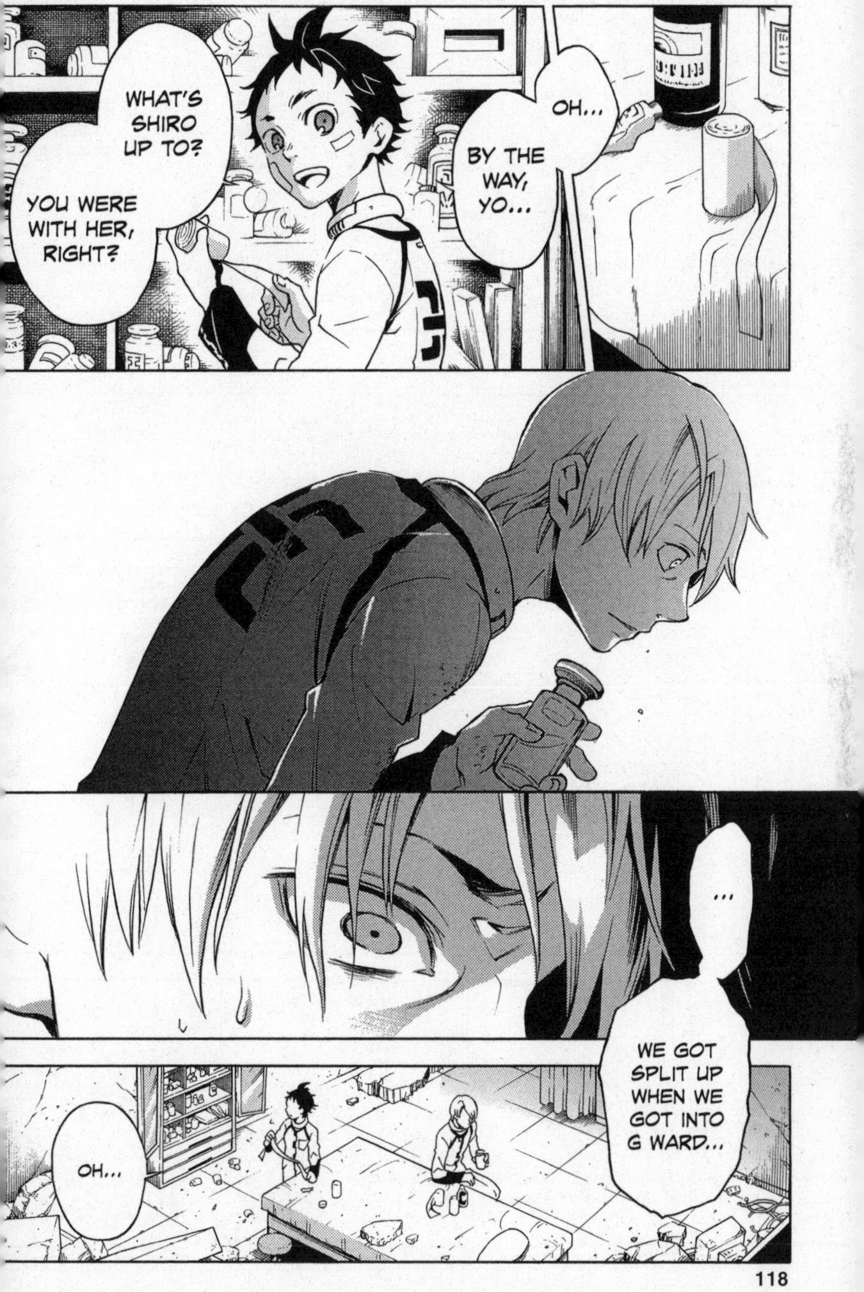
OH... BY THE WAY, YO...
WHAT'S SHIRO UP TO?
YOU WERE WITH HER, RIGHT?
...
WE GOT SPLIT UP WHEN WE GOT INTO G WARD...
OH...

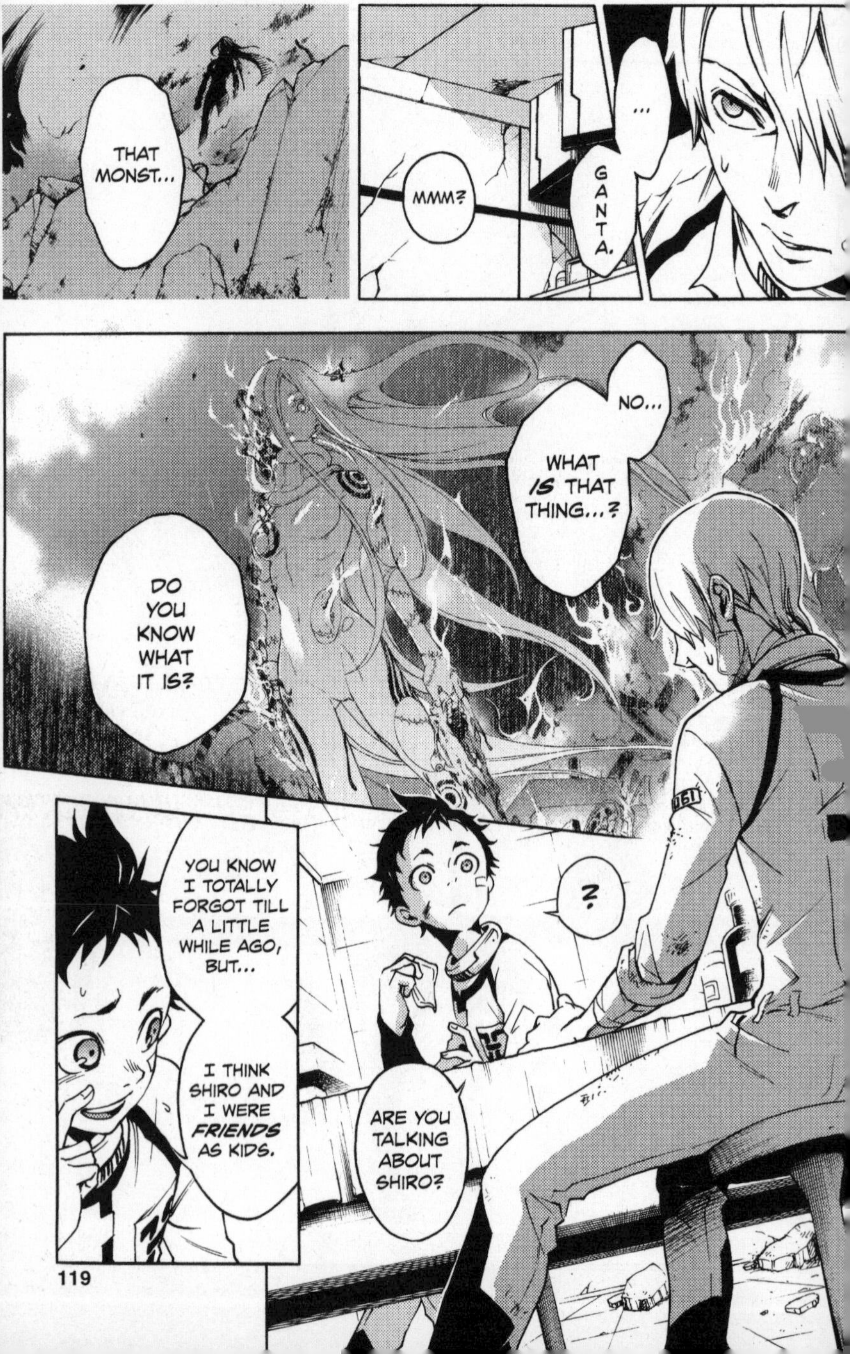
...
GANTA.
MMM?
THAT MONST...
NO...
WHAT *IS* THAT THING...?
DO YOU KNOW WHAT IT IS?
?
YOU KNOW I TOTALLY FORGOT TILL A LITTLE WHILE AGO, BUT...
I THINK SHIRO AND I WERE *FRIENDS* AS KIDS.
ARE YOU TALKING ABOUT SHIRO?

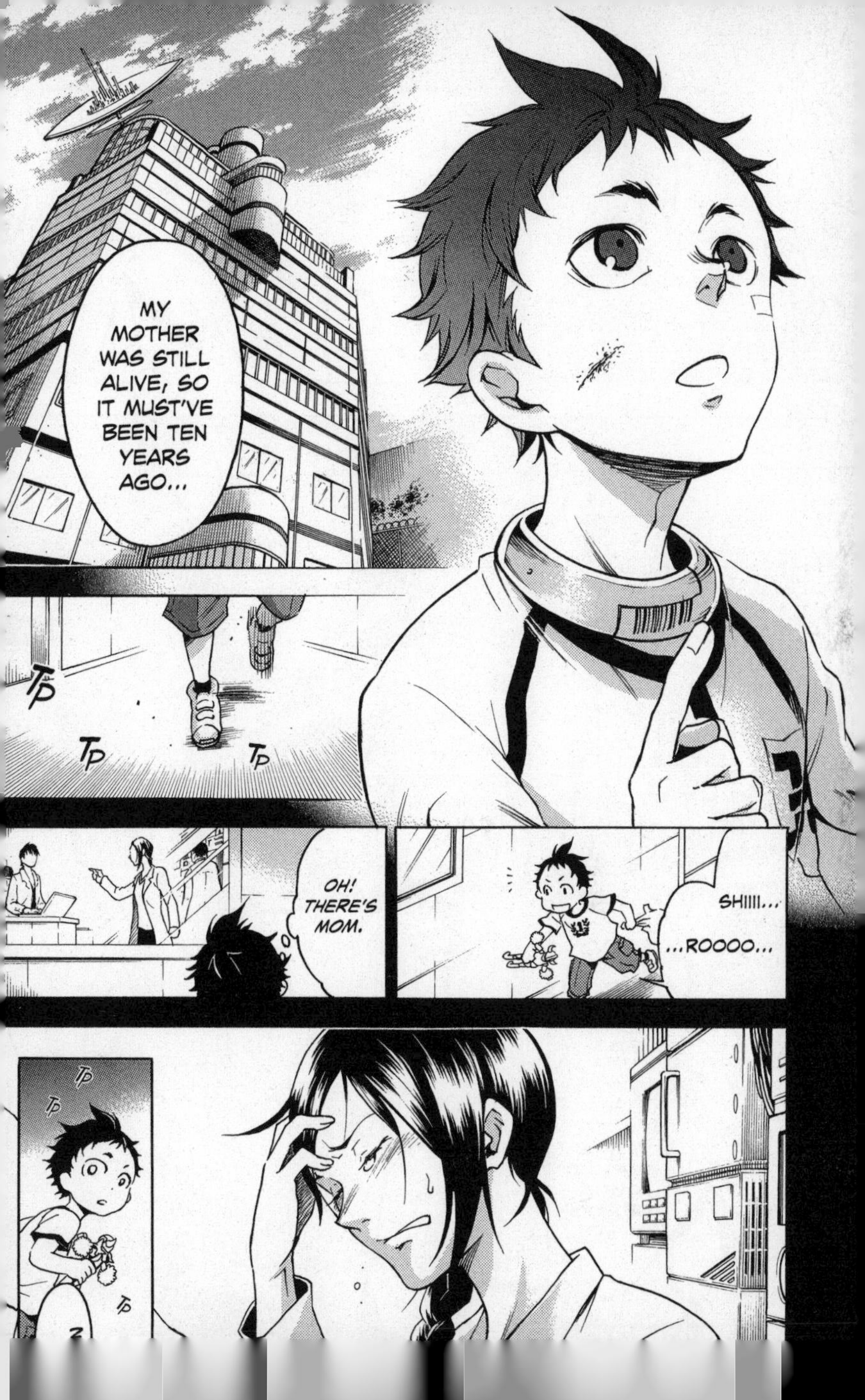
MY MOTHER WAS STILL ALIVE, SO IT MUST'VE BEEN TEN YEARS AGO...
TP
TP
TP
SHIIII...
...ROOOO...
OH! THERE'S MOM.
TP
TP
TP

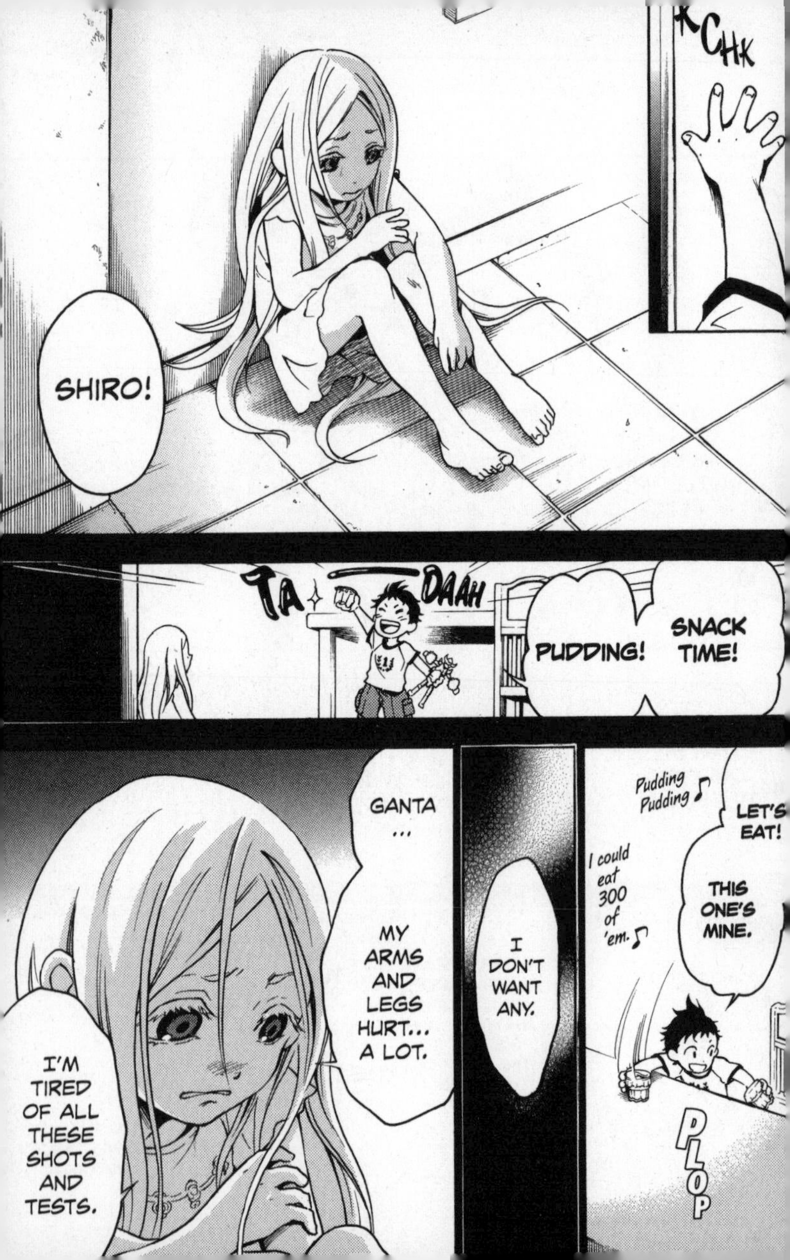
KCHK
SHIRO!
TA DAAH
SNACK TIME!
PUDDING!
Pudding Pudding ♪
LET'S EAT!
THIS ONE'S MINE.
I could eat 300 of 'em. ♪
PLOP
I DON'T WANT ANY.
GANTA ...
MY ARMS AND LEGS HURT... A LOT.
I'M TIRED OF ALL THESE SHOTS AND TESTS.

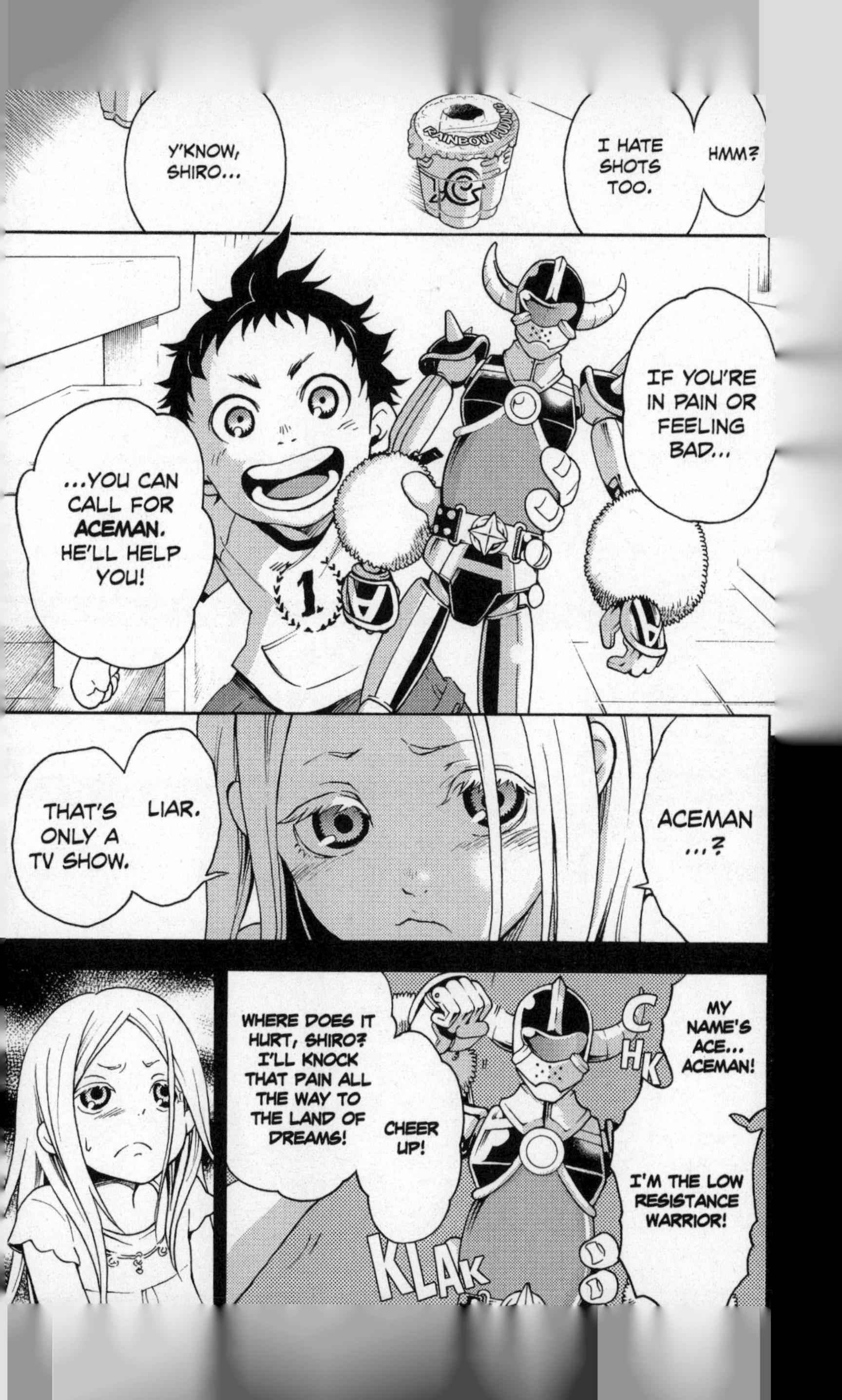
HMM?
I HATE SHOTS TOO.
RAINBOW PUDDING
Y'KNOW, SHIRO...
IF YOU'RE IN PAIN OR FEELING BAD...
...YOU CAN CALL FOR ACEMAN. HE'LL HELP YOU!
ACEMAN ...?
LIAR.
THAT'S ONLY A TV SHOW.
MY NAME'S ACE... ACEMAN!
CHK
WHERE DOES IT HURT, SHIRO? I'LL KNOCK THAT PAIN ALL THE WAY TO THE LAND OF DREAMS!
CHEER UP!
I'M THE LOW RESISTANCE WARRIOR!
KLAK

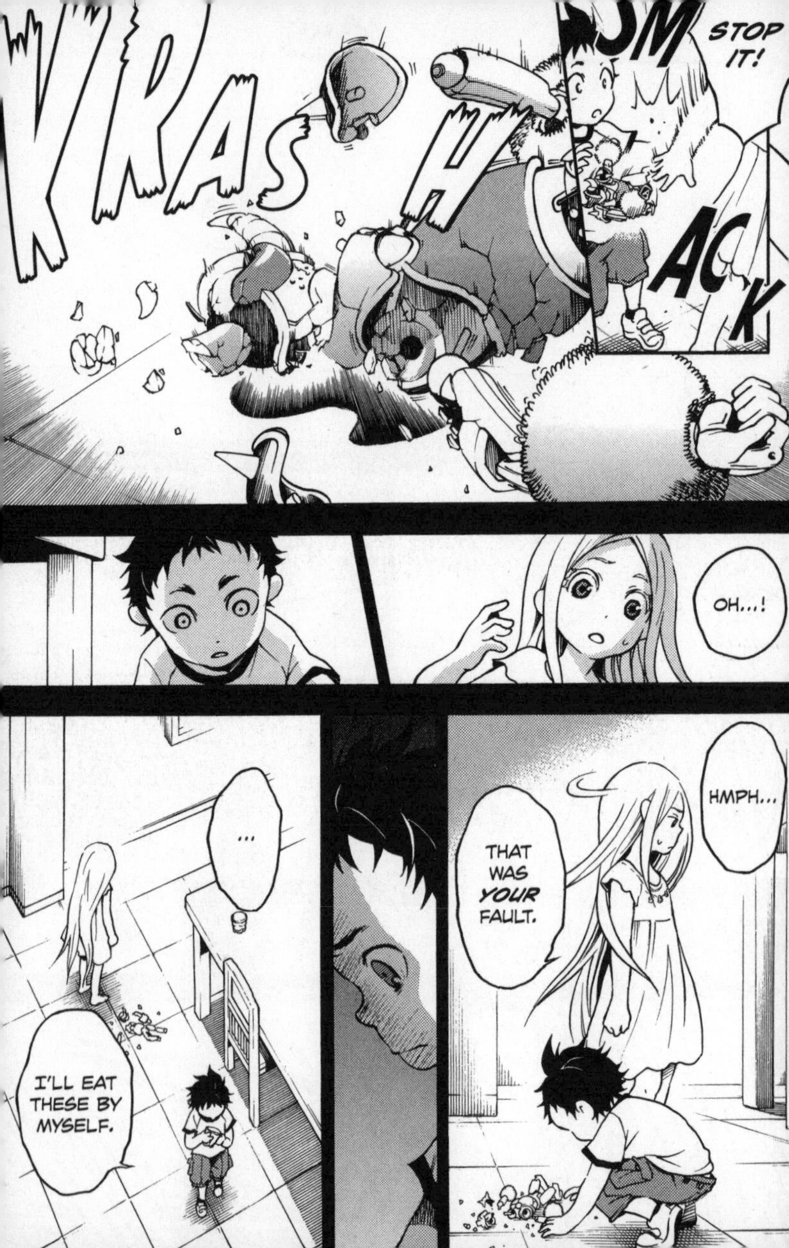
STOP IT!
KRASH
OH...!
HMPH...
THAT WAS *YOUR* FAULT.
...
I'LL EAT THESE BY MYSELF.

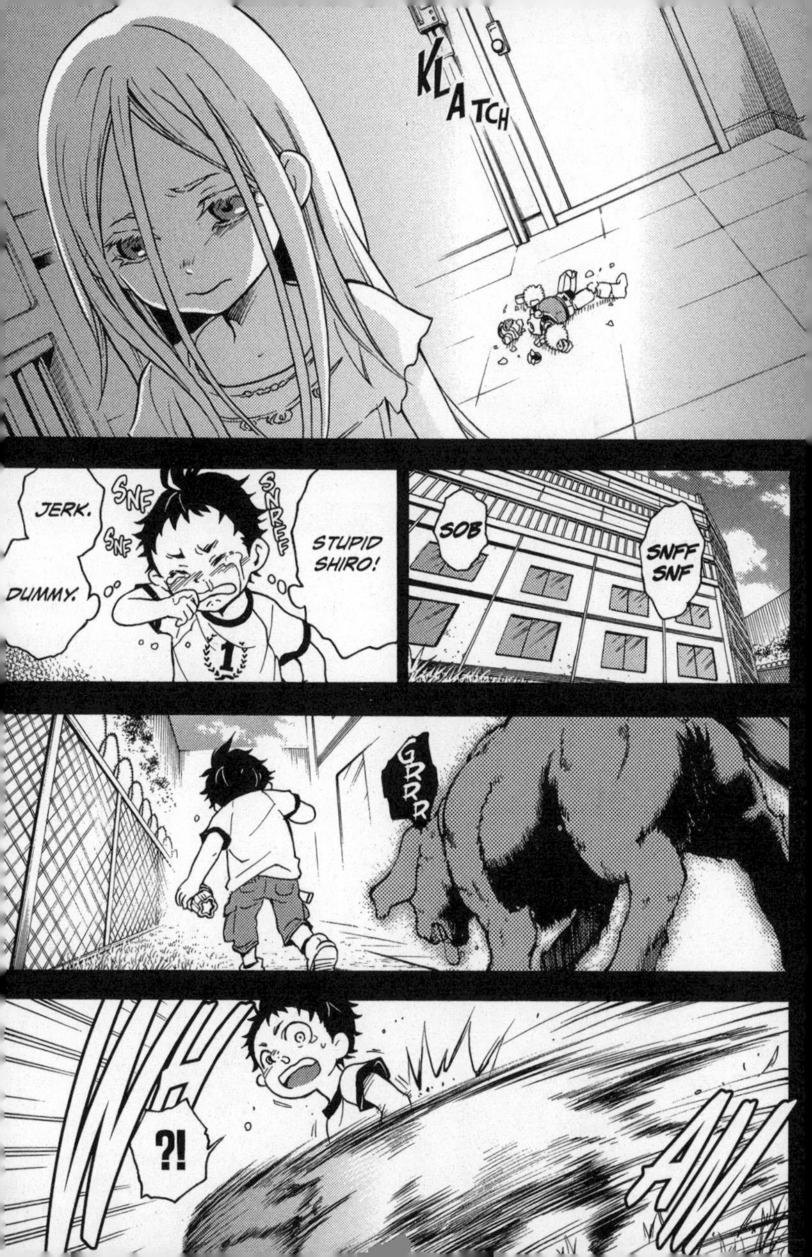
KLATCH
SOB
SNFF SNF
STUPID SHIRO!
SNREFF
SNF
SNF
JERK.
DUMMY.
GRRR
WHAAA
?!

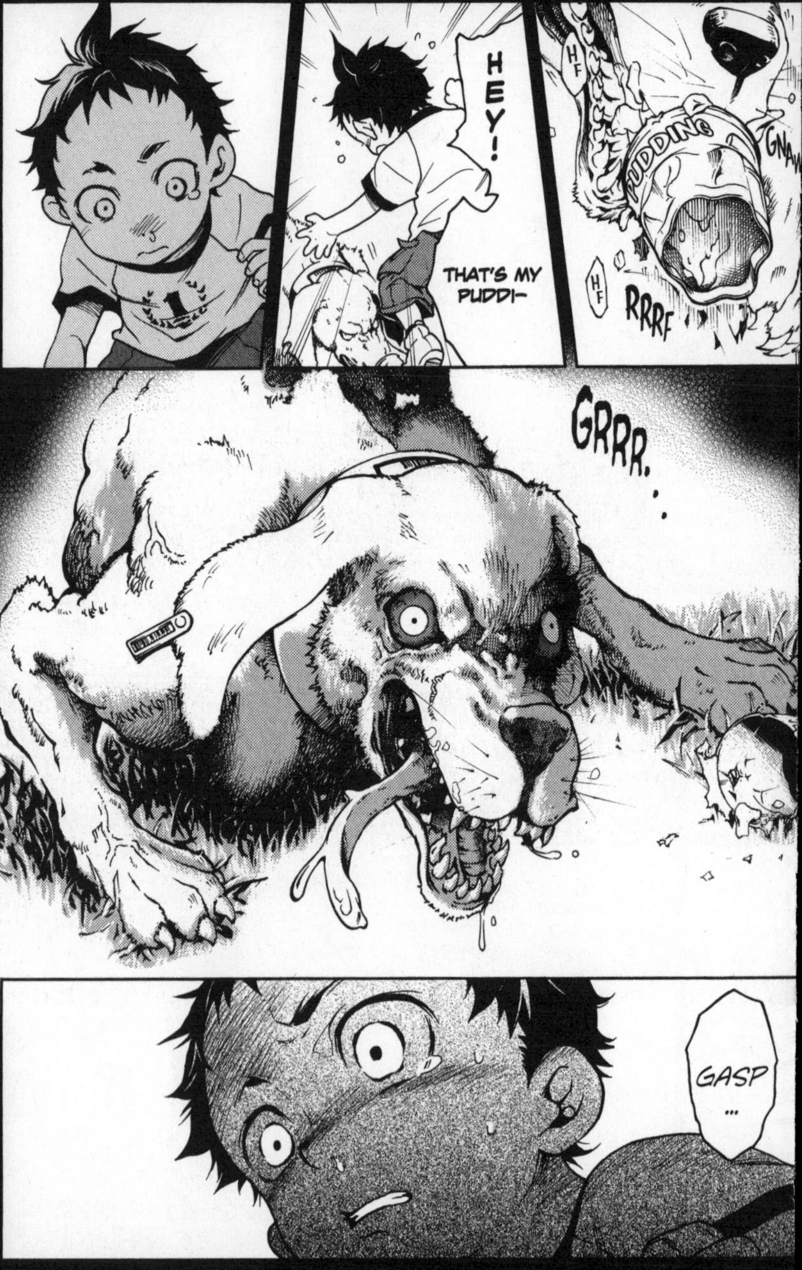
HF
PUDDING
GNAW
HF
RRRF
HEY!
THAT'S MY PUDDI-
GRRR...
GASP
...

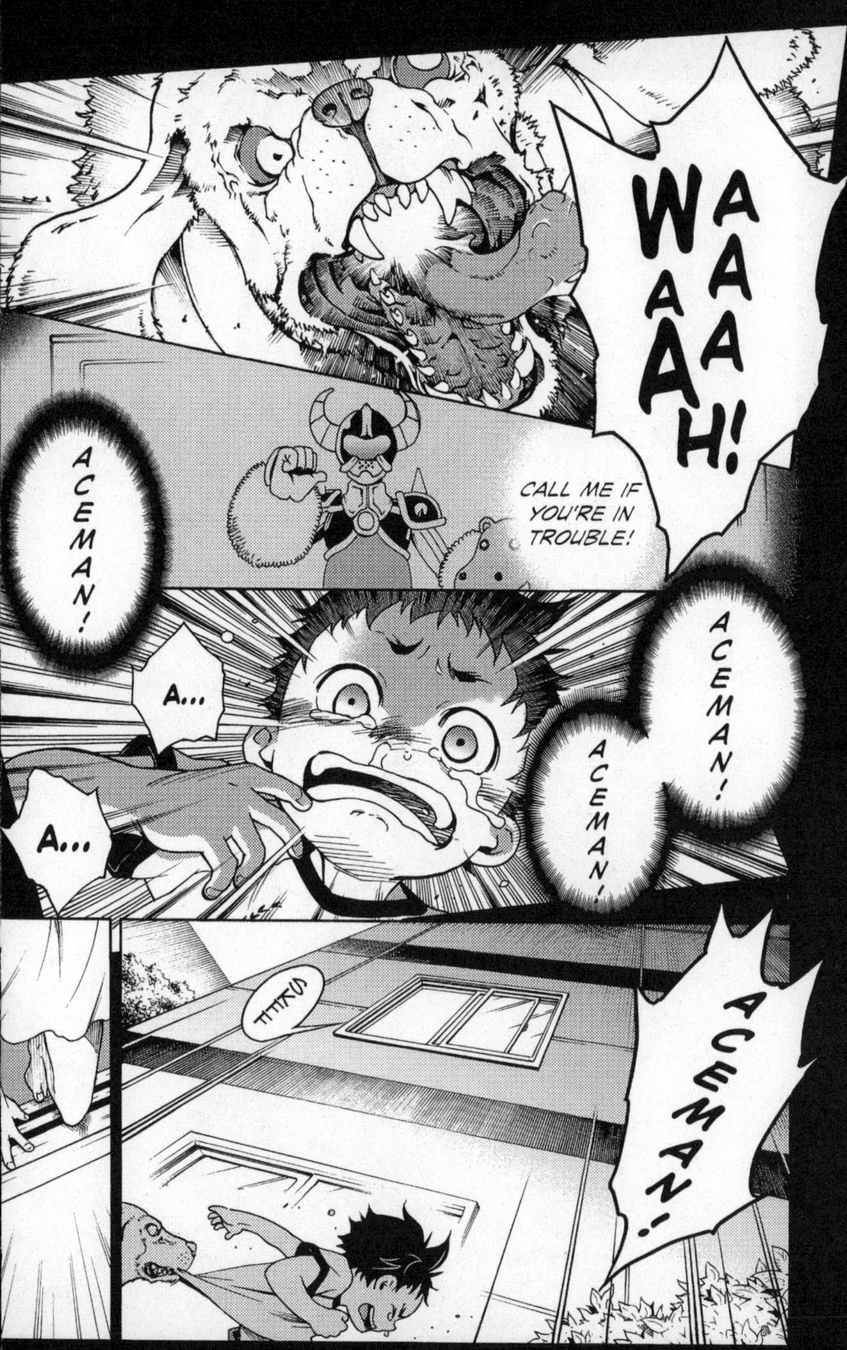
WAAAAAH!
CALL ME IF YOU'RE IN TROUBLE!
ACEMAN!
ACEMAN!
ACEMAN!
A...
A...
ACEMAN!
SKFFF

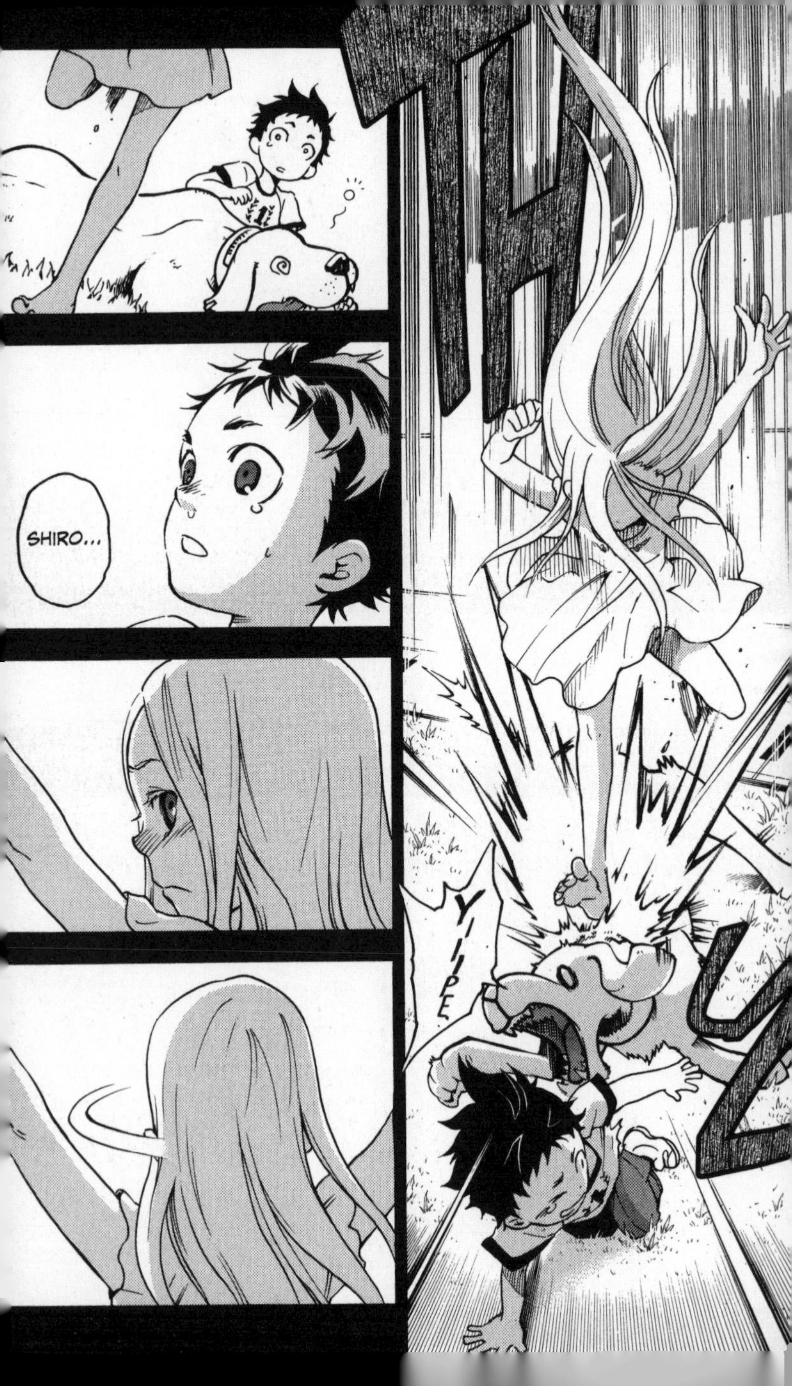
YIIIPE
SHIRO...

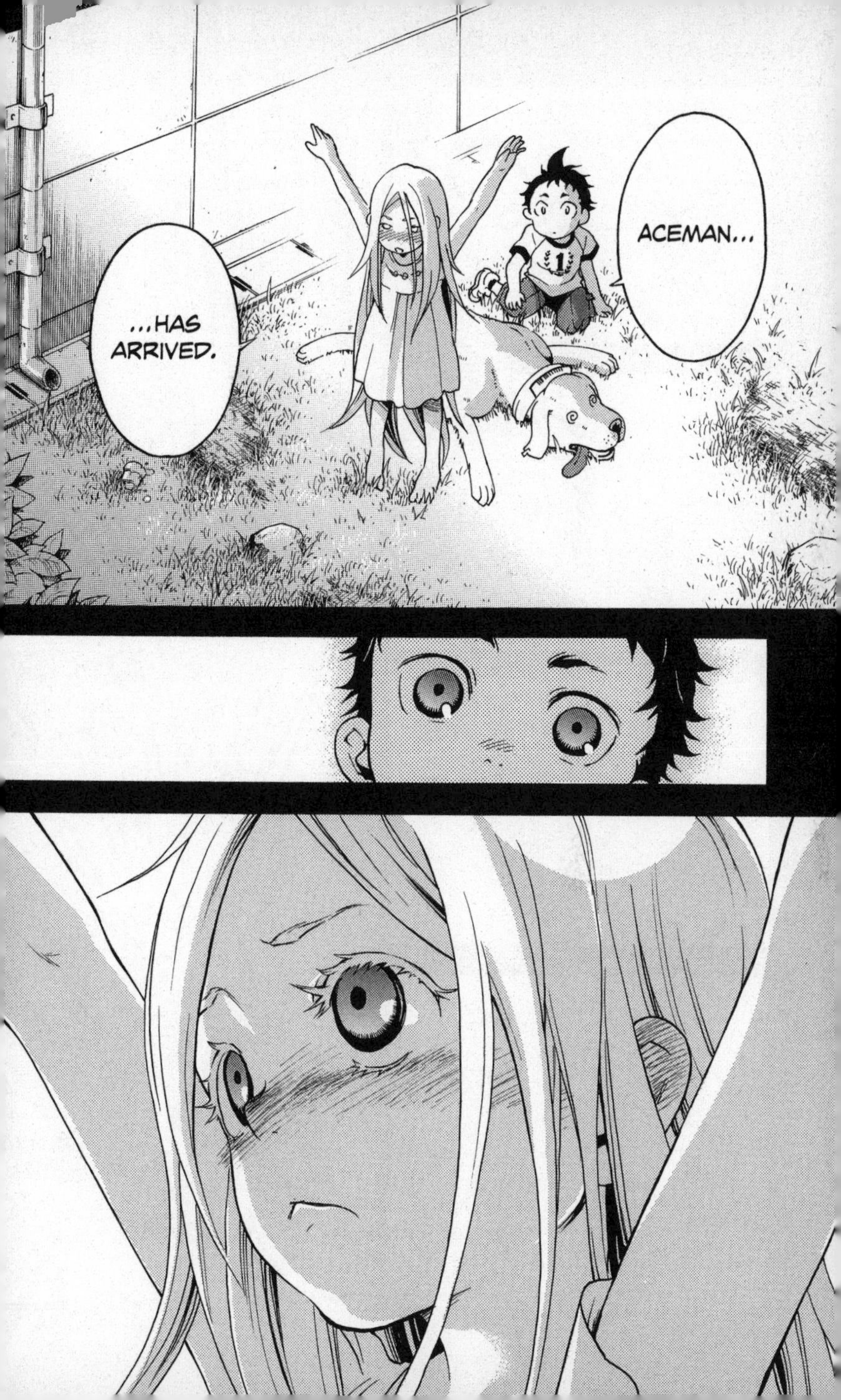
ACEMAN...
...HAS ARRIVED.

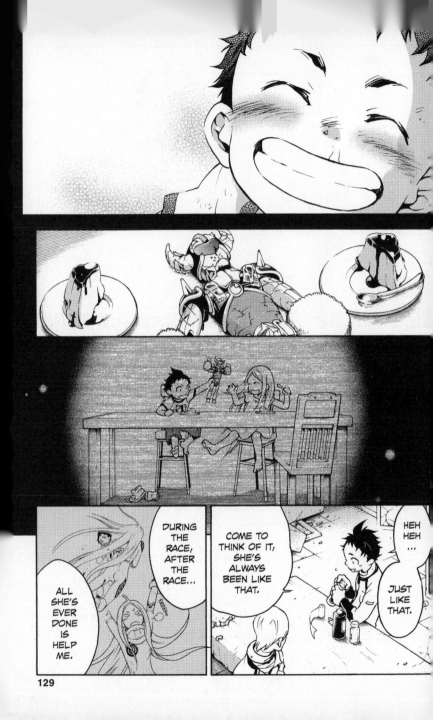

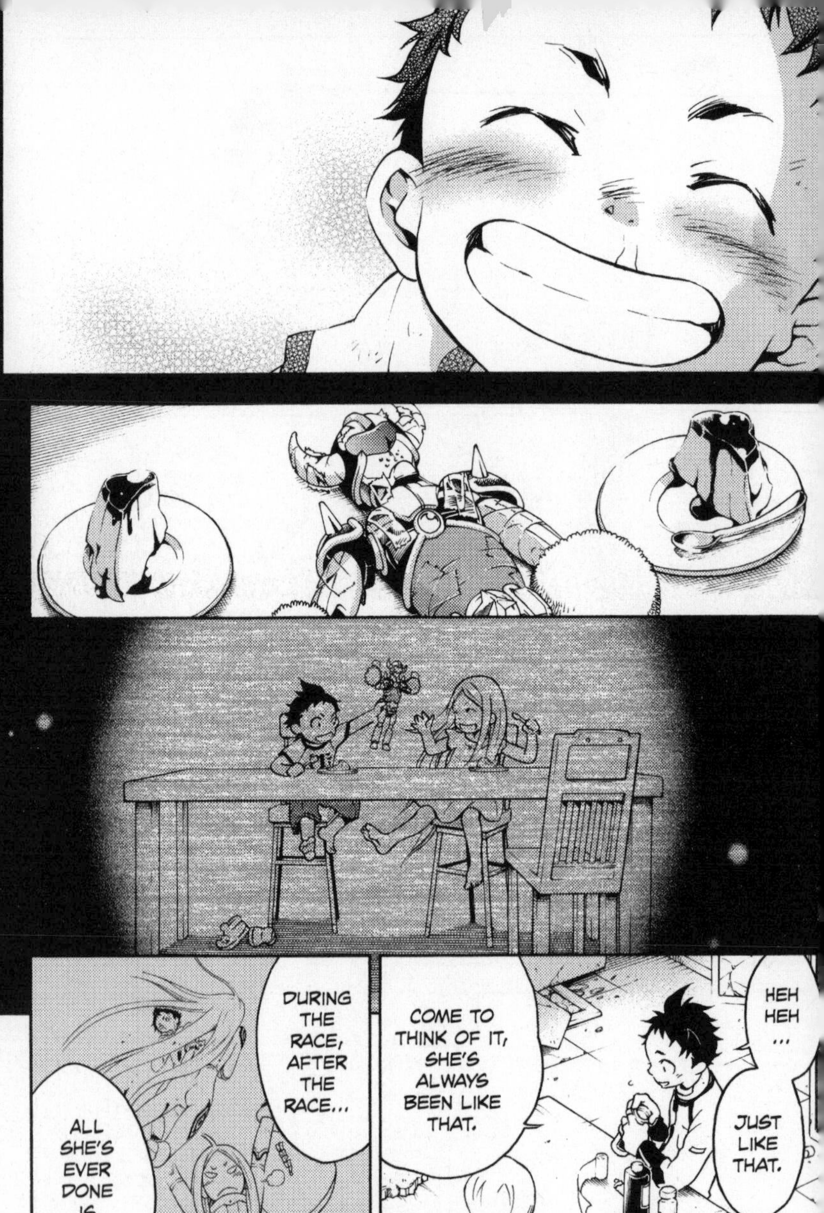
HEH HEH ...
JUST LIKE THAT.
COME TO THINK OF IT, SHE'S ALWAYS BEEN LIKE THAT.
DURING THE RACE, AFTER THE RACE...
ALL SHE'S EVER DONE IS HELP ME.

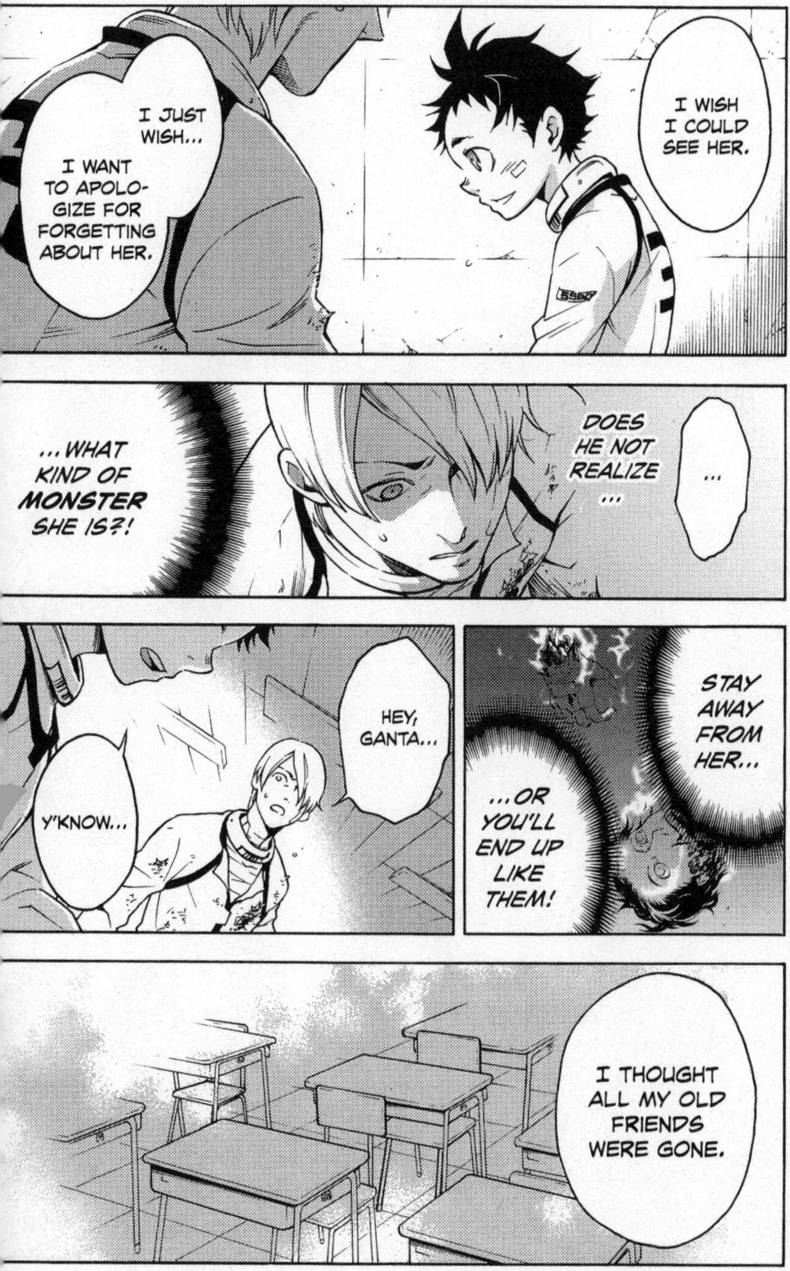
I WISH I COULD SEE HER.
I JUST WISH... I WANT TO APOLOGIZE FOR FORGETTING ABOUT HER.
...
DOES HE NOT REALIZE ...
...WHAT KIND OF MONSTER SHE IS?!
STAY AWAY FROM HER...
...OR YOU'LL END UP LIKE THEM!
HEY, GANTA...
Y'KNOW...
I THOUGHT ALL MY OLD FRIENDS WERE GONE.

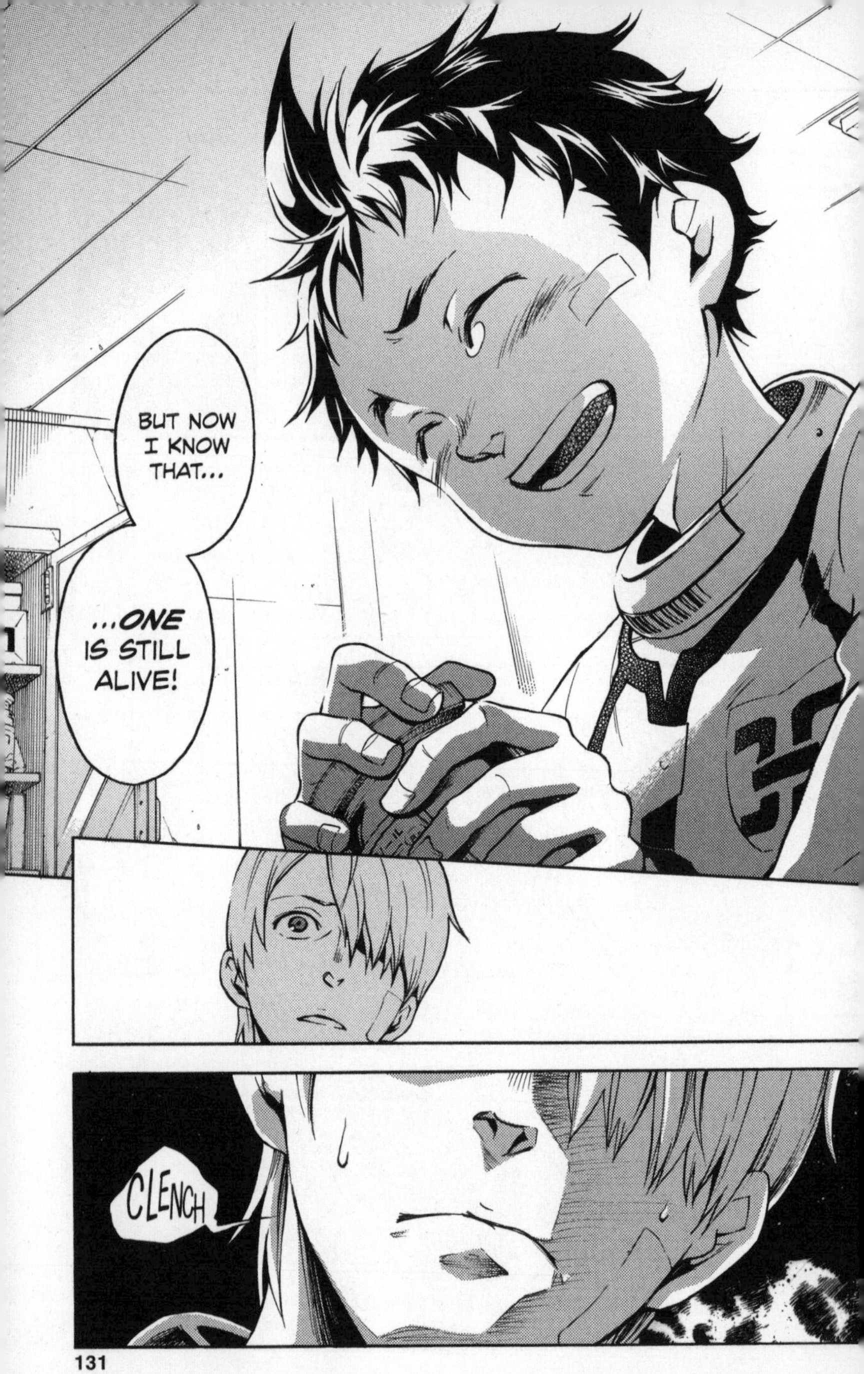
BUT NOW I KNOW THAT...
...ONE IS STILL ALIVE!
CLENCH

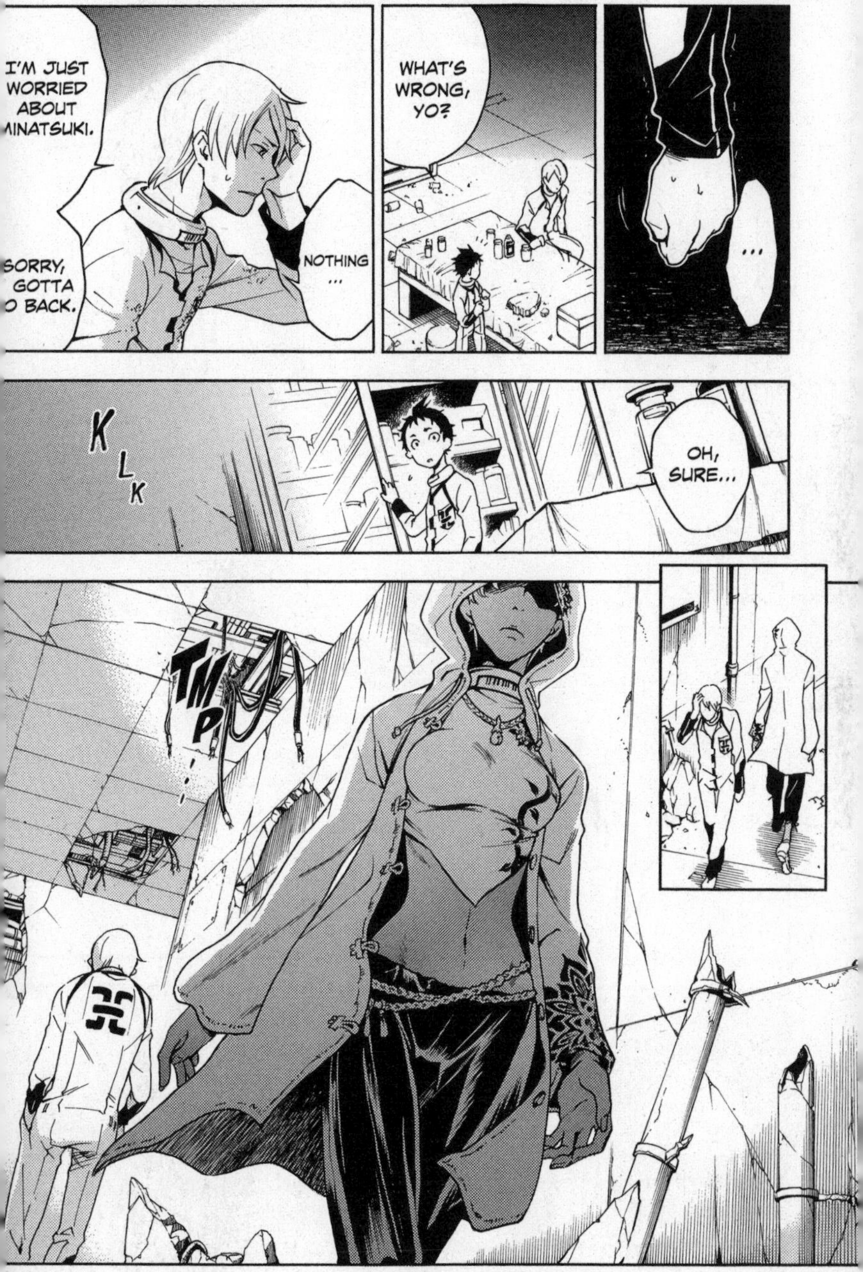
...
WHAT'S WRONG, YO?
NOTHING ...
I'M JUST WORRIED ABOUT MINATSUKI.
SORRY, GOTTA O BACK.
OH, SURE...
KLK
TMP

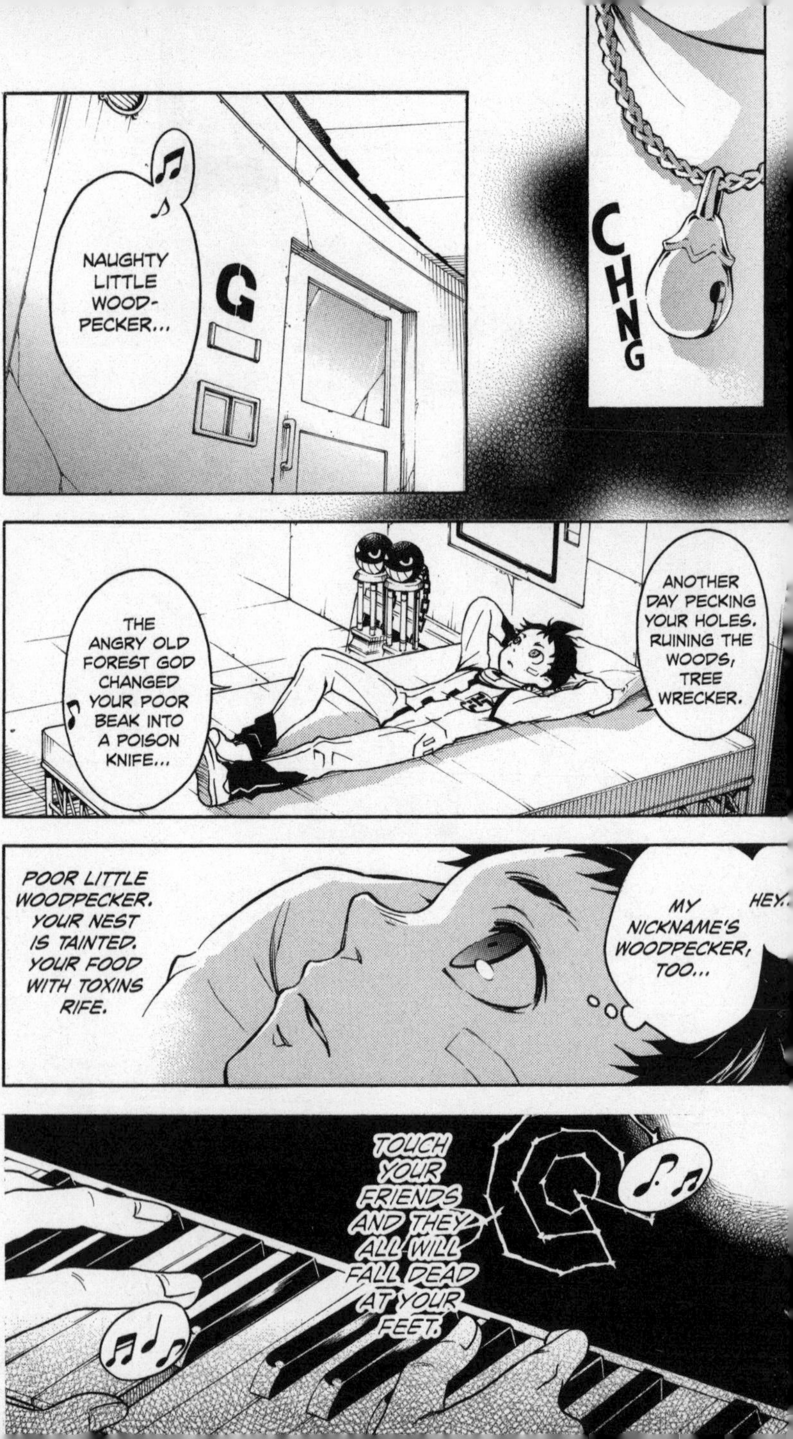
CHNG
G
NAUGHTY LITTLE WOODPECKER...
ANOTHER DAY PECKING YOUR HOLES. RUINING THE WOODS, TREE WRECKER.
THE ANGRY OLD FOREST GOD CHANGED YOUR POOR BEAK INTO A POISON KNIFE...
HEY.
MY NICKNAME'S WOODPECKER, TOO...
POOR LITTLE WOODPECKER. YOUR NEST IS TAINTED. YOUR FOOD WITH TOXINS RIFE.
TOUCH YOUR FRIENDS AND THEY ALL WILL FALL DEAD AT YOUR FEET.

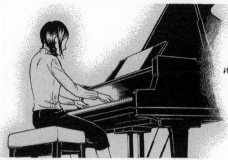

OH, SAD LITTLE WOODPECKER ♪

POISONOUS TEARS, SHINING BRIGHTLY...

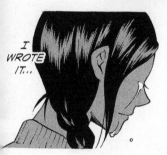

I WROTE IT...

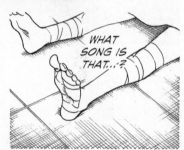

WHAT SONG IS THAT...?

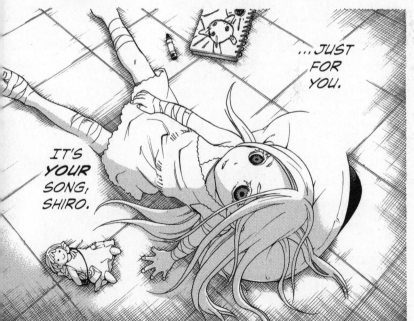

...JUST FOR YOU.

IT'S *YOUR* SONG, SHIRO.

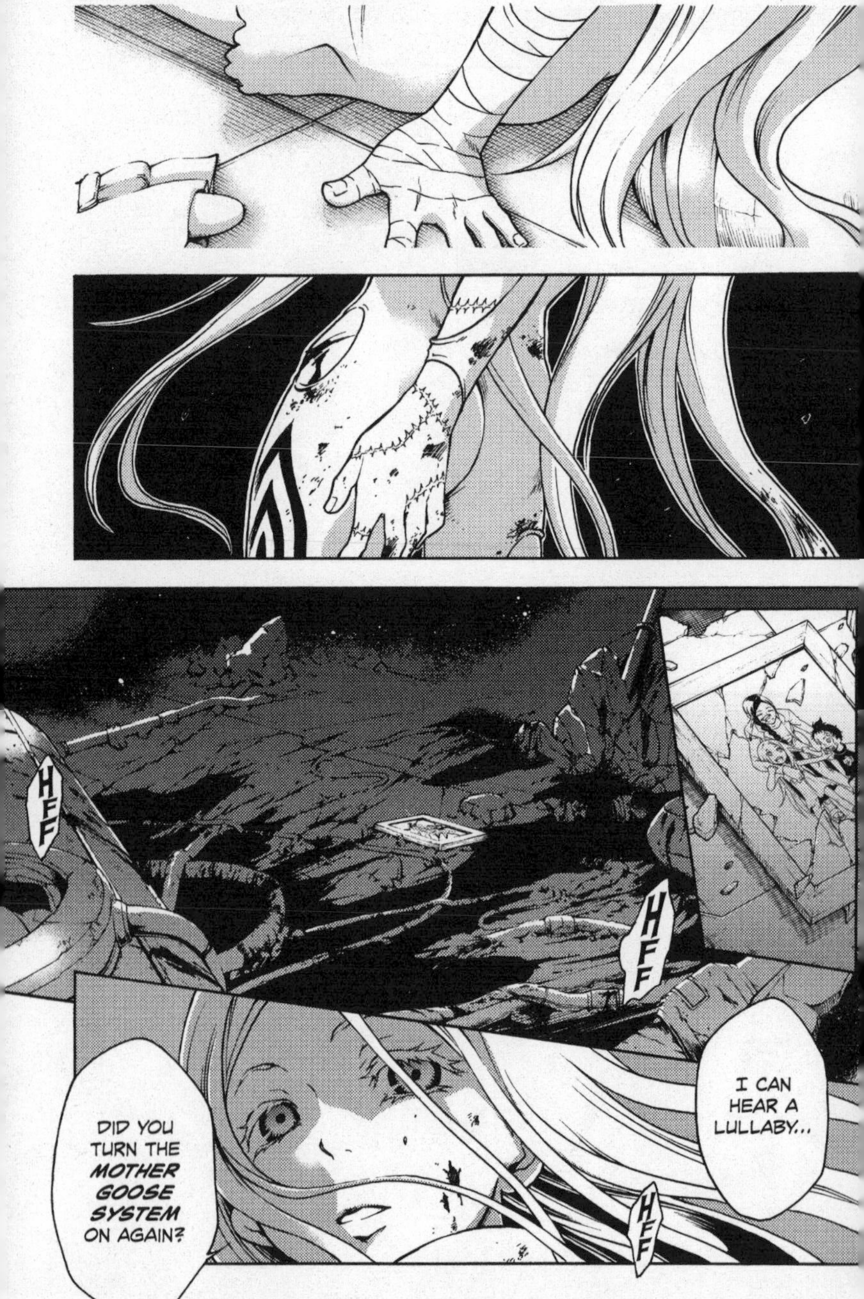
HFF
HFF
I CAN HEAR A LULLABY...
HFF
DID YOU TURN THE *MOTHER GOOSE SYSTEM* ON AGAIN?

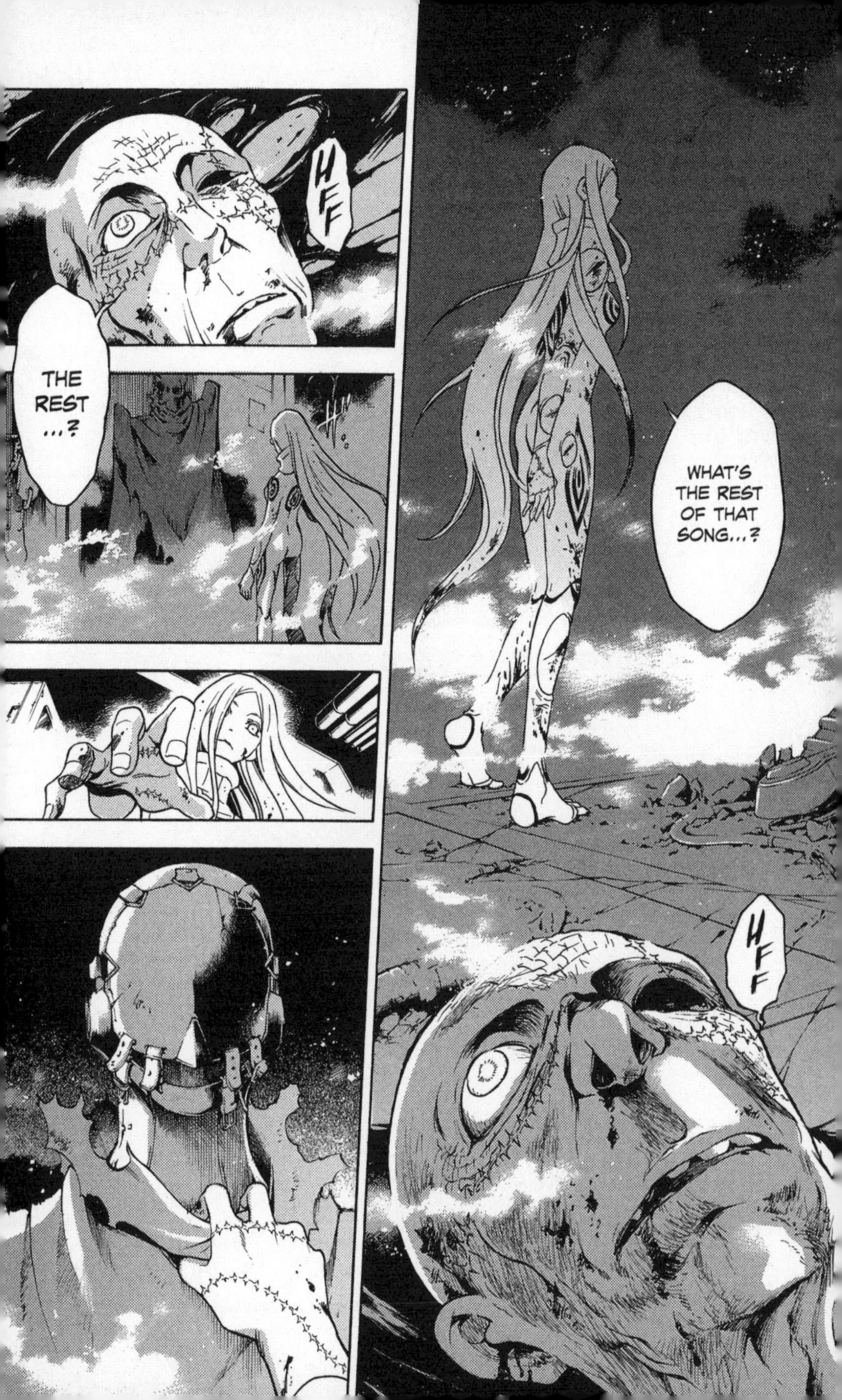
WHAT'S THE REST OF THAT SONG...?
HFF
HFF
THE REST ...?

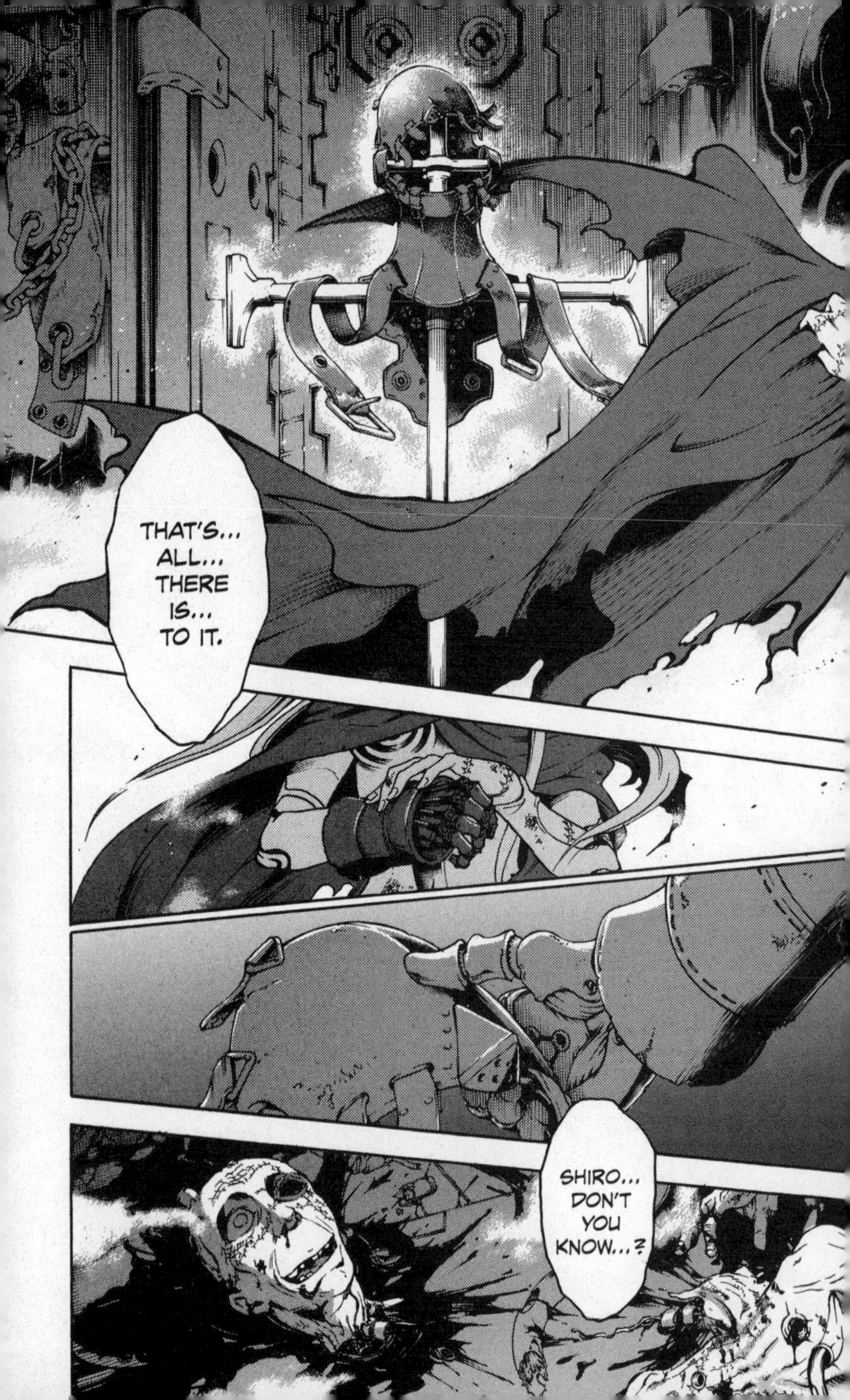
THAT'S... ALL... THERE IS... TO IT.
SHIRO... DON'T YOU KNOW...?

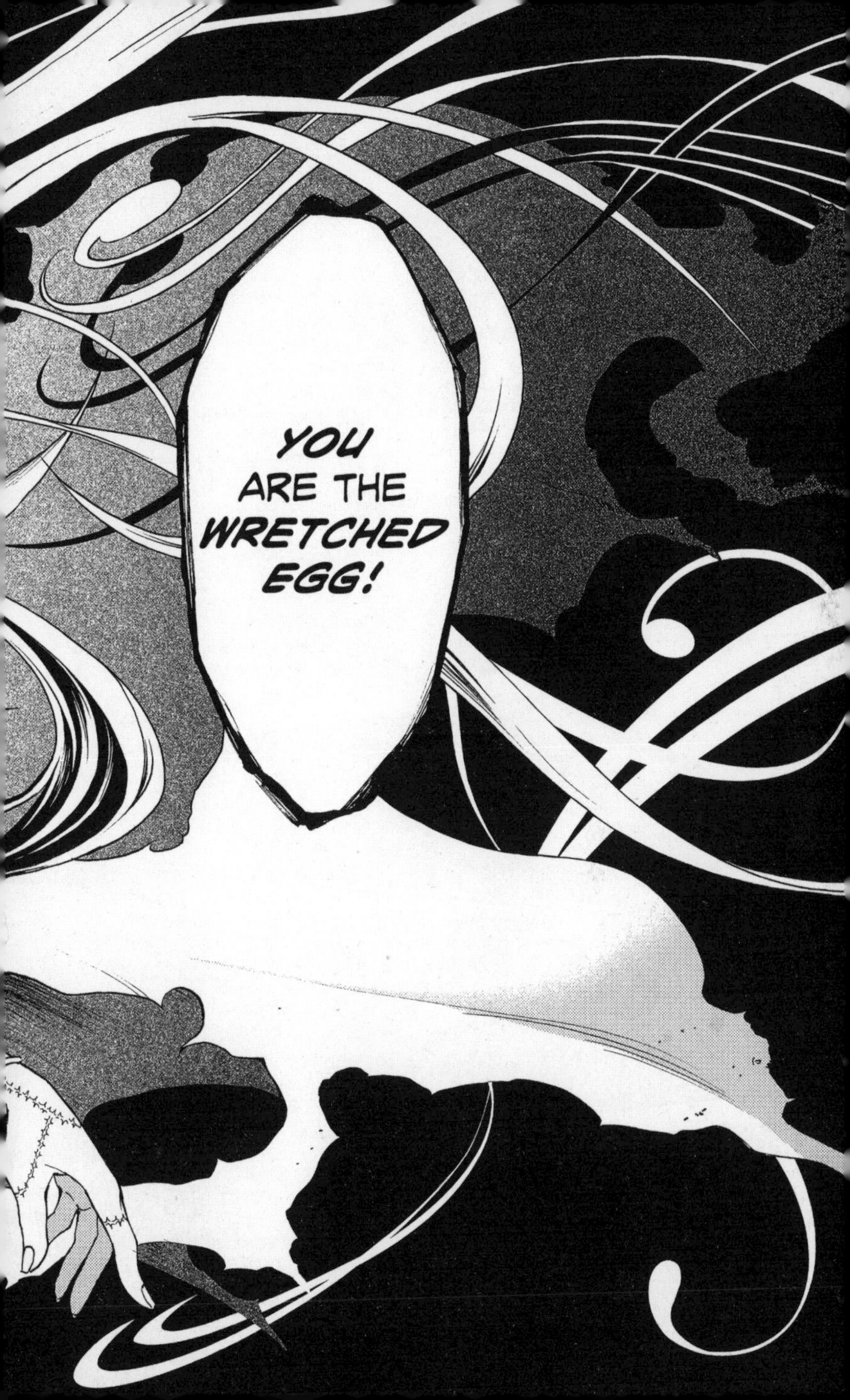
YOU ARE THE WRETCHED EGG!

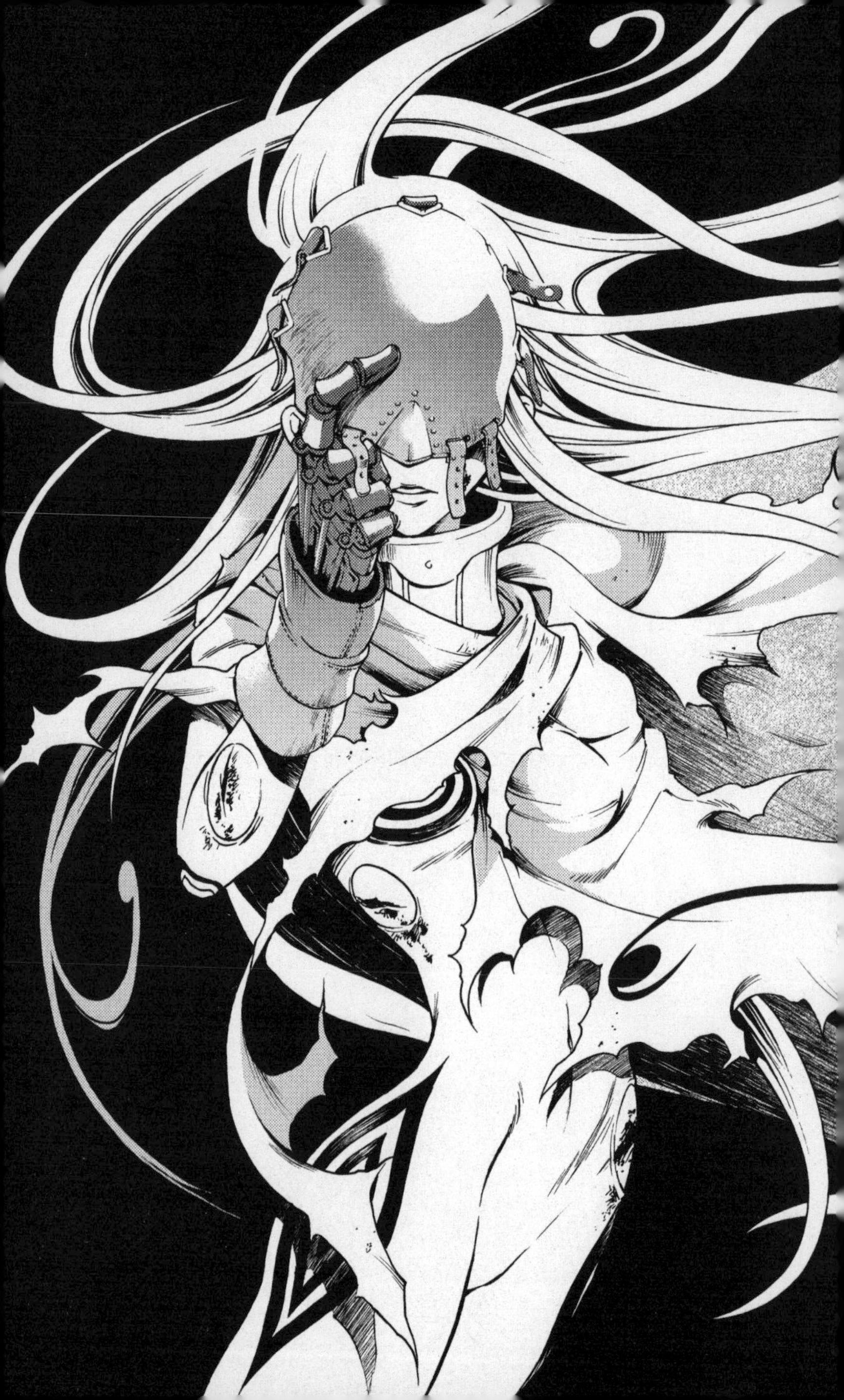

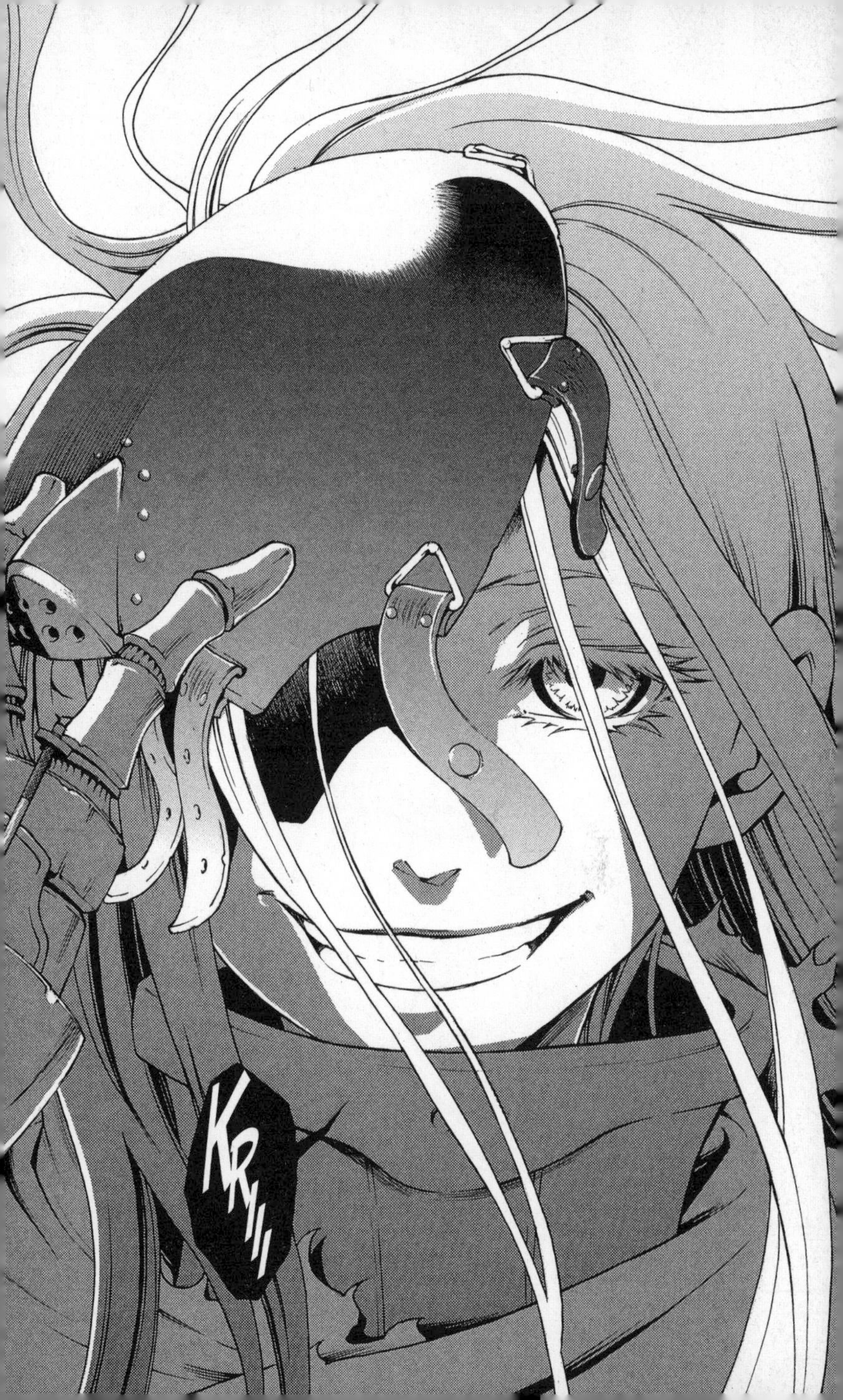
KRIII

DEADM

WONDE

LAND

DEADM

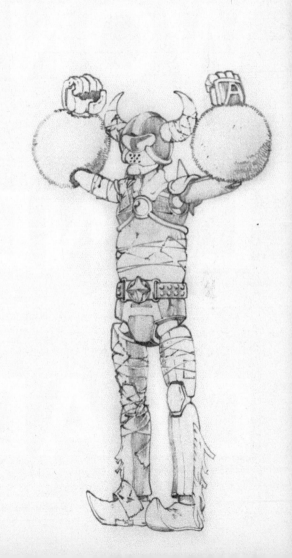

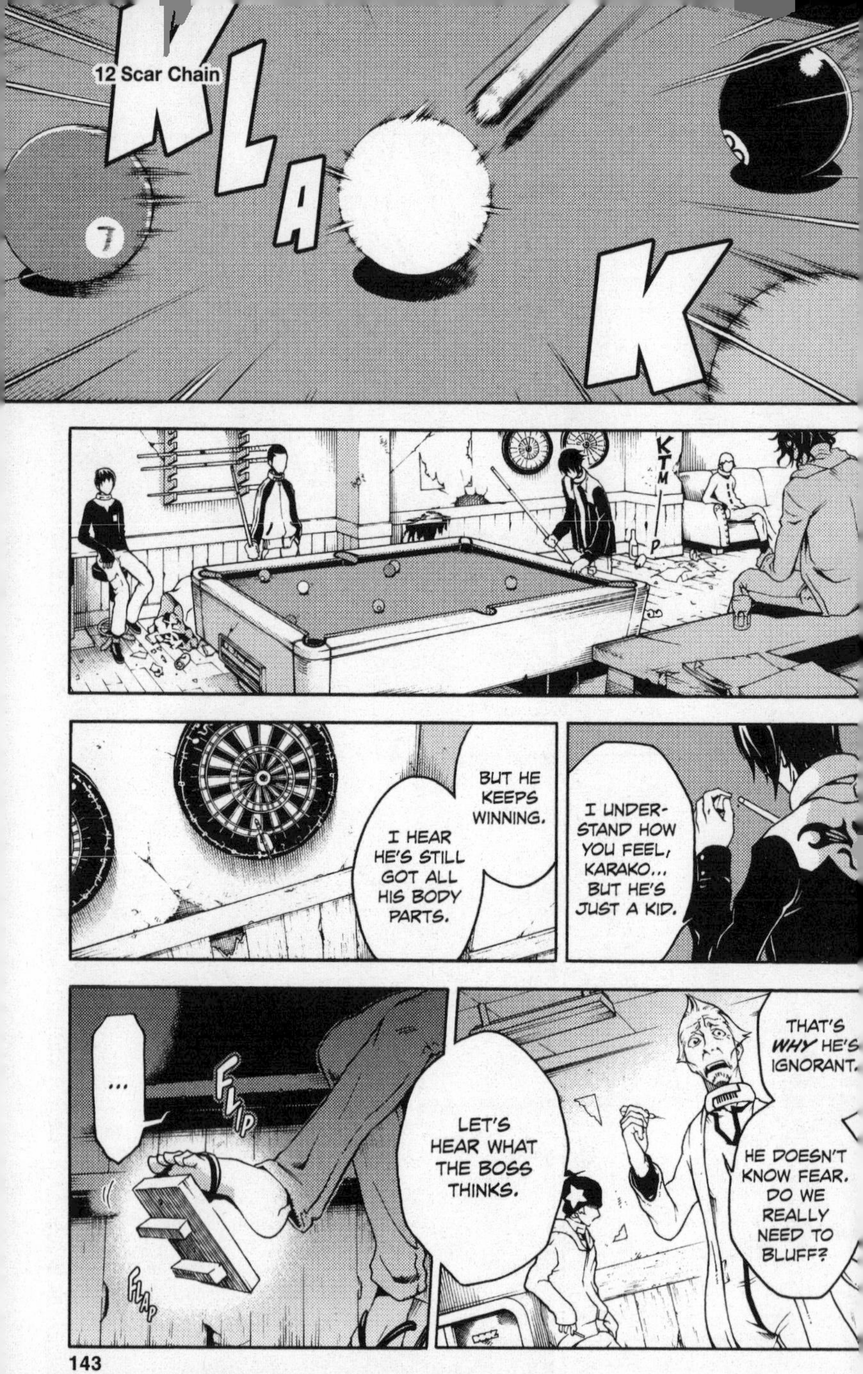
12 Scar Chain
KLAAK
KTMP
I UNDER-STAND HOW YOU FEEL, KARAKO... BUT HE'S JUST A KID.
BUT HE KEEPS WINNING.
I HEAR HE'S STILL GOT ALL HIS BODY PARTS.
THAT'S *WHY* HE'S IGNORANT.
HE DOESN'T KNOW FEAR. DO WE REALLY NEED TO BLUFF?
LET'S HEAR WHAT THE BOSS THINKS.
...
FLIP
FLAP

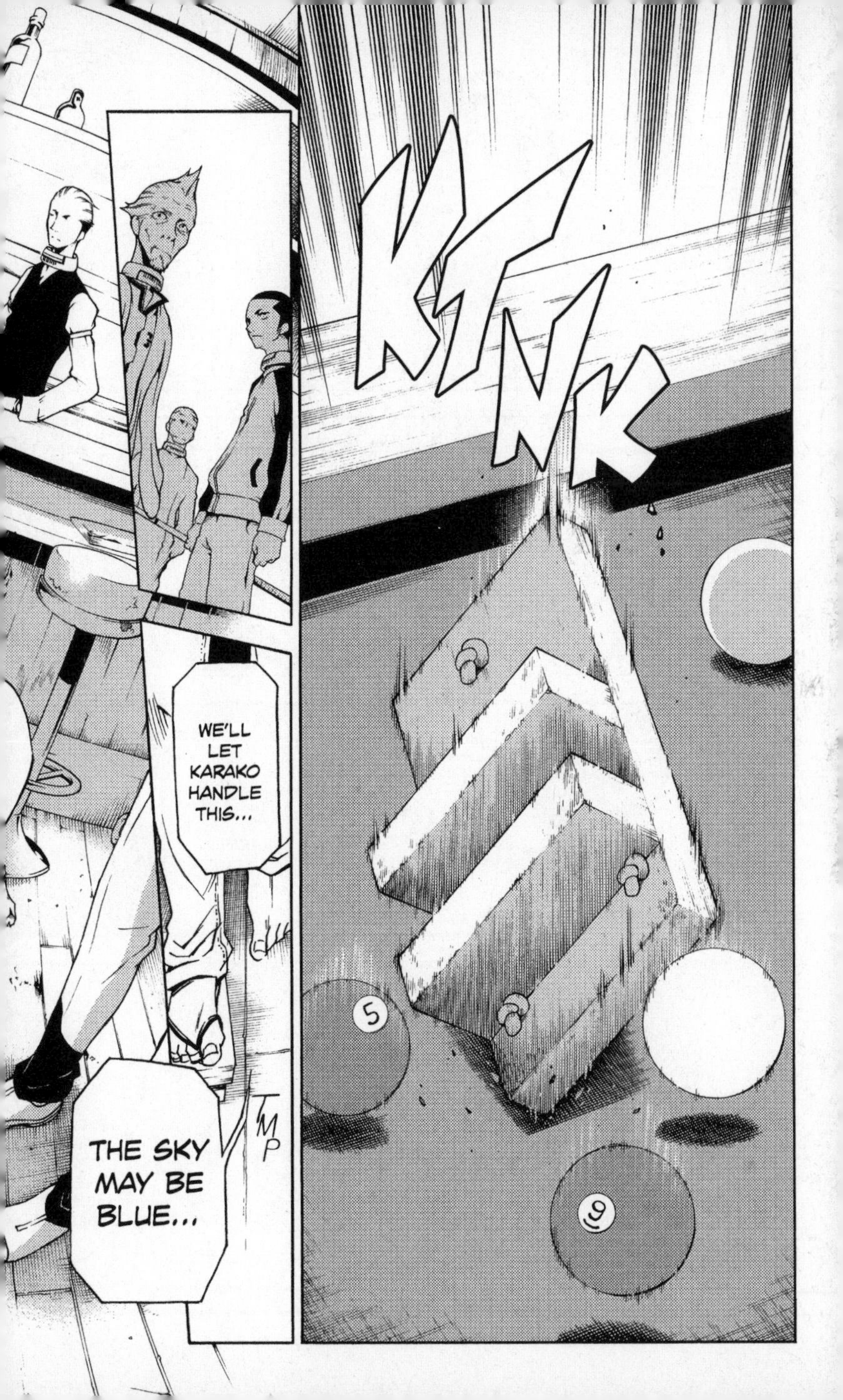

KTNK
WE'LL LET KARAKO HANDLE THIS...
THE SKY MAY BE BLUE...
TMP

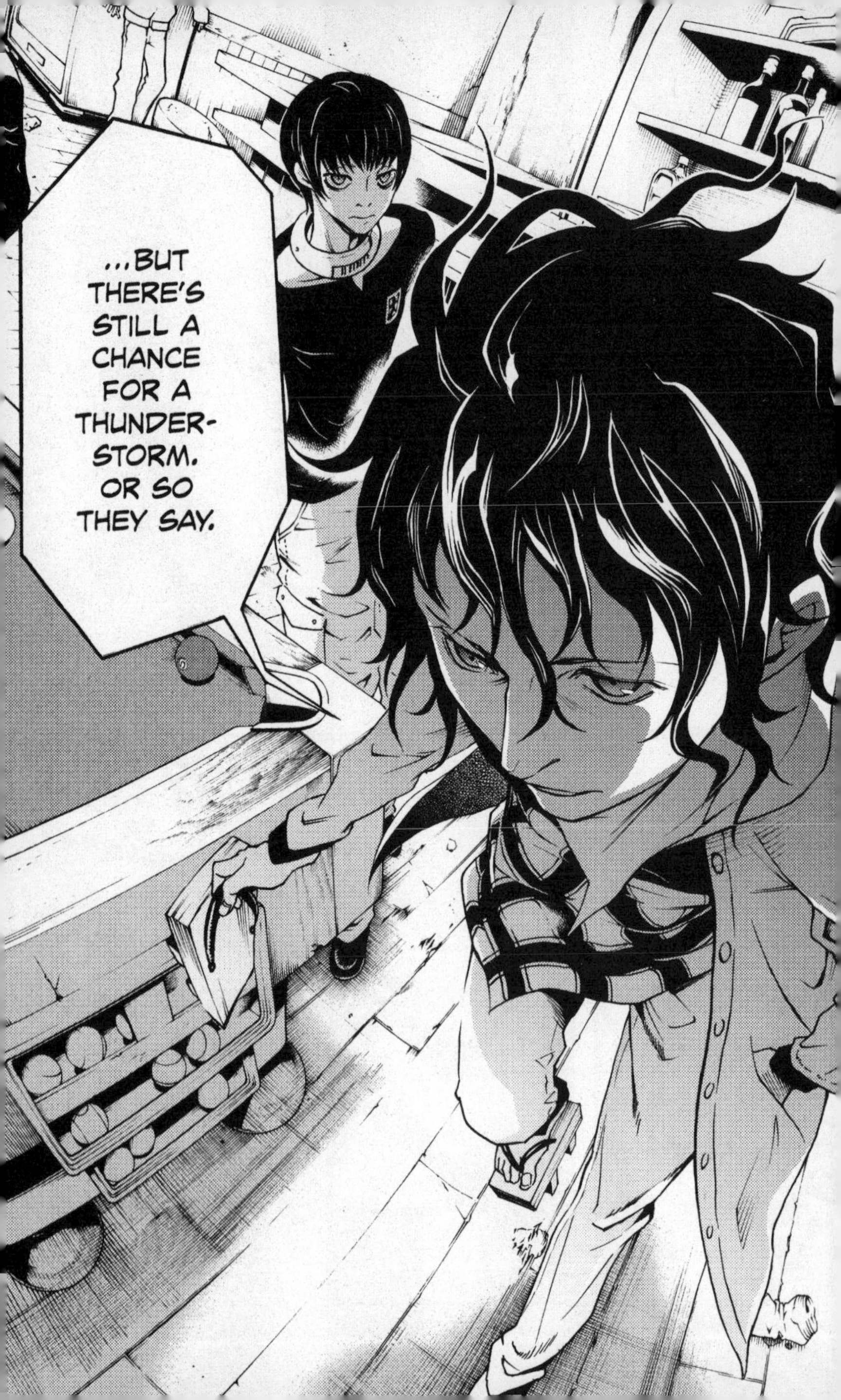
...BUT THERE'S STILL A CHANCE FOR A THUNDER-STORM. OR SO THEY SAY.

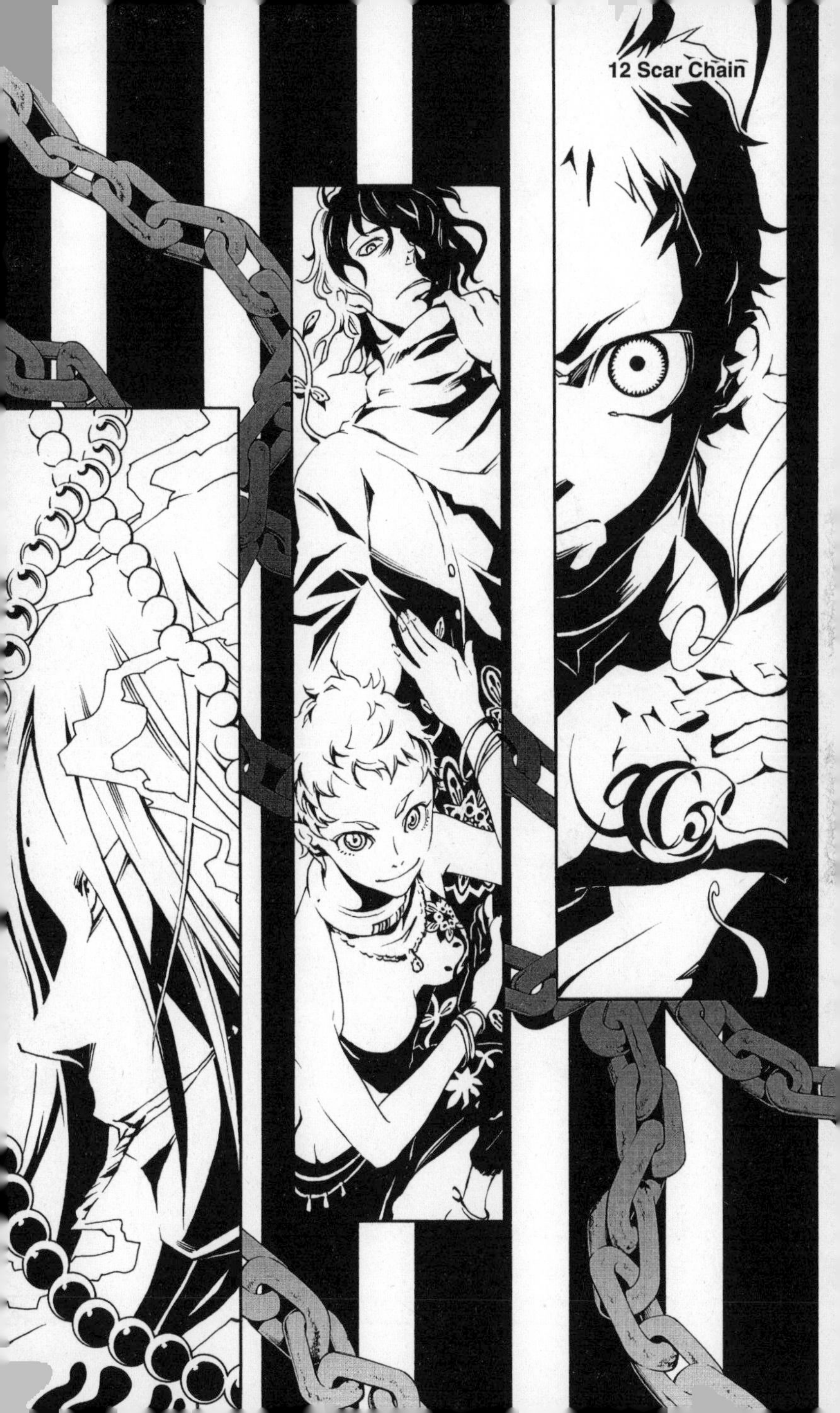
12 Scar Chain

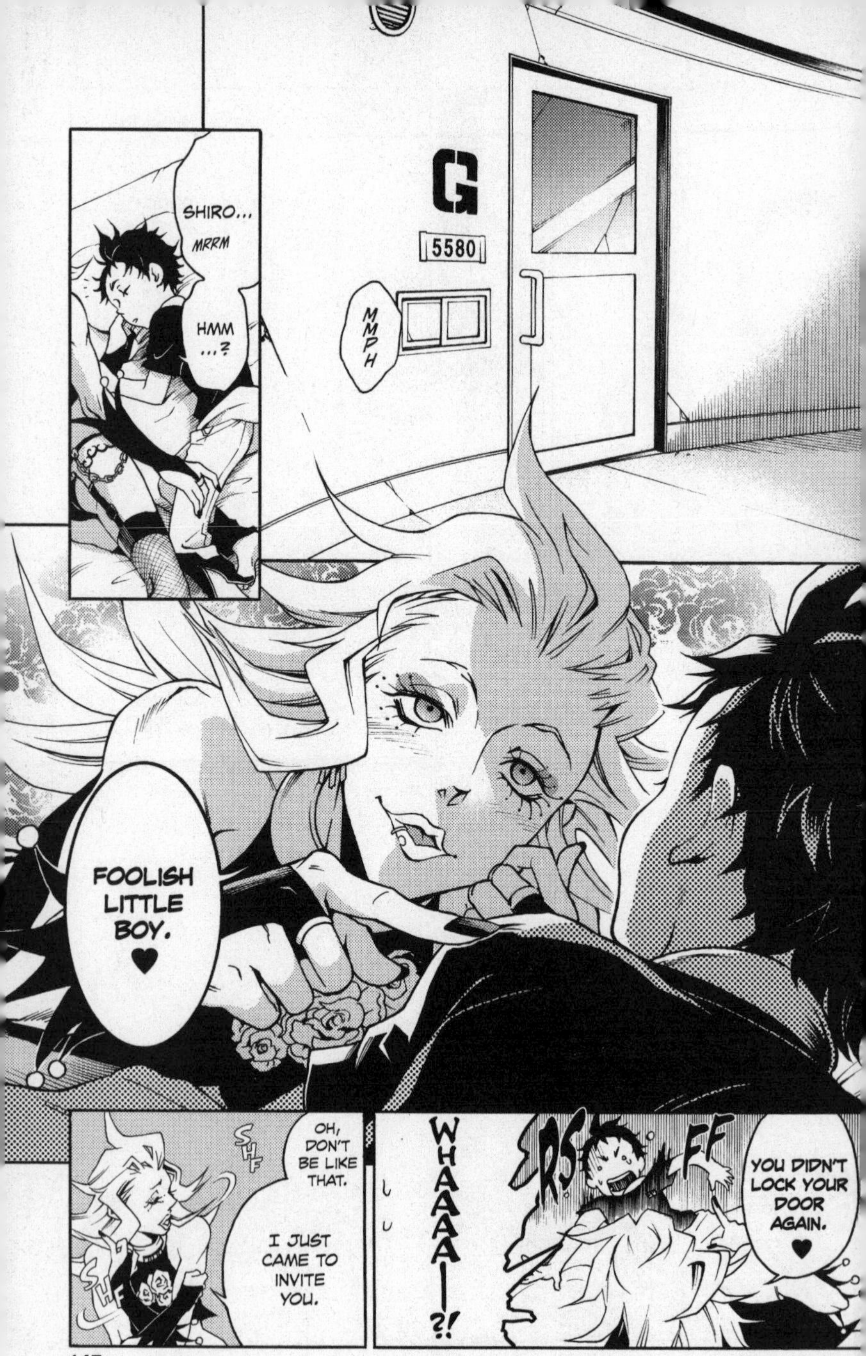
MMPH
SHIRO...
MRRM
HMM ...?
FOOLISH LITTLE BOY. ♥
YOU DIDN'T LOCK YOUR DOOR AGAIN. ♥
WHAAAI—?!
SHF
OH, DON'T BE LIKE THAT.
I JUST CAME TO INVITE YOU.
SHF

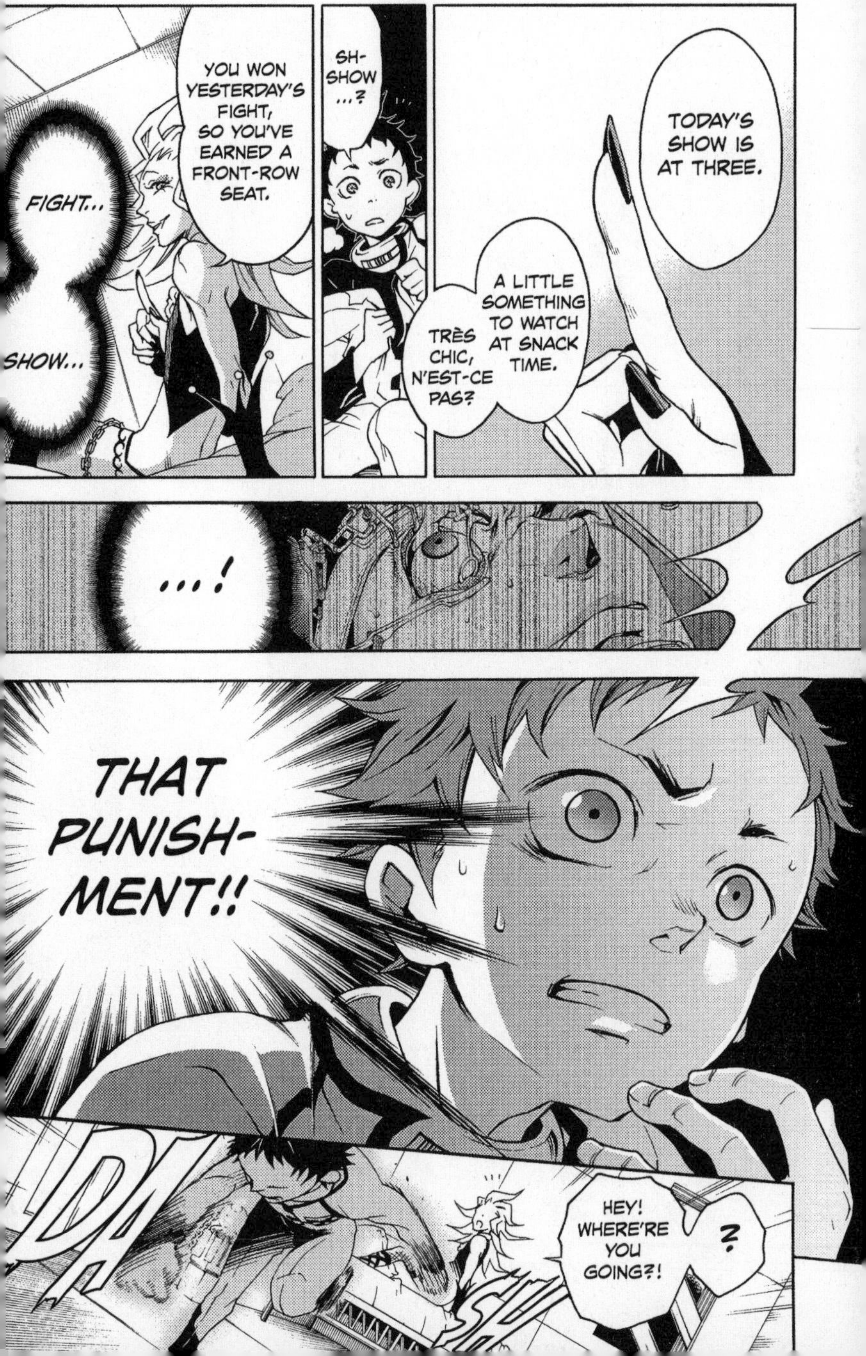
TODAY'S SHOW IS AT THREE.
A LITTLE SOMETHING TO WATCH AT SNACK TIME.
TRÈS CHIC, N'EST-CE PAS?
SH-SHOW ...?
YOU WON YESTERDAY'S FIGHT, SO YOU'VE EARNED A FRONT-ROW SEAT.
FIGHT...
SHOW...
...!
THAT PUNISH-MENT!!
HEY! WHERE'RE YOU GOING?!
?

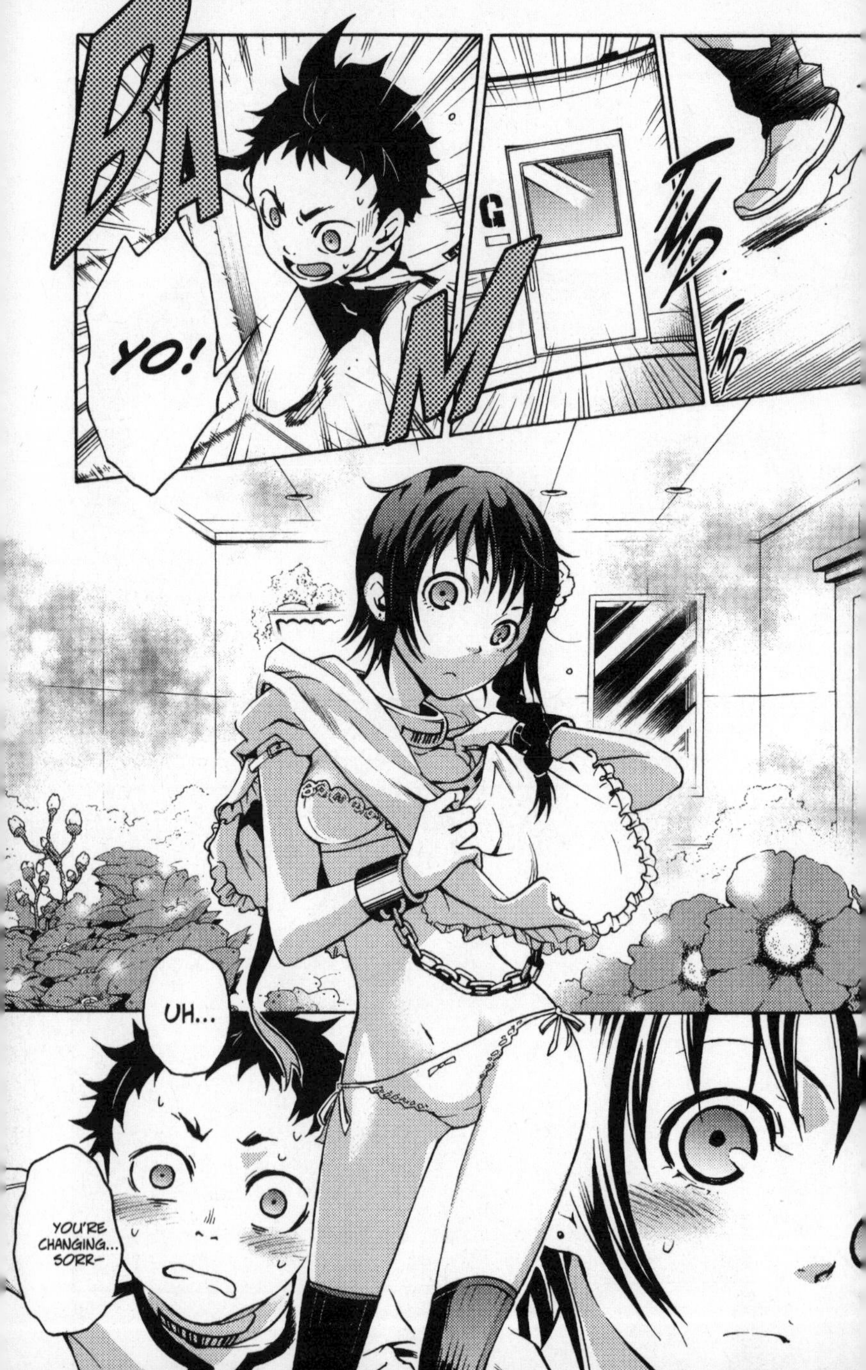
THMP THMP
BAM
YO!
G
UH...
YOU'RE CHANGING... SORR–

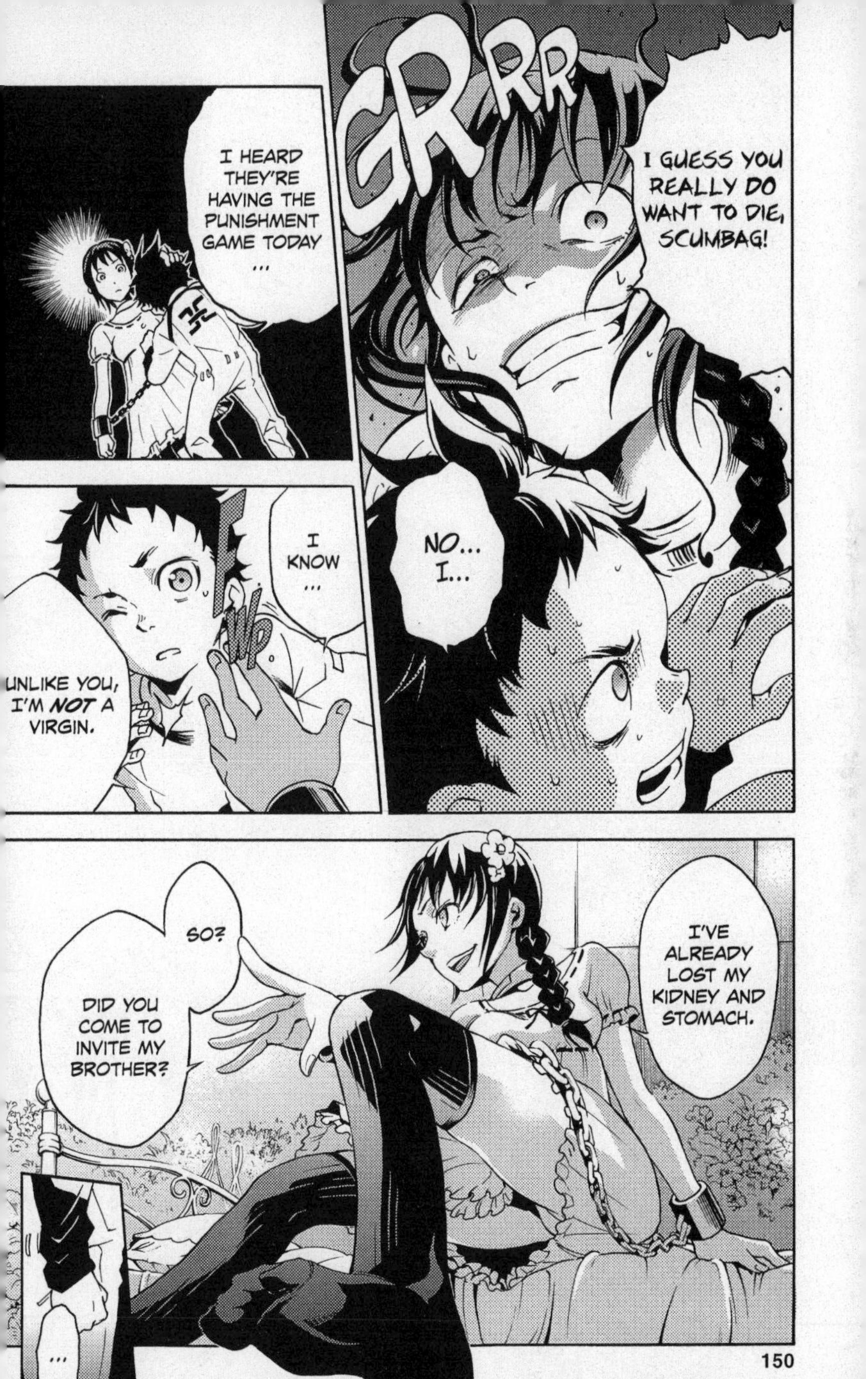
GRRR
I GUESS YOU REALLY DO WANT TO DIE, SCUMBAG!
NO... I...
I HEARD THEY'RE HAVING THE PUNISHMENT GAME TODAY ...
I KNOW ...
UNLIKE YOU, I'M *NOT* A VIRGIN.
I'VE ALREADY LOST MY KIDNEY AND STOMACH.
SO?
DID YOU COME TO INVITE MY BROTHER?
...

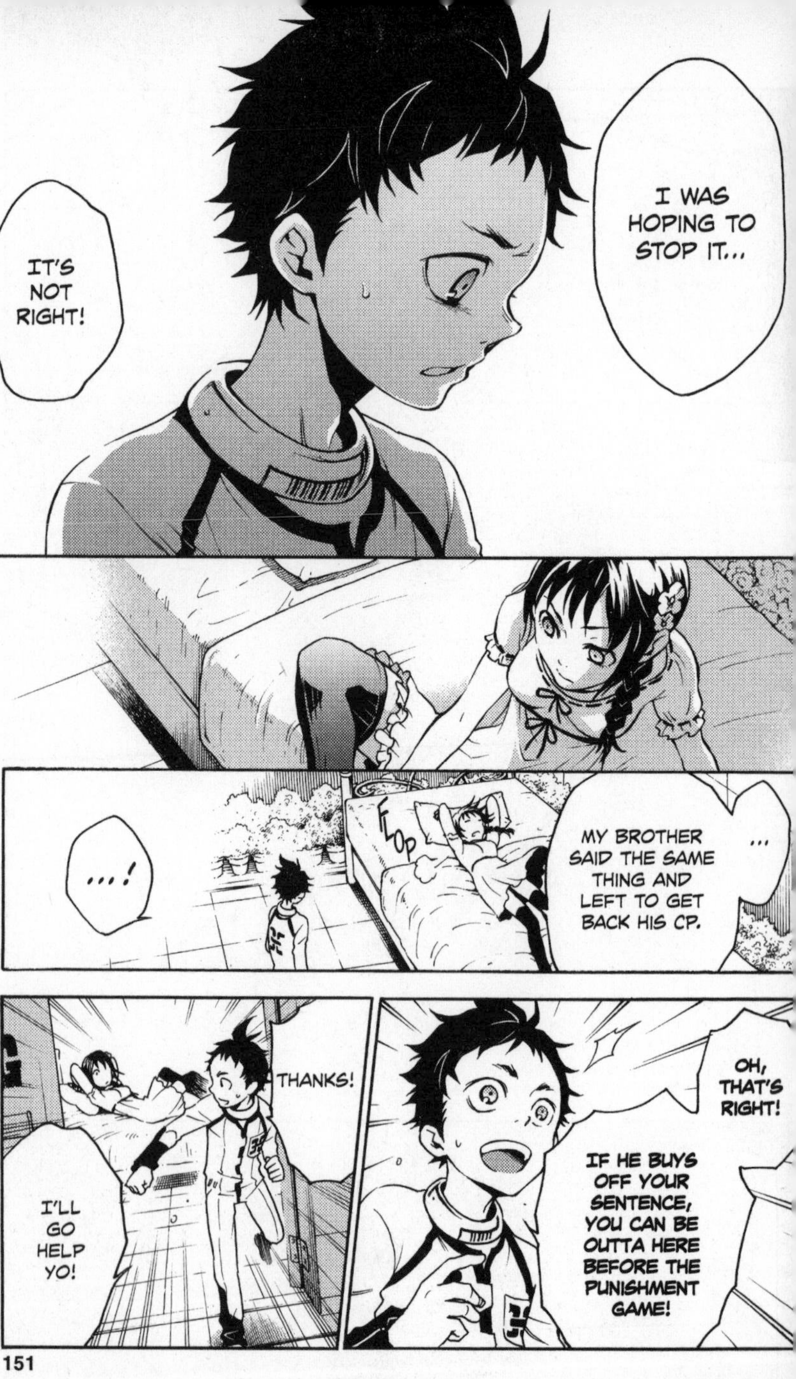
I WAS HOPING TO STOP IT...
IT'S NOT RIGHT!
...
MY BROTHER SAID THE SAME THING AND LEFT TO GET BACK HIS CP.
FLOP
...!
OH, THAT'S RIGHT!
IF HE BUYS OFF YOUR SENTENCE, YOU CAN BE OUTTA HERE BEFORE THE PUNISHMENT GAME!
THANKS!
I'LL GO HELP YO!

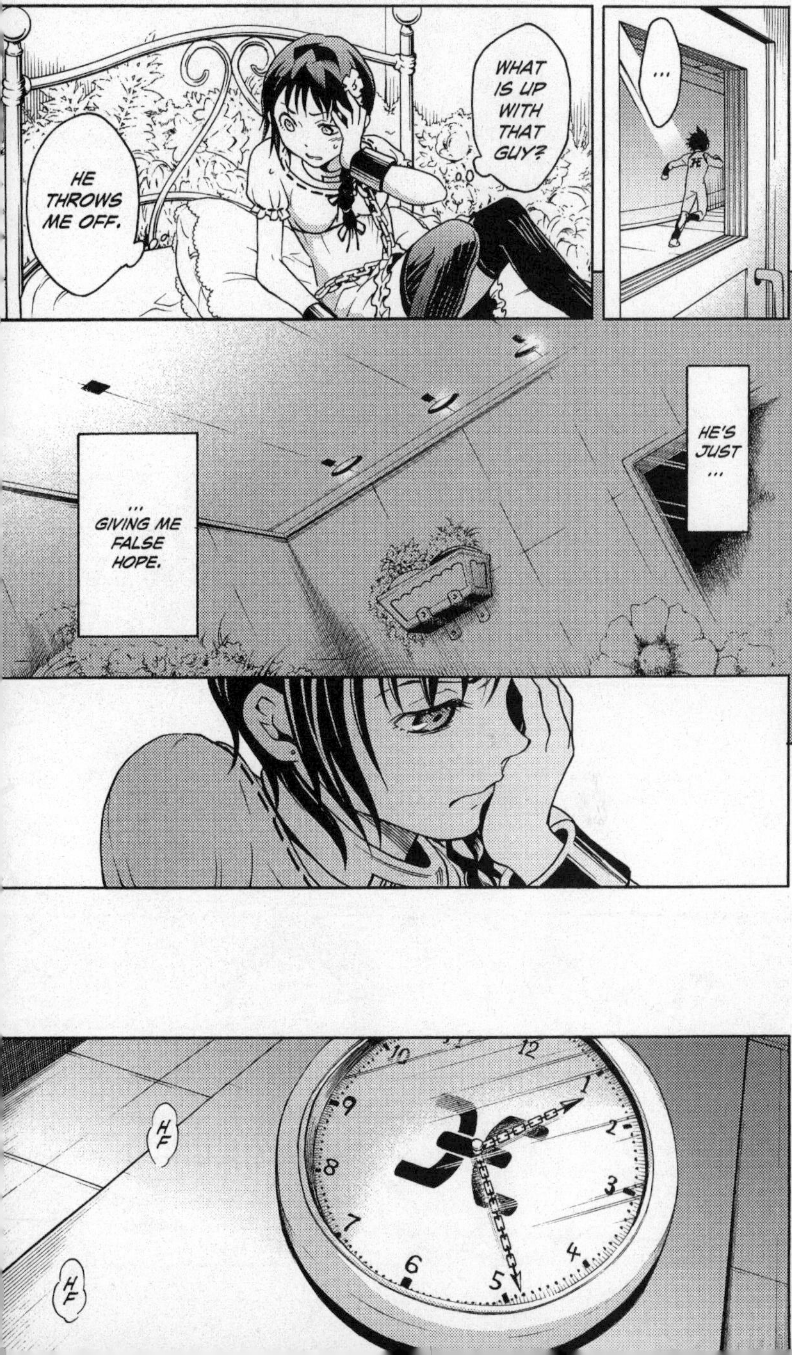
...
WHAT IS UP WITH THAT GUY?
HE THROWS ME OFF.
HE'S JUST ...
... GIVING ME FALSE HOPE.
HF
HF

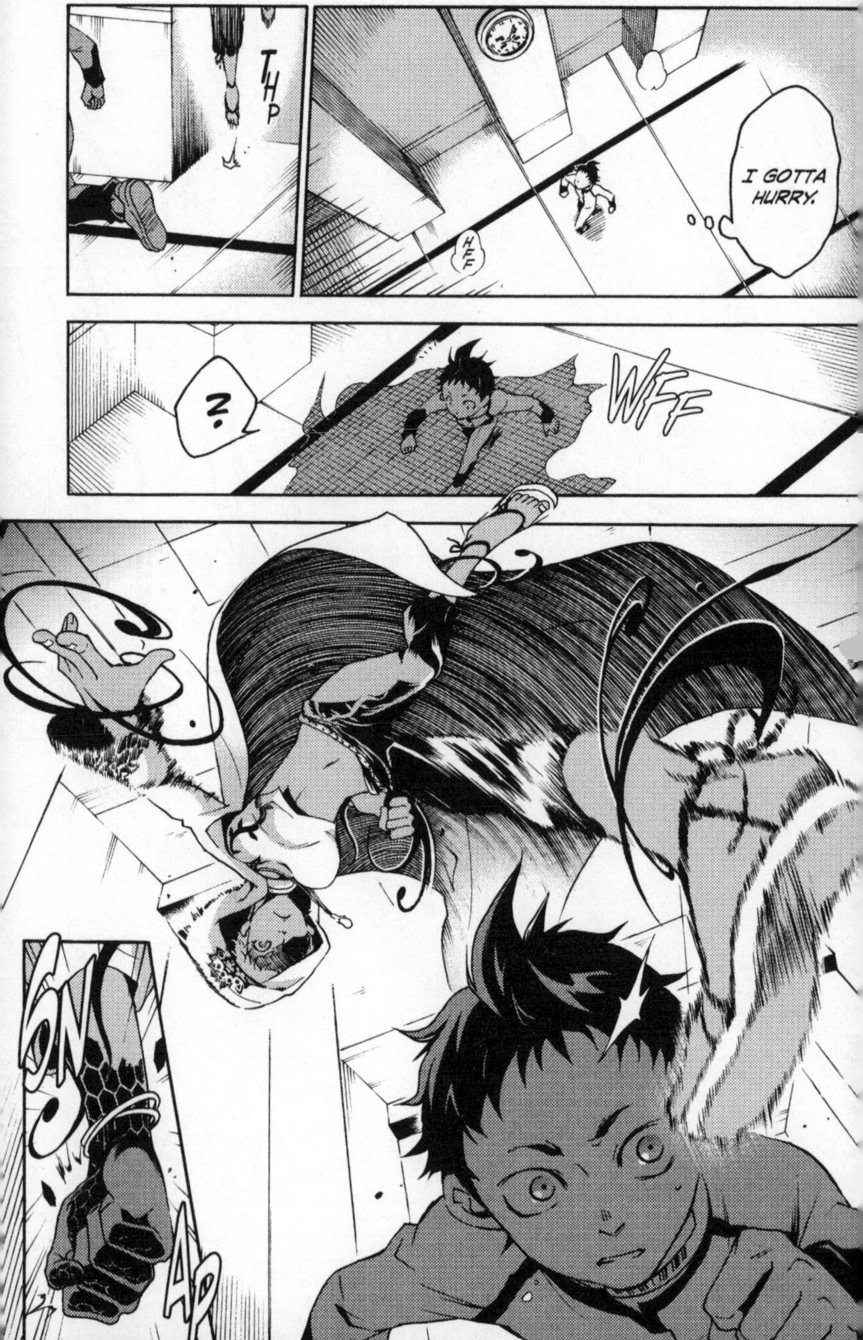
I GOTTA HURRY.
HEF
THP
WFF
?
SNAP

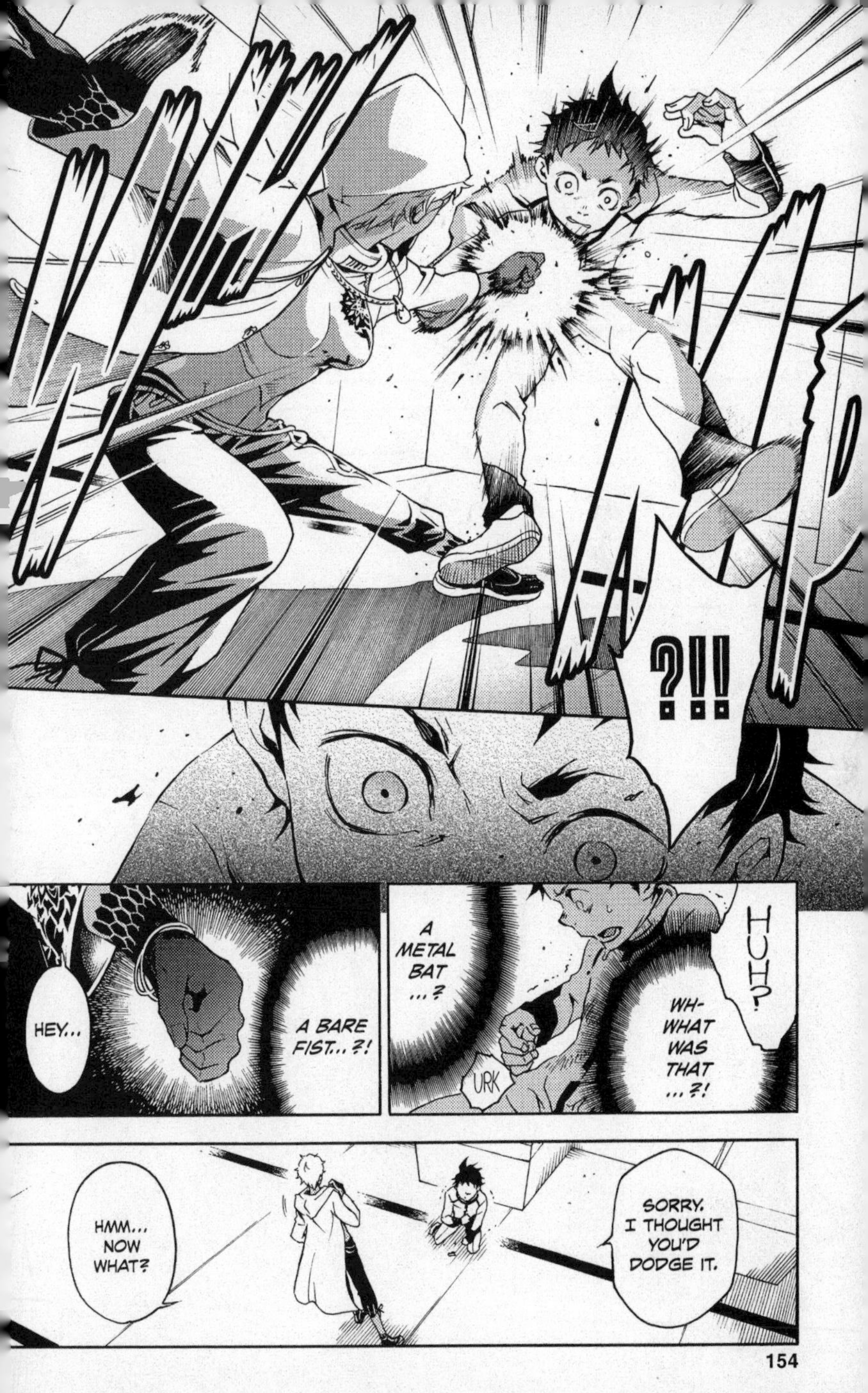
?!!
HUH?
WH- WHAT WAS THAT ...?!
URK
A METAL BAT ...?
A BARE FIST...?!
HEY...
SORRY. I THOUGHT YOU'D DODGE IT.
HMM... NOW WHAT?

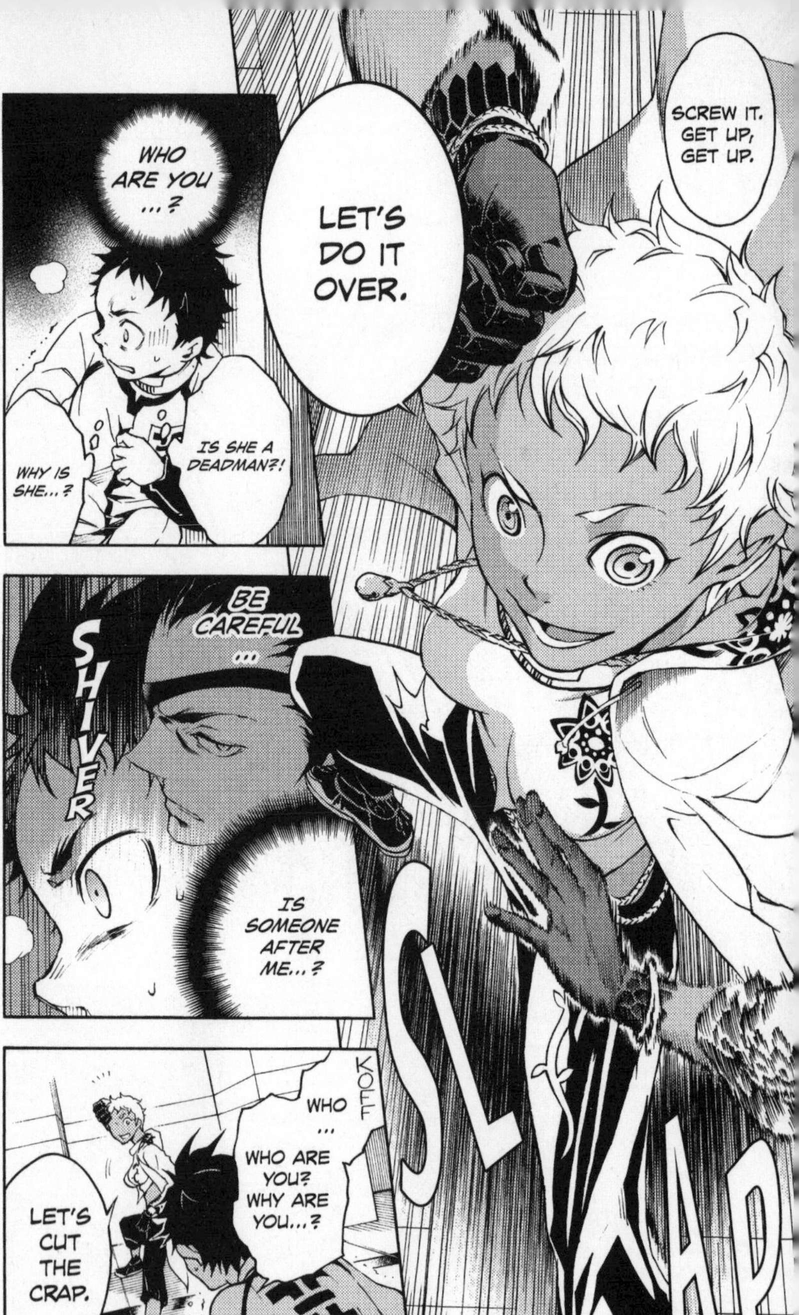
SCREW IT. GET UP, GET UP.
LET'S DO IT OVER.
SLAP
WHO ARE YOU ...?
IS SHE A DEADMAN?!
WHY IS SHE...?
SHIVER
BE CAREFUL ...
IS SOMEONE AFTER ME...?
KOFF
WHO ... WHO ARE YOU? WHY ARE YOU...?
LET'S CUT THE CRAP.

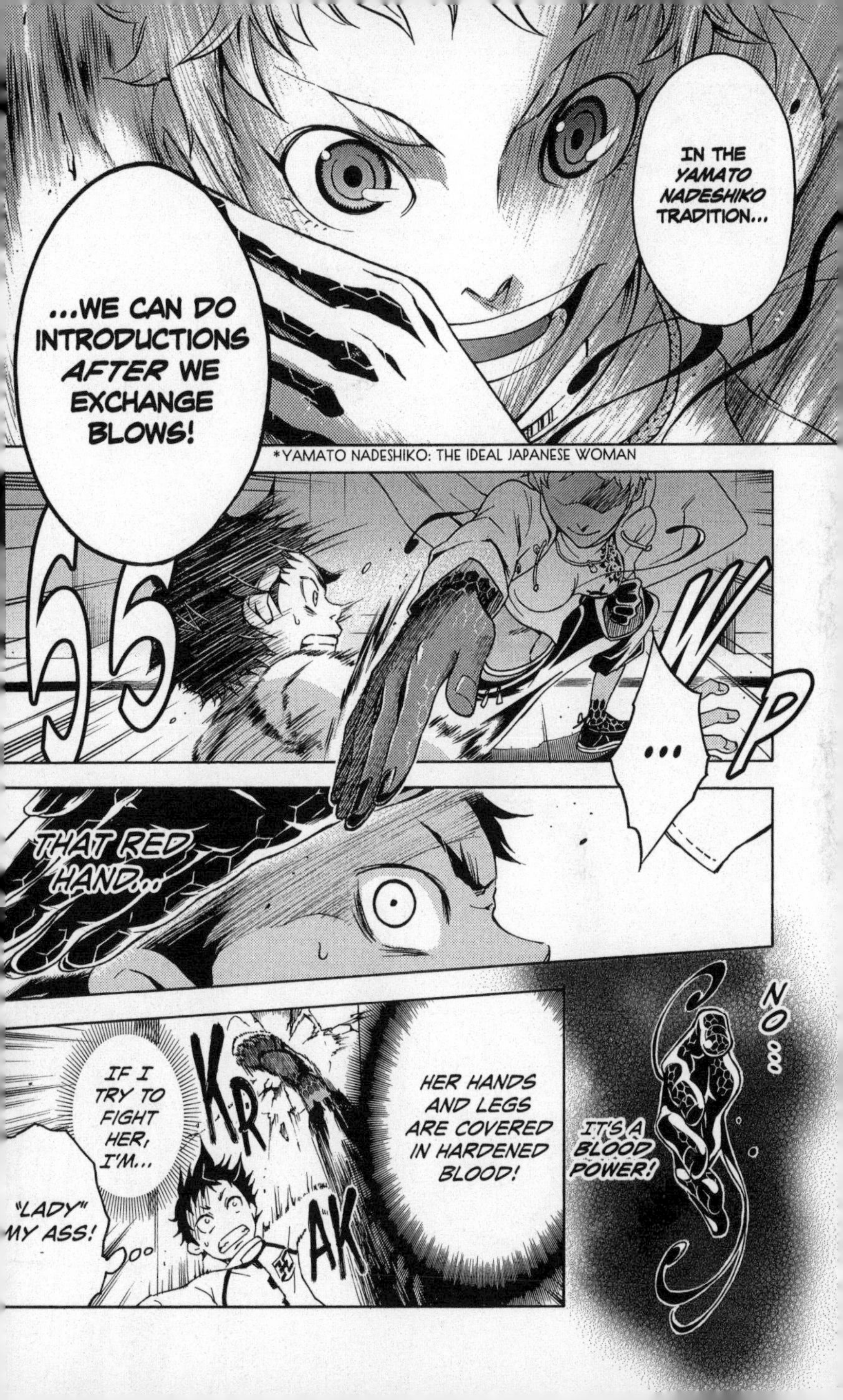
IN THE YAMATO NADESHIKO TRADITION...
...WE CAN DO INTRODUCTIONS AFTER WE EXCHANGE BLOWS!
*YAMATO NADESHIKO: THE IDEAL JAPANESE WOMAN
WIP
...
THAT RED HAND...
NO...
IT'S A BLOOD POWER!
HER HANDS AND LEGS ARE COVERED IN HARDENED BLOOD!
KRAK
IF I TRY TO FIGHT HER, I'M...
"LADY" MY ASS!

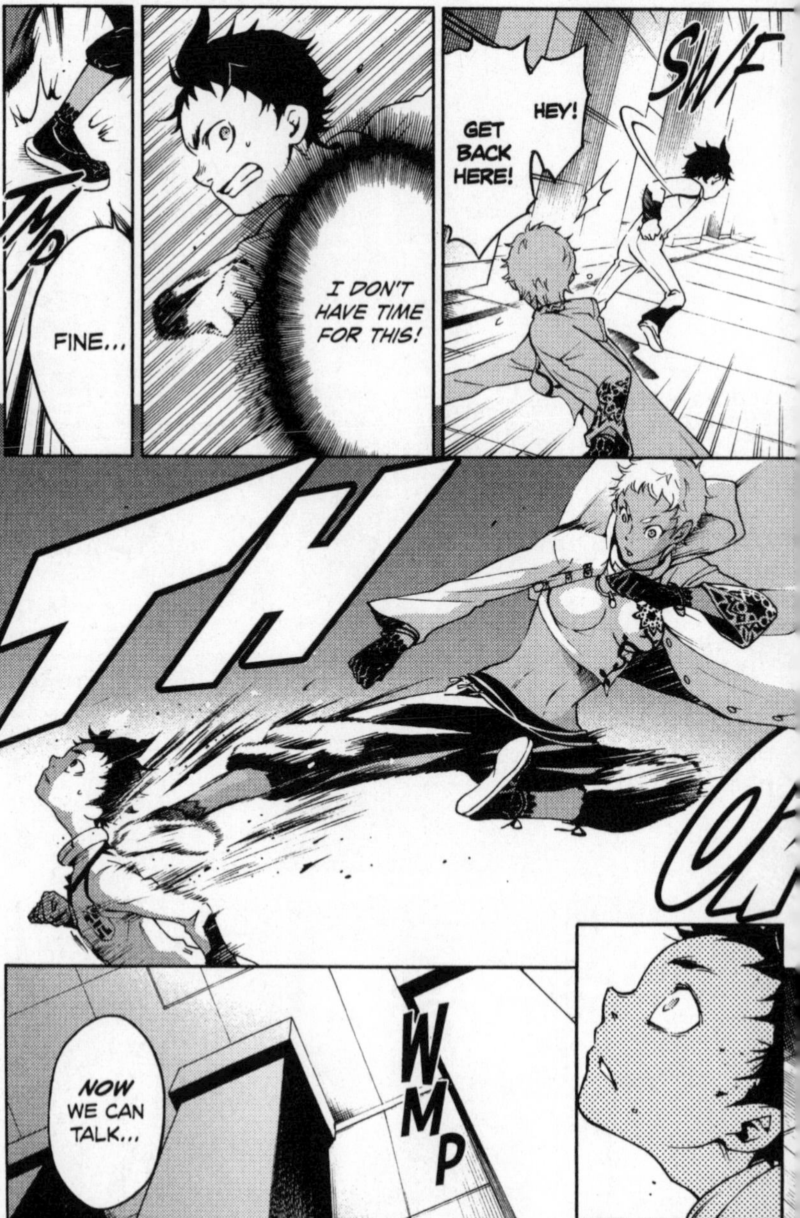
SWF
HEY!
GET BACK HERE!
I DON'T HAVE TIME FOR THIS!
TMP
FINE...
TH
WMP
NOW WE CAN TALK...

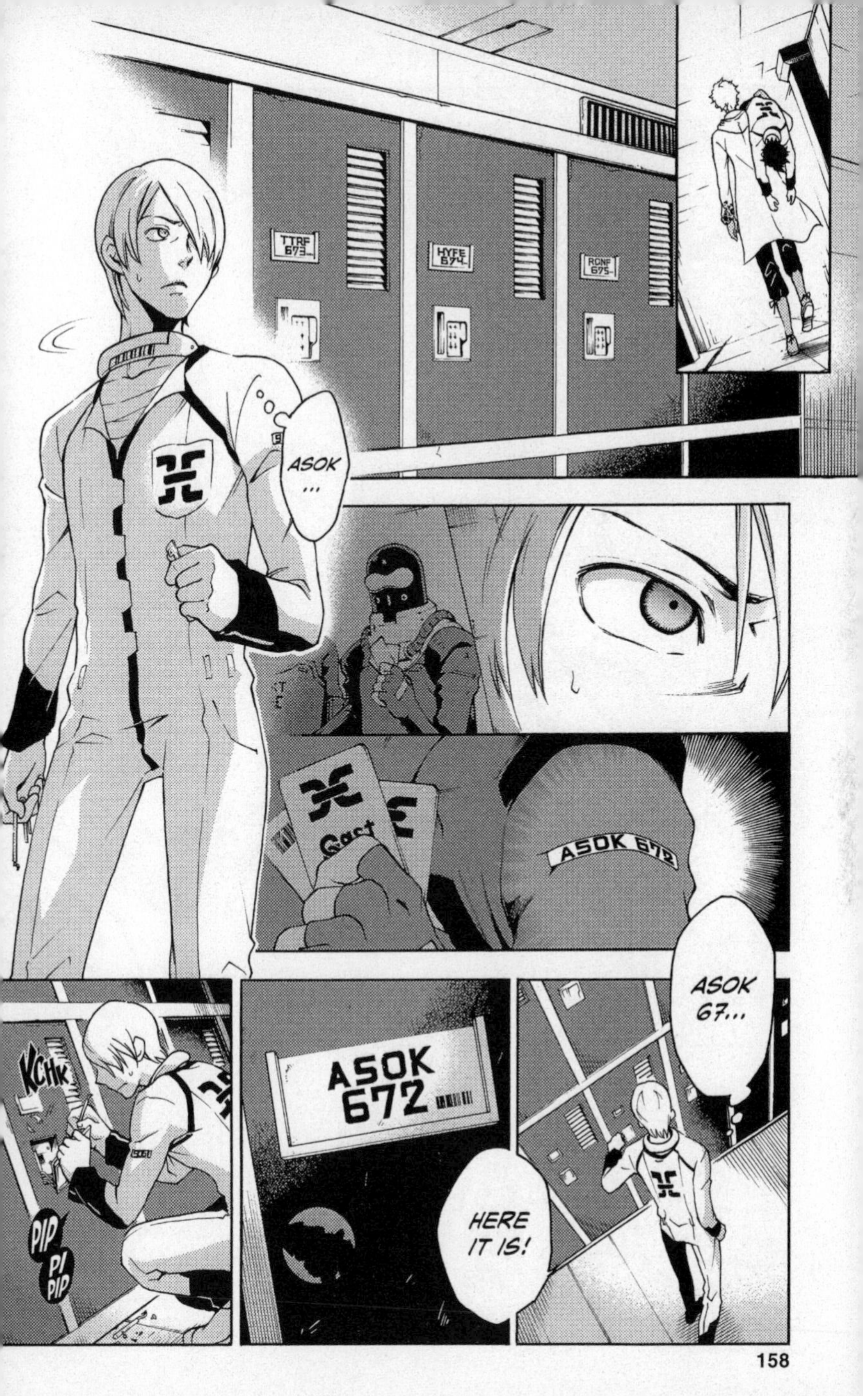
Gast
ASOK 672
TTRF 673
HYFE 674
RONF 675
ASOK ...
ASOK 67...
HERE IT IS!
ASOK 672
KCHK
PIP PI PIP

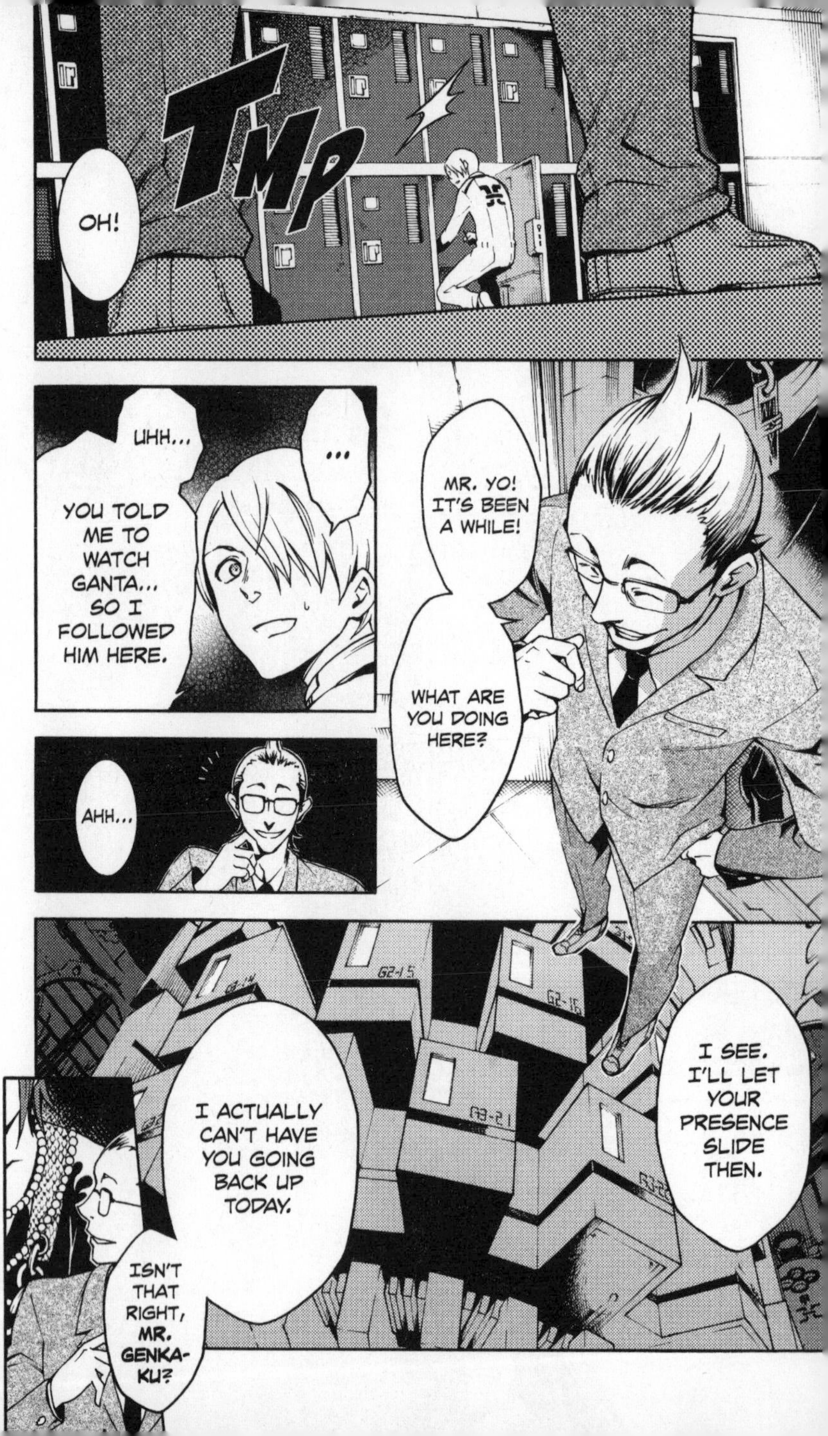
TMP
OH!
MR. YO! IT'S BEEN A WHILE!
WHAT ARE YOU DOING HERE?
...
UHH...
YOU TOLD ME TO WATCH GANTA... SO I FOLLOWED HIM HERE.
AHH...
I SEE. I'LL LET YOUR PRESENCE SLIDE THEN.
I ACTUALLY CAN'T HAVE YOU GOING BACK UP TODAY.
ISN'T THAT RIGHT, MR. GENKAKU?

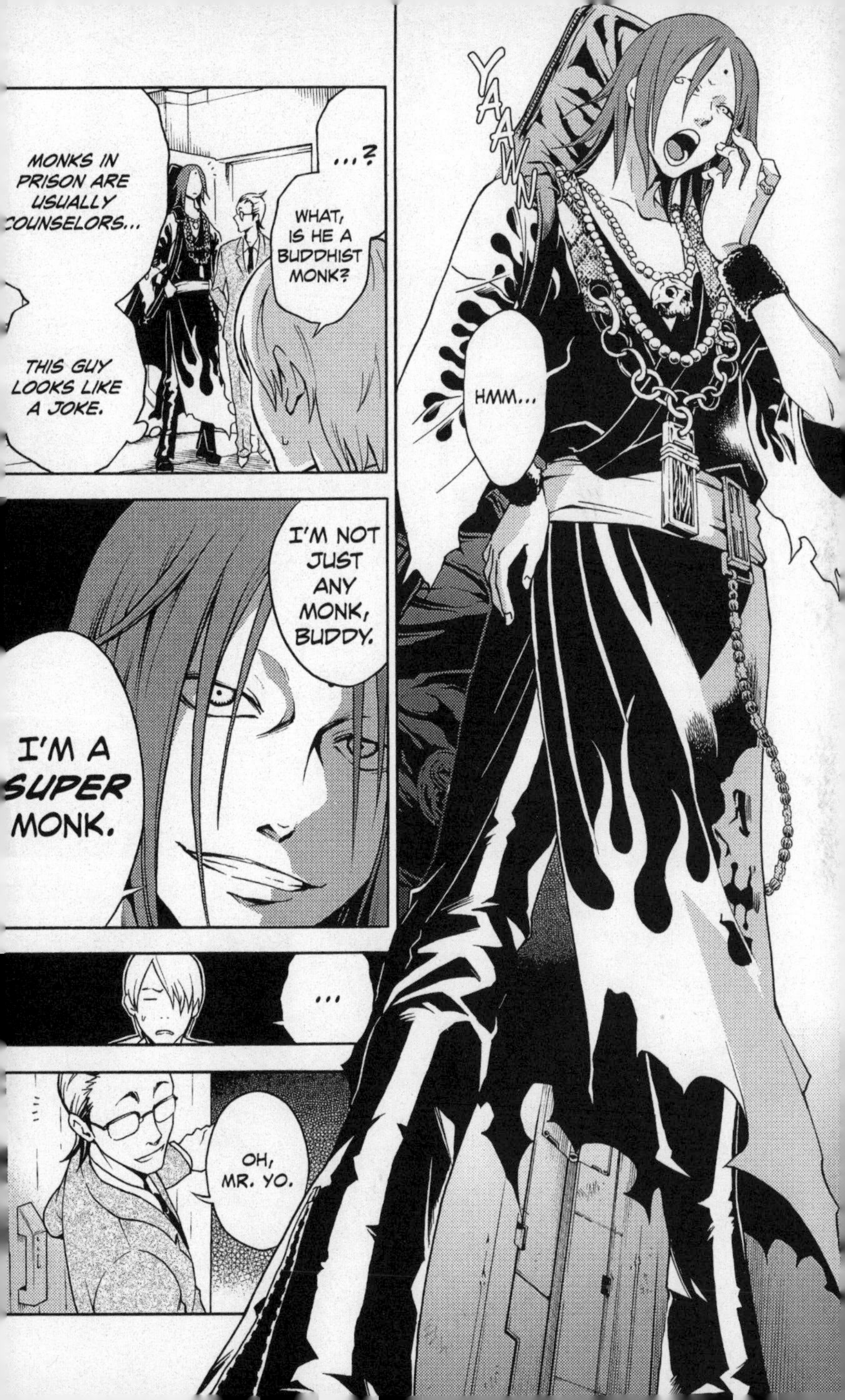
YAAWN
HMM...
...?
WHAT, IS HE A BUDDHIST MONK?
MONKS IN PRISON ARE USUALLY COUNSELORS...
THIS GUY LOOKS LIKE A JOKE.
I'M NOT JUST ANY MONK, BUDDY.
I'M A SUPER MONK.
...
OH, MR. YO.

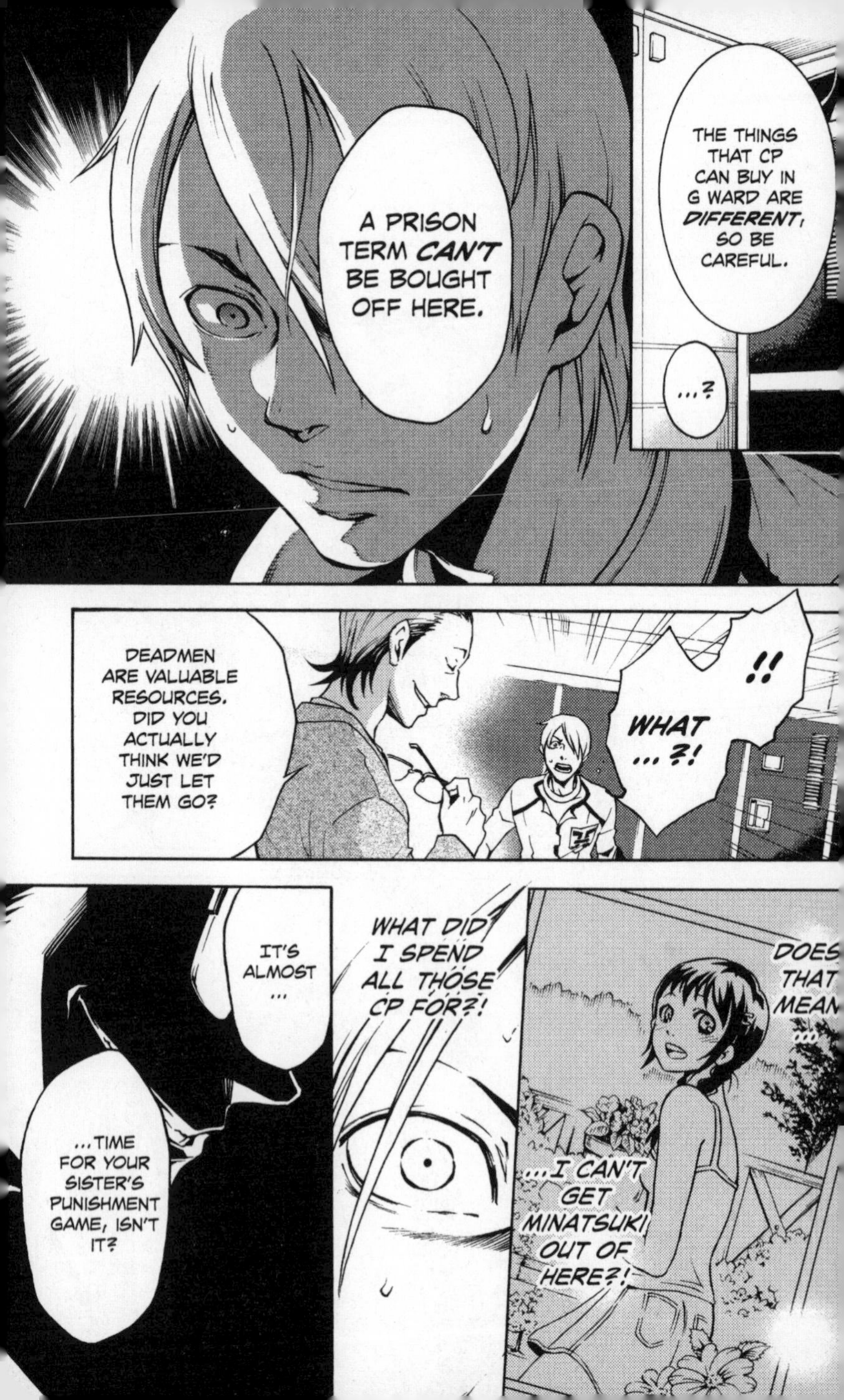
THE THINGS THAT CP CAN BUY IN G WARD ARE *DIFFERENT*, SO BE CAREFUL.
...?
A PRISON TERM *CAN'T* BE BOUGHT OFF HERE.
!! WHAT...?!
DEADMEN ARE VALUABLE RESOURCES. DID YOU ACTUALLY THINK WE'D JUST LET THEM GO?
DOES THAT MEAN...
...I CAN'T GET MINATSUKI OUT OF HERE?!
WHAT DID I SPEND ALL THOSE CP FOR?!
IT'S ALMOST...
...TIME FOR YOUR SISTER'S PUNISHMENT GAME, ISN'T IT?

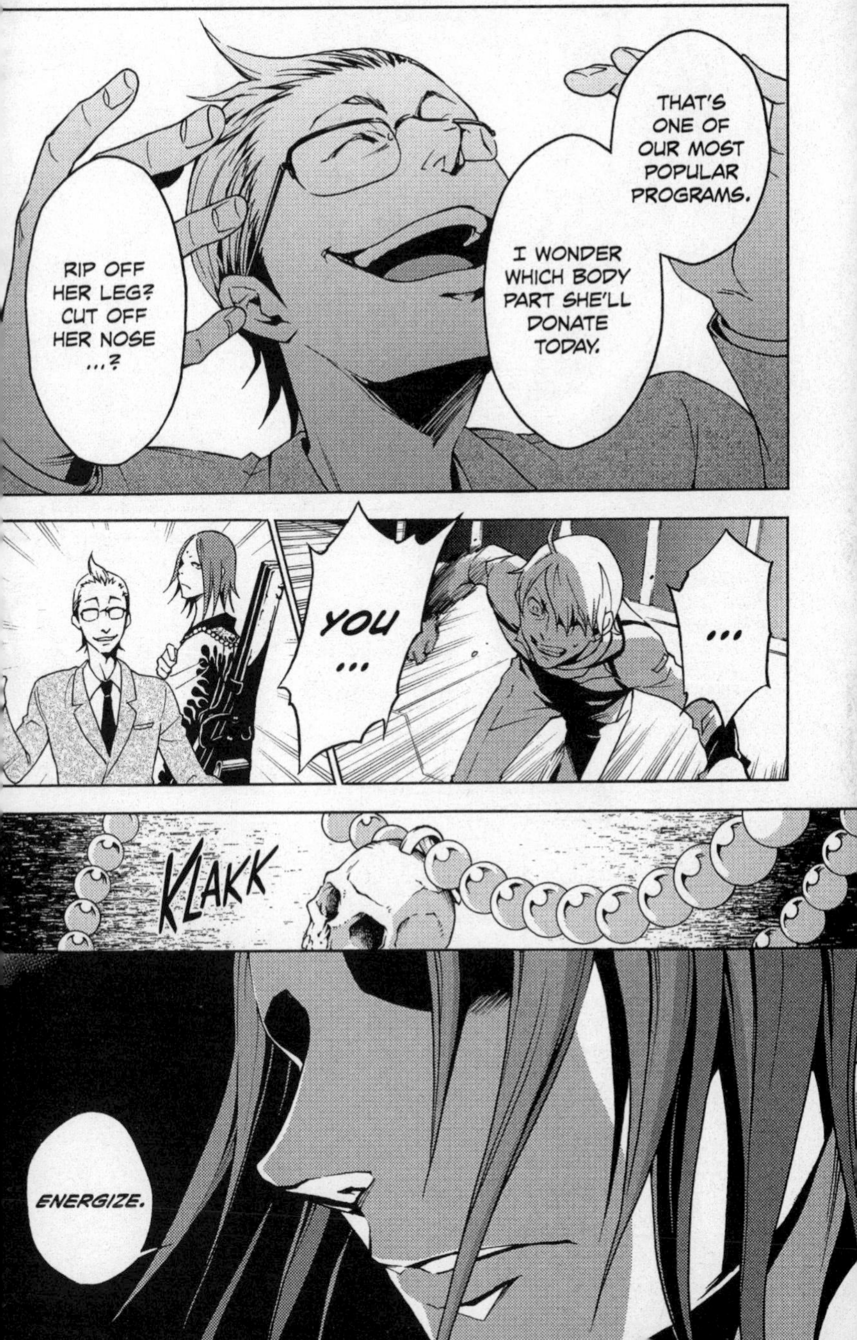
THAT'S ONE OF OUR MOST POPULAR PROGRAMS.
I WONDER WHICH BODY PART SHE'LL DONATE TODAY.
RIP OFF HER LEG? CUT OFF HER NOSE ...?
...
YOU ...
KLAKK
ENERGIZE.

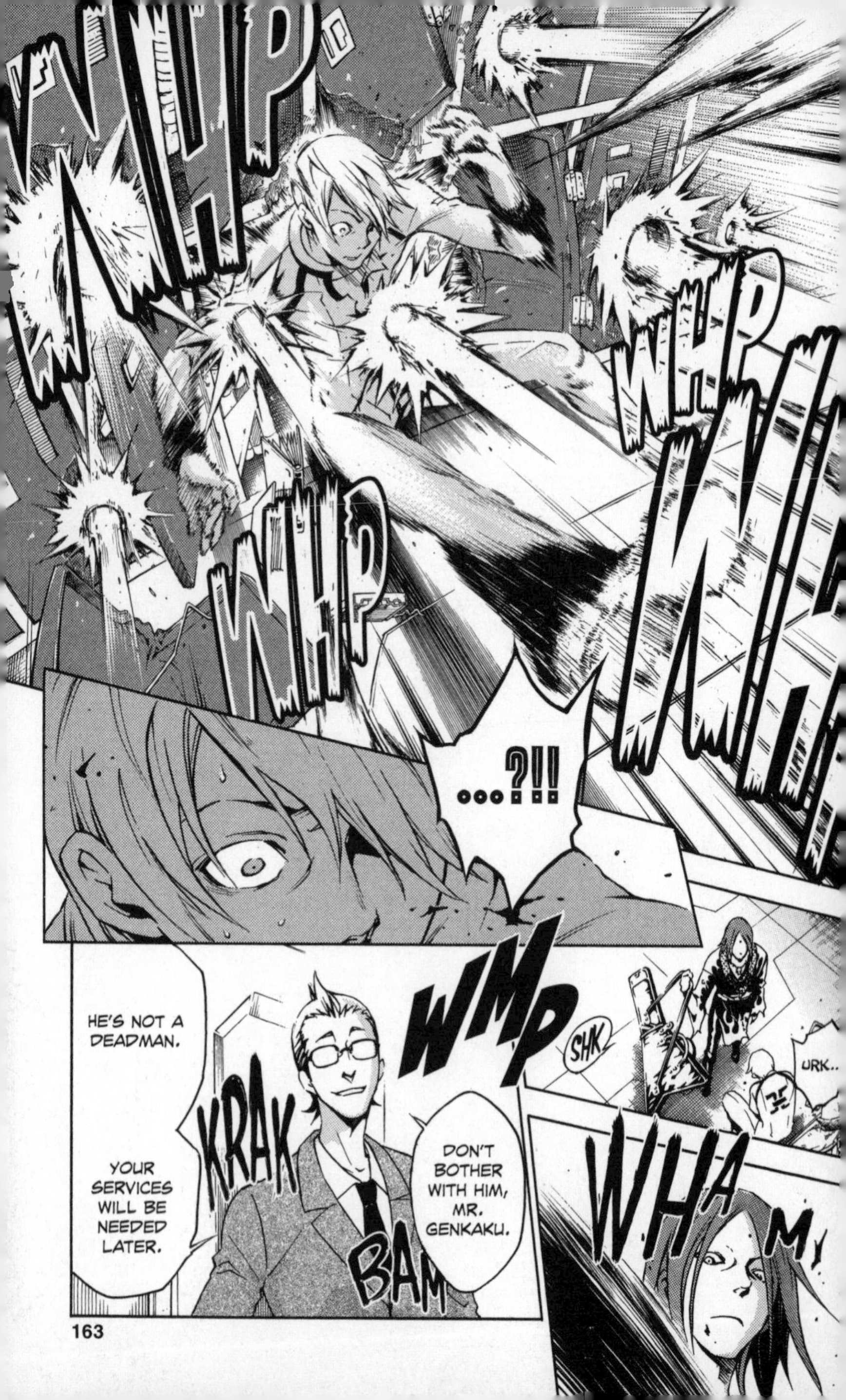
WHIP
WHIP
WHIP
WHAM
...?!!
SHK
URK..
WHAM
WMP
DON'T BOTHER WITH HIM, MR. GENKAKU.
HE'S NOT A DEADMAN.
YOUR SERVICES WILL BE NEEDED LATER.
KRAK
BAM

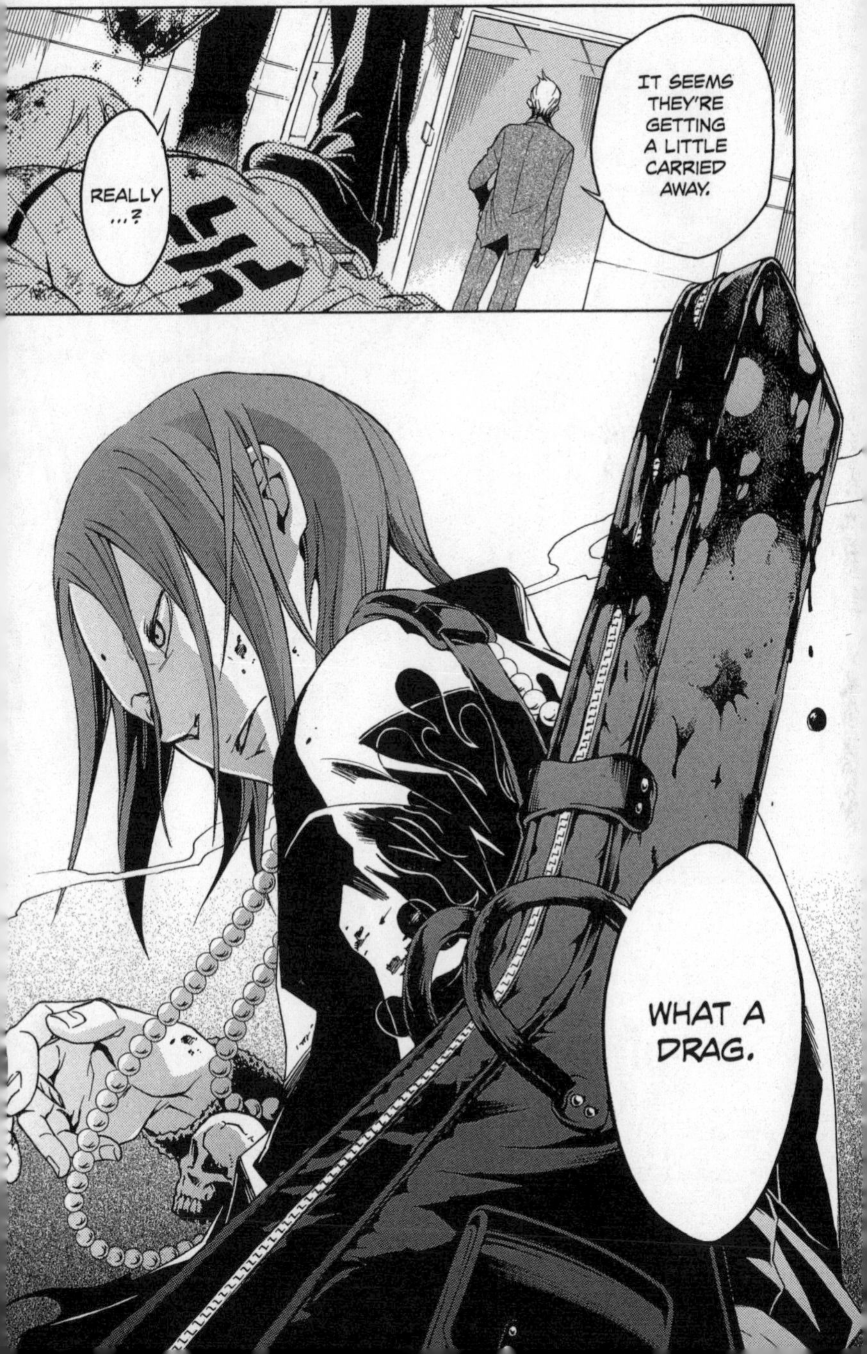
IT SEEMS THEY'RE GETTING A LITTLE CARRIED AWAY.
REALLY ...?
WHAT A DRAG.

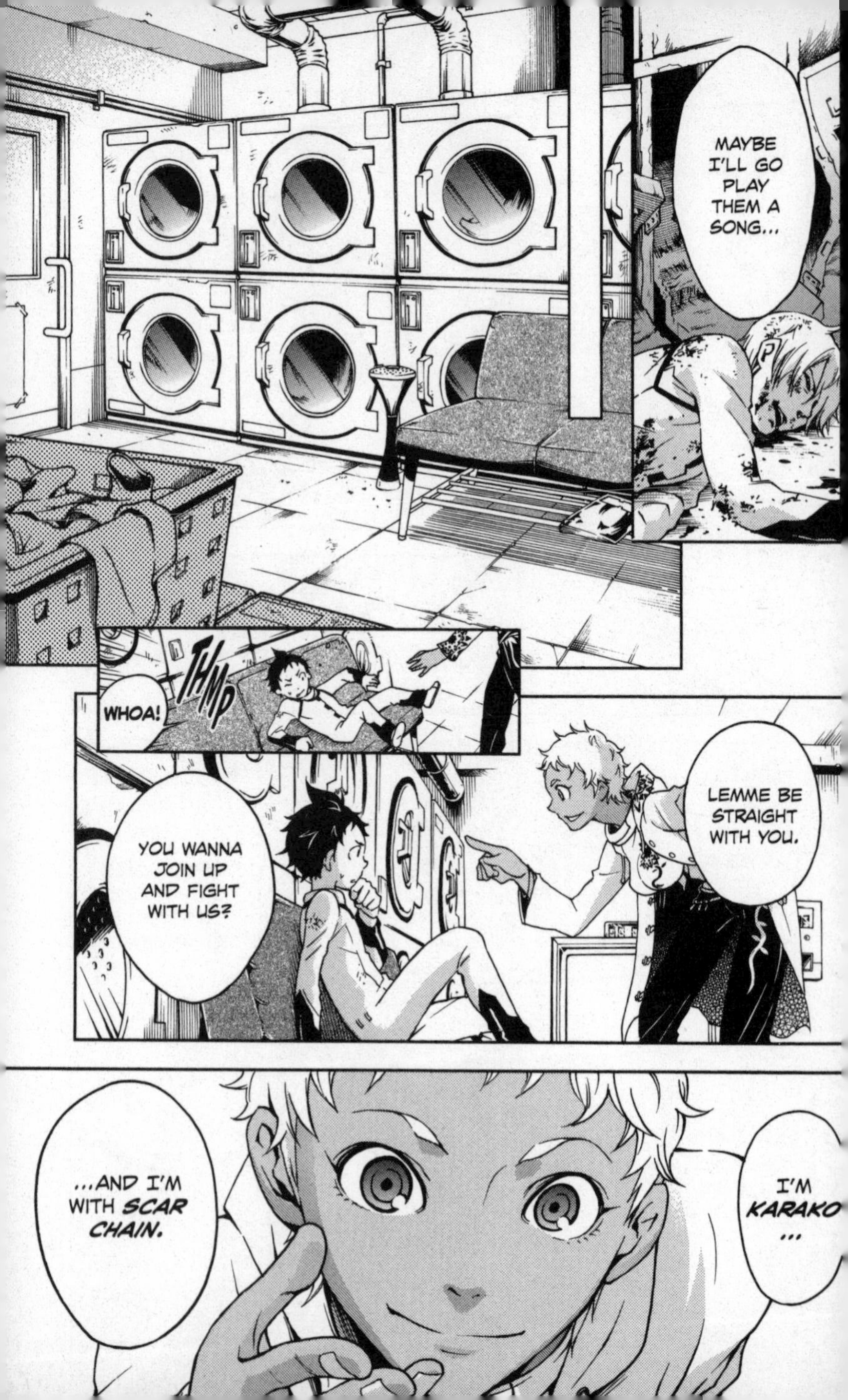
MAYBE I'LL GO PLAY THEM A SONG...
WHOA!
THMP
LEMME BE STRAIGHT WITH YOU.
YOU WANNA JOIN UP AND FIGHT WITH US?
I'M *KARAKO*...
...AND I'M WITH *SCAR CHAIN.*

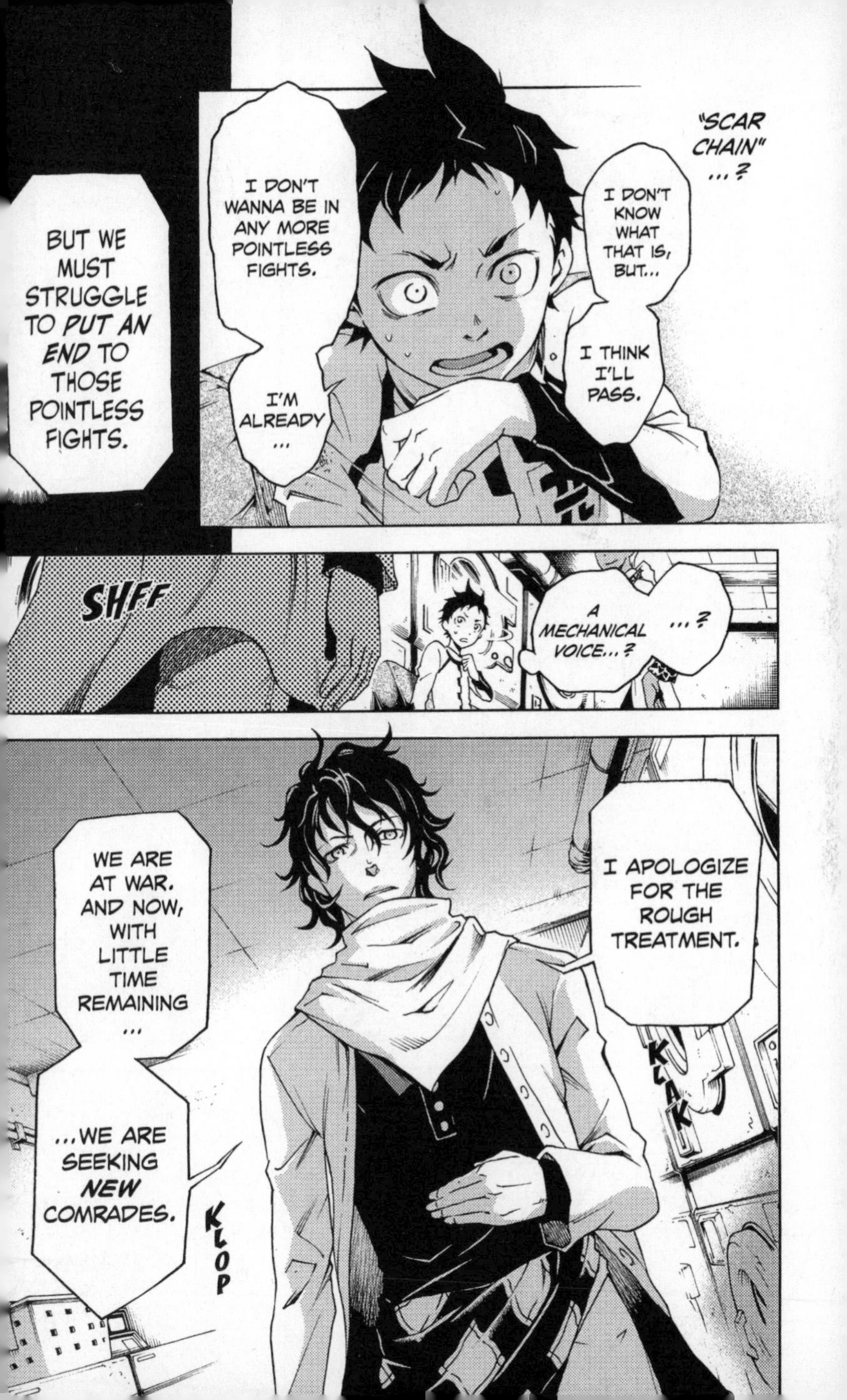
"SCAR CHAIN" ...?
I DON'T KNOW WHAT THAT IS, BUT...
I THINK I'LL PASS.
I DON'T WANNA BE IN ANY MORE POINTLESS FIGHTS.
I'M ALREADY ...
BUT WE MUST STRUGGLE TO *PUT AN END* TO THOSE POINTLESS FIGHTS.
...?
A MECHANICAL VOICE...?
SHFF
KLAK
I APOLOGIZE FOR THE ROUGH TREATMENT.
WE ARE AT WAR. AND NOW, WITH LITTLE TIME REMAINING ...
...WE ARE SEEKING *NEW* COMRADES.
KLOP

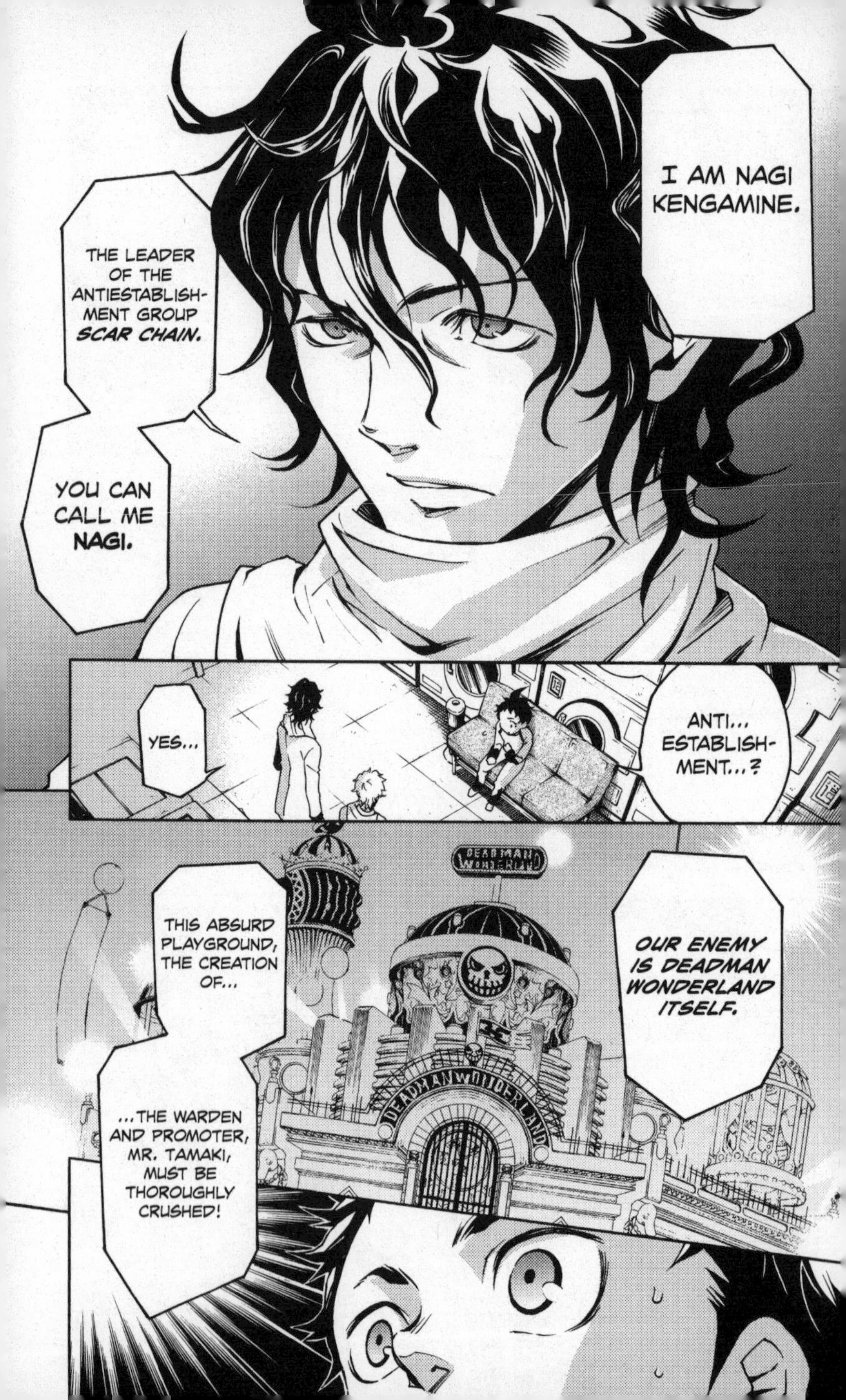
I AM NAGI KENGAMINE.
THE LEADER OF THE ANTIESTABLISHMENT GROUP SCAR CHAIN.
YOU CAN CALL ME NAGI.
ANTI... ESTABLISHMENT...?
YES...
OUR ENEMY IS DEADMAN WONDERLAND ITSELF.
THIS ABSURD PLAYGROUND, THE CREATION OF...
DEADMAN WONDERLAND
...THE WARDEN AND PROMOTER, MR. TAMAKI, MUST BE THOROUGHLY CRUSHED!

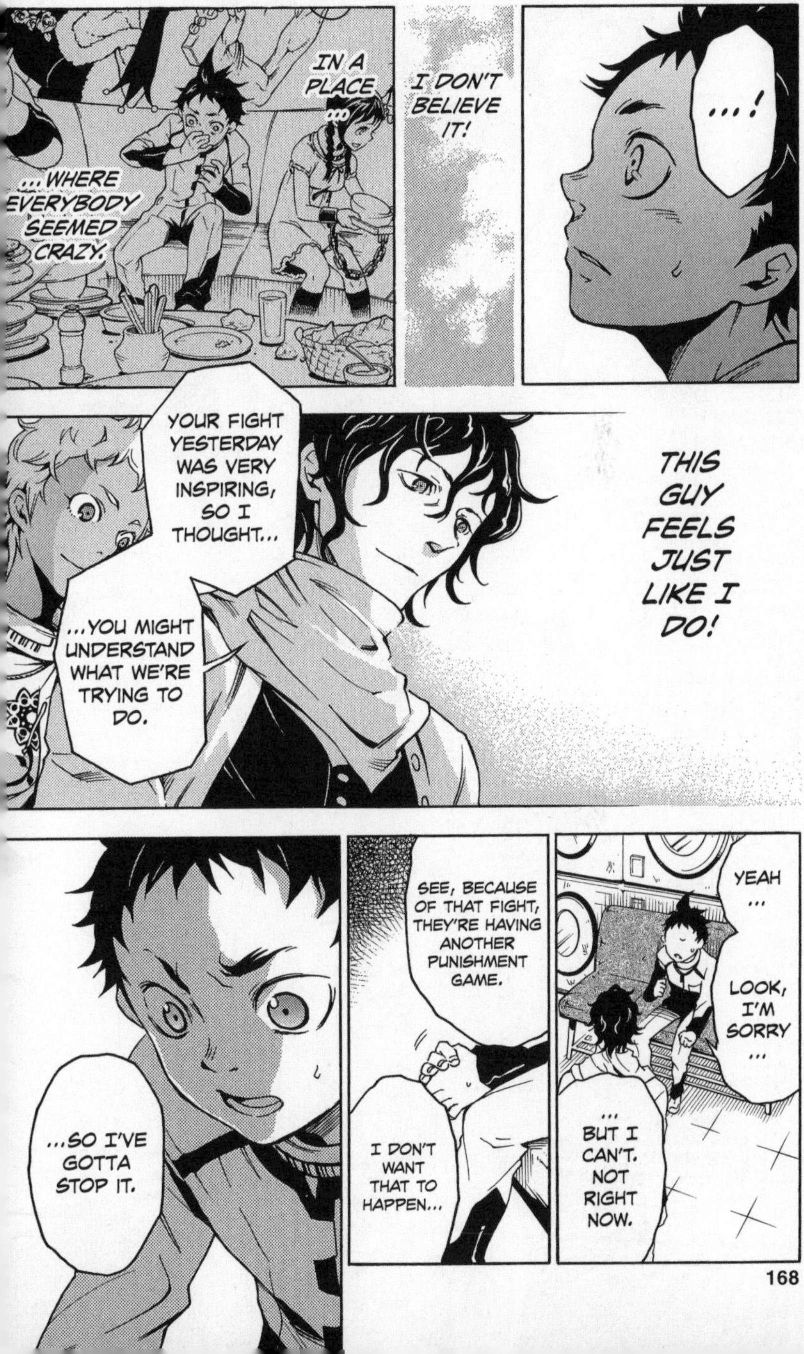
...!
I DON'T BELIEVE IT!
IN A PLACE...
...WHERE EVERYBODY SEEMED CRAZY.
THIS GUY FEELS JUST LIKE I DO!
YOUR FIGHT YESTERDAY WAS VERY INSPIRING, SO I THOUGHT...
...YOU MIGHT UNDERSTAND WHAT WE'RE TRYING TO DO.
YEAH...
LOOK, I'M SORRY...
...BUT I CAN'T. NOT RIGHT NOW.
SEE, BECAUSE OF THAT FIGHT, THEY'RE HAVING ANOTHER PUNISHMENT GAME.
I DON'T WANT THAT TO HAPPEN...
...SO I'VE GOTTA STOP IT.

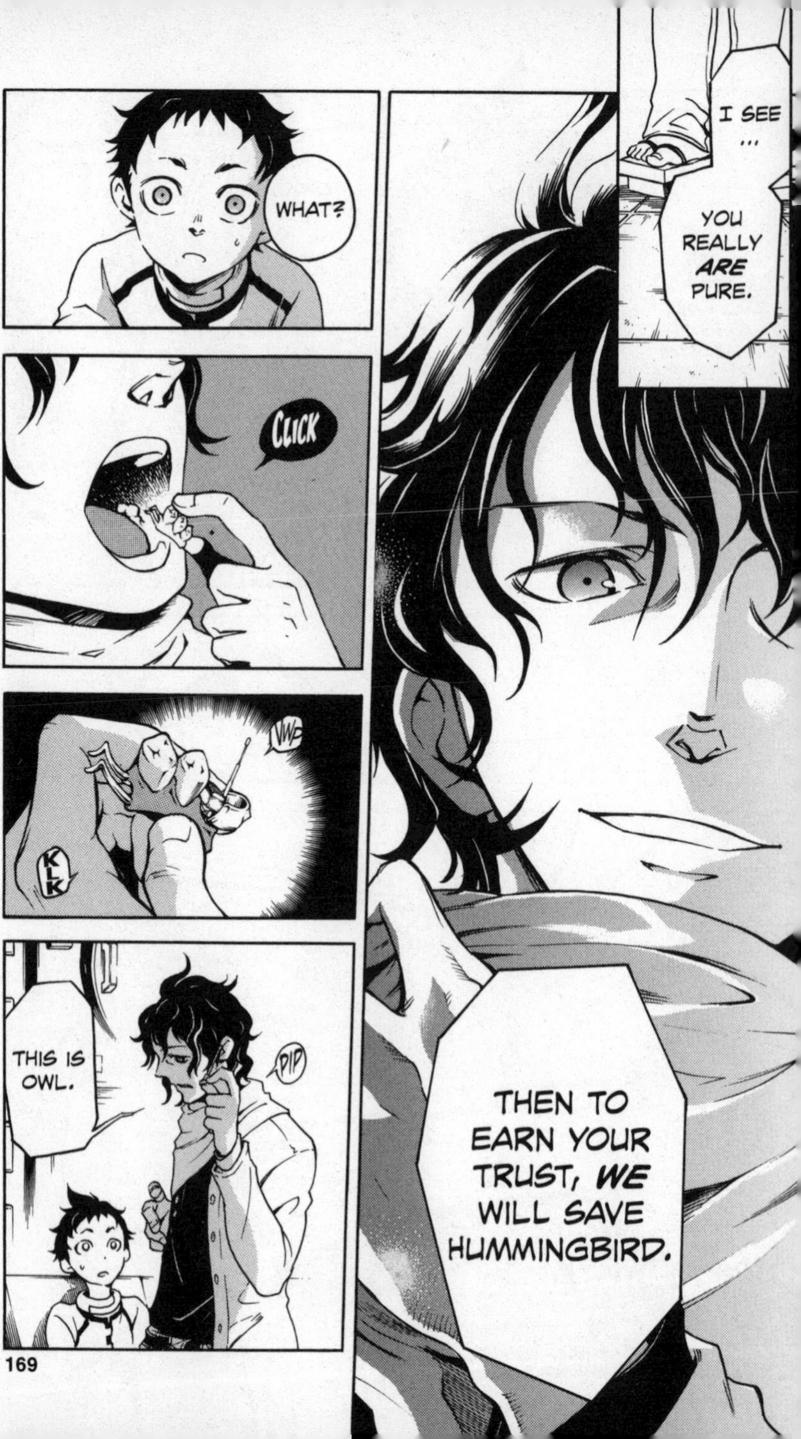
I SEE ...
YOU REALLY ***ARE*** PURE.
THEN TO EARN YOUR TRUST, ***WE*** WILL SAVE HUMMINGBIRD.
WHAT?
CLICK
VWP
KLK
THIS IS OWL.
PIP

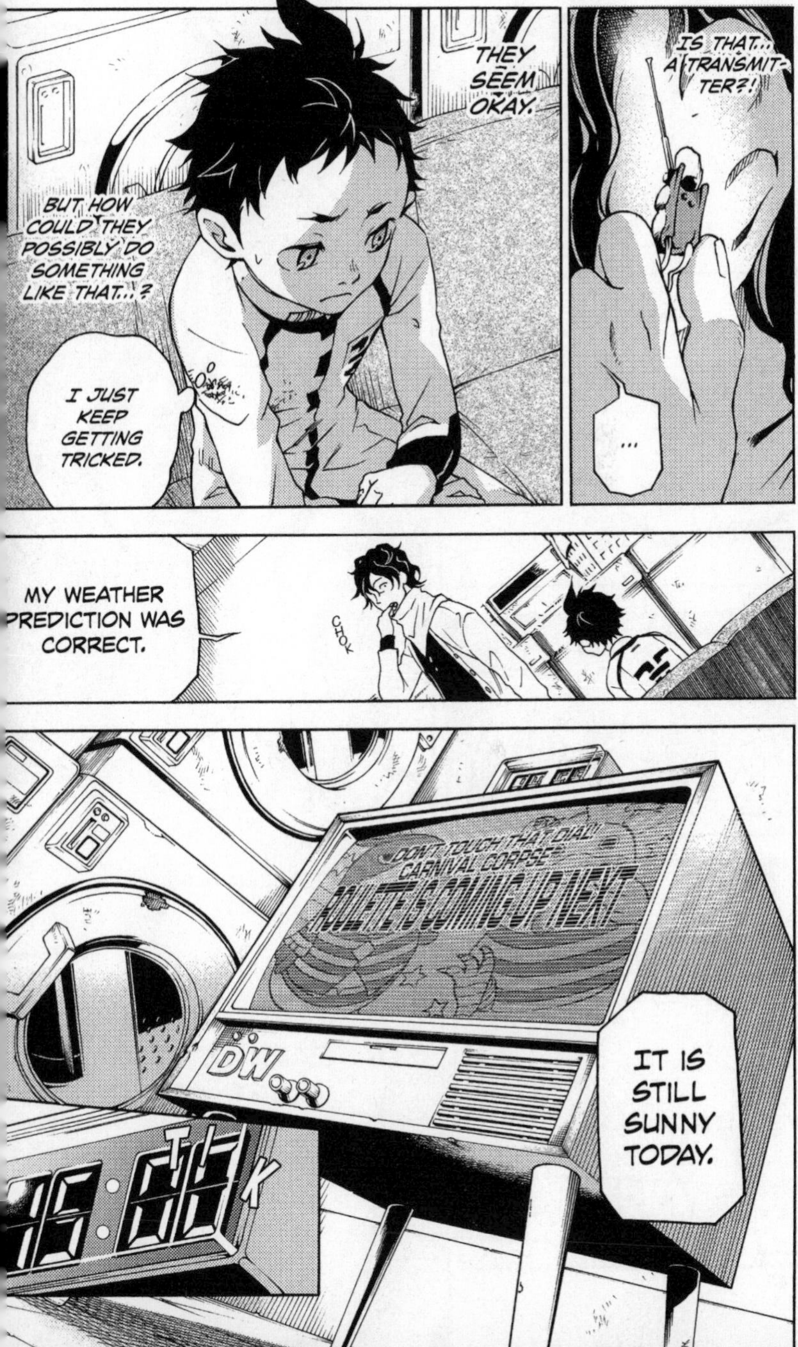
IS THAT... A TRANSMITTER?!
...
THEY SEEM OKAY.
BUT HOW COULD THEY POSSIBLY DO SOMETHING LIKE THAT...?
I JUST KEEP GETTING TRICKED.
MY WEATHER PREDICTION WAS CORRECT.
CHOK
DON'T TOUCH THAT DIAL!! CARNIVAL CORPSE ROULETTE IS COMING UP NEXT
DW
IT IS STILL SUNNY TODAY.

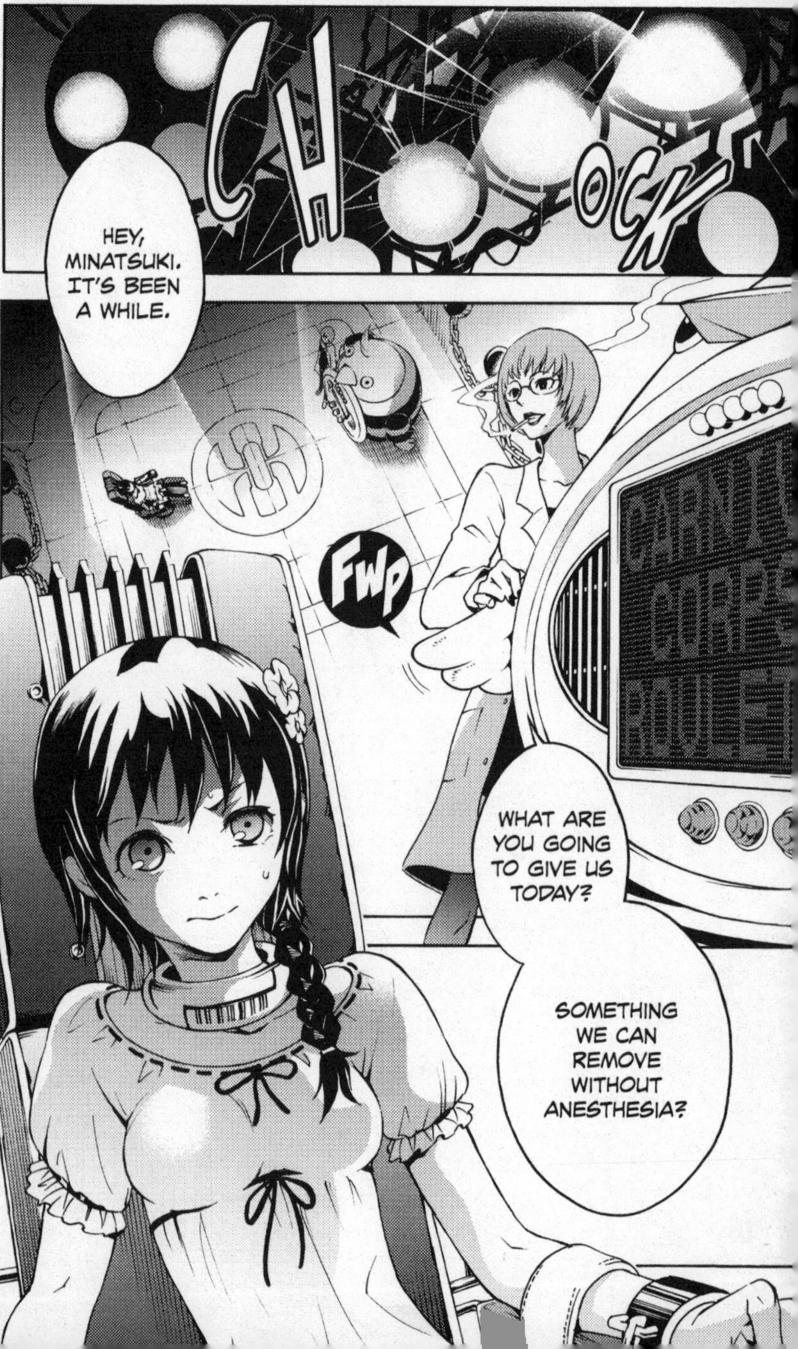
CHOCK
HEY, MINATSUKI. IT'S BEEN A WHILE.
FWP
WHAT ARE YOU GOING TO GIVE US TODAY?
SOMETHING WE CAN REMOVE WITHOUT ANESTHESIA?

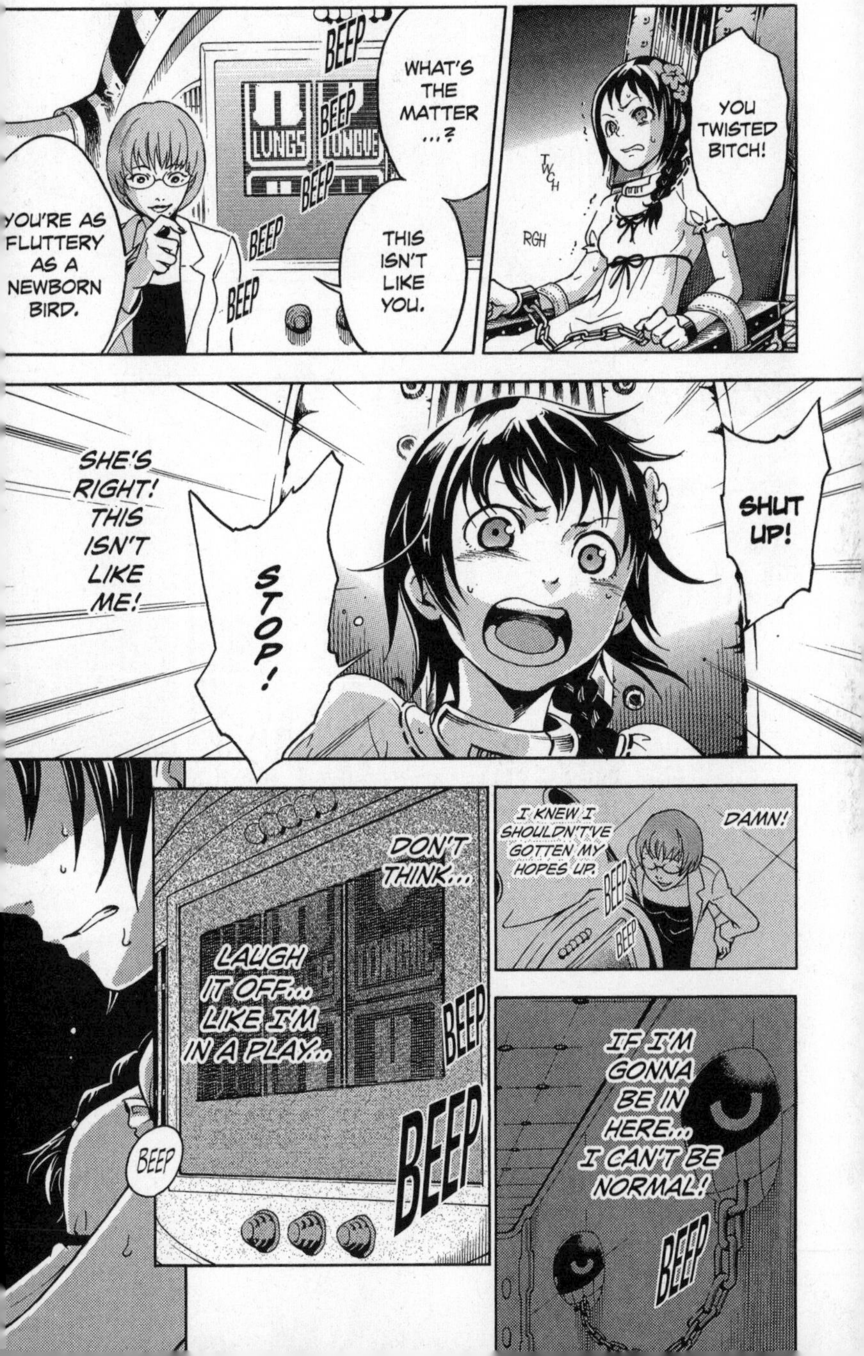
YOU TWISTED BITCH!
TWCH
RGH
BEEP
WHAT'S THE MATTER ...?
LUNGS
BEEP
TONGUE
BEEP
BEEP
BEEP
THIS ISN'T LIKE YOU.
YOU'RE AS FLUTTERY AS A NEWBORN BIRD.
SHUT UP!
STOP!
SHE'S RIGHT! THIS ISN'T LIKE ME!
DAMN!
I KNEW I SHOULDN'T'VE GOTTEN MY HOPES UP.
BEEP
BEEP
IF I'M GONNA BE IN HERE... I CAN'T BE NORMAL!
BEEP
DON'T THINK...
LAUGH IT OFF... LIKE I'M IN A PLAY...
BEEP
BEEP
BEEP

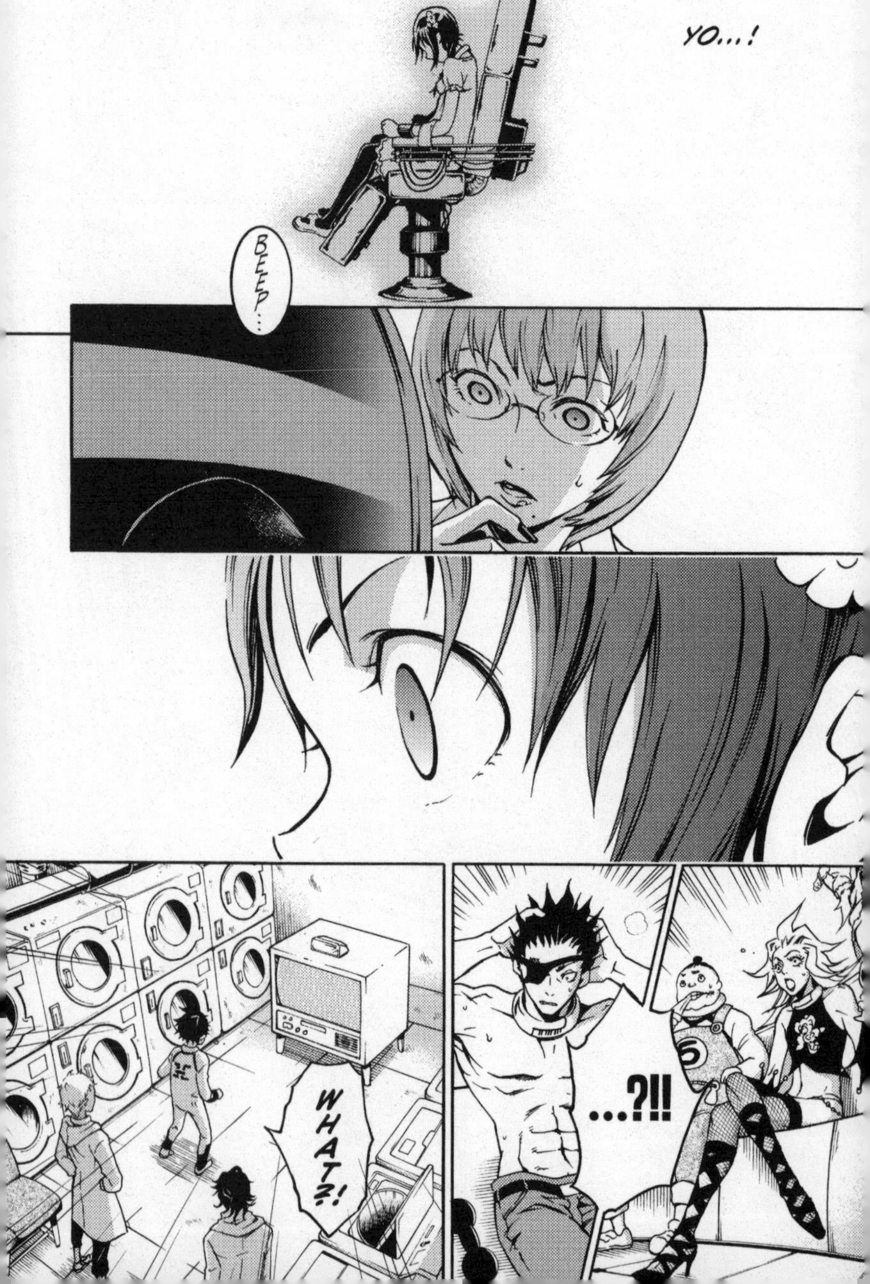
YO...!
BEEP...
...?!!
WHAT?!

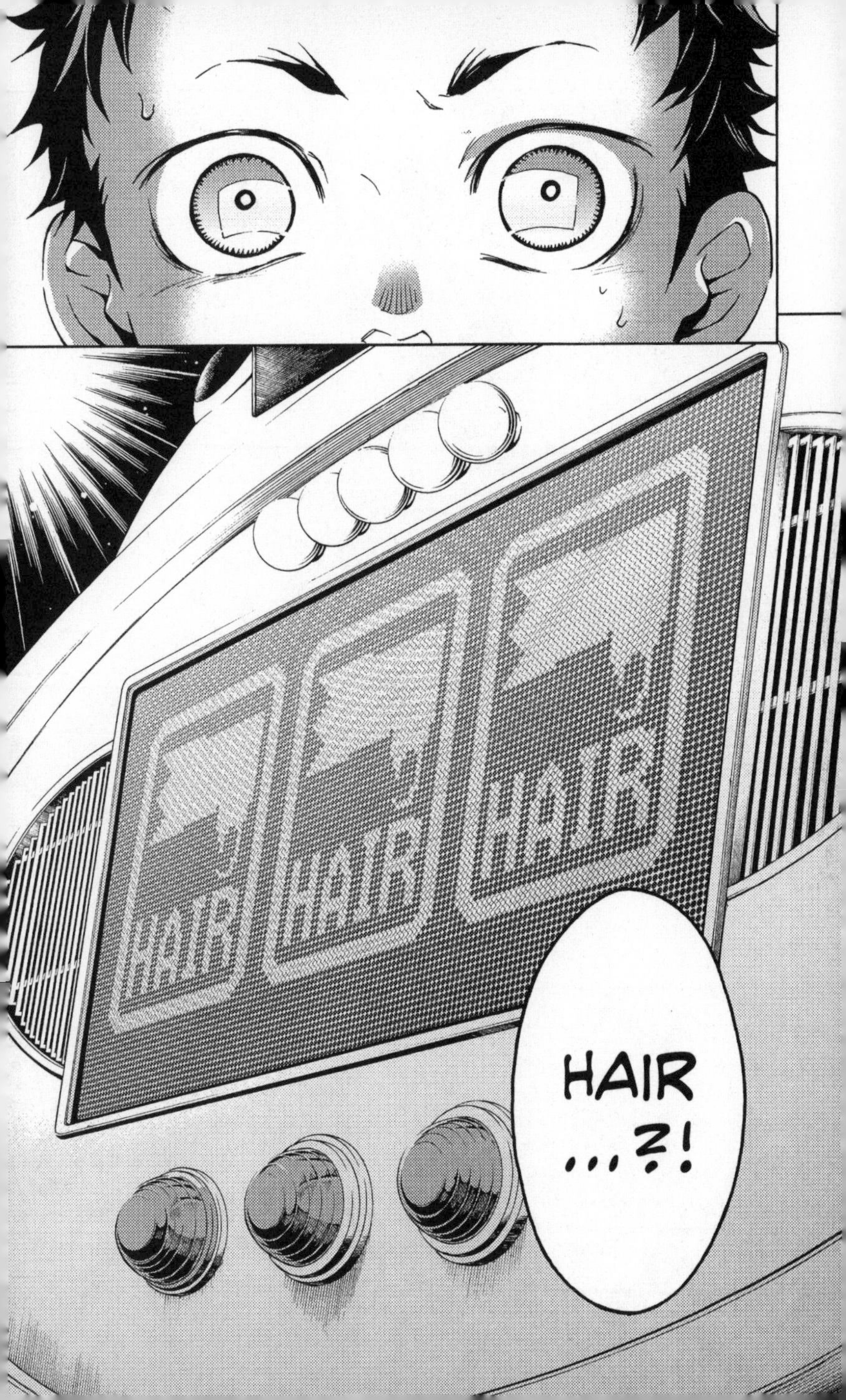
HAIR
HAIR
HAIR
HAIR ...?!

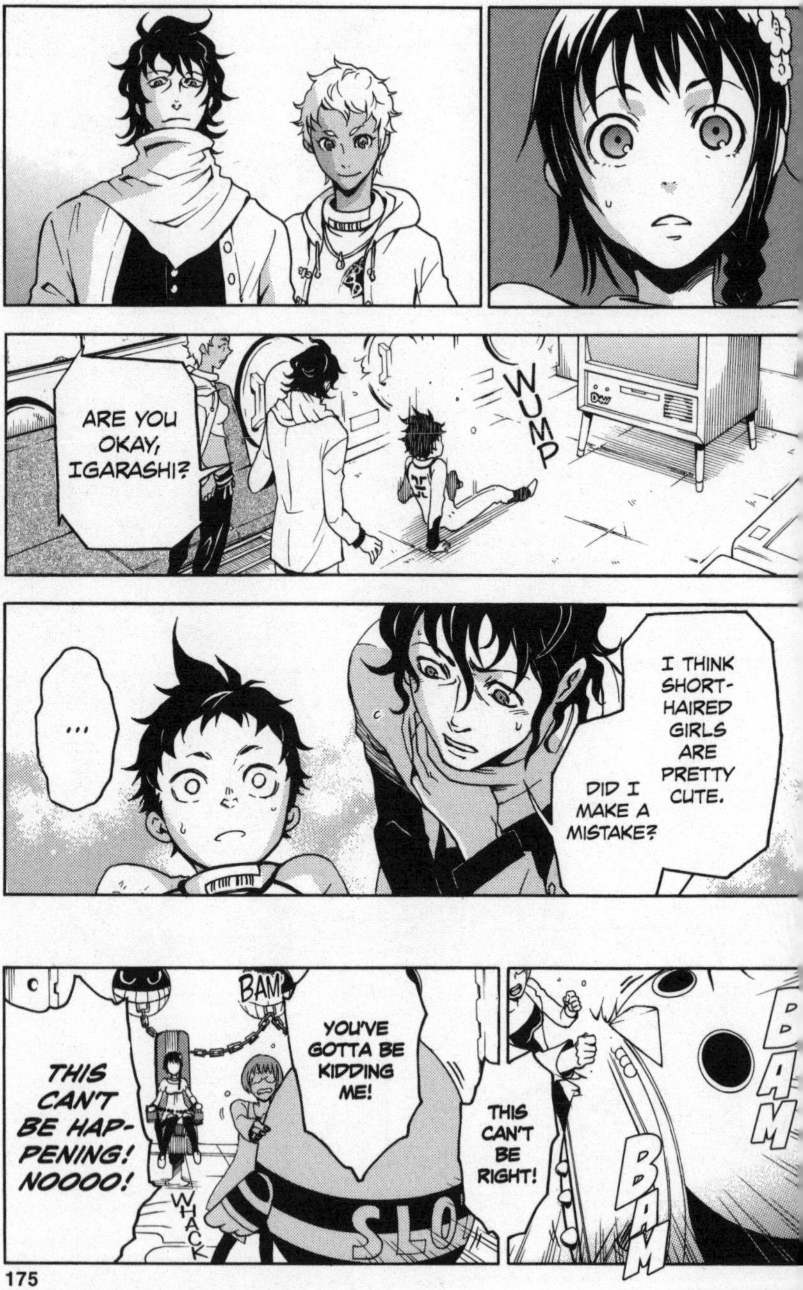
WUMP
ARE YOU OKAY, IGARASHI?
I THINK SHORT-HAIRED GIRLS ARE PRETTY CUTE.
DID I MAKE A MISTAKE?
...
BAM
BAM
THIS CAN'T BE RIGHT!
BAM
YOU'VE GOTTA BE KIDDING ME!
THIS CAN'T BE HAPPENING! NOOOO!
WHACK
SLO

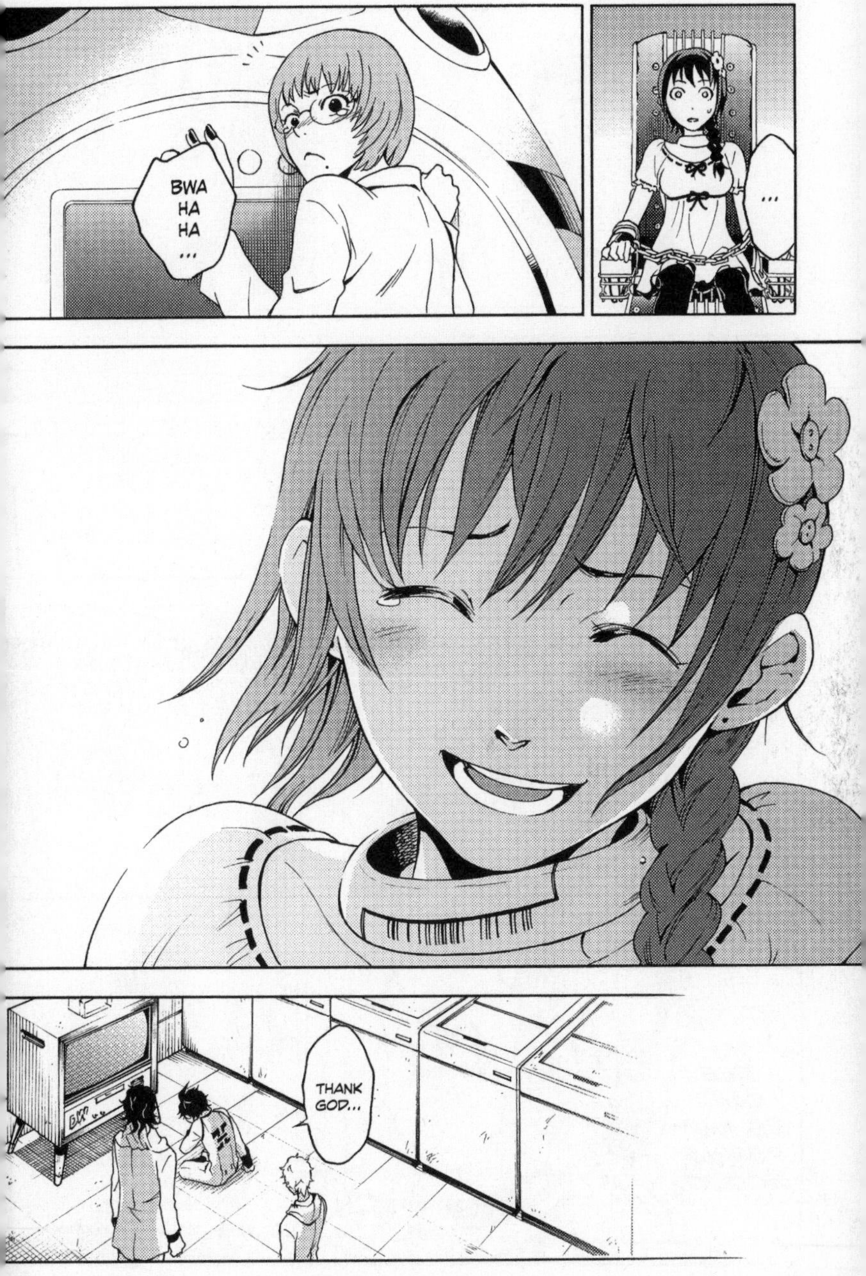
...
BWA HA HA ...
THANK GOD...

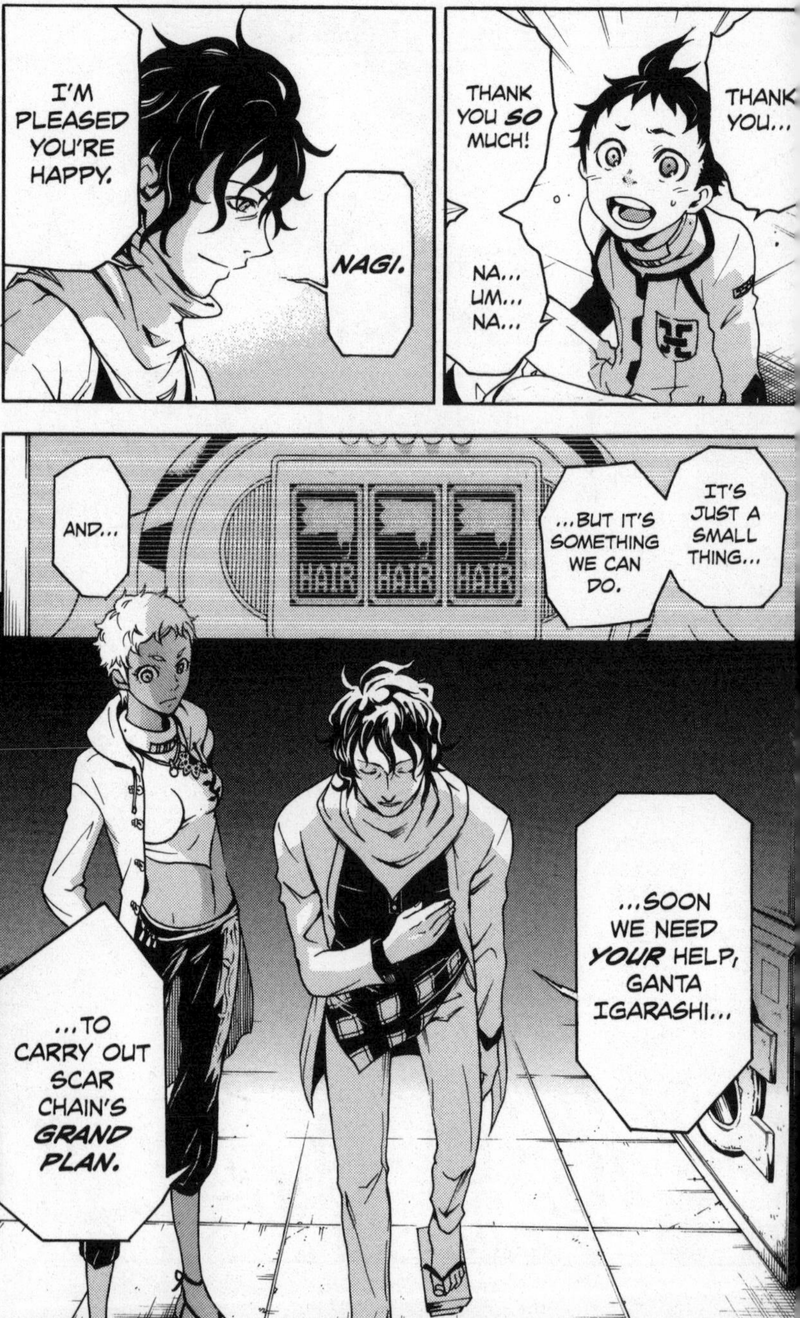
THANK YOU...
THANK YOU *SO* MUCH!
NA... UM... NA...
I'M PLEASED YOU'RE HAPPY.
NAGI.
IT'S JUST A SMALL THING...
...BUT IT'S SOMETHING WE CAN DO.
HAIR
HAIR
HAIR
AND...
...SOON WE NEED *YOUR* HELP, GANTA IGARASHI...
...TO CARRY OUT SCAR CHAIN'S *GRAND PLAN.*

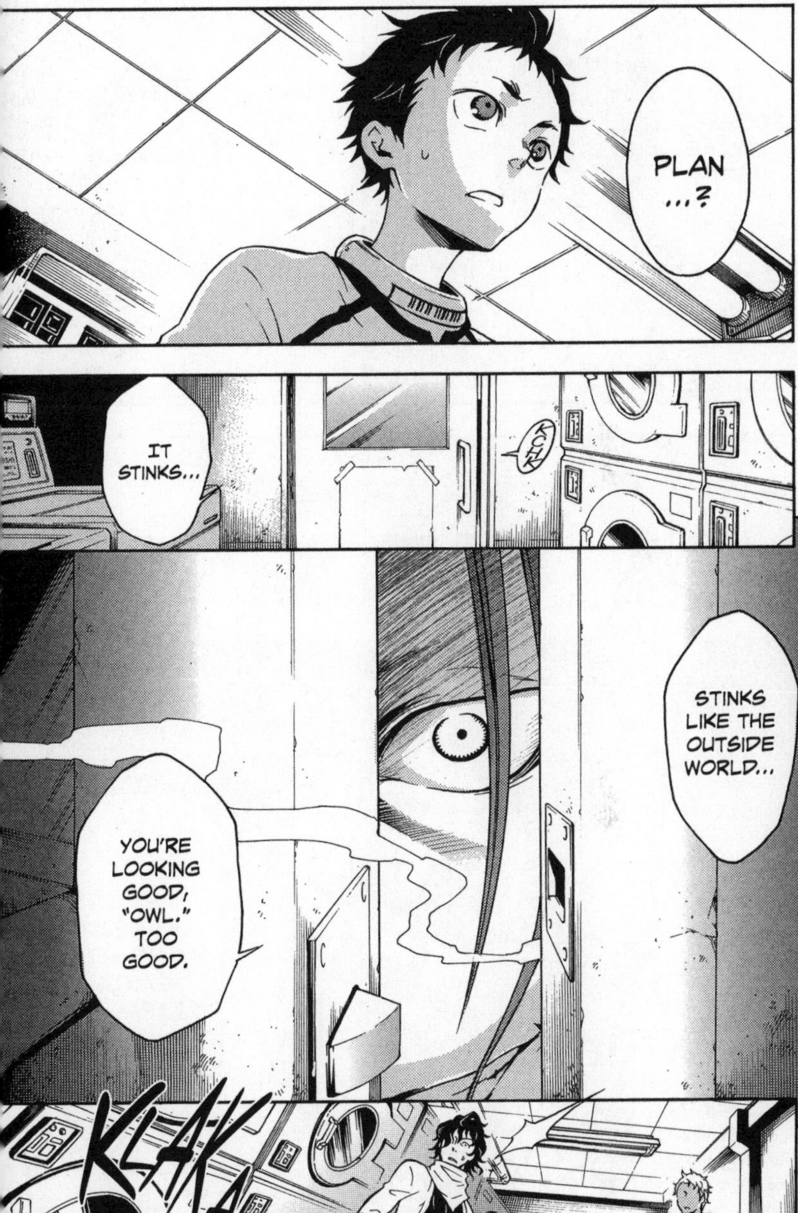
PLAN ...?
KCH
IT STINKS...
STINKS LIKE THE OUTSIDE WORLD...
YOU'RE LOOKING GOOD, "OWL." TOO GOOD.
KLAKA

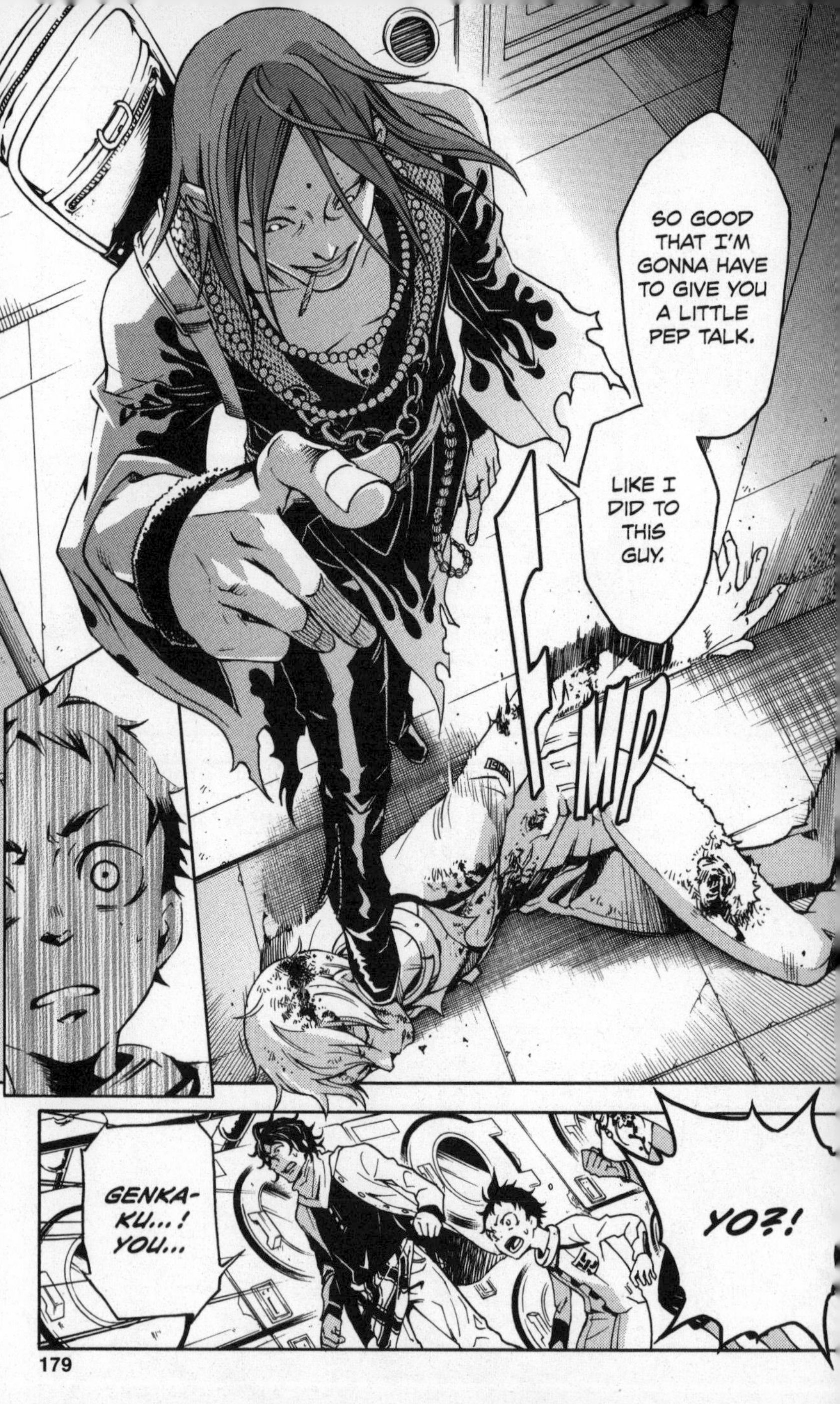
SO GOOD THAT I'M GONNA HAVE TO GIVE YOU A LITTLE PEP TALK.
LIKE I DID TO THIS GUY.
TMP
YO?!
GENKA-KU...! YOU...

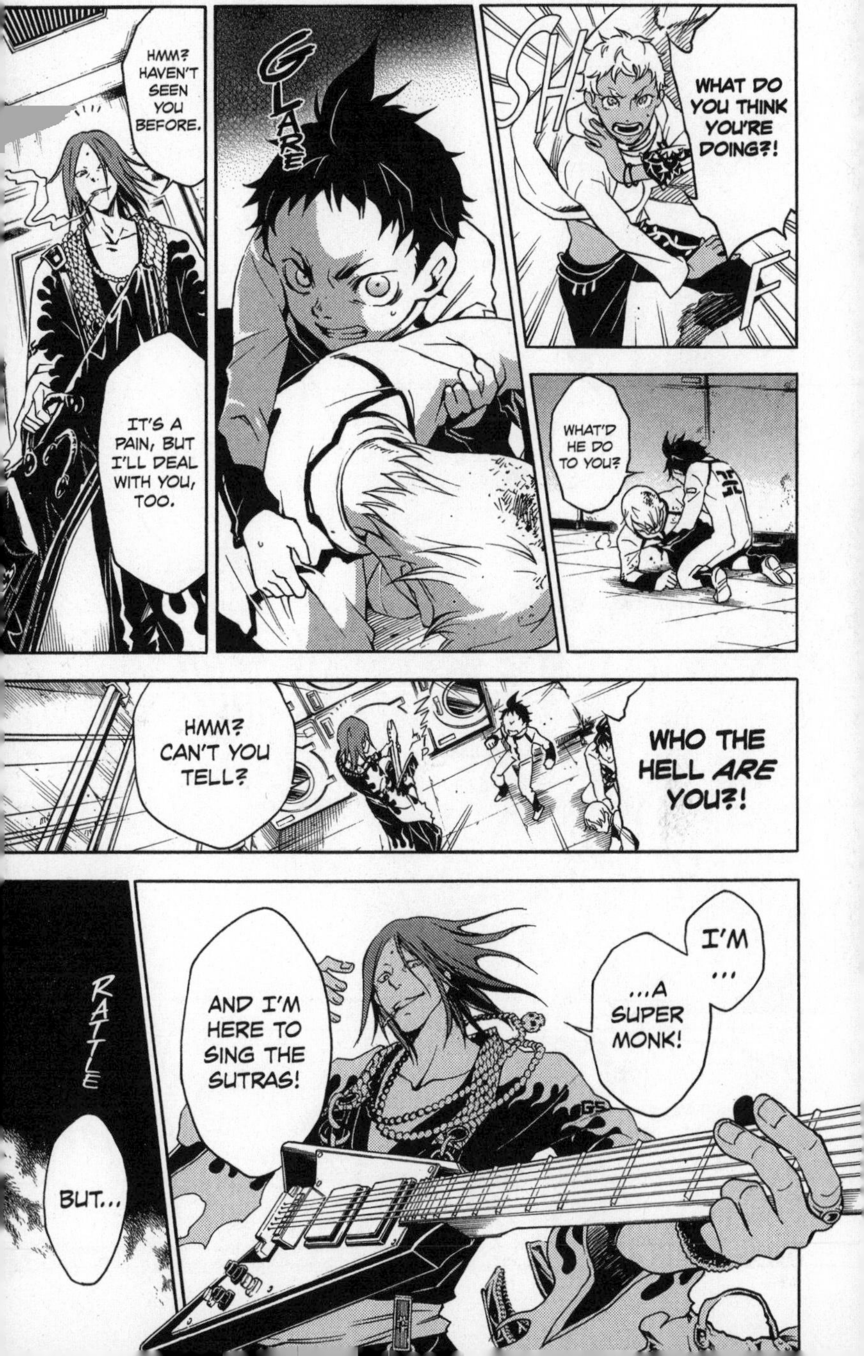
SH
WHAT DO YOU THINK YOU'RE DOING?!
F
WHAT'D HE DO TO YOU?
GLARE
HMM? HAVEN'T SEEN YOU BEFORE.
IT'S A PAIN, BUT I'LL DEAL WITH YOU, TOO.
WHO THE HELL *ARE* YOU?!
HMM? CAN'T YOU TELL?
I'M ...
...A SUPER MONK!
AND I'M HERE TO SING THE SUTRAS!
RATTLE
BUT...

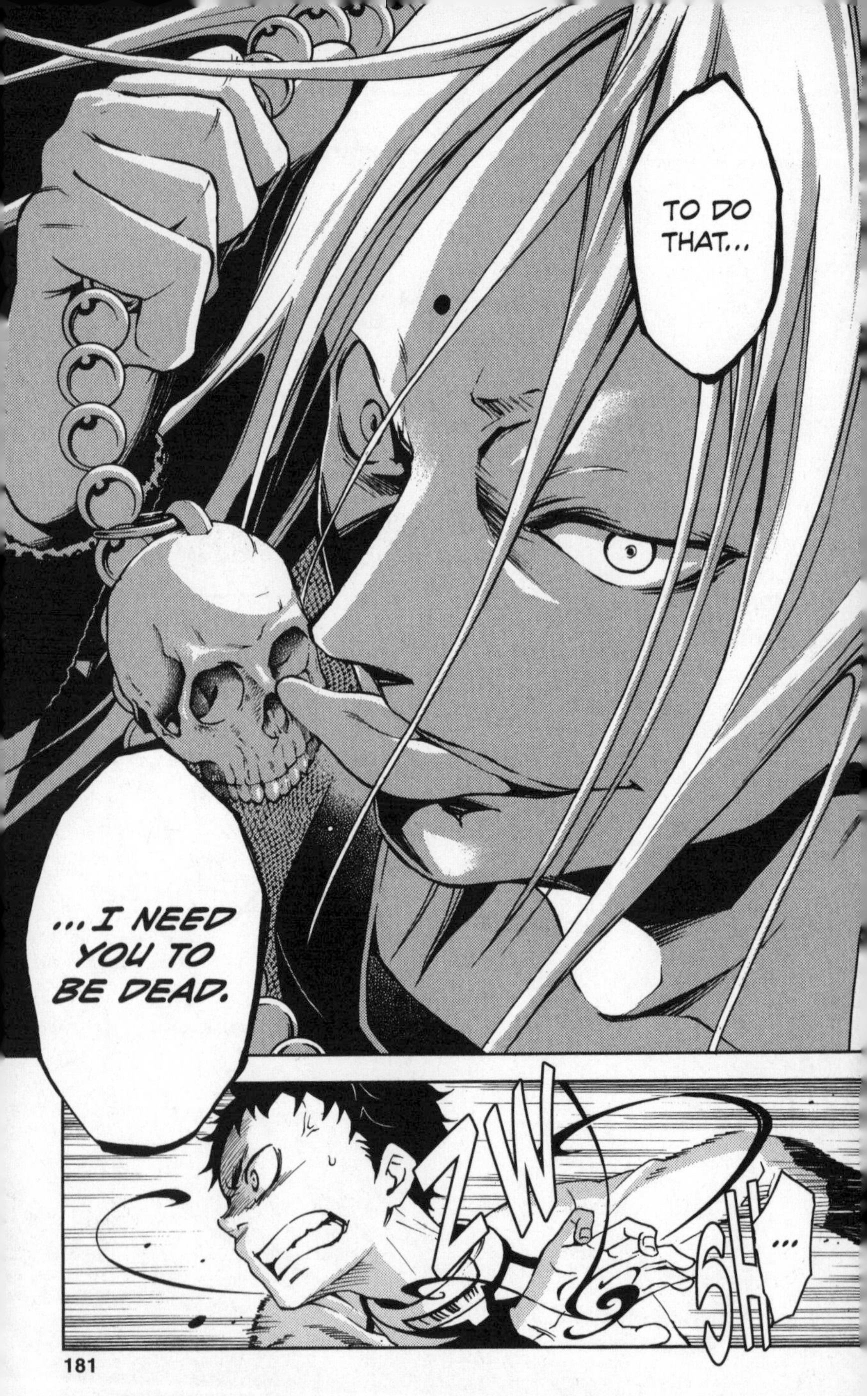
TO DO THAT...
...I NEED YOU TO BE DEAD.
ZWISH...

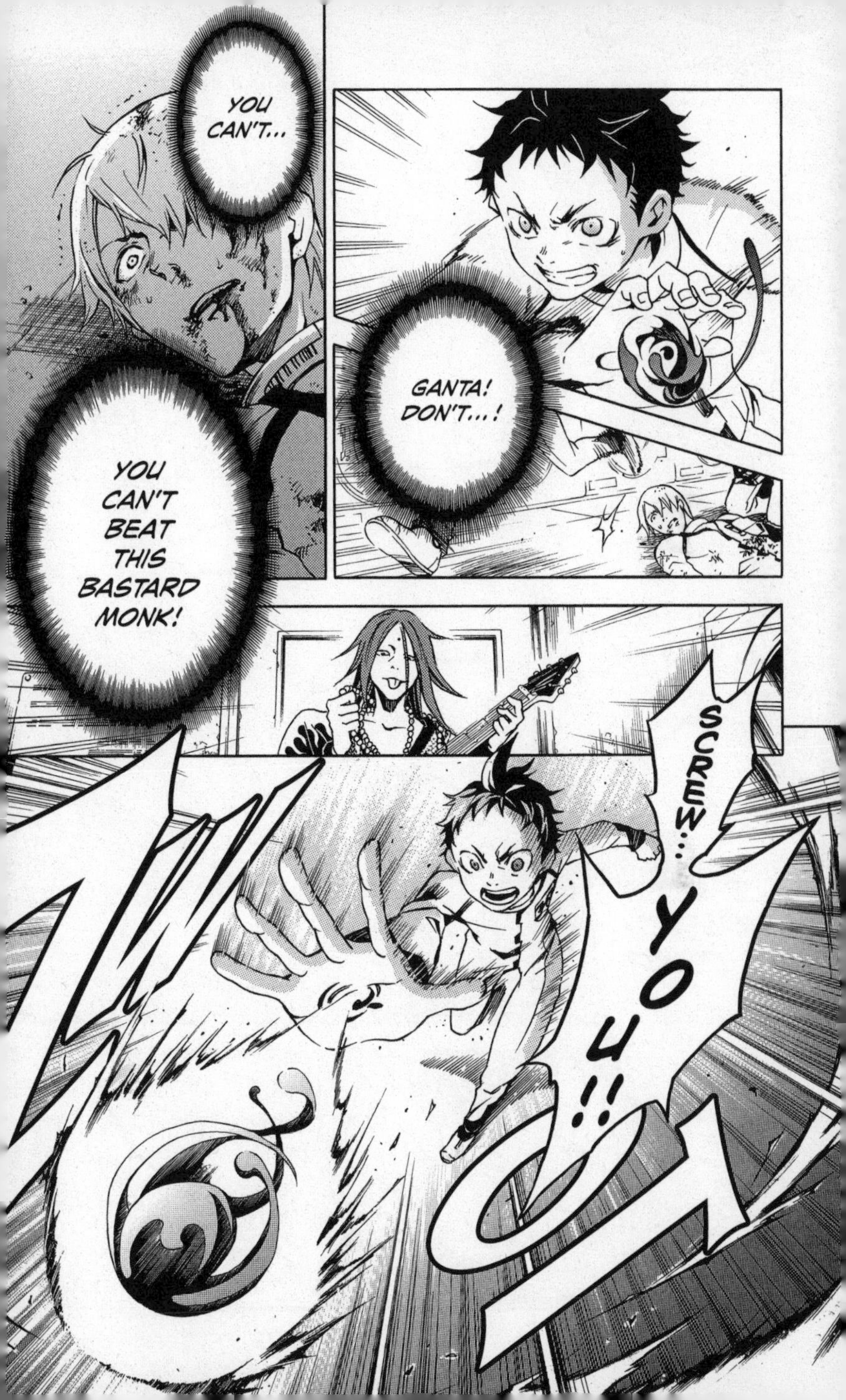
GANTA! DON'T...!
YOU CAN'T...
YOU CAN'T BEAT THIS BASTARD MONK!
SCREW...
YOU!!

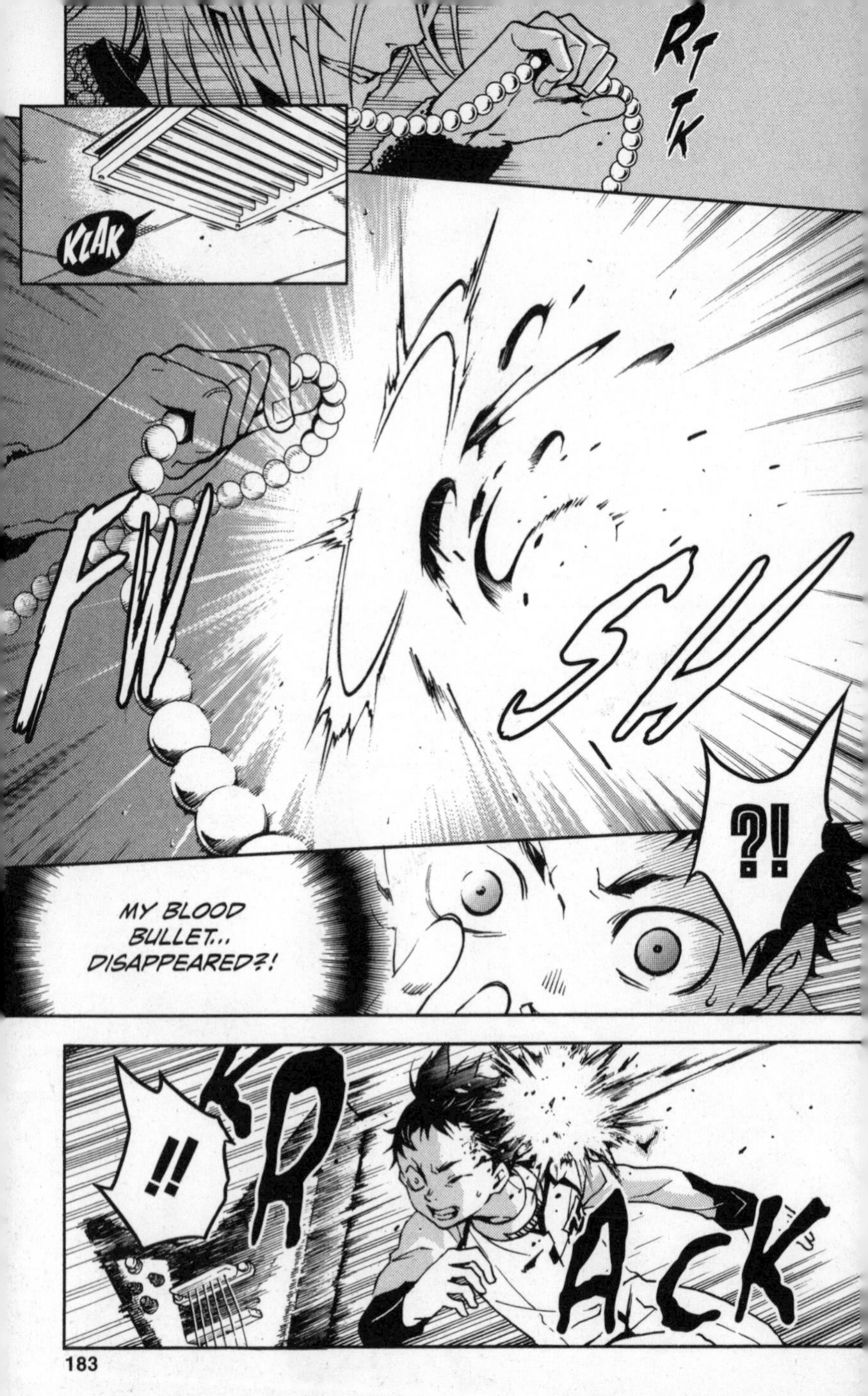
RTTK
KLAK
FWUSH
?!
MY BLOOD BULLET... DISAPPEARED?!
KRACK
!!

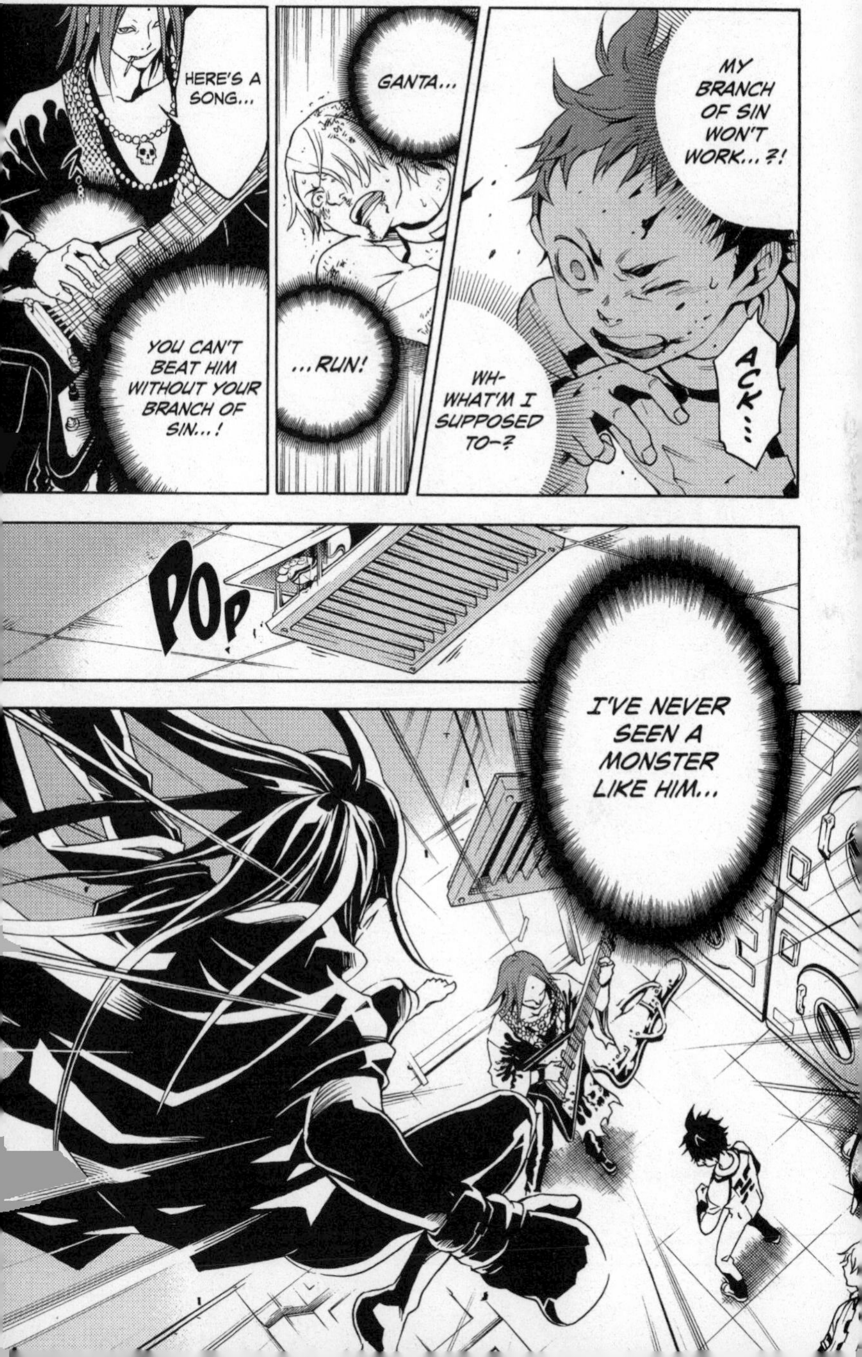
MY BRANCH OF SIN WON'T WORK...?!
ACK...
WH-WHAT'M I SUPPOSED TO-?
GANTA...
...RUN!
HERE'S A SONG...
YOU CAN'T BEAT HIM WITHOUT YOUR BRANCH OF SIN...!
POP
I'VE NEVER SEEN A MONSTER LIKE HIM...

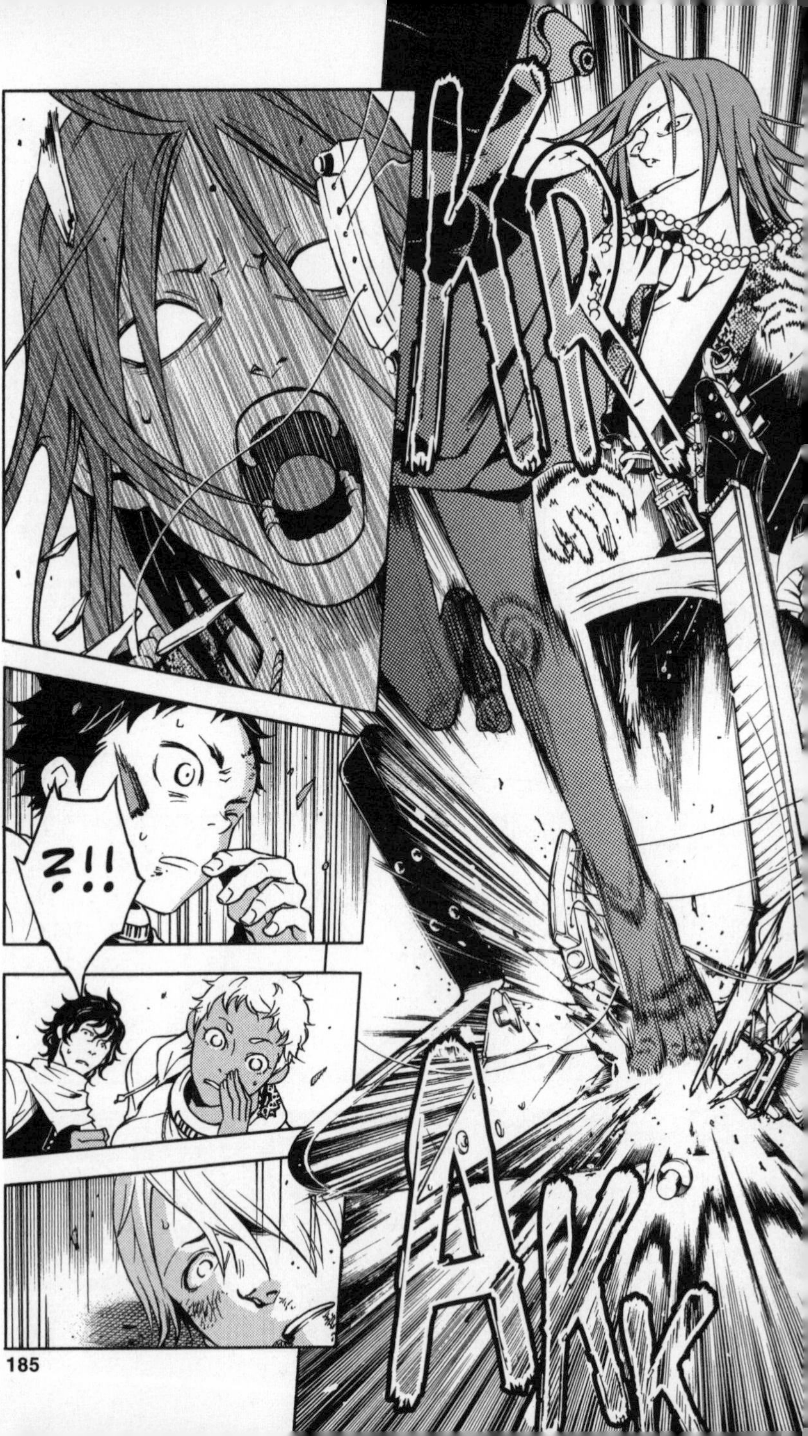
KRAKK
?!!

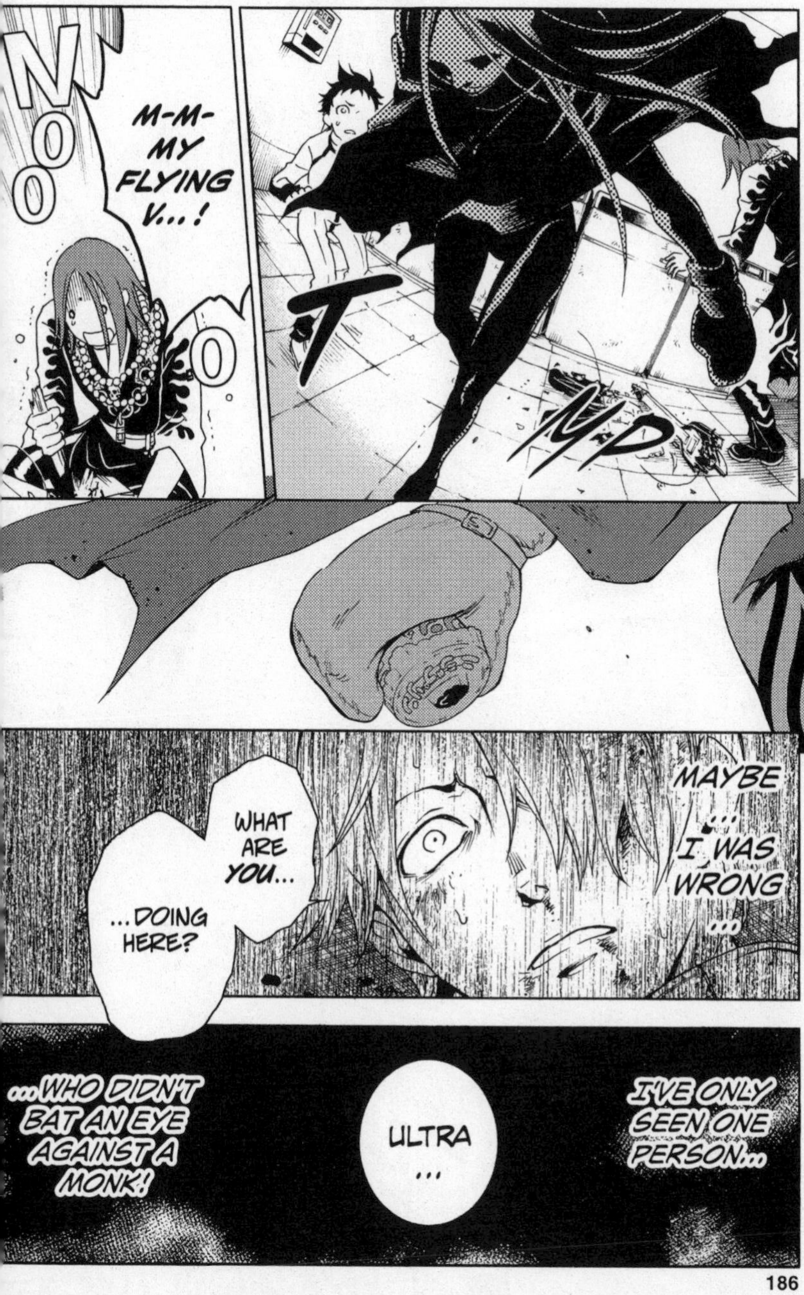
T
MP
NOOOO
M-M-MY FLYING V...!
MAYBE ... I WAS WRONG ...
WHAT ARE YOU...
...DOING HERE?
I'VE ONLY SEEN ONE PERSON...
ULTRA ...
...WHO DIDN'T BAT AN EYE AGAINST A MONK!

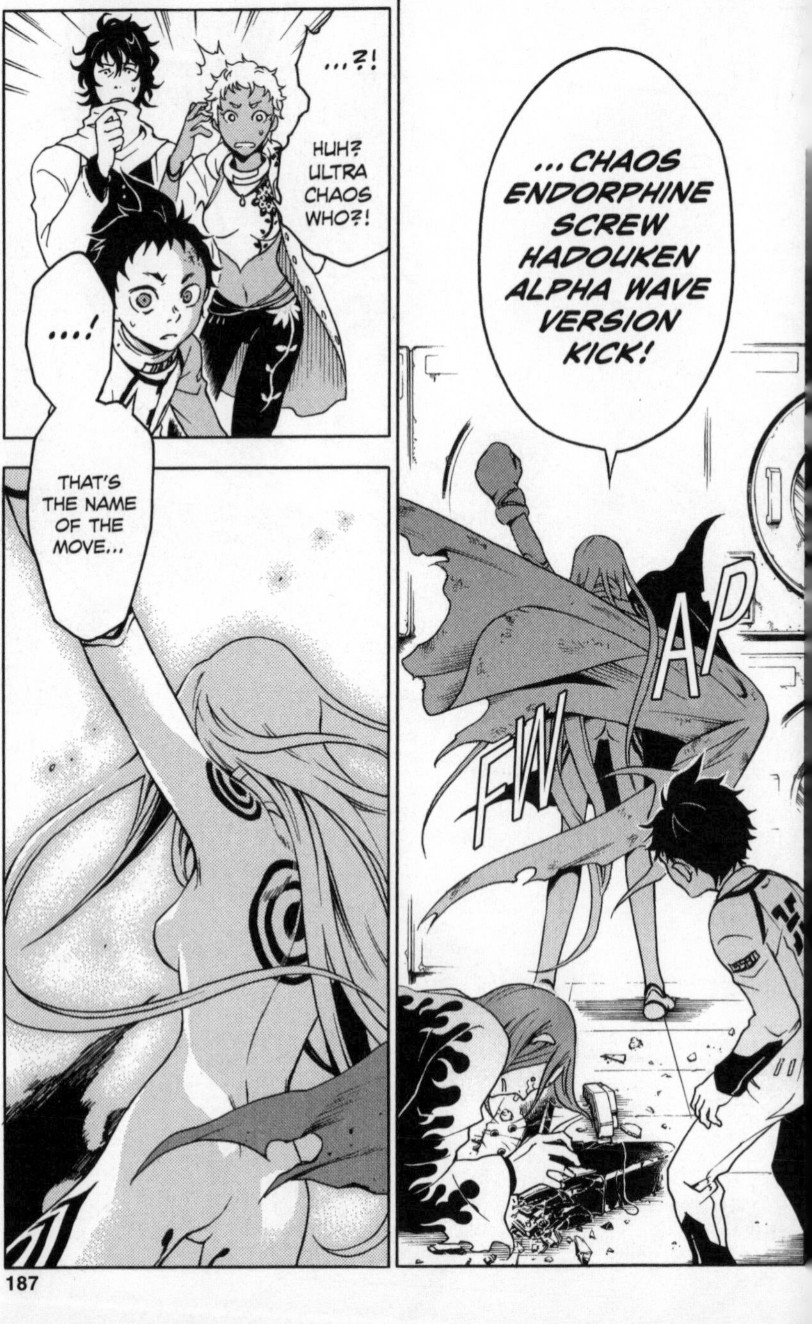
...CHAOS ENDORPHINE SCREW HADOUKEN ALPHA WAVE VERSION KICK!
FWAP
...?!
HUH? ULTRA CHAOS WHO?!
...!
THAT'S THE NAME OF THE MOVE...

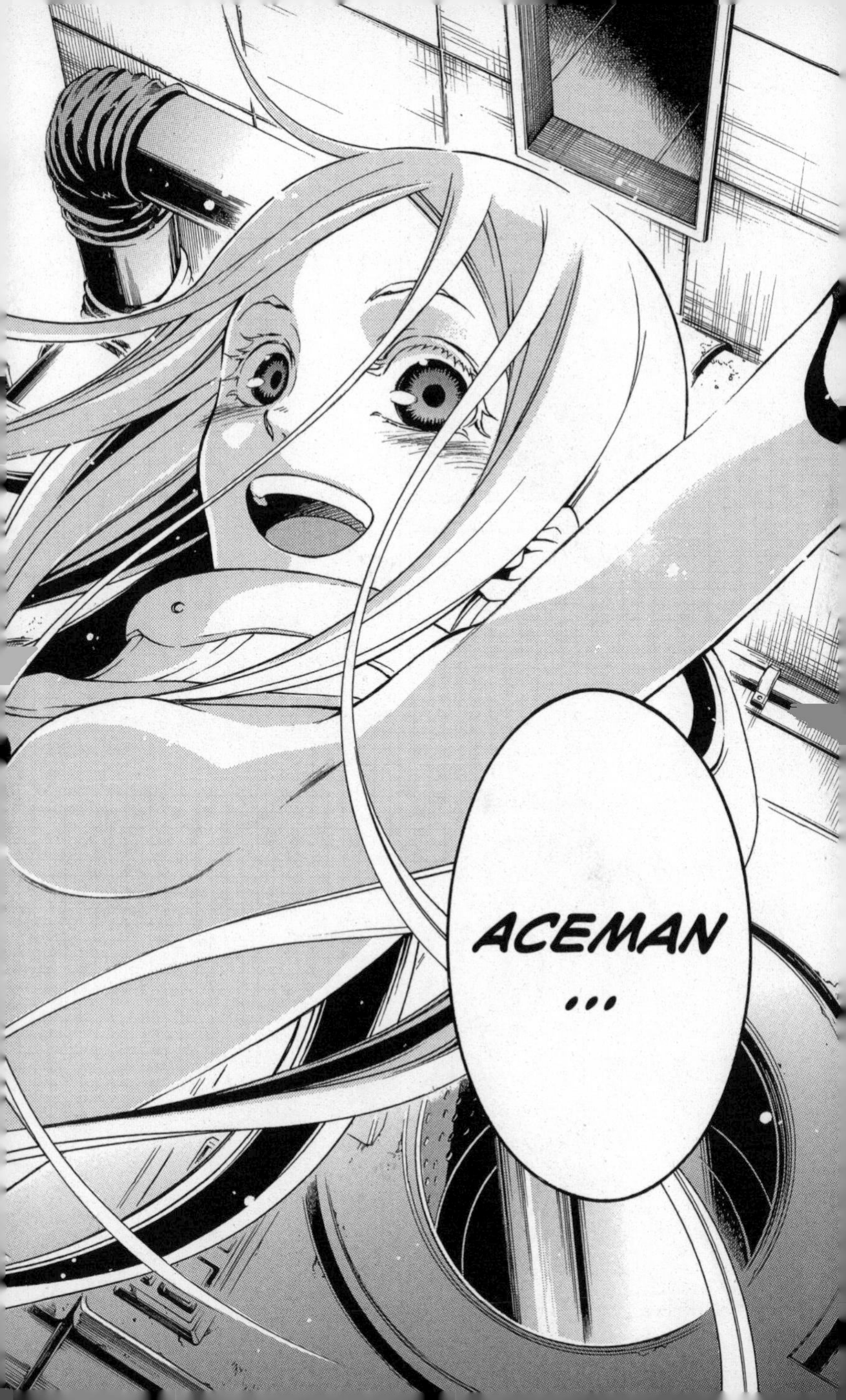
ACEMAN ...

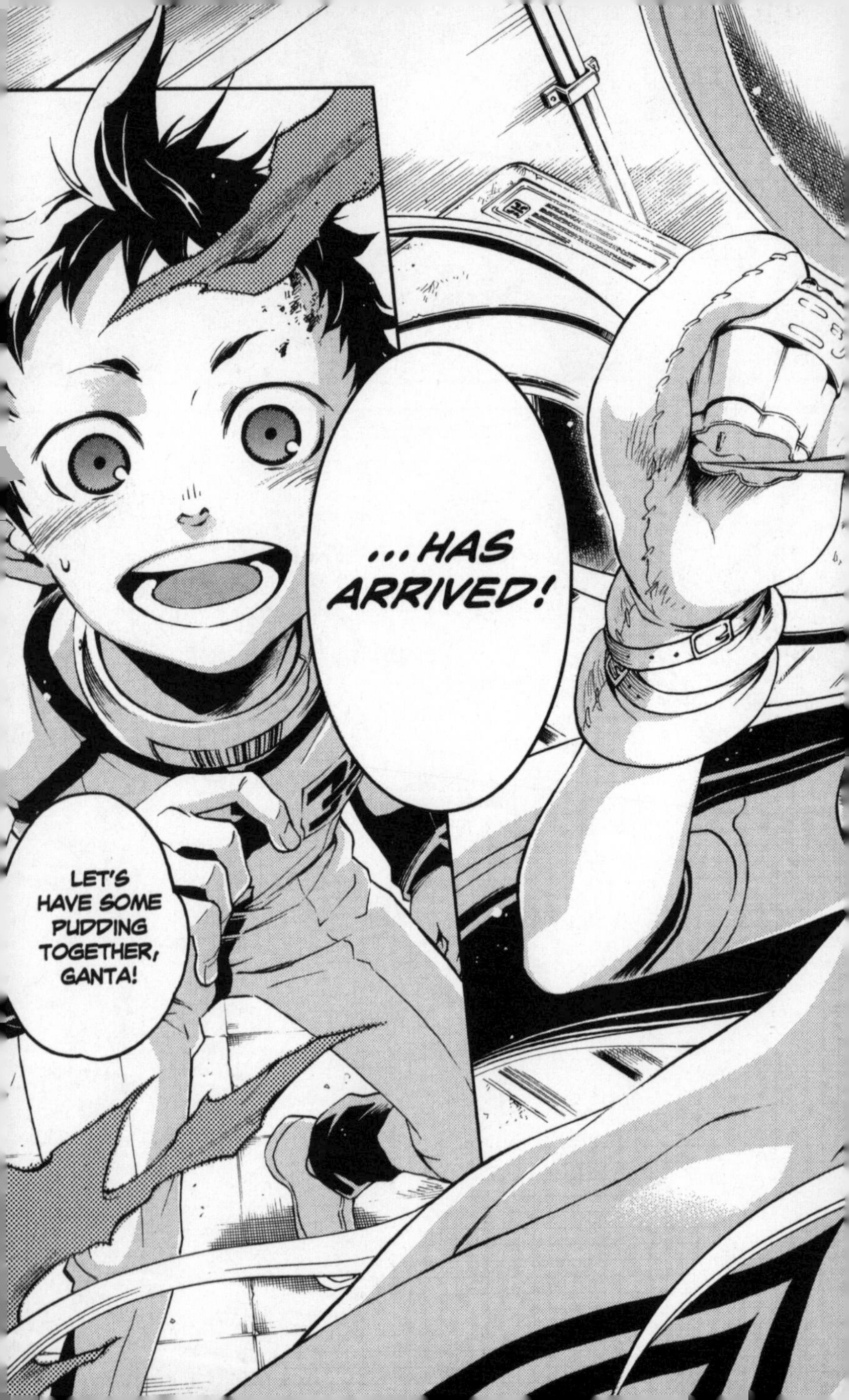
...HAS ARRIVED!
LET'S HAVE SOME PUDDING TOGETHER, GANTA!

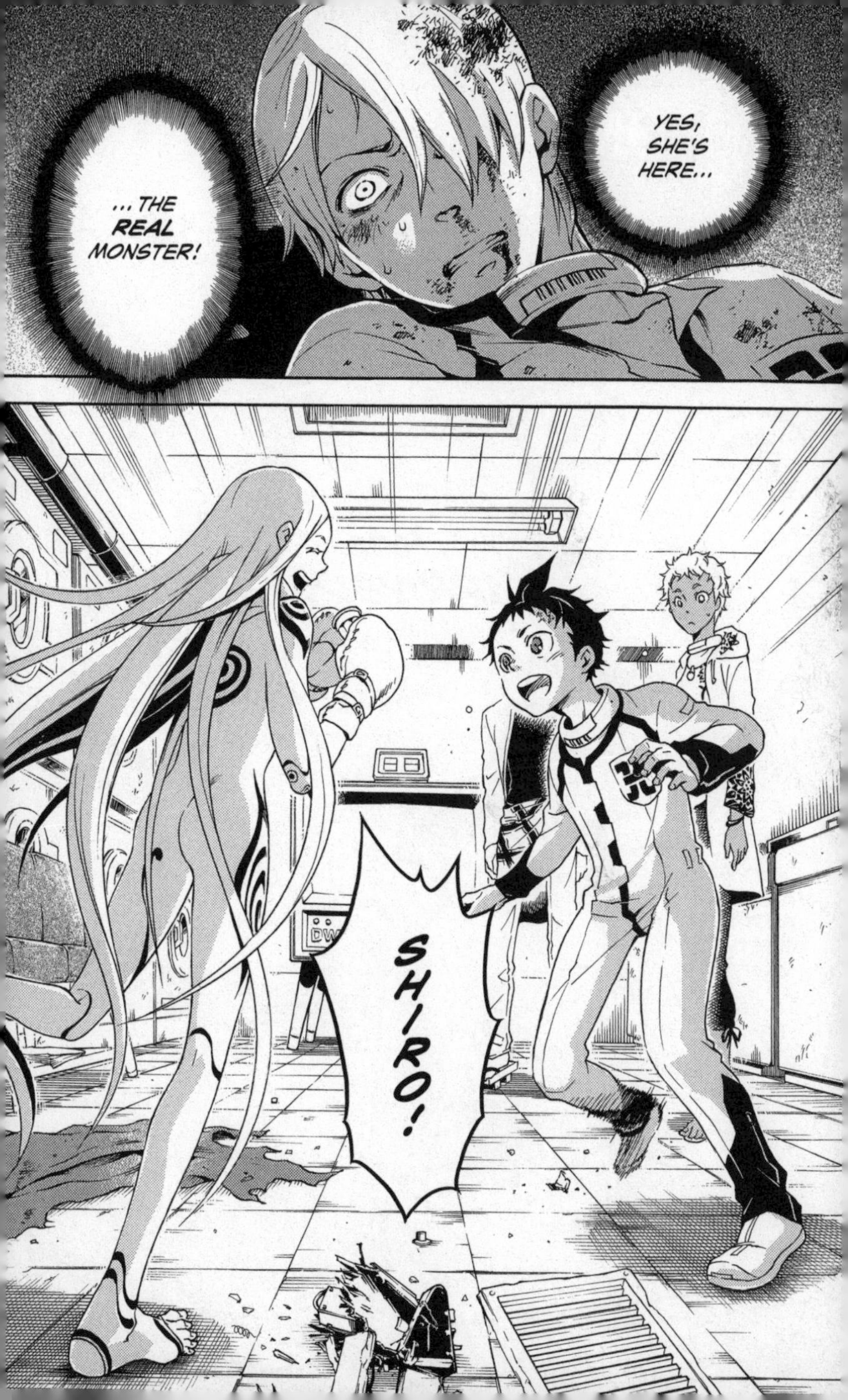
YES, SHE'S HERE...
...THE REAL MONSTER!
SHIRO!

DEADMAN WONDERLAND 3

Jinsei Kataoka
Kazuma Kondou

STAFF

Ryuichi Saitaniya

Shinji Sato

Mamoru Take

Ai Takahashi

Taro Tsuchiya

Toshihiro Noguchi

Takako Nobe

CONTINUED IN VOLUME 04

The Ideal Man

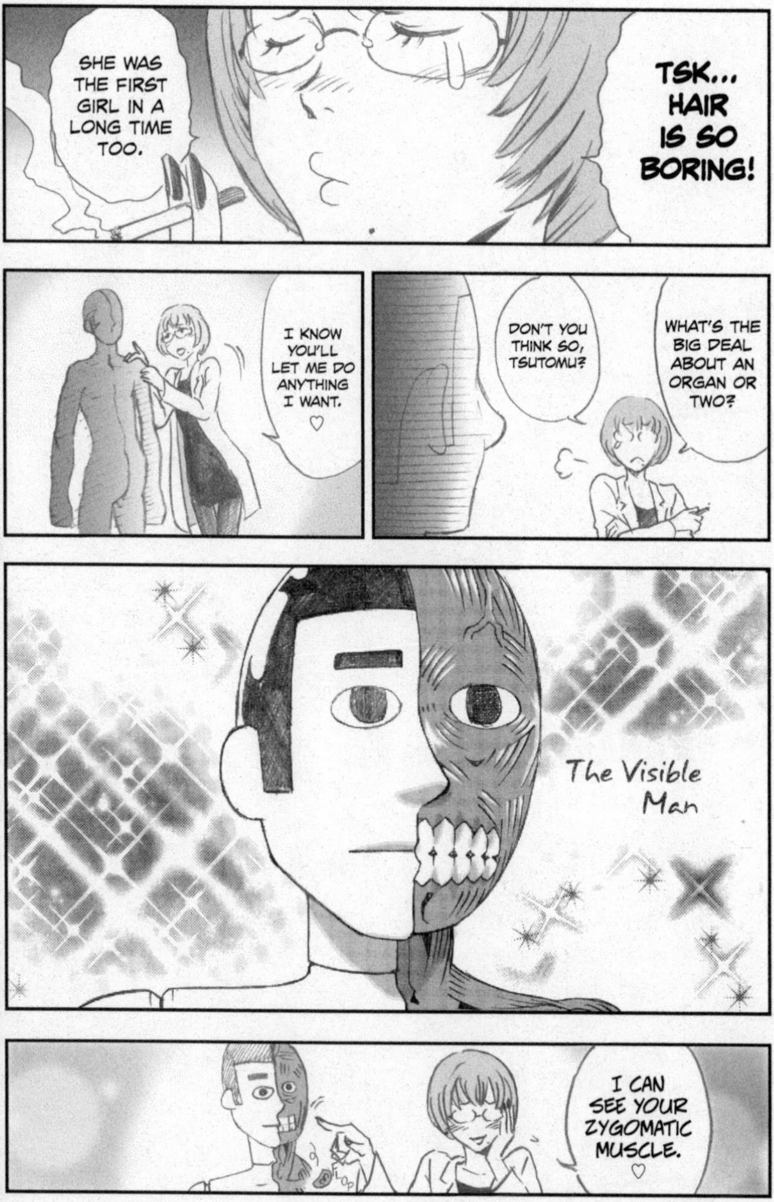
TSK... HAIR IS SO BORING!
SHE WAS THE FIRST GIRL IN A LONG TIME TOO.
WHAT'S THE BIG DEAL ABOUT AN ORGAN OR TWO?
DON'T YOU THINK SO, TSUTOMU?
I KNOW YOU'LL LET ME DO ANYTHING I WANT. ♡
The Visible Man
I CAN SEE YOUR ZYGOMATIC MUSCLE. ♡

Smirk

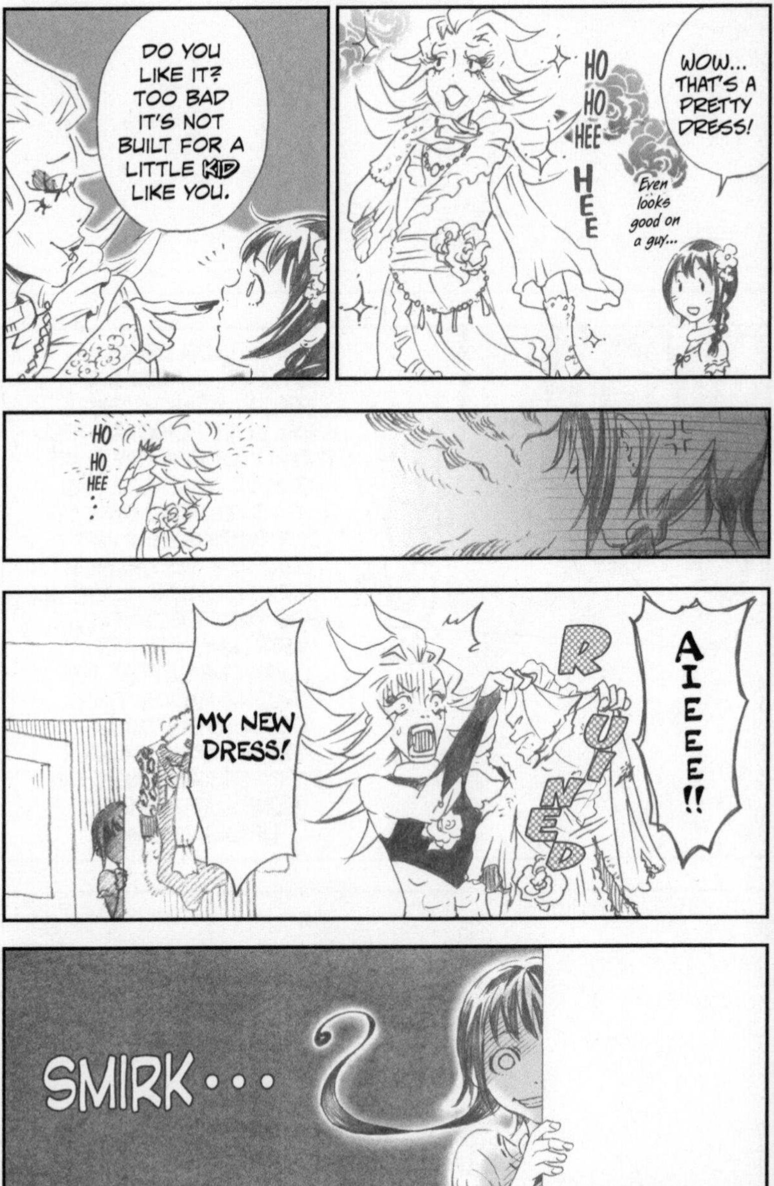
WOW... THAT'S A PRETTY DRESS!
HO HO HEE HEE
Even looks good on a guy...
DO YOU LIKE IT? TOO BAD IT'S NOT BUILT FOR A LITTLE KID LIKE YOU.
HO HO HEE...
AIEEE!!
RUINED
MY NEW DRESS!
SMIRK...

Our Hero Aceman

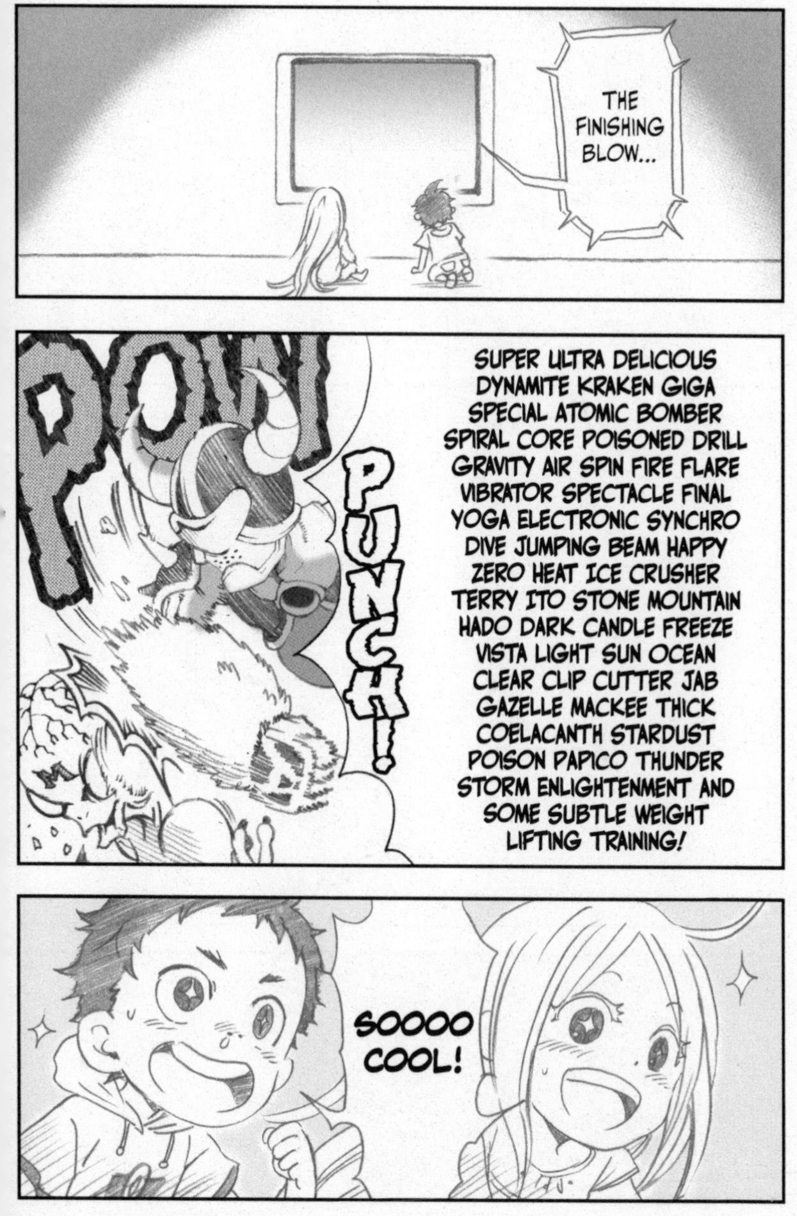
THE FINISHING BLOW...
SUPER ULTRA DELICIOUS DYNAMITE KRAKEN GIGA SPECIAL ATOMIC BOMBER SPIRAL CORE POISONED DRILL GRAVITY AIR SPIN FIRE FLARE VIBRATOR SPECTACLE FINAL YOGA ELECTRONIC SYNCHRO DIVE JUMPING BEAM HAPPY ZERO HEAT ICE CRUSHER TERRY ITO STONE MOUNTAIN HADO DARK CANDLE FREEZE VISTA LIGHT SUN OCEAN CLEAR CLIP CUTTER JAB GAZELLE MACKEE THICK COELACANTH STARDUST POISON PAPICO THUNDER STORM ENLIGHTENMENT AND SOME SUBTLE WEIGHT LIFTING TRAINING!
PUNCH!
POW
SOOOO COOL!

Tee Hee

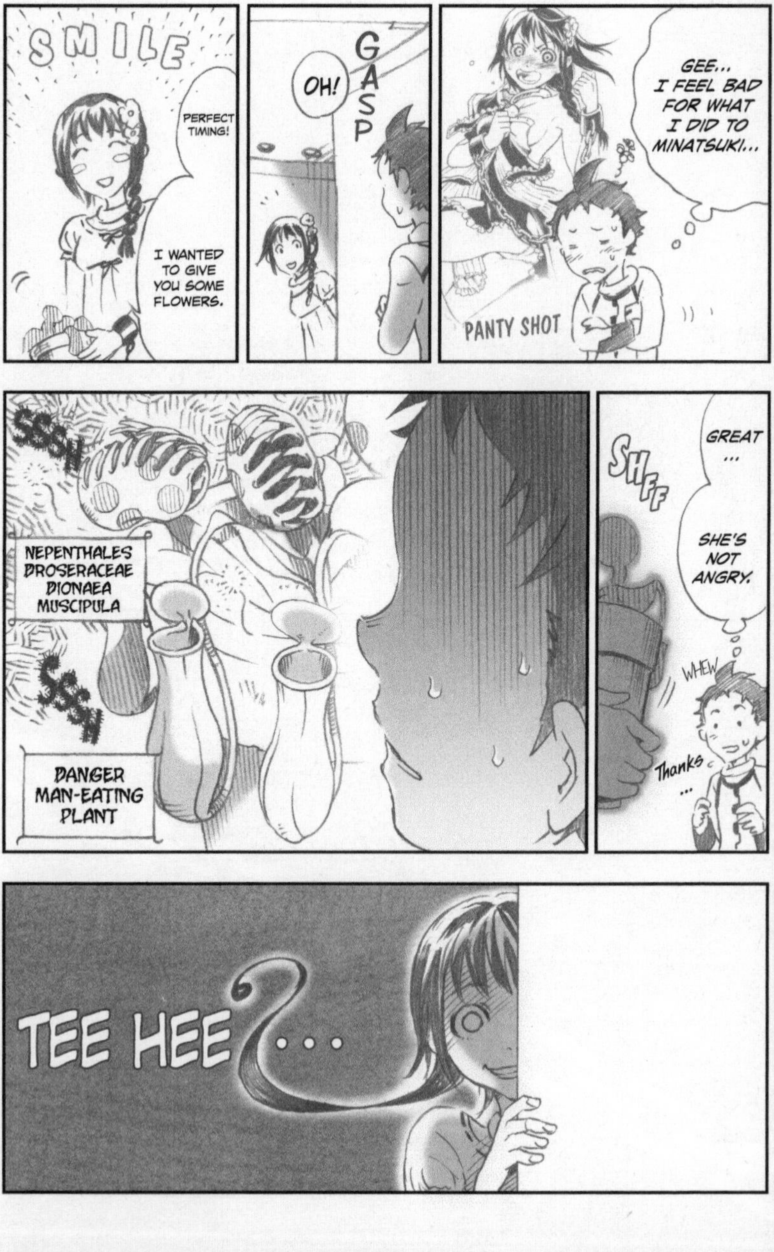
GEE... I FEEL BAD FOR WHAT I DID TO MINATSUKI...
PANTY SHOT
OH!
GASP
SMILE
PERFECT TIMING!
I WANTED TO GIVE YOU SOME FLOWERS.
SHFF
GREAT... SHE'S NOT ANGRY.
WHEW
Thanks...
SSSH
NEPENTHALES DROSERACEAE DIONAEA MUSCIPULA
SSSH
DANGER MAN-EATING PLANT
TEE HEE...

DEADM☠N WONDERLAND

DEADMAN WONDERLAND
VOLUME 3
VIZ MEDIA EDITION

STORY & ART BY
JINSEI KATAOKA, KAZUMA KONDOU

DEADMAN WONDERLAND VOLUME 3
©JINSEI KATAOKA 2008 ©KAZUMA KONDOU 2008
EDITED BY KADOKAWA SHOTEN
FIRST PUBLISHED IN JAPAN IN 2008 BY KADOKAWA CORPORATION, TOKYO.
ENGLISH TRANSLATION RIGHTS ARRANGED WITH KADOKAWA CORPORATION, TOKYO.

TRANSLATION/JOE YAMAZAKI
ENGLISH ADAPTATION/STAN!
TOUCH-UP ART & LETTERING/JAMES GAUBATZ
DESIGN/SAM ELZWAY
EDITOR/MIKE MONTESA

PRINTED IN THE U.S.A.

PUBLISHED BY VIZ MEDIA, LLC
P.O. BOX 77010
SAN FRANCISCO, CA 94107

10 9 8 7 6 5 4 3 2 1
FIRST PRINTING, JUNE 2014

www.viz.com